On Max Horkheimer

On Max Horkheimer

New Perspectives

edited by Seyla Benhabib, Wolfgang Bonß, and
John McCole

The MIT Press   Cambridge, Massachusetts   London, England

This book was set in Baskerville by Maple-Vail Composition Services and printed and bound in the United States of America.

Library of Congress Cataloging-in-Publication Data

On Max Horkheimer : new perspectives / edited by Seyla Benhabib, Wolfgang Bonss, and John McCole.
    p. cm.—(Studies in contemporary German social thought)
  "Bibliography of Max Horkheimer's works" : p.
  Includes bibliographical references and index.
  ISBN 0-262-02355-5
   1. Horkheimer, Max, 1895–1973. 2. Philosophy and social sciences. 3. Social sciences—Philosophy. 4. Critical theory. I. Benhabib, Seyla. II. Bonss, Wolfgang. III. McCole, John (John Joseph), 1954– . IV. Series.
B3279.H847406   1993
193—dc20   93-20516
                                                                                      CIP

Contents

1

Introduction
Max Horkheimer:
Between Philosophy and Social Science

John McCole, Seyla Benhabib, and Wolfgang Bonß

The German social philosopher Max Horkheimer (1895–1973) was among the initiators and founders of the Institut für Sozialforschung, the early home of the Frankfurt School.[1] With his appointment as professor of social philosophy in 1930, he also officially became director of the institute. As was customary upon being installed in a university chair, he delivered an inaugural lecture in January 1931, "The Present Situation of Social Philosophy and the Tasks of an Institute for Social Research."[2] In this address he formulated the conceptual framework for that unique blend of philosophy and empirical social research that would later become known as the critical theory of the Frankfurt School. For Horkheimer, the foundation and point of reference for a critical social theory was materialism of the kind represented by Marxian social analysis, but he was equally convinced that a materialism capable of diagnosing contemporary social trends could be developed only by overcoming the all too frequently dogmatic application of Marxism, as well as the fragmentation of the specialized academic disciplines. His goal was a new form of interdisciplinary work, in which "philosophers, sociologists, political economists, historians, and psychologists join together . . . to pursue philosophical questions directed at the big picture with the most refined scientific methods, to reformulate and sharpen these questions in the course of their work, to devise new methods, and yet not lose sight of the larger context."[3]

The program of integrating empirical research and theoretical reflection announced in these words did in fact constitute the characteristic feature of the institute's work between 1930 and 1937, guiding research and publications that were pathbreaking for the Weimar Republic and beyond. In 1931 the first empirical surveys on the political attitudes of workers and white-collar employees in Germany were begun,[4] and in 1932 the first issue of the now-legendary *Zeitschrift für Sozialforschung* appeared, with its programmatic articles on the role of economics, psychology, history, and cultural theory in the framework of the interdisciplinary materialism envisaged by the Institute.[5] This inaugural issue also testifies to Horkheimer's success in recruiting members of a rising generation of philosophers, scholars, and social scientists who were as yet unknown but would later achieve eminence in their fields. Erich Fromm, Herbert Marcuse, and Leo Löwenthal joined the Institute between 1929 and 1932; beginning in 1935 Walter Benjamin received a stipend and published regularly in the *Zeitschrift;* and in 1938 Theodor Adorno, who had been closely associated with the Institute since the late 1920s, became an official member as well.[6] It might be argued, then, that Horkheimer's singular achievement was to combine the roles of programmatic social theorist, manager of the collective projects of a social-scientific research institute, editor of its journal, and, not seldom, personal mediator among this remarkably talented group.

Max Horkheimer was born near Stuttgart in 1895, the only son of an upwardly mobile Jewish entrepreneurial family. His father, Moritz Horkheimer, had worked his way up from modest beginnings to become a prosperous textile manufacturer and had also achieved considerable public recognition, including various civic honors. Horkheimer's parents were part of a German-Jewish generation who could still feel that they were essentially German citizens whose religious confession happened be Judaism.[7] They did maintain religious and cultural practices that provided the young Horkheimer with a firm basis for his Jewish identity; his mother kept a kosher household, and the family lived "in a somewhat strict, not orthodox, but conservative Jewish atmosphere."[8] By the end of his life, Horkheimer would come to see his parental home as something of an archetype of the bourgeois, patriarchal family in the era of liberalism. He remembered his father as stern and domineering yet earnestly dedicated to the family's welfare and his mother as "a particularly loving woman."[9] Traces of this idealized image can be found interwoven with his sociological analyses of the decline of the modern family. Yet it stands in marked contrast to passages from his early journals and novels in which he accused his parents of vicious hostility toward him.[10]

The young Horkheimer had to fight a protracted struggle to free himself from his family's plans for him. His father had designated him as his successor in running the family business, and in 1910 he was removed from secondary school, a year before completing his degree, to begin an apprenticeship in the factory. In late adolescence, three things fueled Horkheimer's bitter conflict with his parents. The first was his outrage at the sufferings of workers, for whom he had now become directly responsible. Horkheimer was tormented by the conviction that his own comforts and possibilities were being purchased at the cost of exploiting the labor of others.[11] He vented his outrage and probed his conscience in novellas and diaries. This formative experience would remain one of the essential spurs to his intellectual activity.[12] The second was his relationship with Friedrich Pollock. They met in 1911 and almost immediately formed a lifelong friendship, complete with a written contract that regulated how and even when they would make joint decisions and work out their differences. Horkheimer was impressed by the cool, reserved bearing that enabled Pollock to disregard social convention, and their relationship provided a refuge where he could nurture his opposition to the world of his parents and his class. Together they made their first acquaintance with philosophy—Spinoza, Kant, and Schopenhauer—and read works of literary naturalism and social protest: Ibsen, Strindberg, Zola, Tolstoy, Kropotkin, Karl Kraus, and contemporary Expressionism, including Franz Pfemfert's left-wing journal, *Die Aktion*. The pathos of Expressionist protest left a lasting mark on the tone of his work.[13] Finally, in 1916, Horkheimer began a relationship with Rose Riekher that represented his first open challenge to his parents' world. In their eyes she was an unsuitable match on all counts: she was his father's secretary, eight years older than Max, the daughter of a bankrupt hotel owner, and a Christian. Their relationship—which, like his friendship with Pollock, proved to be lifelong—precipitated years of open confrontation with his parents.

Although he entered the military in 1916, Horkheimer was exempted from service at the front on medical grounds, and it was from a sanatorium in Munich that he experienced the demise of the German Empire and the postwar upheavals. Horkheimer now began to translate his acute sense of injustice into political terms. He had rejected the war from the beginning, but the November revolution and the councils movement played a key role in politicizing his opposition to bourgeois society. He became convinced that there were social and political forces at work that promised to eradicate exploitation more effectively than the pathos of moral appeals. This discovery of society went together with his discovery of Marxism, which from the first seemed to him the best guide to explain the social and political upheavals he was witnessing. Nevertheless, throughout his life Horkheimer remained circumspect about any public engagement in politics and even, until the late 1920s, about openly professing his Marxist sympathies. During these years his politics remained, as one observer has put it, "more or less a private matter."[14]

After the war, Horkheimer began his studies in Munich and then moved to the new university in Frankfurt. During the Weimar Republic Frankfurt provided a rich climate for those interested in social philosophy in the broadest sense. In addition to the newly founded Institute for Social Research, there were circles around the seminars of Paul Tillich and, later, Karl Mannheim; at the Freies Jüdisches Lehrhaus, Franz Rosenzweig was promoting a renaissance of Jewish culture; and the Frankfurt Psychoanalytic Institute offered lectures and seminars.[15] At first Horkheimer pursued work in both psychology and philosophy. He quickly established a close relationship with Hans Cornelius, a neo-Kantian who held the only full professorship for philosophy at Frankfurt. Cornelius's encouragement and patronage were decisive in convincing Horkheimer to pursue philosophy and in promoting the rapid development of his career. It was on Cornelius's recommendation that he went to Freiburg in 1920–1921 to study with Edmund Husserl, where he also met Husserl's young assistant, Martin Heidegger. Although he already doubted that he could agree with Heidegger's basic positions, he was duly impressed by what he saw as the genuine, nonacademic impulse to Heidegger's thinking. The encounter with Heidegger provided an early impetus to the process by which Horkheimer gradually began distancing himself from the sort of neo-Kantianism represented by Cornelius. Following the collapse of his plans for a doctoral dissertation on the psychology of visual perception, Cornelius proposed that he submit a study of "The

Antinomy of Teleological Judgment" in Kant. His career now advanced rapidly. Upon completion of the dissertation in 1923, Cornelius named him to the prestigious position of his assistant; just two years later, in 1925, Horkheimer submitted his *Habilitationsschrift*, a broader study of Kant's *Critique of Judgment*, and became a *Privatdozent*, or unsalaried lecturer.[16]

During the late 1920s Horkheimer lectured regularly on the history of philosophy, steadily expanding the scope of his work, and he began to move beyond formal and idealist paradigms by reading the history of philosophy in terms of a Marxian model of historical materialism adopted from *The German Ideology*.[17] At the same time, he was recording an extensive collection of private notes and aphorisms, which he later published under the title of *Dämmerung* (Twilight) (1934). It was in these years that the marriage of Marx and Schopenhauer, so characteristic of Horkheimer's work, took place.[18] This turn in Horkheimer's thinking accorded with a more general philosophical movement of the 1920s: the rising generation rejected what they now regarded as formalism in favor of more engaged philosophical stances, whether existential philosophy or critical Marxism. In Horkheimer's work this took the form of constructing an alliance between Schopenhauerian pathos and progressive social philosophy. What they shared, to Horkheimer's way of thinking, was a relentless critique of any transfiguration of suffering—this was one of the keys to his affinity for materialism—and an attempt to ground human solidarity on a shared experience of suffering and creaturely finitude. These principles provide what may be the most consistent themes underlying his work throughout its many transformations.[19]

When Carl Grünberg was forced by ill health to give up the directorship of the institute, Horkheimer, by now regarded as the heir apparent, was named director in 1930, at age thirty-five. At the same time, he was appointed to a newly created chair for social philosophy at the university, culminating a steady rise through the academic ranks that contrasts markedly with the careers of the institute's other members. Horkheimer moved quickly to establish a new character and direction for the institute, initiating major changes in its personnel, the focus of its work, and its guiding conception of social research. He gathered around him a circle of close collaborators whom he often referred to as the institute's "Interieur." Their backgrounds and interests clearly set them off from the previous members: none came out of the labor movement, none had been active in party politics, and all came from Jewish backgrounds, though their families represented a wide range of relationships to Judaism. The new guard's interests indicated the directions in which Horkheimer looked to expand the institute's work. Under Grünberg it had focused squarely on political economy and on the history of socialism and the labor movement. Now Erich Fromm was to guide the integration of psychoanalysis and social psychology into the institute's social analysis; Herbert Marcuse would reinforce Horkheimer's own pursuits in philosophy; Leo Löwenthal would be responsible for literature and Theodor Adorno (not yet officially a member) for music. The older lines of work were not discontinued, but they tended to fall into the background of the institute's research program. Finally, Horkheimer projected a new conception of social research, which he outlined in his 1931 inaugural lecture and continued to elaborate in programmatic contributions to the *Zeitschrift* in the course of the 1930s. The interdisciplinary program he envisioned would overcome the "chaotic specialization" of the disciplines and mediate splits between philosophy and empirical research and, ultimately, theory and practice.

Putting these changes into practice required Horkheimer to play several roles. Intellectually, he advanced his own distinctive conception of interdisciplinary materialism or, as he later called it, "critical theory," and he drew out its philosophical implications, demarcating it against the philosophical currents of the time. He also had to coordinate the work of a diverse group of talents. This meant that although his own model might enjoy quasi-official status due to his authority as director, in practice there was an implicit tolerance for alternative paradigms. Adorno's model of a nonintentionalist "interpretive philosophy," inspired by Benjamin, was one example, and beyond the inner circle, Wittfogel, Grossman, and Neumann continued to work with a model closer to orthodox Marxism.[20] Horkheimer's ability to accommodate what might have been regarded as contradictions or inconsistencies was not just a matter of making pragmatic concessions. In no small measure, it was made possible by his characteristic style of thinking: he operated not in terms of rigorous internal consistency but aporetically, constructing frameworks in which the complementary contradictions of competing programs could be made explicit and productive.[21] The balance between an animating vision and diverse perspectives was nowhere more apparent than in the *Zeitschrift für Sozialforschung*. As the institute's house organ and the platform for its program, it presented a distinctive persona among the schools of social analysis in the 1930s, yet it also incorporated contributors with an impressively broad range of orientations—not only in its articles but in its extensive book review section as well.[22] As an organizer of talents and distributor of the institute's resources, Horkheimer also held the strings of personal relationships among the members. Their dependence on the institute's support has led some critics to see it as a "patriarchally structured enclave of social criticism in the lap of bourgeois society."[23]

Finally, as director, Horkheimer was also responsible for managing the institute's practical affairs.[24] From the beginning of his tenure he was forced to do so under the most difficult of conditions. He had no illusions about the danger posed by the rise of the radical right and immediately began establishing branch operations in Geneva and London while transferring the institute's assets abroad to ensure its survival. His fears soon proved to be well founded. In March, 1933 the institute's headquarters in Frankfurt was occupied and closed by the police; the following month Horkheimer was dismissed from his chair at the university under the law that purged the civil service of Jews and political undesirables. The institute moved first to provisional quarters in Geneva and then, in 1934, to New York City, where a building on Morningside Heights was provided by Columbia University.

The 1930s proved to be Horkheimer's most productive period as a theorist. He generated a steady stream of essays for the *Zeitschrift*, contributing major statements to every volume.[25] He also displayed an extraordinary single-mindedness in keeping the institute's theoretical and empirical projects going. Nevertheless, the institute's work was clearly marked by the experience of exile. It should not be forgotten that it was in exile that the so-called Frankfurt School actually developed its identity. The difficulties that Horkheimer and his collaborators faced are suggested by the fact that during its most productive years, the institute was based in New York, producing a German-language journal that was published in Paris. Under these conditions and given the situation in Germany, it was extremely dif-

John McCole, Seyla Benhabib, and Wolfgang Bonß

ficult to conduct empirical research. Important projects like *Studies on Authority and the Family* (1936), however significant their findings, remained incomplete. The exigencies of exile had other, less immediately obvious effects as well. For all practical purposes, the institute gradually tended to contract to the members of Horkheimer's inner circle, and out of consideration for its guest status in a country not known for its hospitality to socialism, it frequently practiced a kind of self-censorship in its publications by toning down political language it feared might be abrasive. All of these tendencies were arguably present in Horkheimer's management of the institute in any case, but the pressures of exile undoubtedly accentuated them. Finally, the steady deterioration of the political situation also left its mark on his work.[26] Particularly in the first months of the war, signs of despair became palpable in essays such as "The Jews and Europe" and "The Authoritarian State."

In 1941 Horkheimer decided to relocate farther west, to Santa Monica, California, a move that put an end to the nexus of working relationships he had managed to sustain in New York. The institute now contracted to a rump consisting of Horkheimer, Adorno, and Pollock. With this second westward migration, critical theory was also entering a new phase, in which it would be shaped more by Adorno than by Horkheimer. The product of their conversations in California was a manuscript originally titled "Philosophical Fragments" (1944), which they published after the war as *Dialectic of Enlightenment* (1947).[27]

When the war was over, Horkheimer at first remained based in the United States, coordinating a research project on anti-Semitism sponsored by the American Jewish Committee. But he was also beginning to receive overtures from Frankfurt—both the city and the University. After considerable hesitation, he decided, in 1948, to accept the invitation to return the institute to Frankfurt, and by 1951 it was able to move into new quarters. The "Café Max," as students called it, was back in business. Of the institute's former insiders, only Pollock and Adorno came with him. Among Horkheimer's motives for returning was his hope that the institute could contribute to building a democratic political culture in Germany, but Horkheimer never again succeeded in striking a balance among his various roles as he had under the objectively far more precarious conditions of the 1930s. He now achieved considerable academic prominence, serving as rector of the

University of Frankfurt from 1951 to 1953 (the first Jew ever to hold this position at a Germany university) and receiving numerous civic honors. His public stance was thoroughly pragmatic, and the institute did important work: it contributed to the reestablishment of social research in Germany, promoting the introduction of new techniques in the social sciences while trying to keep alive the connection with "the great tradition of European philosophy and sociology." It also helped to train a generation of students who went on to shape the intellectual debates of the 1960s and 1970s.

By now Horkheimer's pragmatism was not so much a matter of political caution and self-censorship as the expression of a change of heart, never fully acknowledged, about liberal democracy. Nevertheless, his reservations remained. His private notes from these years renewed his concern with human suffering as a spur to social solidarity, and his affinities with the philosophy of Schopenhauer took on a new resonance. But now Horkheimer did not mediate these themes with a program of social research in any cogent way, nor did he reconcile the radical, totalizing critique of Enlightenment developed in *Dialectic of Enlightenment* with his earlier, and continuing, identification with its traditions and goals. He was either unwilling or unable to develop a third paradigm in which aporias such as these could be resolved productively. Although he had never been an author of large, synthetic statements, he also produced nothing comparable to his remarkable series of programmatic essays for the *Zeitschrift* in the 1930s. Instead, his work was divided between occasional pieces and private notes, which were published only posthumously.[28] His position increasingly centered on the theme of preserving a "longing for the totally Other" (*Sehnsucht nach dem ganz Anderen*)[29] in a totally administered world, or taking up a stance "For Non-Conformism," the title of his final aphorism in *Notizen*. This stance both attracted the student movement of the 1960s and eventually led to acrimonious tensions with part of it. Behind the disjointedness of Horkheimer's roles lay his ambivalent, uncomfortable relationship with the society of the postwar Federal Republic, a discomfort heightened by the more positive sense of Jewish identity he had meanwhile developed. By his own account, the persecution of the the Jews in the 1930s led him to exchange his "rebellious instincts" against Judaism for an identification with the victims and a new appreciation for the particular qualities of

Jewish social and cultural solidarity.[30] In fact, Horkheimer continued to hedge his bets on Germany. He carefully maintained his U.S. citizenship, and from 1954 to 1959 he held a guest professorship at the University of Chicago. After retiring in 1959, he retreated to his home in Montagnola, Italy, and passed away in 1973 at the age of seventy-eight.

In view of Horkheimer's role as the founding father of critical theory, it is surprising that his work is so little known and studied. Compared to the proliferation of studies on Marcuse, Adorno, and Benjamin, Horkheimer has been relatively neglected in the scholarly literature. He has sometimes been seen through the lens of journalistic memory, appearing as a historical witness whose lifetime spanned the rise and fall of the Weimar Republic, the rise and fall of National Socialism and the Third Reich, the mass annihilation of the European Jews, and postwar reconstruction in the Federal Republic.[31] Frequently, he has been assigned an organizational rather than a theoretical role in his capacity as the "dictatorial" director of the Institute.[32] And many interpreters have implied that, compared to Adorno, he was always the lesser theorist, overshadowed in the collaboration with his brilliant junior colleague.[33]

   In some ways Horkheimer himself helped to promote such interpretations, for after his postwar return to Germany, he hesitated to identify himself with his earlier work. Jürgen Habermas recalls that in the reconstructed Institute of the 1950s, not only the Institute's own projects of the 1930s but even the *Zeitschrift für Sozialforschung* were virtually unknown; apparently Horkheimer kept the Institute's only copy of the *Zeitschrift* in the basement, in a crate that was nailed shut.[34] But once Horkheimer's essays from the 1930s were republished in 1968 in a two-volume set, *Kritische Theorie*, followed two years later by a reprint of the entire *Zeitschrift für Sozialforschung*, the outlines of the early institute's complex research strategy gradually became clear. Against the background of the newly edited materials that have continued to appear since then, it is not surprising that the early phases of the institute's research program have received increased attention. As it has become clear that there was (and is) more than one conception of critical theory,[35] the evaluation of Horkheimer's place in the development of the Frankfurt School has changed accordingly.

Horkheimer is now viewed as the creator of a unique theoretical program that conceptualized an innovative process of interaction between philosophy and the social sciences. Particularly his early addresses and writings (1931–1937) reveal his originality as a thinker and highlight the significance of the program of materialist, interdisciplinary research that he advocated in those years.[36]

This new perspective on Horkheimer's work is significant because it demonstrates that what has come to be known as critical theory actually encompasses multiple paradigms that cannot be seamlessly translated into one another. At the beginning of the 1930s at least two contrasting alternatives can be distinguished. In counterpoint to the interdisciplinary materialism that Horkheimer advocated in his 1931 inaugural address, Adorno later that year set out his own vision in his own inaugural lecture as *Privatdozent* in philosophy at Frankfurt. The alternative program Adorno presented in "The Actuality of Philosophy" differed from Horkheimer's on two essential points.[37] On the one hand, Adorno was skeptical about the claims of philosophy and much more critical than Horkheimer of the conceptual structure of Western rationality, which he characterized as "identity philosophy." Whereas Horkheimer insisted on the normative potential of the concept of reason developed in the Western philosophical tradition, in Adorno's view this potential had now broken down irrevocably. And that was why, in turn, the interdisciplinary collaboration of social philosophy and social research offered no viable alternative. For Adorno, there could be no general, positive solutions, and in particular all hopes for an internal reform of the social sciences were bound to prove futile.

Adorno's version of critical theory, with its turn to aesthetics and cultural criticism, increasingly prevailed from the end of the 1930s onward. But a demonstration that this development was by no means inevitable in fact preceded the intellectual historians' rediscovery of Horkheimer's early essays and addresses. A case in point can be seen in the development of Jürgen Habermas's work. Beginning in the early 1970s, Habermas rejected Adorno's aesthetic orientation and began arguing for a reorientation of critical theory toward a renewed collaboration between philosophy and the social sciences. From 1971 to 1983, through his position at the Starnberg Max Planck Institute, he also had at his disposal the institutional basis needed to put this reorientation into practice. In this context Habermas proposed the program of a reconstructive science, in which the insights of philosophy and the results of empirical social research would be synthesized in a new way. Like Horkheimer, he drew upon the most advanced social-scientific approaches, such as the work of Niklaus Luhmann and Jean Piaget, which were to be appropriated, integrated, and pushed further, theoretically as well as empirically.

One may debate whether what Habermas accomplished at the Starnberg Institute is comparable to the achievements of the Institute for Social Research under Horkheimer's directorship, but the project itself is in many respects more a resumption of Horkheimer's program of interdisciplinary materialism than a continuation of the intervening phases of critical theory. Habermas's strong affinity for Horkheimer's original program in spirit, if not in detail, is clear in his *Theory of Communicative Action.*[38] At the end of both the first and second volumes, he explicitly places himself within the tradition of Horkheimer's program, at the same time demarcating his position against that of Adorno. Whereas Adorno is moved closer to the postmodern camp, Horkheimer's approach is presented as having lost none of its relevance.[39] It deserves to be reactivated, Habermas argues, because it makes possible a reformulation of critical theory corresponding to the state of development meanwhile achieved by the social-scientific disciplines.

Recent research has made us aware of intraparadigmatic disputes in critical theory, such as that between Adorno and Horkheimer, as well as interparadigmatic breaks in its history, as between Adorno and Habermas. With reference to Horkheimer, these tensions and fissures can now be defined more precisely than before, thanks to the publication of Horkheimer's *Gesammelte Schriften* since 1985.[40] The previously unpublished material now available enables us better to appreciate both the breadth of his work and its originality. The importance and distinctiveness of Horkheimer's version of critical theory may already have been recognized, but study of the *Gesammelte Schriften* will play an important role in the emerging reevaluation of Horkheimer's work and of his place in the history of critical theory.

This book presents to an English-language audience some of the most important results of this ongoing reevaluation. The contributions have been collected and solicited with three purposes in mind. First, we want to present the breadth, depth, and complexity of Horkheimer's conception of philosophy and the social sciences in the years from 1931 to 1937. Second, through a series of detailed analyses, we want to assess the insights and illusions of Horkheimer's pivotal 1937 essay, "Traditional and Critical Theory," which came to stand as the manifesto for an entire school of thought. Finally, we want to highlight several crucial but previously underilluminated themes, issues, and episodes in Horkheimer's life and work. Our goal has been to shed light on salient aspects of Horkheimer's work rather than to cover his thought as a whole. Although the chapters have been organized thematically, they also run more or less parallel to the development of his thought, with part I concentrating on the early phase between 1931 and 1937 and part II beginning with 1937 and leading up to *Eclipse of Reason* of 1944.[41]

Part I opens with "Max Horkheimer's Intellectual Physiognomy," in which Alfred Schmidt maintains that running throughout Horkheimer's life and oeuvre is a pessimistic materialism, which Horkheimer learned from Arthur Schopenhauer. Schopenhauer's emphasis on our finitude as mortal creatures and his belief in the contingency of the universe allow Horkheimer to distance himself from the more rationalist and optimistic philosophies of history of Kant and Hegel. Horkheimer combines the themes of finitude and contingency with Marxian materialism. Materialism in this context does not mean only or primarily a theory of society but also a vision of human life, rooted in finitude, open to suffering and unpredictability. Schmidt is careful to distinguish Horkheimer's "metaphysical pessimism" from his equally forceful critique of the metaphysical systems of German philosophy of late 1920s and early 1930s. Throughout his life, Max Horkheimer fought against two currents of thought: the dogmatic metaphysics of "meaning creation" (*Sinngebung*) and the antitheoretical positivism of the empirical sciences.

Horkheimer's conceptual strategy of repudiating metaphysical systems while being equally critical of antitheoretical forms of positivism are also the central themes of the essays of Jürgen Habermas and Hauke Brunkhorst. According to Habermas, the only complete intellectual program Horkheimer ever worked out was his program of an "interdisciplinary materialism." This program receded after 1937, as Adorno's critique of identity logic and a much more pessimistic conception of reason began to dominate Horkheimer's work. Habermas argues that the break with the program of interdisciplinary materialist research continued into *Dialectic of Enlightenment* and shaped Horkheimer's later years.

Brunkhorst's essay, "Dialectical Positivism of Happiness: Horkheimer's Materialist Deconstruction of Philosophy," documents aspects of this interdisciplinary materialism. According to Brunkhorst, the real meaning of Horkheimer's materialism is not the overcoming of philosophy but its social-scientific transformation. Brunkhorst outlines a typology of the changing meanings of materialism and idealism for Horkheimer. The essay concludes by considering the ethical implications of Horkheimer's concept of materialism, and particularly the claim that all ethics is rooted in individuals' longings for happiness on the one hand and their capacity for compassion for the suffering of the living on the other.

Wolfgang Bonß further analyzes the conceptual program of an interdisciplinary materialist social research. Horkheimer criticized the established practices of the social sciences in particular for their fragmentation and specialization; interdisciplinary materialism, therefore, does not imply a syncretic synthesis of existing disciplines and theorems but rather a reconfiguration of the existing disciplines with an eye to producing a picture of "the present as a concrete totality."

Thomas McCarthy and Wolf Schäfer in their contributions expand the exclusive focus on the internal analysis of Horkheimer's thought characteristic of the previous essays and situate Horkheimer's views in broader intellectual contexts. McCarthy is interested in reviving Horkheimer's critique of metaphysical reason of the early 1930s, in the light of the postmodernist and posttranscendentialist attacks on reason today. McCarthy maintains that although Horkheimer, like today's antimetaphysicians, was against the globalizing and universalizing approaches of system builders, nonetheless he did not view the "rootedness" of thought in human action and interests as sufficient reason to dismiss claims to the validity of such thinking. Horkheimer distinguished between "contextualizing" and "judging validity claims." McCarthy also laments the fact that despite this auspicious beginning Horkheimer's program went awry after 1937. The aporias of Horkheimer's later work may derive from the fact that at that point he subscribed to a more foundationalist concept of justification, which in turn led him to more intense pessimism that such claims to rationality could ever be realized.

Wolf Schäfer begins his essay on John Desmond Bernal and Max Horkheimer by reflecting on a well-known topos of Marxian social theory. Marx, and many Marxists after him, frequently saw the domination of nature, and the degree of control over natural processes reached by the natural sciences of his day, as an example to be emulated by social theory and practice in their attempts both to comprehend society and to control social processes. Schäfer notes that Horkheimer's work up to and including his essay "Traditional and Critical Theory" is dominated by such science-optimism. The later Horkheimer performs, however, a near reversal of his early position, moving from an optimism about natural science to an equally one-sided pessimism. Schäfer establishes an unusual contrast between Horkheimer and the British scientist and writer John Desmond Bernal (1901–1971) to show how "dehumanization" can mean such radically different things. For Bernal, dehumanization refers to a fictional process of progressive disembedding from the human body, a technoscientific frontier of leaving our earthly existence behind; for Horkheimer, the humanist, dehumanization refers to the increasing sense of loss of meaning and freedom in a fully administered universe, in which the natural sciences are fully complicitous. These radically divergent attitudes are viewed by Schäfer as exemplifying the gap between the "two cultures" of natural science and humanities to which C. P. Snow has called our attention.

Part II of this volume begins with two essays focusing on the social-scientific aspects and deficiencies of Horkheimer's "Traditional and Critical Theory." According to Axel Honneth, Horkheimer equivocated between two concepts of human activity in his best-known essay, much as Marx had in the *Economic and Philosophical Manuscripts of 1844*. On the one hand, Horkheimer modeled his understanding of human activity on that of world-shaping and transforming physical labor; on the other hand, he continued to mean by activity "critical-political" praxis as well. In "Horkheimer's Original Program: The Sociological Deficit of Critical Theory," Honneth argues that this equivocation is part of a philosophy of history of macrosubjectivity, within the framework of which the "social," the sphere of everyday social action and interaction, disappears. Hence the "sociological deficit" of early critical theory, which sought a synthesis of political economy and psychoanalysis while neglecting the domain of social interactions, associations, and habits.

A number of contributions to this volume, such as Habermas's, Brunkhorst's, and McCarthy's, locate the sources of Horkheimer's later pessimism in avoidable and unfortunate theoretical turns taken by Horkheimer from the mid-1930s onward. Moishe Postone and Barbara Brick turn from epistemology and the philosophy of science to political economy in Horkheimer's work. Horkheimer's pessimism, they argue, cannot be explained by the historical events of his day alone. Rather, a much more fundamental paradigm change in critical theory is at work here under the influence of Friedrich Pollock's thesis of "state capitalism." State capitalism is seen as a system of the integration of the economic and the political that eventually eliminates all social conflict and contradictions. If this were so, however, it would mean that social critique could no longer be anchored in the contradictory social totality; it would lose its moorings in the social. Postone and Brick examine the faulty logic of Pollock's thesis of "state capitalism," distinguishing it in the process from what they consider a more adequate Marxian method of social criticism.

In "Remarks on the Development of Horkheimer's Work," Habermas argues that the theoretical differences between Adorno and Horkheimer are reflected in the text of *Dialectic of Enlightenment*. While the introductory chapter and the chapter on "Juliette, or Enlightenment and Morality" come from Horkheimer's pen, the chapters on Odysseus and the culture industry bear Adorno's stamp. These theoretical differences between Adorno and Horkheimer are the focus of Stefan Breuer's "The Long Friendship: On Theoretical Differences between Adorno and Horkheimer." Breuer, like Honneth, analyzes and highlights the rationalist metaphysics of labor that colors Horkheimer's conception of critical theory, and traces it back to Georg Lukács's work. According to Breuer, once he gave up this metaphysics, Horkheimer could no longer distinguish his position from that of conservative cultural criticism. Adorno, however, rejected such metaphysics from the beginning; his reflections on "sociation" *(Vergesellschaftung)* and on second nature are the material on which Breuer constructs his theses.

If one compares Alfred Schmidt's thesis with those of Honneth, Postone and Brick, and Stefan Breuer, one sees that they emphasize the continuity of elements of rationalist metaphysics in Horkheimer's thought, whereas Schmidt focuses on Horkheimer's metaphysical pessimism. Such pessimism is certainly not antirational, but neither does it posit any utopias of reconciliation of reason, freedom, and happiness, as the German idealists did. Herbert Schnädelbach's essay "Max Horkheimer and the Moral Philosophy of German Idealism" throws light on these issues by approaching the question of Horkheimer's relation to German idealism not through his philosophy of history but through his reflections on morality. Much of what Horkheimer said about morality belonged not to a systematic doctrine of ethics but to a sociology of morality. Nonetheless, Schnädelbach discovers in Horkheimer's work a "materialistic moral philosophy," distinct from the deontological, universalistic, and rationalistic conceptions of ethics characteristic of German idealism. "For Horkheimer," writes Schnädelbach, "morality only occurs where men profess their commitment to feelings of 'indignation, compassion, love, and solidarity.'"

The significance of emotions, needs, and sensuous images in Horkheimer's writings are also at the center of Mechthild Rumpf's contribution, " 'Mystical Aura': Imagination and Reality of the 'Maternal' in Horkheimer's Writings." In *Dialectic of Enlightenment*, Horkheimer and Adorno suggested that the process of enlightenment, which unleashed the human domination over external nature, must be accompanied by a process of sublimation for the individual. External relations of domination were internalized by the subject to produce "the self, the identical, purposive, virile character of man."[42] In Horkheimer's reflections on the maternal and maternal love, Rumpf sees an alternative model of individual psychosexual development suggested by Horkheimer. In the traces of the maternal, she seeks "aspects of the constitution of the subject that resist the separation of reason and sensuality, of self and other, aspects in which a rupture of the subject-object structure is implicit." This feminist rereading of Horkheimer brings to light hitherto neglected but fascinating aspects of his thought.

It is one of the central theses of *Dialectic of Enlightenment* that instrumental rationality could not comprehend the otherness of the other except by reducing the other to an object to be manipulated. Otherness could only be comprehended insofar as it could also be appropriated. The phenomenon of anti-Semitism is seen by Adorno and Horkheimer in this light as the desperate attempt to eliminate the Jews, after the Nazis stamped them as the bearers of an insufferable otherness within German-Christian culture. This quasiontological analysis of anti-Semitism, however, had not been Horkheimer's view earlier. Dan Diner's article, "Reason and the 'Other': Horkheimer's Reflections on Anti-Semitism and Mass Annihilation," is devoted to an analysis of Horkheimer's changing reflections on anti-Semitism, from the orthodox Marxism of his 1939 essay, "The Jews and Europe," to his later prayer "that the murderer not triumph over the innocent victim."

The final two contributions in this volume turn to the place of art and the aesthetic for Horkheimer. Whereas Martin Jay elucidates Horkheimer's views by contrasting them with those of Siegfried Kracauer, Georg Lohmann discovers the presence of the aesthetic in the dense, philosophical text of *Eclipse of Reason.* Jay documents Horkheimer's unswerving modernism, his rejection of avant-garde as well as mass art, and his continuing emphasis on the autonomous individual as a measure of the value of the aesthetic. Lohmann approaches a similar conclusion through a careful analysis of the measuring rods of Horkheimer's method of critique. For Horkheimer the only normative basis of social criticism is the experience of individual suffering, a negative phenomenon, rather than the positive experience of self-actualization. Self-actualization remains an elusive ideal that only the aesthetic can redeem.

As can readily be seen from the preceding discussion, the authors of this volume do not share a common assessment of the viability and cogency of Horkheimer's thought for present concerns in the realms of epistemology, ethics, sociology, political economy, or aesthetics. What unites them is a shared sense that Horkheimer's integration of the results of the specialized sciences with philosophical reflection to produce a unique form of theorizing was highly significant. It is this interaction between philosophy and social science that has receded from the horizon of theorizing in the Anglo-American context since the mid-seventies and has given way to the dominance of cultural studies over social theory, of discourse analysis over concrete social and historical research. To be sure, recalling and reexamining Horkheimer's original insight of interdisciplinary materialism alone will not change this constellation of our current cultural and theoretical universe. It may, however, prompt a new generation of readers to reconsider the interplay between philosophy and social science that was formulated over half a century ago by this unique and unusual intellectual, and which, in the form of the critical theory of the Frankfurt School, has become the source for one of the most challenging theoretical traditions of this century.

Notes

1. On the founding of the Institute for Social Research see Paul Kluke, *Die Stiftungs-universität Frankfurt am Main, 1914–1932* (Frankfurt, 1972), and Ulrike Migdal, *Die Frühgeschichte des Frankfurter Instituts für Sozialforschung* (Frankfurt, 1981); and for bio-graphical portraits, Wilhelm van Reijen and Gunzelin Schmid Noerr, eds., *Grand Hotel Abgrund: Eine Photobiographie der Kritischen Theorie* (Hamburg, 1990).

2. "Die gegenwärtige Lage der Sozialphilosophie und die Aufgaben eines Instituts für Sozialforschung," in Horkheimer, *Gesammelte Schriften* (Frankfurt, 1988), 3:20–35; English translations: "The State of Contemporary Social Philosophy and the Tasks of an Institute for Social Research," in Stephen Bronner and Douglas Kellner, eds., *Critical Theory and Society: A Reader* (New York, 1989), 25–36, and in Horkheimer, *Between Philosophy and Social Science: Selected Early Writings* (Cambridge, 1993).

3. Ibid., in *Gesammelte Schriften* 3:29–30; in *Critical Theory and Society,* 32.

4. See Erich Fromm, *Arbeiter und Angestellte am Vorabend des Dritten Reiches. Eine sozial-psychologische Untersuchung,* ed. Wolfgang Bonß (Stuttgart, 1980).

5. The *Zeitschrift für Sozialforschung* replaced previous director Carl Grünberg's *Archiv für die Geschichte des Sozialismus und der Arbeiterbewegung* as the institute's official journal. It appeared quarterly for a total of nine volumes (vol. 1: Leipzig, 1932; vols. 2–7: Paris, 1933–1938; vols. 8–9: New York, 1939–1941); beginning in 1940 with vol. 8, no. 3, it appeared as *Studies in Philosophy and Social Science.* A facsimile reprint was published in 1970 and again in 1980 in a paperback edition. See the Bibliography.

6. The political economist Friedrich Pollock should also be mentioned; Horkheimer delegated to him the institute's day-to-day administrative and financial affairs. Löwen-thal also served as editor-in-charge of the *Zeitschrift.*

7. Horkheimer's parents refused to leave Germany until 1939, despite the accelerating persecution of the Jews, the confiscation of the family business and villa, and their son's warnings. His father wrote to him that their family had been "in Germany longer than that of Herr Hitler," who was Austrian. Helmut Gumnior and Rudolf Ringguth, *Max Horkheimer* (Reinbek, 1973), 11.

8. Horkheimer, "Das Schlimme erwarten und doch das Gute versuchen" (conversation with Gerhard Rein, 1972), in *Gesammelte Schriften* (Frankfurt, 1985), 7:443. On Horkheimer's changing attitude toward his Jewish identity in relation to his work, see the essay by Dan Diner in this book, chapter 13.

John McCole, Seyla Benhabib, and Wolfgang Bonß

9. Ibid., 442.

10. For a discussion of the relationship between Horkheimer's ambivalences about his own parents and his conception of the "maternal," see the essay by Mechthild Rumpf in this book, chapter 12.

11. Horkheimer expressed his sense of guilt and outrage with particular vehemence in a letter to his cousin Hans: "Who is complaining about suffering? You and I? We are cannibals complaining that the flesh of those we slaughter gives us stomachaches. . . . you sleep in beds and wear clothes produced by people who are starving, people we drive with the tyrannical whip of our money, and you don't know how many women have fallen at the machine that produces the material for your 'cutaway.' . . . It's downright ridiculous, as if a butcher in the slaughterhouse were to brood about his white apron getting bloody." Unpublished letter, Horkheimer Archive, Stadts- und Universitätsbibliothek Frankfurt, cited by Gumnior and Ringguth, *Max Horkheimer*, 7–9.

12. Horkheimer, *Gesammelte Schriften* 1: "*Aus der Pubertät. Novellen und Tagebuchblätter,*" *1914–1918* (Frankfurt, 1988). For commentary, see chapter 2 in this book.

13. Rolf Wiggershaus, *Die Frankfurter Schule: Geschichte, Theoretische Entwicklung, Politische Bedeutung* (Munich, 1986), 62, 125.

14. Ibid., 60.

15. The intellectual culture of Frankfurt in the 1920s is portrayed in Wolfgang Schivelbusch, *Intellektuellendämmerung: Zur Lage der Frankfurter Intelligenz in den zwanziger Jahren* (Frankfurt, 1982).

16. Ironically, in the same year Horkheimer was responsible for a negative evaluation of Walter Benjamin's manuscript, *The Origin of German Trauerspiel,* which sealed the failure of Benjamin's own attempt to secure a position at Frankfurt. Horkheimer never acknowledged this during his lifetime. The story has now been reconstructed by Burkhardt Lindner, "Habilitationsakte Benjamin. Über ein 'akademisches Trauerspiel' und über ein Vorkapitel der 'Frankfurter Schule' (Horkheimer, Adorno)," in *LiLi. Zeitschrift für Literaturwissenschaft und Linguistik* 14, 53/54 (1984): 147–65.

17. Horkheimer's detailed lecture notes for his late 1920s lecture courses on the history of philosophy are now available as volumes 9 and 10 of Horkheimer, *Gesammelte Schriften* (Frankfurt, 1987).

18. On the importance of Schopenhauer throughout Horkheimer's work, see the essay by Alfred Schmidt in chapter 2 of this book.

19. On these themes, see in particular the essays by Alfred Schmidt, Hauke Brunkhorst, Georg Lohmann, and Herbert Schnädelbach in this book.

20. Differences between Adorno and Horkheimer are discussed below. On the continuing role played by Marxian political economy in the institute, see Alfons Söllner, *Geschichte und Herrschaft: Studien zur materialistischen Sozialwissenschaft, 1929–1942* (Frankfurt, 1978); David Held, *An Introduction to Critical Theory: Horkheimer to Habermas* (Berkeley/Los Angeles, 1980); Wiggershaus, *Die Frankfurter Schule;* and the essay by Barbara Brick and Moishe Postone in chapter 9 of this book. Those outside the Institute's inner circle did not always see it as particularly flexible, as is shown by Benjamin's disagreements over his project on nineteenth-century Paris and his essays on Baudelaire. On the pro-

cess of establishing consensus among the members of the core, see Leo Löwenthal's recollections in *Mitmachen wollte ich nie: Ein autobiographisches Gespräch mit Helmut Dubiel* (Frankfurt, 1980), 86–96.

21. On this aporetic tendency in Horkheimer's thinking, see chapters 3–5 in this book.

22. See Alfred Schmidt, "Die *Zeitschrift für Sozialforschung:* Geschichte und gegenwärtige Bedeutung," in *Zeitschrift für Sozialforschung,* facsimile reprint (Munich, 1970), 1:5–63, and Jürgen Habermas, "Die Frankfurter Schule in New York," in *Philosophisch-politische Profile* (Frankfurt, 1981), 411–25.

23. Wiggershaus, *Die Frankfurter Schule,* 168.

24. Wiggershaus's *Die Frankfurter Schule* was the first study to use archival material to give a detailed account of Horkheimer's practical strategies. Much of the author's account has a debunking tone, as when he describes Horkheimer's strategy for saving the institute's assets in 1932–1933 as "not heroic, in fact not even particularly cunning . . . but successful" (152).

25. For a chronological list of Horkheimer's articles in the *Zeitschrift,* see the Bibliography.

26. See Helmut Dubiel, *Theory and Politics: Studies in the Development of Critical Theory* (Cambridge, Mass., 1985), for a systematic account of how responses to historical events were linked to changes in the orientation of Horkheimer and his collaborators.

27. For an analysis that distinguishes the voices and contributions of the two authors of *Dialectic of Enlightenment,* see the essay by Jürgen Habermas in this book.

28. See Horkheimer, *Notizen 1950 bis 1969 und Dämmerung: Notizen in Deutschland* (Frankfurt, 1974), now also available in *Gesammelte Schriften* (Frankfurt, 1991), vol. 6, as "Notizen 1949–1969." These notes are discussed in chapter 2 in this book.

29. See "Die Sehnsucht nach dem ganz Anderen" (conversation with Helmut Gumnior, 1970), in *Gesammelte Schriften* (Frankfurt, 1985), 7:385–404.

30. Horkheimer, "Das Schlimme erwarten," 444–45.

31. See Gumnior and Ringguth, *Max Horkheimer.*

32. For instance, see Held, *Introduction to Critical Theory.*

33. For this view, see Wiggershaus, *Die Frankfurter Schule.*

34. See Habermas, "Die Frankfurter Schule in New York," 415.

35. See Martin Jay, *The Dialectical Imagination: A History of the Frankfurt School and the Institute of Social Research, 1923–1950* (Boston, 1973); Dubiel, *Theory and Politics;* Söllner, *Geschichte und Herrschaft;* Wolfgang Bonß and Axel Honneth, eds., *Sozialforschung als Kritik: Zum sozialwissenschaftlichen Potential der Kritischen Theorie* (Frankfurt, 1982); and Alfred Schmidt and Norbert Altwicker, eds., *Max Horkheimer heute: Werk und Wirkung* (Frankfurt, 1986).

36. The translations available in *Critical Theory: Selected Essays* (New York, 1972) have now been supplemented by a new set of translations in *Between Philosophy and Social*

Science: Max Horkheimer's Early Essays. For a listing of the contents of these volumes, see the Bibliography.

37. "Die Aktualität der Philosophie," in Adorno, *Gesammelte Schriften* (Frankfurt, 1973), vol.1; English translation: "The Actuality of Philosophy," *Telos* 31 (1977). On the differences between Adorno's and Horkheimer's agendas, see Jay, "Positive and Negative Totalities: Implicit Tensions in Critical Theory's Vision of Interdisciplinary Research," in Jay, *Permanent Exiles* (New York, 1985), and chapter 10 in this book.

38. Habermas, *Theorie des kommunikativen Handelns,* 2 vols. (Frankfurt, 1981); English translation: *The Theory of Communicative Action,* 2 vols. (Boston, 1984).

39. This is all the more remarkable since for biographical reasons Habermas might have been expected to look to Adorno rather than to Horkheimer: whereas Horkheimer rejected his aspirations for a *Habilitation,* Adorno took up his cause and helped to arrange his *Habilitation* at Marburg with Wolfgang Abendroth.

40. Max Horkheimer, *Gesammelte Schriften,* ed. Alfred Schmidt and Gunzelin Schmid Noerr (Frankfurt, 1985–   ). To date (1993), fourteen of the projected eighteen volumes have appeared; three volumes of letters and a concluding volume with an index and bibliography are still in preparation. For a listing of the individual volumes, see the Bibliography.

41. *Eclipse of Reason* was published in 1947; its five chapters were originally delivered as a series of lectures, "Society and Reason," at Columbia University in February and March, 1944.

42. Horkheimer and Adorno, *Dialectic of Enlightenment* (New York, 1972), 33; see Horkheimer, *Gesammelte Schriften,* vol. 5 (Frankurt, 1987), 56.

I

Science, Methodology, and Research Paradigms in the Development of Horkheimer's Work

2

Max Horkheimer's Intellectual Physiognomy

Alfred Schmidt

Countless, luminous spheres in infinite space, around each of which whirl perhaps a dozen smaller, illuminated spheres inwardly molten, covered with a congealed, cold crust, on which a film of mould has produced living, knowing beings: this is the empirical Truth, the Real, the World.
—*Arthur Schopenhauer*

Periodizations in biography and intellectual history can easily seem arbitrary. Nevertheless, if handled carefully, they are an indispensable aid to historians. This is especially true when dealing, as in the case of Max Horkheimer, with a complex life's work whose actual intentions, which cannot be fixed to an abstract position, at first remain inaccessible to contemporary readers. Horkheimer's intellectual biography can be clearly divided into six stages. The first consists of the novellas and diary entries written during World War I, which have been published under the title *Aus der Pubertät* (From Puberty).[1] Moral protest against social injustice, utopian desire for a better world, and pessimistic metaphysics, mindful of the ultimate futility of all human endeavor, stand side by side, unreconciled, in these remarkable literary ventures of his youth. They are nourished, as Horkheimer stressed in his old age, by the "desire for truth and for a correct life"; ethical and religious imperatives appear here as "motives which are either immediate prescriptions for the individual or which he negates."[2] The young Horkheimer lacks that scientific knowledge of social reality that would have nuanced his rebellious thoughts. He advocates "unconditional . . . loyalty to one's belief."[3] His novellas, rent by the painful gap between the ideal and reality, portray the merciless fate of uncompromising virtue "in this world."[4] The ensnarement of humanity in eternal nature and an unswerving struggle against temporal injustice are already central in his thinking. As essential as he finds it that the "unjust distribution of goods" be abolished, he nevertheless wonders whether even the "fulfillment of the boldest utopias" would not leave the "great torment" untouched, "because the core of life . . . is torment and dying"[5] or whether the "transcendental significance" of even "humanitarian, compassionate action"[6] does not become problematic once the "worldly and infernal mechanism"[7] has been seen through.

Clearly Horkheimer's adolescent writings, taking Schopenhauer's metaphysics of will (radicalized here and there) as their point of departure, anticipate essential traits of his later conceptions. "I had long been intimate with metaphysical pessimism," Horkheimer observed retrospectively in 1968. "I owe my first acquaintance with philosophy to the works of Schopenhauer; my relationship to Hegel and Marx and my desire to understand and change social reality have not extinguished my experience of his philosophy, despite the political contradictions involved."[8] Conceptual motifs from Marx and Schopenhauer— the latter standing for the *malum metaphysicum,* metaphysical evil, the former the *malum physicum,* material evil—are played out against each other on all levels of critical theory, because the "just society" is always also "a goal that is implicated with the idea of guilt,"[9] not only with that of a scientifically controllable total process.

Horkheimer's years as a student and graduate assistant (1919–1925) make up the second stage of his intellectual development. During this period he was influenced by his teacher in Frankfurt, Hans Cornelius, under whom he took his doctorate with a dissertation "On the Antinomy of Teleological Judgment" ("Zur Antinomie der teleologischen Urteilskraft," 1922). His *Habilitation* followed in 1925 with "Kant's *Critique of Judgment* as the Link between Theoretical and Practical Philosophy" ("Kants *Kritik der Urteilskraft* als Bindeglied zwischen theoretischer und praktischer Philosophie"). Cornelius, originally a pupil of Mach and Avenarius, characterized the "epistemological clarification of the world picture and the elimination of specious metaphysical problems" as the "first commandment of the need for philosophical clarity."[10] His "transcendental systematics" combines psychological and sensualistic elements with Kantian motifs. Horkheimer's precise, useful knowledge of positivist epistemologies (which are difficult to dissociate from neo-Kantianism) and his fundamentally antidogmatic position, which preserves Kant's achievements, took shape during this period. Nevertheless, he was soon to lose faith in the orthodox university philosophy at Frankfurt. What concerned him above all were substantial, metaphysical questions. As he wrote to his future wife in November 1921, "What must be sought are not formal laws of knowledge, which at bottom are most unimportant, but rather material statements about our life and its sense." [11]

During his years as a *Privatdozent* (1926–1930), Horkheimer succeeded in breaking out of academic pigeonholes and developed the conception of philosophy to which he henceforth remained committed. This third phase is characterized by his resolute transition to Marxism, whose explosive force he had already become aware of during the revolutionary developments of the postwar years. The radicality of the position Horkheimer had now reached was reflected in *Dämmerung* (Twilight), a volume of aphorisms published only later (1934), in Switzerland, under the pseudonym Heinrich Regius; it was to play an important role during the late 1960s, at least in Germany, in the political consciousness formation of student protest groups. These "occasional jottings," as Horkheimer all too modestly described them, lead into the categories of critical theory.

Horkheimer's thinking maneuvers from the outset between two fronts: against meaning-constitutive, dogmatically proclaimed metaphysics, and against anti-conceptual positivism, which abstractly denies any meaning whatsoever that extends beyond the here and now. For Horkheimer, just as thought cannot be restricted to immediate utility, so there can be no pure desire for knowledge, removed from material reality. Those who pretend to pursue a "disinterested striving for truth" are laboring under an ideologically loaded "philosophical delusion." [12] Thought pursued "for thought's sake" has "lost its sense, which is to be a means of improving the human condition." [13] Moreover, such a "pursuit of truth" contradicts its own claims inasmuch as "it necessarily replaces truth with a phantom: the absolute, i.e. transcendent truth." [14]

When Horkheimer repeatedly stresses that "metaphysics" is impossible—which may appear odd—he understands it as the quintessence of theological and rationalist claims to make positive judgments about an absolute. On the other hand, however, "statements about the randomness, finitude, and senselessness of the visible world [are] possible."[15] But Horkheimer refuses to follow Kant's theory of ideas in interpreting "the criteria of necessity, infinity, and meaningfulness involved . . . in such negations . . . as guarantees for the existence of the eternal in the human soul."[16] About this there can be no haggling: such criteria remain a "human, all-too-human" thought, "which dies and is scattered along with those who form it."[17] We are the ones who take it into our heads to oppose an eternal, absolutely good, and just authority to the countless evils of the sensually experienceable world, as much out of fear and mistrust as from hope. Whenever our statements overstep the contingent and temporally limited, they are "equally justified and unjustified."[18] For Horkheimer, the "senselessness of the world," which is obvious to anyone who sees things unerringly, follows particularly from the fact that no supertemporal symbolic force accrues to the difference between a morally good and a morally bad life; this "gives the lie to metaphysics, i.e. its meaningful interpretation." But then this can irritate "only those . . . who lead a humane life out of fear of some lord and not out of compassion with humanity."[19]

Horkheimer states all this without cynicism, as a "sad recognition."[20] Only to the extent that human beings, who are radically finite beings, succeed in making concrete reason prevail in the historical world does this world become more than the "play of blind nature."[21] Our fears, needs, and ephemeral happiness are utterly external to the material universe. "Goodness" and "justice" are not inherent in the cosmos, which is "gloomy and pitiless."[22] Humanity is alone.

Such reflections link Horkheimer's materialism with the philosophy of Schopenhauer. It is true that Schopenhauer rejects the kind of materialism that presents itself as "absolute physics," on both epistemological and ethical grounds.[23] But he is unable to sustain the incompatibility of materialism with metaphysical thinking, which he proclaims so emphatically at first, inasmuch as he accuses Kant of having too hastily identified metaphysics with a priori knowledge: "In that case one would . . . have to have proved that the material for solving the riddle of the world can by no means be found within the world, but is only to be sought outside it, in something one can only reach via the guiding thread of those forms conscious to us a priori. But as long as this has not been proved we have no grounds, in this most important and difficult of all tasks, for shutting off the richest of all sources of knowledge—internal and external experience—in order to operate solely with forms devoid of content."[24] What Schopenhauer calls the "deciphering of the world"[25] proves to be correspondingly concrete. Thus, he underscores the creaturely frailty and the deficiencies of humanity, just as the great materialists of the French Enlightenment had done. This, according to Schopenhauer, not some autonomous drive for knowledge, is the source of the "need for metaphysics."[26] People are metaphysical animals only because they are previously physical animals: "Doubtless the knowledge of death, along with reflection on the sufferings and afflictions of life, give the strongest impetus . . . to metaphysical interpretations of the world. Were our lives endless and painless, it might not occur to anyone to ask why the world is there and why it is constructed as it is."[27]

From Schopenhauer's perspective we can better understand the point of Horkheimer's blunt rejection of "metaphysics." In its own way, it is a metaphysically materialistic insight into the physical finitude and fragility of all that is human.[28] The themes of official metaphysics, by contrast, unmask themselves from the outset by "the way they frame the question" and the "more or less cultivated tone of their treatment."[29] One immediately notices that its proponents are scarcely "impressed by what torments humanity."[30] What official philosophers and humanistic scholars report "about mind, cosmos, god, being, freedom . . . about art, style, personality, form, epochs, indeed about history and society," is irreproachably objective; "suffering or even outrage over injustice, or sympathy with the victims"[31] is foreign to them. That which metaphysicians, concerned with timeless objectivity, present as the true essence of being is obviously "the kind of thing that one can investigate and live in view of without becoming outraged by the existing social system. The sage, who sees to the heart of things, may be able to draw all sorts of philosophical, scientific, and ethical consequences . . . but his view of class relationships is hardly sharpened. Indeed, the fact that this ascent to the eternal can be made under the existing class relationships justifies such conditions all the more to the extent that the metaphysician ascribes absolute value to this ascent."[32] He elevates people above the morass of the everyday, granting them access to a higher reality that has precedence over the merely empirical and thereby helping them, amid the prevailing order of things, to their true vocation.

Yet there is no unified, spiritual ground—undergirding, productive, meaning-constitutive—that embraces empirical, spatially and temporally determinate reality, whether human or natural. This sums up the Marxist critique leveled by Horkheimer's *Twilight* at the ontologically revived metaphysics of the 1920s. Its proponents, first and foremost Martin Heidegger, incline to take up concepts originating in everyday language and life and convert them into dematerialized form. Shorn of their historical and scrutable contents, they are accorded the (ideological) dignity of expert ascertainments of the *condition humaine*.[33] By then Horkheimer already saw through the apologetic role of the official philosophers, who "prefer to set up a system of values rather than of perversions of value *[Unwerte]* . . . and would rather concern themselves with 'man as such' than human beings in particular, with Being as such than with their own being."[34] However much Horkheimer despises the "abominable, ghastly realm"[35] of the bourgeois metaphysics of the time, he holds fast all the more to the idea of a rationally established humanity. This idea links him, if in a peculiarly ambivalent way, with the conceptual world of German idealism. German idealism provided him with a more material conception of philosophy than that of his contemporaries. His source, Schopenhauer—at once Kantian and Kant critic—insists (as did Hegel, with whom Schopenauer so grimly feuded) that "the world . . . , precisely as an appearance, is the manifestation of that which appears," of the thing-in-itself. "The thing-in-itself must therefore express its essence . . . in the world of experience, and thus . . . be interpretable . . . out of the material of experience, not its mere form. Accordingly . . . philosophy is . . . the correct, universal comprehension of experience itself, the true interpretation . . . of its content. This is the Metaphysical, . . . which is merely clothed in appearances and veiled in forms."[36] Note that the materialist Marx, whose political intentions were diametrically opposed to Schopenhauer's, was no more ready to accept "reality" in the spirit of naive realism. He explicitly characterized it as a "world of appearances."[37] In his view, scientific procedure consists in penetrating the "surface of appearances";[38] science must "detect the inner essence and form" of the total process of capitalism "through and behind the appearances."[39]

This linkage between Schopenhauer and Marx is entirely substantial and not simply a formal analogy. It deserves emphasis because it entered into Horkheimer's philosophy without becoming immediately apparent. It extends beyond epistemology to metaphysics and moral philosophy as well. Both thinkers teach the unconsciousness and blindness of the course of the world. Marx, of course—in this he was indebted to Kant—restricted this negative state of affairs to the "prehistory" of humanity, which, he hoped, could be ended by revolution. His theory envisions humanly socialized individuals "making their own history," "with a collective will, according to a unified plan."[40] Schopenhauer, far more skeptical, sees in the historical process "only the same thing constantly repeated, under other names and in other guises"; any attempt by believers in progress "to comprehend world history as a well-planned whole"[41] is reprehensible Hegelianism. Schopenhauer thereby renounces not only metaphysical theories but unified theories of history as such. He regards the assumption of transindividual structures and tendencies with insuperable mistrust: "Even the most general in history, after all, is only singular and individual—a long epoch, for instance, or a major occurrence; the relation of the particular to the general is that of the part to the whole, not that of the instance to the rule—as is fitting of all the sciences, which deliver concepts, not mere facts."[42]

Of course—and Horkheimer proceeds from this assumption—it will not do simply to criticize the obvious shortcomings of the purely narrative interpretation of history, which reduces its course to the sum of individual events. Implicit in Schopenhauer's insistence that historiography must deal with the "absolutely singular and individual"[43] is a materialist protest against the conformistic metaphysics that plays down or even transfigures individual suffering by integrating it into the allegedly meaningful totality of the course of history. By contrast, as shown by the origins precisely of Marx and Engels, the philosophical and political transition to materialism consists first and foremost in criticizing woolly universals and attending to the genuine afflictions "of the real, individual person."[44] It is quite a different matter that the founders of Marxism, as opposed to the metaphysician of the will, did not remain standing at that "base" (arrived at polemically, as yet with a Feuerbachian tint) but expanded it into the economic, developmentally lawful basis of social history.

Yet by virtue of the fact that Horkheimer appropriates historical materialism from a Schopenhauerian point of view from the very beginning, he is protected against any pantheistic mystification of History (with a capital H) as a self-activating, teleologically self-unfolding substance.[45] The economic laws Marx discovered, according to Horkheimer, signify only that the elements of socialism "are present in a certain way in capitalism"—as objective "tendencies."[46] Even so, the "stock of experience on the basis of which we assume that the tendencies will actually prevail . . . [is] very slight."[47] But Horkheimer does not think well of the wise skepticism of those who respectfully "incorporate" Marx as a neutral "cultural asset" into the history of philosophy. Insofar as Marx is made into "just another philosopher," his doctrine surrenders its objective and, more important, its moral binding force. For the "observation," which is correct in itself, "that socialism does not 'follow' from Marxist theory, even if it . . . were to be desirable, has the effect"—when made skeptically—of a "scientific and moral argument in favor of capitalism."[48] For Horkheimer, the consequence is not resignation but a combative "profession of the practice that theory is in need of." "Marx," as he still writes at the time, "discovered the law of the dominant, inhuman order of things and showed the lever which must be applied to create one more human."[49]

Skepticism, in turn, is the expression of academic thinking that persists in self-satisfied contemplation. Its contrary, as Horkheimer stresses, is not just another theoretical posture, an optimistically proclaimed dogma, but engagement in historical practice itself. The mere certainty of salvation has no edge over bourgeois skepticism: "The illusion that socialism will come about with natural necessity is scarcely less of a danger to correct action than skeptical disbelief. . . . The socialist order of society . . . is historically possible; yet it will be realized not by the immanent logic of history, but by humanity schooled in theory and bent on improvement—or else it will not be realized at all."[50]

Horkheimer's fundamental reflections on the proletarian politics of the 1920s also take place within this context. He accuses the reformist

Social Democrats of having "lost the insight that an effective improvement of human conditions within the bounds of capitalism is impossible."[51] Even when they do not reject specifically theoretical work out of hand, they tend "to discredit . . . all determinate concepts and views . . . and to smear everything with the same grey color of relativism, historicism, sociologism."[52] Averse to the materialistic dialectic, they set up "relativizing or questioning as such"[53] as an absolute. In so doing, the ideologists of *Realpolitik* fail to satisfy even their own positivistic creed of soberly taking account of the facts; their knowledge of these facts also falls prey to a miserable relativism. The reformists present themselves as "impartial and free of illusions."[54] But their "love of the 'concrete' " is bound to remain hopeless; the changing of the social totality opens up "only to the interest which arises from practice." Their concept of concretion disappears without remainder in the "material with which they fill their schemas; they do not organize it by consciously choosing sides in the historical struggle, but believe themselves to float above it."[55] Conversely, although Communist theorists profess Marxist principles, in their writings these principles do not take on a "timely form . . . by virtue of the mass of material worked through theoretically . . . but are clung to undialectically."[56] Communist politics turns out to be correspondingly doctrinaire. Frequently disregarding real circumstances, it "exhausts itself . . . in unavailing commands and moralizing reprimands of the disobedient and disloyal."[57] Here, empty categories; there, unconceptualized fact mongering. The political impotence and the schism of the German working class is theoretically reflected in the "isolation of the two moments of the dialectical method from one another: knowledge of the facts and clarity of principle."[58]

Horkheimer's sociological notes on the left-wing parties in the Weimar Republic are important in two respects. They are instructive as to the precarious political locus of later critical theory and—and this is the more comprehensive aspect—they show that for Horkheimer, from the very beginning, socialism is not a question of social technique but essentially an ethical idea. The way a scholar confronts the historical task of replacing class society with a more just order indicates "the degree of his morality."[59] The "realization of socialism" is for Horkheimer nothing less than the "form" that morality "has assumed at present,"[60] without this detracting from the analytical significance of scientific materialism. To attain what is socially desirable, the revolutionary forces are in need of a precise study of economic conditions. Yet it is not the automatic course that these conditions follow but solely the well-considered action of those who are suffering that can bring about a better state of things: "a rationally organized, socialist society that regulates its own being."[61] The early Horkheimer is convinced of the objective possibility of breaking the alien rule of capitalism and of making united individuals into the masters of their fate: "If human beings would consciously take charge of their social living process and replace the struggle between capitalist concerns with a classless, planned economy, then the effects of the process of production on . . . their relations could also be overseen and regulated."[62]

The decades from 1930 to 1950 comprise those stages of Horkheimer's development that shaped his image, and that of the critical theory he founded, in the consciousness of the general public. The first of these decades, which can be considered the fourth stage, extends from 1930, when he was appointed to the chair in social philosophy created for him in Frankfurt, to 1941, the year he moved to California. To this extraordinarily productive period belong such important studies as *The Origins of the Bourgeois Philosophy of History* (1930); "Hegel and the Problem of Metaphysics" (1932), which first appeared in the *Festschrift für Grünberg;* and above all the great essays in the *Zeitschrift für Sozialforschung,* including "Materialism and Metaphysics" (1933), "Materialism and Morality" (1933), "Remarks on Philosophical Anthropology" (1935), "Egoism and the Freedom Movement" (1936), and the programmatic "Traditional and Critical Theory" (1937).[63] Based on the notion of an empirically supported "social philosophy," Horkheimer during this period arrived at a specific concept of "social research" and, finally, from there, at the conception of critical theory that guided the formation of the Frankfurt school.

By contrast, the decade 1940–1950, the wartime and postwar years, is characterized by substantial sociological studies on racism, ethnocentric prejudice, ideologies, and modes of behavior and also by negative works on the philosophy of history, such as "Reason and Self-Preservation" (1942), *Eclipse of Reason,* and (with Adorno) *Dialectic of Enlightenment,* the latter two both published in 1947.[64] Whereas in the 1930s Horkheimer identified critical theory with the conceptual structure of "dialectical materialism,"[65] seeing himself within a framework warranted by the history of theory[66] despite his distance from Communist party politics, during the fifth stage of his activity, this framework proves to be inadequate. In view of the "contradiction between the evident interests of the masses and the fascist politics . . . to which they enthusiastically [allow] themselves to be harnessed,"[67] it becomes necessary to enrich critical theory with psychoanalytic categories. Not that Freud had previously been neglected in Horkheimer's circle. The first issue of the *Zeitschrift für Sozialforschung* included a considerable article by Fromm on the methods and tasks of an "analytical social psychology." But only now does the "reciprocal influence of society and psychology"[68] move to the center of the theory. Of course socioeconomic pressures, Freud's "vital necessities," remain primary. It will not do to extenuate social antagonisms by "reducing them unmediatedly to human, merely internal processes."[69] But those pressures—and here Freud concretizes the Marxian doctrine—propagate themselves "in unconscious socio-psychological processes which bring people to internalize such pressures and to accept the loss of freedom."[70]

In Horkheimer's work during his years in California, two things went along with the energetic adoption of Freudian insights into the materialist conception of history, which can then be maintained less rigidly: a rigorous critique of late capitalist mass culture and, inasmuch as the latter stands under the dictate of reflectionless self-preservation, a certain corrective to Marx with respect to the autonomy of philosophy. In the great tracts of the 1930s Horkheimer also stresses that the Marxist doctrine of society preserves

the legacy of philosophy itself, over and above that of German idealism; it is not just some research hypothesis that proves its usefulness in the predominant order of business, but an inseparable moment in the historical effort to create a world which satisfies the needs and forces of humanity. For all the reciprocal influence between critical theory and the academic disciplines, critical theory never aims at a mere increase in knowledge as such, but rather at the emancipation of humanity from enslaving conditions. As opposed to the operation of the modern academic disciplines, . . . critical theory . . . has remained philosophical even as a critique of economics. Its object is the reversal of the concepts which govern the economy into their opposites: of fair exchange into deepening of social injustice, of the free market economy into the rule of monopoly. . . . At issue is . . . the historical movement of the epoch, which should be brought to a close.[71]

At this time, Horkheimer sees the intrinsically philosophical moment in Marx's system not in any particular object completely different from those of the individual disciplines but in the fact that its "driving motive" is "knowledge of the historical course of the totality."[72] He still assumes that there is such a structured, conceptually comprehensible course leading to a historically higher state of affairs, at least in principle. In the materialistic unity of science and philosophy, the former—notwithstanding the rejection of merely descriptive empiricism—ultimately takes precedence.[73] Philosophy is nothing definite in itself for Horkheimer during this period but rather, as for Marx himself, a moment in the critique of political economy.[74]

Philosophy claims quite a different rank in Horkheimer's later thinking. Without ever explicitly breaking with the premises and results of Marx's *Capital*, he increasingly mistrusts the materialistically conceived succession of stages of world history. As he writes in 1942, as long as world history "proceeds on its logical course, it does not fulfill its human vocation."[75] It remains unmastered fate. In view of the dwindling chances for practical political intervention, as well as the growing helplessness of the individual in the face of collective forces, the "social function of philosophy," as Horkheimer put it in the 1940 essay under the same title, is altered essentially. As before, this function consists in "criticism of the prevailing state of affairs."[76] Yet its reference to Marxist economics has grown pale in his thinking. Philosophy, which thereby wins a greater measure of autonomy than conceded to it in the originally Marxist context, must "prevent human beings from losing themselves to those . . . forms of behavior instilled in them by society as organized at present."[77] In a corresponding formulation in *Dialectic of Enlightenment*, a fully philosophical work, "The prevailing order of things compels people not merely by means of physical force and material interests, but through overpowering suggestion. Philosophy is not synthesis; it is neither a fundamental nor a comprehensive science. It is the effort to resist suggestion, the determination to achieve intellectual and real freedom."[78]

A more detailed discussion of Horkheimer's works from 1930 to 1950 can be dispensed with here.[79] What has been said should suffice to contribute to a better understanding of the notes that arose during the years 1949 though 1969. Their philosophical content can now be considered. Let us first recall the political and intellectual conditions under which they were recorded. The most important biographical data from this period can be recounted quickly. In 1950 the Frankfurt Institute resumed its work under Horkheimer, who returned from Los Angeles to Germany; a year later, the Institute took up quarters in its new building. From 1951 to 1953 he acted as rector of the University of Frankfurt; from 1954 to 1959 he held a guest professorship at the University of Chicago, retiring in 1959. He left Frankfurt and lived until his death at Montagnola, in Tessin. The political situation confronting Horkheimer upon his return was, until well into the 1960s, that of a decidedly restorational postwar Germany, which, rearmed and integrated into the Atlantic alliance, was becoming the most important theater of the cold war, if only for geographical reasons. Facing the West in those years of sharpest confrontation was an aggressive Stalinist ideology and military power. Marxism, already brutally repressed during the National Socialist period, continued to be out of the question for considerable segments of the population (including the organized workers), who equated it with the Soviet system.

Under these circumstances, for the circle around Horkheimer there could no longer be any question of continuing to insist on the unity of critical analysis and revolutionary action, a unity that had already been precarious but now was becoming entirely dubious. The historical locus of theory was changing; immediate utility now made it suspect. "Action for action's sake," Horkheimer wrote in 1946, "is in no way superior to thought for thought's sake."[80] The hope that at least the democratic peoples, after their military victory over barbarism, would "work out and put into practice the principles of humanity in the name of which the sacrifices of the war were made"[81] was not fulfilled. At the time, he was already conscious of the problematic character of modern progress, the major theme of his philosophy of history after the war: "Even as technical knowledge expands the horizon of man's thought and activity, his autonomy as an individual, his ability to resist the growing apparatus of mass manipulation, his power of imagination, his independent judgment appear to be reduced. . . . Thus progress threatens to nullify the very goal it is supposed to realize: the idea of man."[82]

In view of all this, sociological theory and research, which are founded on social philosophy, become an attempt to grasp deep-rooted anthropological transformations and to arm the individual against delusionary, prejudiced thought and behavior—a goal more modest than that of the earlier approach. This is to be its contribution to the maturity of politically enlightened humanity in its striving for a just, rationally ordered world. However, this requires a "connection between broad perspectives and responsible, rigorous individual work," as Horkheimer once again underscored on the occasion of the reopening of the Frankfurt Institute in 1951.[83]

Let us dwell for a moment on Horkheimer's programmatic ideas, which reflect the spirit in which he took up his academic work in the Germany of the 1950s. "We see in the social sciences," he said,

an element of that urgently relevant humanism whose unfolding is currently bound up with the question of the future of humanity. . . . The student of modern sociology learns the grounds for the opinion of others, for the differing behavior of other nations, religions, and political systems. . . . Genuine liberality is a product of insight. One who is sociologically educated is less inclined to allow himself to be blinded to the rest of the world by a totalitarian propaganda machine. . . . Nevertheless, social insight is . . . not . . . to be confused with relativism. . . . The mind that concerns itself with ultimate questions has always . . . inquired into . . . the flow, the interdependency, and the conditionality of finite moments. . . . In speaking of the broad perspectives which must always be bound to individual work, I mean that embedded in . . . the sociological attitude . . . there is always an intention that transcends society as it is. . . . A certain critical attitude . . . belongs, so to speak, to the profession of the social theorist; and precisely this critical element, which grows out of the most positive thing there is—hope—is what makes the sociologist unpopular. To educate the student to withstand this tension with the prevailing state of things . . . to make him social in the true sense—which also includes being able to bear standing alone—is perhaps the . . . ultimate goal of education as we conceive of it.[84]

These views were to remain binding for Horkheimer. They were extended and modified, particularly during the 1960s, by an important moment that relates his late philosophy back to the early novellas and journals: the explicit adoption of Schopenhauer into critical theory. Previously, Schopenhauer's metaphysics of will—as part of the Western European Enlightenment—had been present as an undercurrent in Horkheimer's writings.[85] Now, however, he devoted to it a series of positive studies that originated as lectures. In 1955, "Schopenhauer and Society" appeared; in 1961, "The Relevance of Schopenhauer"; 1967, "Religion and Philosophy"; 1971, "Pessimism Today"; and 1972, "Remarks on Schopenauer's Thought in Relation to Science and Religion."[86] Horkheimer, precisely as a sociologist, saw Schopenhauer's greatness in his strict "nominalism with respect to society."[87] As "in nature," Schopenhauer observes in *The World as Will and Representation*, "only the species are real, whereas the *genera* are mere abstractions, so in humankind only the individuals and their life histories are real, whereas peoples and their life are mere abstractions."[88] Schopenhauer spurns the myth of the nation, that brutal collective that disdains the individual. The unwavering interest of Schopenhauer's philosophy is dedicated to that individual, to its striving for happiness and its suffering, although—and precisely because—he teaches, on the other hand, that we are subject to the veil of the Maya: space and time, which constitute the *principium individuationis* (principle of individuation), are subjective; they do not belong to the thing in itself, which is why the multiplicity of restlessly driven human beings (and of things in general) proves to be an empty appearance. That which Schopenhauer proclaimed epistemologically and metaphysically—the nullity of the individual—has been ratified, according to Horkheimer, by the course of recent history: "That which is taking place in the current era, the decline in the social significance of the individual, his increasing replaceability, is logical according to Schopenhauer's philosophy; in any case, the doctrine of the absurdity of the fear of death, of the vanity of the human ego's existence, is thereby confirmed."[89]

Seen through Horkheimer's lens, what has happened would justify a pessimism far more radical than Schopenhauer's. The consolation of his philosophy, which is related to Christian belief—that the return of those who negate their egoistic, blind, vital drives into the undifferentiated unity of the world will is "a kind of salvation"[90]—is still too affirmative. The late Horkheimer's fundamental idea is that

there remains only the longing, endangered by progress itself, that is common to those who know of the misery of the past, the injustice of the present, and the prospect of a future bereft of all spiritual meaning. This longing could . . . lay the foundation of a solidarity which, in an undogmatic fashion, includes theological moments. Linked with its ultimately negative attitude would be . . . what is known as "critical theory." Those bound by their longing would be able to say nothing about any absolute or intelligible realm, about god and salvation; knowledge . . . could not be proclaimed as absolute truth; yet they could indicate what, in view of progress which is paid for dearly and nonetheless necessary, is to be changed or retained for the purpose of easing suffering. Theoretical pessimism could be . . . combined with a praxis which, mindful of what is universally bad, nevertheless seeks to improve whatever possible. Its own judgment of good and bad will not count as absolute truth for those active in this solidarity. They are constantly aware of the relativity of one's own judgment, insofar as it does not limit itself to ascertaining facts.[91]

A precise interpretation of Horkheimer's often misunderstood late philosophy must proceed from this modest, but humane perspective—a perspective that is oriented analytically toward Marx, metaphysically toward Schopenhauer, and yet transcends them both. It is not an abrupt break with the preceding stages of his thought but rather a dialectical sublimation of them. Troubled by the doubt, which can indeed be substantiated, "whether the realm of freedom, once realized, must not necessarily prove to be its opposite: the automatizing of society and of human behavior," Horkheimer attempts "to reflect" the current state of the world "in the awareness of that contradiction, without surrendering the thought of the Other."[92]

Horkheimer's late materialism is negative. It reflects an age in which it looks as if the human species (an emphatic concept in the language of Feuerbach and Marx) wished to attain the pitiful "status of a particularly skillful, ingenious animal breed."[93] Thus, he places a question mark behind the hedonistic components of traditional (and sometimes vulgar) materialism. The relative right to reject it becomes obvious in view of a society that "in everything thinks, next to power, only of the standard of living. . . . It is true that one who is sated may not scold one who is hungry, and wants to live, as a materialist. The question is: in those places where there is already enough available for a passable life, is not the principle that things must always get better and better a dangerous folly?"[94] What use is the abundance of goods if the autonomous subject becomes a "romantic concept"?[95]

This leads us back to the social-theoretical aspect of Horkheimer's materialism. His critique of technical progress "denounces the dissolution of *Geist* and of the soul, the victory of rationality, without flatly rejecting it."[96] As much as Horkheimer guards against offering prescriptions, he interprets the falsity of progress largely as the expression of a mode of production that remains as contradictory as ever. There can be no question of the Marxist theory of crisis being obsolete: "Precisely those elements of the business cycle through which the crisis is held off—the war economy in peacetime; the aid for the celebrated 'underdeveloped,' which in truth is a further aspect of the war economy; and above all the 'blooming' of leisure time—do not merely veil the spreading sickness of society in its present form, but rather are symptoms of it."[97] Horkheimer insists on the analytical force of the categories of Marx's critique of political economy; the "so-called science of economics" has "nothing to match them."[98] What seems problematic to him in Marx, who provided "a most highly rational foundation for understanding the development of society,"[99] is his optimistic philosophy of history—the assumption that in the postcapitalist era, which is unquestionably approaching, social equality will be reconciled with fully unfolded individual freedom. It is this doubt that expresses itself in Horkheimer's concept of the administered world. Those striving today for the "right society" must adopt into "their critique of the prevailing order . . . the loyalty to freedom, which is to be preserved."[100]

Philosophy finds itself engaged at present in a kind of rearguard action. Given the state of history, it necessarily takes on utopian and eccentric traits. Philosophers see themselves referred back to "general formulations, such as Kant's on the final goal of universal history."[101] Setting forth immediately useful slogans, which would be no better than the plain, pragmatic spirit of the prevailing order, is not the task of philosophy. The individual, especially the philosophizing individual, can bring about little; "He is nevertheless able, in theory and practice, to intervene in the course of development by contributing, through the use of timely methods, to the formation of untimely collectives, which are able to preserve . . . the individual."[102]

The final aphorism of the *Notizen* is entitled "For Nonconformism." It could stand over the life's work of this truly European thinker, in the sense imprinted upon the concept by Nietzsche and Thomas Mann. The present can learn from Horkheimer that the struggle for what is better must be conducted without self-deception or lying. He is a philosopher with staying power, an enemy of solutions that are quick because they are ideologically lasting. Nor does he mimic the speech of those who stand close to him politically. In Horkheimer's intellectual existence, the idea of the independently judging, enlightened subject is once again incarnated. His hallmark is the capacity for incorruptible criticism, even of his own ideas, to which he nonetheless remained true.

Translated by John McCole

Notes

Horkheimer's texts are cited and English translations, where available, are cross-referenced according to the following key (in some cases the translations have been modified):

> *N = Notizen 1950 bis 1969 und Dämmerung: Notizen in Deutschland* (Frankfurt, 1974); *DD = Dawn and Decline: Notes 1926–1931 and 1950–1969* (New York, 1978) (contains selections from *Notizen* and *Dämmerung*).

> *KT = Kritische Theorie. Eine Dokumentation*, vols. I, II (Frankfurt, 1968); *CT = Critical Theory: Selected Essays* (New York, 1972).

> *DA = Dialektik der Aufklärung. Philosophische Fragmente* (Frankfurt, 1969); *DE = Dialectic of Enlightenment* (New York, 1972).

> *KV = Zur Kritik der instrumentellen Vernunft* (Frankfurt, 1967); *Eclipse = Eclipse of Reason* (Oxford, 1947); *CIR = Critique of Instrumental Reason* (New York, 1974).

1. Horkheimer, *Aus der Pubertät*, ed. and with an afterword by Alfred Schmidt (Munich, 1974).

2. Ibid., "Nachwort," 7.

3. Ibid., 7.

4. Ibid., 8.

5. Ibid., 165.

6. Ibid., 337.

7. Ibid., 349.

8. *KT*, I:xiii/*CT*, ix.

9. *KT*, I:xiii/*CT*, ix.

10. Hans Cornelius, *Einleitung in die Philosophie* (Leipzig/Berlin, 1921), vi.

11. Unpublished letter, Horkheimer Archive, Stadts- und Universitätsbibliothek, Frankfurt.

12. *N*, 272, 273/*DD*, 53.

13. *N*, 273/*DD*, 53.

14. *N*, 273/*DD*, 54.

15. *N*, 334/*DD*, 101.

16. Ibid.

17. Ibid.

18. *N*, 335/*DD*, 102.

19. Ibid.

20. *N*, 334/*DD*, 101.

21. *N*, 336/*DD*, 102.

22. Ibid.

23. Arthur Schopenhauer, *Die Welt als Wille und Vorstellung*, in *Sämtliche Werke*, ed. Arthur Hübscher (Wiesbaden, 1949), 3:195. English: Schopenhauer, *The World as Will and Representation* (New York, 1969).

24. Ibid., 2:506f.

25. Ibid., 3:204.

26. Ibid., 176.

27. Ibid., 176f.

28. On this point, see my essay, "Adorno: Ein Philosoph des realen Humanismus," in *Theodor W. Adorno zum Gedächtnis*, ed. Hermann Schweppenhäuser (Frankfurt, 1971), esp. 67–75.

29. *N*, 352/*DD*, 111.

30. *N*, 263/*DD*, 46.

31. N, 352f./*DD*, 111.

32. *N*, 263/*DD*, 45.

33. Horkheimer must have found it a sheer mockery of the anonymous, very empirically caused suffering of the lower classes when in 1929, the first year of the world economic crisis, he came upon the following definition, which fancies itself radical, in Heidegger's *Being and Time*: "The unity of the transcendental structure of the inwardmost neediness of being in man has received the designation of 'care' " (ibid., 320). In *The Twilight of the Idols*, Nietzsche, to whom Horkheimer owed decisive impulses, rebuked the "idiosyncrasy" of idealist philosophers that consists in "confusing the last things with the first. They put that which comes at the end—unfortunately! for it shouldn't come at all!—the 'highest concepts,' meaning the most general, emptiest concept, the last puff of vaporized reality, at the beginning *as* the beginning. This in turn is only an expression of their way of honoring things: the higher *may* not grow out of the lower, it *may* not have *grown* at all. . . . Originating out of something else counts as placing values in doubt." Friedrich Nietzsche, *Götzendämmerung* (Stuttgart, 1954), 96.

34. *N*, 288/*DD*, 67.

35. *N*, 296/*DD*, 73.

36. Schopenhauer, *Sämtliche Werke*, 3:204.

37. Karl Marx, *Das Kapital* (Berlin, 1953), 3:67.

38. Ibid., 63.

39. Ibid., 194. "Social research," as Horkheimer wrote in agreement with Marx, "strives for knowledge of the total social process and therefore posits that a conceptually accessible structure of effective forces can be discerned beneath the chaotic surface of events." "Vorwort," *Zeitschrift für Sozialforschung* 1 (1932), 1.

40. Engels to Heinz Starkenberg, January 25, 1894, in Karl Marx and Friedrich Engels, *Ausgewählte Briefe* (Berlin, 1953), 560.

41. Schopenhauer, *Sämtliche Werke*, 3:507, 505.

42. Ibid., 503.

43. Ibid., 502.

44. Karl Marx and Friedrich Engels, *Die heilige Familie*, in *Werke* (Berlin, 1959), 2:7.

45. This motif becomes even more important in later stages of Horkheimer's development. As he wrote in *The Origins of the Bourgeois Philosophy of History* (1930), with a pronouncedly anti-Hegelian accent: "A completely successful explanation, a thorough knowledge of the necessity of a historical event, can become a means by which we, who act, bring reason into history; but history has no reason when considered 'in itself': it is not some sort of 'essentiality,' neither 'spirit,' to which we would have to bow, nor power. Rather, it is a conceptual summary of events that result from the human social process. No one is called to life or killed by 'history'; history neither sets tasks nor accomplishes them. The pantheistic hypostatization of history as a uniform, substantial essence is nothing but dogmatic metaphysics." Horkheimer, *Anfänge der bürgerlichen Geschichtsphilosophie* (Frankfurt am Main, 1971), 69/*BPSS*.

46. *N*, 251/*DD*, 35.

47. Ibid.

48. *N*, 252/*DD*, 36.

49. Ibid.

50. *N*, 253/*DD*, 37; see also *N*, 323/*DD*, 94.

51. *N*, 284/*DD*, 63.

52. *N*, 284/*DD*, 64.

53. Ibid.

54. *N*, 285/*DD*, 64.

55. Ibid.

56. *N*, 283/*DD*, 63.

57. Ibid.

58. *N*, 285/*DD*, 64. The tense, productive unity of theoretical, categorial work and empirical study, discussed here on the political level, remained binding for later critical theory as a whole. "Social research," which aims at "contemporary human reality," as Horkheimer wrote in the foreword to the first issue of the *Zeitschrift* in 1932, "will not be able to do without synoptic conceptual formulations . . . but as opposed to broad currents of contemporary metaphysics, its categories do not exclude further illumination and justified contradiction by empirical research. However little overarching conceptual summaries can be dispensed with in scientific work, such summaries must never close off this work in advance by taking the place of the problems to be solved." "Vorwort," *Zeitschrift für Sozialforschung* 1 (1932): III.

59. *N*, 252/*DD*, 36.

60. Ibid.

61. *N*, 270/*DD*, 51.

62. *N*, 269/*DD*, 51. In this (which also accords with his later development), Horkheimer sees Marxian theory as being closer to Kant than is commonly admitted. This interpretation is justified especially by Kant's brief works on the philosophy of history. Thus, in his "Idea for a Universal History with a Cosmopolitan Purpose," Kant characterizes the previous, unmastered progression of historical stages in a way similar to Marx and Engels: " Since men neither pursue their aims purely by instinct, as the animals do, nor act in accordance with any integral, prearranged plan like rational cosmopolitans, it would appear that no law-governed history of mankind is possible. . . . We can scarcely help feeling a certain distaste on observing their activities as enacted in the great world-drama, for we find that, despite the apparent wisdom of individual actions here and there, everything as a whole is made up of folly and childish vanity, and often of childish malice and destructiveness." Kant, "Idea for a Universal History with a Cosmopolitan Purpose," in Hans Reiss, ed., *Kant's Political Writings* (Cambridge, 1970), 41–42.

63. [Editors' note: For publication information on these texts, see the Bibliography.]

64. [Editors' note: For publication information on these texts, see the Bibliography.]

65. On this point, cf. *KT*, I:150, 268; *KT*, II:196/*CT*, 248; *KT*, II:257/*BPSS*.

66. "Because materialist science," as Horkheimer wrote in 1933, entirely in Lenin's sense, "never leaves its goals out of account, it lacks the character of apparent impartiality; rather, it is deliberately accentuated. What matters to it is not so much originality as extending the theoretical experience that . . . has already been had." *KT*, I:108f./ *BPSS*.

67. Max Horkheimer and Theodor W. Adorno, "Vorrede" to *Freud in der Gegenwart* (Frankfurt am Main, 1957), ix.

68. Ibid.

69. Ibid., x.

70. Ibid., ix.

71. *KT*, II:193f., 195/*CT*, 245f., 247.

72. *KT*, II:195/*CT*, 247.

73. On this point, see Horkheimer's "Vorwort" to the first issue of the *Zeitschrift für Sozialforschung* (1932), I–III.

74. Cf. *KT*, II:194/*CT*, 246; *KT*, II:270.

75. Max Horkheimer, "Autoritärer Staat," in *Gesellschaft im Übergang*, ed. Werner Brede (Frankfurt, 1972), 34.

76. *KT*, II:304/*CT*, 264. In the same article, Horkheimer emphatically rejects the unconditional reduction of philosophy to sociology as a specialized science: "The stereotypical application of the concept of ideology to every conceptual system ultimately rests on the notion that there is no philosophical truth—and therefore no truth at all—for humanity, that all thought is "bound to being *[seinsgebunden]*. . . .This attitude toward philosophical ideas does not include, for instance, examining them objectively; it . . . limits itself to attributing them, in a more or less complicated fashion, to a social group." Far from clarifying the "social function of philosophy," the sociology of knowledge "itself has such a social function: to buy off the courage of thought that points to the future and forestall its practical tendencies."

77. *KT*, II:304/*CT*, 265. The reevaluation of the status of philosophy begun by Horkheimer at the end of the 1930s also expressed itself in the fact that the last issues of the *Zeitschrift für Sozialforschung* appeared, in English, under the title *Studies in Philosophy and Social Science*.

78. *DA*, 260/*DE*, 243.

79. Horkheimer's thought in this period is presented in more detail in the following works: Gian Enrico Rusconi, *La teoria critica della società* (Bologna, 1968); Martin Jay, *The Dialectical Imagination: A History of the Frankfurt School and the Institute of Social Research, 1923–1950* (Boston, 1973); Alfred Schmidt, *Zur Idee der Kritischen Theorie. Elemente der Philosophie Max Horkheimers* (Munich, 1974); and in the essays in this book.

80. *KV*, 14/*Eclipse*, vi.

81. *KV*, 13/*Eclipse*, v.

82. *KV*, 13/*Eclipse*, v–vi.

83. *Institut für Sozialforschung an der Johann Wolfgang Goethe-Universität Frankfurt am Main; Ein Bericht über die Feier seiner Wiedereröffnung, seine Geschichte und seine Arbeiten* (Frankfurt, 1952), 11.

84. Ibid., 10–12.

85. This holds above all for the manner of their reception of Marx's materialism (cf. my study, *Zur Idee der Kritischen Theorie*, 45). Horkheimer was otherwise clear about the fact that Schopenhauer "thoroughly, ideologically mystified [his] living on an income," as can be seen in *Dämmerung* (*N*, 352/*DD*, 111).

86. "The Schopenhauer lectures," writes Arthur Hübscher, "have no mere episodic place in Horkheimer's body of work; they . . . testify to a resolute . . . continuation of approaches to be found in his early publications. . . . Horkheimer's late work stands under the sign of a sober unmasking of a reality which can be dealt with neither by a utopian faith in progress nor a flight into traditions that have lost their strength." Arthur Hübscher, 55. *Schopenhauer-Jahrbuch für das Jahr 1974* (Frankfurt, 1974), 88. On Schopenhauer's role in Horkheimer's philosophy, cf. also Werner Post, *Kritische Theorie und metaphysischer Pessimismus. Zum Spätwerk Max Horkheimers* (Munich, 1971).

87. Max Horkheimer, *Sozialphilosophische Studien*, ed. Werner Brede (Frankfurt, 1972), 72.

88. Arthur Schopenhauer, *Die Welt als Wille und Vorstellung*, in *Sämtliche Werke*, 3:505ff.

89. Max Horkheimer, *Sozialphilosophische Studien*, 149, 142.

90. Ibid., 143.

91. Ibid.

92. *KV*, 9/*CIR*, ix–x. "Critical thinking," as it says in the same spirit in the new edition of *Dialectic of Enlightenment*, "which does not stop short of criticizing progress, calls today for engagement on behalf of the residues of freedom, of the tendencies to real humanity, even if these seem helpless against the broad trend of history." *DA*, IX/*DE*, ix–x.

93. *N*, 215f./*DD*, 237; on this point, cf. also the aphorism "Der Fluch der Endlichkeit" ("The Curse of Finitude"), *N*, 106f.

94. *N*, 156.

95. *N*, 197/*DD*, 225.

96. *N*, 218/*DD*, 238.

97. *N*, 193.

98. *N*, 207/DD, 231; cf. also *N*, 27/*DD*, 130.

99. *N*, 207/*DD*, 231.

100. *N*, 206/*DD*, 230; on this point, cf. also *N*, 210, 212/*DD*, 233, 234.

101. *N*, 79; on this, cf. also *N*, 61/*DD*, 148.

102. *N*, 219/*DD*, 240.

3

Remarks on the Development of Horkheimer's Work

Jürgen Habermas

Horkheimer occupies a unique position within the circle of Frankfurt theoreticians who in the 1930s came together in an intimate, school-founding collaboration in New York. As director of the Institute for Social Research and as editor of the *Zeitschrift für Sozialforschung,* he not only held all the strings in his hand from an organizational point of view, Friedrich Pollock notwithstanding; he was also recognized as the uncontested *spiritus rector* of the common research program. The other side of this unique position is less often noticed: Horkheimer's own philosophical work cannot be as easily detached from the collective achievements of the group of emigrant intellectuals gathered around him as can that of some of his co-workers. He remains more strongly bound than the other members to the collective-singular subsequently called the Frankfurt School. I recall this circumstance not because I am interested in questions of individual attribution but rather for substantive and biographical reasons.

Between 1932 and 1941 Horkheimer invested almost all his theoretical drive and intellectual energy in the interdisciplinary realization of the materialist research program whose contours took shape in *Studies on Authority and Family* and in the *Zeitschrift für Sozialforschung,* down to its book review section. The unfolding of Horkheimer's philosophy through this cooperative endeavor with economists, psychologists, legal experts, historians, and sociologists—especially sociologists of music and literature—was based on a philosophical conviction that was not shared by the other members of the Institute, or at least was not the principal motive for their work. Certainly all were of the conviction that Marxist social theory must be freed from the orthodox fetters of the Second and Third International and placed in an unprejudiced relation to the bourgeois social sciences established in the meantime. All the Institute's members also agreed that the previous perspective of an emancipated society, still grounded in the philosophy of history, would establish a connection between the disciplines and change the orientation of work in the individual disciplines. But only Horkheimer joined a transformed and highly individual understanding of philosophy to this program of interdisciplinary materialism. He wanted to continue philosophy by other means, namely, the social sciences. The social scientists were not especially interested in this, and the philosophers in the circle, Adorno and Marcuse, probably did not take it completely seriously. For Horkheimer the concept of materialism always carried a connotation critical of philosophy; it signified postmetaphysical thinking. Following Marx, Horkheimer believed that the very form of philosophical thought had come to an end in Hegel's philosophy; idealism, which sought to retain the traditional form of philosophy after Hegel, had hardened into an ideology and served above all to conceal concrete misery and individual suffering under glorified universal categories. Like Marx, Horkheimer believed that philosophy could save its truth-content only by becoming practical. But Horkheimer, more skeptical than Marx from the start, found himself in a situation in which hopes of an imminent transformation had been historically precluded. Thus, the intermediary step of reconstructing and developing a scientific theory immune to idealistic mystification acquired its own importance. Indeed, in light of the need to preserve the essential contents of philosophy, which had reached its end, social theory acquired a new meaning. Horkheimer sought the sublation *(Aufhebung)* of philosophy in social theory; transformation into the social sciences offered the only chance of survival for philosophical thought. Hauke Brunkhorst has examined this "materialist deconstruction of philosophy" in detail. He has shown that in the productive phase of his life, Horkheimer was an "antiphilosopher" in a manner different from Adorno and Marcuse.[1]

Thus, the fact that Horkheimer's philosophical work at that time passes over into the collective work of his circle is not due to an arbitrary decision to assume the role of scientific organizer. Rather, it constitutes an original, anti-Heideggerian response to the "end of metaphysics." As long as philosophy cannot be actualized, it must be transferred to another medium in order not to degenerate into ideology—and for Horkheimer this medium should be the social sciences gathered, fused, and renewed in the reflector of a critical theory of society. Through this idea, Horkheimer's theoretical achievement was joined to his role as director of the Institute and editor of the *Zeitschrift*. The biographical consequences that the termination of this collaboration had for Horkheimer's work can also be explained on the basis of this substantive connection. It is these consequences that I wish to consider in this chapter. The claim that Horkheimer's scientific productivity was concentrated in the 1930s, especially in his major contributions to the *Zeitschrift für Sozialforschung*, is not without justification. In the joint work with Adorno that followed between 1941 and 1944, it was still strong enough to enable him to carry out the turn to a negativistic philosophy of history. But in the almost three decades after the war, his productivity was peculiarly inhibited, appearing only in occasional writings, as Alfred Schmidt puts it, and in the posthumously published notes that Horkheimer recorded between 1949 and 1969.

Anyone who wants to take up the intentions of Horkheimer's materialism and pursue them in today's altered theoretical contexts must refer to the substance of his work, which appeared before the end of the war; if an author's work is to be assessed, he has the right to have his major contribution taken seriously. But I begin with something more incidental, a question of intellectual biography: how can one account for the disparateness of Horkheimer's later philosophy, as represented by the *Notizen*?[2] These notes are shot through with contradictions. Of course, the philosophy of history that was shaped by the critique of instrumental reason sets the tone: the fate of the Western world—of its vision of the rational association of autonomous, undamaged individuals—seems sealed by the triumph of a totalitarian form of life. But at the same time the author holds fast with a defiance born of despair, and sometimes even an abrupt naiveté,[3] to the liberal heritage of the era of the Enlightenment. Again and again Horkheimer stops himself short: "Regression seems to be the only goal of progress. And yet that thought is wicked so long as there is still suffering that can be eliminated through progress" (*N*, 137). On the one hand, Horkheimer believes that critique is impossible if its historical basis slips away. It must pay for the loss of its pragmatic moment "with an empty utopianism" (*N*, 39/*DD*, 137–38). On the other hand, he finds a thoroughly positive sense in this utopian turn of critique, with its return from the philosophy of Hegel to that of Kant. Under the title of "Utopian Regression" he writes:

Since Being, that interest which transcends its own perpetuation, can no longer fulfill itself in the history of society in which he [the individual] lives . . . it becomes at once more concrete, inasmuch as he learns that humanity, and not just a part of it, can be put right; and also more abstract, since its own work is separated from its goal by an infinitely long, unforeseeable path. He is thrown back on general formulations, such as Kant's formula on the end of cosmopolitan history. (*N*, 79)

These obvious contradictions, which are by no means dialectical and which Horkheimer did not even try to eradicate, could initially be taken to mean that in his late philosophy, an unresolved tension appears between motifs from two different phases, as if the more practical impulses of the 1930s were fighting off the historical vision of the *Dialectic of Enlightenment*. This explanation may not be entirely wrong; materialist skepticism remains a constant attitude in the thought of Horkheimer the moralist. But it is too simple. The only completed conception that Horkheimer ever worked with was that of interdisciplinary materialism, but this program is cogent only under two presuppositions: the fallible social sciences must in fact be able to carry the burden of the strong theoretical claims in which the intentions of the great philosophers are supposed to live on, and the course of history must ensure that the critical attitude, from which the interdisciplinary work first gained its perspective, arises objectively out of social conflicts and is reproduced and disseminated. Helmut Dubiel has shown in detail how Horkheimer's confidence in both of these presuppositions had been exhausted by the beginning of the 1940s.[4] From that time on, his thought lacked a unifying bond.

I pursue Horkheimer's further development in three steps. First, I cite the reasons that impelled him to move toward Benjamin's conception of history and to seek a closer working relationship with Adorno. Then, with a brief glance at Adorno, I recall that in *Dialectic of Enlightenment* the intentions of the two authors by no means flawlessly coincide. Finally, I return to my original question and consider those contradictions that caused Horkheimer, in his late phase, to distance himself from *Dialectic of Enlightenment* as well; in any case, he quarreled with the inescapable fate of an instrumental reason inflated to a false totality.

I

In April 1941, as Hitler's armies were on the march, apparently unstoppably, Horkheimer emigrated to California. How significant this turn in his life was is clear from the facts. With the Institute's quarters on Morningside Heights, the inner circle of the Institute's members, and the final issue of the *Zeitschrift für Sozialforschung*, Horkheimer was leaving behind a world he had organized and intellectually inspired. He stepped out of the framework in which his rare combination of talents had found their realization. In those years, Horkheimer must have been quite imposing as a person and as an intellectual stimulator, original thinker, philosopher, and scientific administrator; otherwise, he would have not been able to hold together over the years so many productive and highly talented thinkers who differed so much in temperament, background, and orientation.

Just prior to the beginning of his work on *Dialectic of Enlightenment*, in 1941 and in the winter of 1941–1942, Horkheimer wrote two essays that contain the deeper reasons for leaving the New York Institute and entering into an exclusive collaboration with Adorno.[5] "The Authoritarian State" and "The End of Reason"[6] were published in a privately printed volume, dedicated to Benjamin, together with Benjamin's "Theses on the Philosophy of History," which Hannah Arendt had rescued from Paris and brought to New York for Adorno.[7]

"The Authoritarian State" belongs to the studies on National Socialism completed between 1939 and 1942 and is obviously influenced by Pollock's theory of state capitalism.[8] Here Horkheimer outlines a view of the future that explains why the authors of *Dialectic of Enlightenment* considered it a simple fact that humanity would sink into a new barbarism. If the Institute had so far conceived of fascism in orthodox terms as the transition from monopoly capitalism to state capitalism, and thus as the future of liberalism, National Socialism now appears as an unstable hybrid that will be worn down and replaced by the "integral statism" of Soviet state socialism. The latter is "the most con-

sistent form of the authoritarian state" ("AS," 300/"AuthSt," 101)—
Stalinism as the future of fascism. This integral statism abandons the
practice of racism and puts an end to factional struggles, competition
for power, and, generally, the remainders of a world not yet totally
administered. The bureaucratic net is spread completely over society;
the control of the secret police extends to the last cell. Horkheimer,
in 1941, anticipated Orwell's vision: "The selection of those who are
sent to the camps becomes more and more arbitrary. Whether the
number of inmates increases or decreases, or whether one might for
a time be able to afford not to refill the empty places of the murdered, actually anyone could be in the camps" ("AS," 303/"AuthSt,"
103).

The place where this essay was published was by no means accidental. Here Horkheimer backed away from the materialist conception
of history and took up Benjamin's line. He now considered it equally
possible that the growth of productive forces would bring about or
liquidate socialism. What was once understood by "socialism" seems
to have lost any intrinsic connection with historical progress. Revolutionary hope no longer has any mooring in the world; it has become
utopian in the bad sense—in any case, dislocated. The hope that there
is a dialectical tension within the historical process itself has proved
empty. But if the only goal is to break out of the continuum of history,
then historically observable tendencies lose any serious interest. Only
invariable calamity and oppression are worth studying; all that deserves attention is a structure of domination that monopolizes progress in the form of instrumental reason. Nietzsche, not Marx, points
the way. Not a historically informed theory of society but a radical
critique of reason that denounces the intimate connection between
reason and domination must explain "why humanity, instead of entering into a truly human condition, is sinking into a new kind of
barbarism" (*DA*, 1/*DE*, xi). This was already the theme of the essay
"The End of Reason," in which Horkheimer gives old ideas a new
characteristic twist.

In his early work on the bourgeois philosophy of history and social
philosophy, Horkheimer had traced the process by which objective
reason is reduced to subjective reason. He was always interested in
how, under the conditions of emerging bourgeois society, the concept
of reason was defined in terms of individual self-preservation and

"led back to its instrumental meaning." He established a connection between bourgeois egoism and the instrumentalization of reason for monadic self-interest. But this instrumental reason appeared as only a by-product of the bourgeois epoch; it still pointed beyond itself to a postbourgeois form of society that would redeem the promise once provided by substantive reason. Horkheimer had given up this hope.

With the rise of fascism and of a future that would bestow integral statism upon it, the bourgeois idea of reason appears in another light: liberal society represents the last phase of an irreversible (or so it seemed) process of the self-destruction of reason. A few years earlier, in "Materialism and Morality," Horkheimer had still held that the idea of a society worthy of humanity, in which any sort of autonomous morality would lose its basis and its purpose, would arise as a consequence of the Kantian moral philosophy itself. Now there remains only the lament that "the concept of the individual, to which the idea of autonomy was connected despite all the tensions involved, has not withstood industrialization" ("VS," 334/"EndR," 36). Along with bourgeois egoism, individual conscience also disintegrates. The moral law loses its addressees: "The agent to whom it is addressed has been liquidated. Morality had to disappear because it did not fulfill its own principle" ("VS," 335/"EndR," 36). Horkheimer would go on to develop this idea in the excursus on "Juliette, or Enlightenment and Morality." The proximity to Benjamin's critique of progress, which uncovers only totalitarian traits in the Enlightenment, is unmistakable.

Although Adorno was already involved in editing the proofs of "The End of Reason," both of the essays Horkheimer published in the Benjamin memorial volume testify to the fact that Horkheimer's interest in a direct collaboration with Adorno arose from the course of his own development. Adorno had taken up Benjaminian motifs from the beginning of his work, but for Horkheimer, these became significant only at the beginning of the 1940s, under the pressure of political experiences.

II

The collaborative work on *Dialectic of Enlightenment* took place during the period when the intellectual biographies of Horkheimer and Adorno most closely coincided, a time when their two life courses intersected. Although after the war Horkheimer and Adorno always assured one another that their thoughts were "one," this obscured the uniqueness of the constellation between November 1941, when an impatient Adorno moved to Santa Monica to join Horkheimer, and May 1944, when they completed work on the manuscript they presented to Pollock on his fiftieth birthday. Such assurances covered up differences that had always existed between their positions, differences that receded only during those years of intensive collaboration. The deeper reasons for this temporary rapprochement resulted more from Horkheimer's development than from Adorno's. On the one hand, *Dialectic of Enlightenment* marks a break with the program pursued in the *Zeitschrift für Sozialforschung;* on the other, it fits seamlessly into the continuity of a way of thinking later characterized as negative dialectics.[9] In making his publishing decisions in the 1950s and 1960s, Adorno could ignore the original contexts of his works, even those dating to the Weimar period, and raise them all to a moment of almost identical simultaneity, since his whole work branched out from its early roots without a break. In fact, his late philosophy draws its essential motifs from the early writings.[10]

The preface to *Dialectic of Enlightenment* opens with the authors' confession of skepticism about science. Their previous work, they assert, had been oriented to the established pursuit of science and learning and thematically connected to specific disciplines; they had limited themselves to "the critique and pursuit of specialist knowledge." But "the fragments that we have collected here, however, show that we have had to abandon that trust" (*DA*, 1/*DE*, xi). In fact, it was only Horkheimer who, with these words, was recanting the program of his inaugural address as director of the Institute, as well as the program developed in the *Zeitschrift für Sozialforschung.* Adorno had never had much confidence in sociology and the specialized disciplines. In his inaugural address as a lecturer in Frankfurt, delivered at approximately the same time as Horkheimer's inaugural address, he had already drawn a sharp distinction between philosophy and science: "The idea of science is research; that of philosophy, interpretation."[11] Even if sociology, like some clever cat burglar, should someday succeed in stealing half-forgotten and almost lost things from the dilapidated house of metaphysics, it would not be able to keep the booty for long, since only philosophy can recognize the true value of those treasures.

It was not even Horkheimer's original intention that *Dialectic of En-lightenment* remain a collection of fragments. He had planned a systematic work, and had previously made use of conventional forms of presentation. By contrast, Adorno was convinced from early on that fragmentary representation was the only suitable form for philosophical thought. Philosophy has no method, no hermeneutic at its disposal. It must decipher the fantasy-laden traces and mazes of a deformed reality and respond with presence of mind to "fleeting, vanishing hints within the enigmatic figure of what is."

Moreover, the young Adorno had already adopted two motifs from Benjamin: negative totality and natural history, on the one hand, and the affinity between myth and modernity, on the other. In *Dialectic of Enlightenment* these are joined with Horkheimer's idea of reason reduced to the function of self-preservation. The text, however, is by no means a seamless web: the authorship of the individual chapters is by no means undivided. Gretel Adorno once confirmed my suspicion, which is at any rate obvious to careful readers: the title essay and the chapter on de Sade are predominantly attributable to Horkheimer, while the chapters on Odysseus and the culture industry belong to Adorno. The differences are not only stylistic.

The greatest difference can be seen in how the two authors responded to the aporia broached in the Preface. If enlightenment is caught up in an irresistible process of self-destruction, then on what does the critique that determines this base its right to such a diagnosis? Since Nietzsche, the answer has always been the same: the radical critique of reason proceeds self-referentially; critique cannot simultaneously be radical and leave its own criteria untouched.

Horkheimer is troubled by this aporia. He shies away from the conclusion that the very act of enlightened knowledge is affected by the process of self-destruction, depriving it of its liberating effect. He would rather entangle himself in contradictions than give up his identity as an enlightener and fall into Nietzscheanism. The old trust was obstinately reaffirmed in the preface: "Enlightenment must reflect on itself if humanity is not to be totally betrayed" (*DA,* 5/*DE,* xv).

But interestingly, in the text itself, evidence of this position is found only in those chapters in which Horkheimer's hand is visible—for example, an insistence on the power of theory, intensified to an almost eschatological degree;[12] the belief in the antiauthoritarian tendency of the Enlightenment;[13] and the formulaic invocation of a self-transcending Enlightenment.[14] Admittedly, these affirmative tendencies emerge clearly only in *Eclipse of Reason*, for which Horkheimer alone was responsible. Here Horkheimer does not hesitate to lower the sights of a totalizing critique of reason that seriously implicates itself, in order not to deprive the dialectic of enlightenment of its own enlightening function:[15] "Reason can realize its reasonableness only through reflecting on the illness of the world as produced and reproduced by man; in such self-critique, reason will at the same time remain faithful to itself, by holding fast to the principle of truth, which we owe to reason alone, and by appealing to no other motive."[16]

Adorno, faced with the aporia of the self-referential critique of reason, was better able to keep his composure because he could bring another motif into play. He did not need to depend solely upon the enlightening power of philosophical criticism but could let his thinking circulate within the paradoxes of an identity logic that denies itself and yet illuminates from within. That is, for him the genuine aesthetic experience of modern art had opened up an independent source of insight.[17] A work immediately preceding the collaboration with Horkheimer already contained that construction of truth, appearance, and reconciliation that would later become decisive for Adorno's two-tracked late philosophy: the essay on Schönberg, written in 1940 and published in 1948 as the first part of his *Philosophy of Modern Music*.[18] Mimesis, that nonrational potential of an ancient reason distorted by the imperatives of self-preservation, is silently preserved by the utopian content of artistic beauty but stands mute and in need of interpretation. This establishes a relation of mutual reciprocity of aesthetics, art, and negative dialectics that contains what philosophical criticism can no longer guarantee: the anarchistic hope that one day the negative totality will still be burst asunder as if struck by lightning.[19]

III

The differences between Horkheimer and Adorno, present in *Dialectic of Enlightenment* but never worked out, clarify part of the hesitant behavior that so characteristically distinguished Horkheimer from Adorno after his return to Germany, even in their publication policies. Whereas immediately after the war—with his *Philosophy of Modern Music, Minima Moralia, Prisms,* and *Dissonances*—Adorno returned to works from the 1930s and 1940s and thus kept *Dialectic of Enlightenment* present as a background model, Horkheimer hesitated on the German edition of his *Eclipse of Reason* until 1967. The essays and lectures published in the 1950s and 1960s display a remarkably indecisive productivity, which perhaps reveals new tones but no new approaches—and certainly no identification with what he had produced so far. Horkheimer's hesitation applied to both previous phases of his intellectual biography, the collaboration with Adorno in California no less than the work of the New York circle.

From the beginning of the 1960s Horkheimer considered making his essays from the *Zeitschrift für Sozialforschung* publicly available. At first he dismissed the plan; the reasons are found in a letter of refusal to the publishing house S. Fischer dated June 1965.[20] Yet in April 1968 they appeared after all. A Preface to the new edition reiterates the distance that Horkheimer had already expressed in his letter: "If early theoretical efforts appear without the author having placed them in relation to contemporary insights, then he has surrendered the claim to substantive validity" (*KT,* II:ix). A peculiar shift in temporal perspective is contained in the remark that the goal of a just society has been barred "since the end of the war." In fact, by the beginning of the 1940s, Horkheimer had already broken with the position represented in his essays of the 1930s. Thus, much in the Preface to the new edition remains unintelligible unless one is clear that in the 1968 edition two distancings coincide: *Dialectic of Enlightenment* is intended as well. Resisting Adorno's pleas, Horkheimer delayed issuing a second edition of the book, long out of print, until after 1968.

I have already given the deeper reason for this hesitation: Horkheimer was stymied by the aporia of a self-referential critique of reason mentioned in the Preface to *Dialectic of Enlightenment.* Unlike Adorno, he could not take recourse to the mimetic content disguised in the esoteric works of modern art, nor did he want, like Nietzsche's followers, to slip into irrationalism. Of course, the "terror with which the rationalized, automated, and administered world takes its course" (*KT,* I:xi) leaves no room for doubt about the totality of an inflated instrumental reason. But Horkheimer wished to remain true to his original impulse: "to remain, in an adverse present, mindful of the other" without taking refuge in divine wisdom. But how is philosophical criticism still supposed to have any confidence in its relation to the wholly other? The 1965 letter to the Fischer Verlag, in which he had initially refused the republication of his older work, closes with an impressive confession: "My hesitation arises from the difficulty . . . of renouncing belief in any imminent realization of the ideas of Western Civilization, yet nevertheless standing up for that idea—without providence, and even against its supposed progress" (*KT*, II:xi). Horkheimer's late philosophy, kept in the form of journal notes, circles around this aporia.[21]

From what one can gather, the older Horkheimer did not return to religious faith, but religion now appears as the only agency that—if it only could command assent—would permit distinguishing between truth and falsity, morality and immorality. It alone could still grant life a meaning that transcends mere self-preservation. In a note that reads like a later continuation of his correspondence with Benjamin from the mid-1930s, Horkheimer wrote: "The atrocity I commit, the suffering I do nothing to stop, survive after the moment in which they occur only in human memory and are extinguished with it. It makes no sense at all to say that they continue to be true. They no longer exist, they are no longer true: the two are the same. Unless, that is, they be preserved—in God. Can one grant that and still seriously lead a godless life? That is the question philosophy raises" (*N*, 11/*DD*, 120). Earlier, in 1937, Benjamin had asked more or less the same question, and Horkheimer had soberly answered that the slain are really slain. In an essay from that period, he explained further: "All these wishes for eternity and for the onset of universal justice and goodness are shared by materialist and religious thinkers, in contrast to the impassivity of the positivist attitude. But if the latter is assuaged by the thought that desires will be fulfilled anyway, then the former are permeated by a feeling of the boundless forsakenness of humanity, which is the only true answer to an impossible hope" (*KT*, I:372). At that time Horkheimer was still confident that critical social theory is capable of converting the rational content of the philosophical tradition into the medium of science. It is the same tenacious postmetaphysical thinking that compels the older Horkheimer to consider not mere philosophy—not even in the form of negative dialectics—but theology as the only alternative to a desolate positivism. Yet this consideration still leads to no affirmative result. In a further note Horkheimer says about critical theory: "It has replaced theology, but found no new heaven to which it can point, not even a heaven on earth. Of course, it cannot rid itself of the idea; therefore, there will always be those who ask that it point the way to one. As if it were not precisely its own discovery that the heaven to which one can show the way is no heaven at all" (*N*, 61/*DD*, 148).

That Horkheimer should invoke theology, even if only hypothetically, is only logical once the philosophy of history has not only lost its historical basis but, extended into a totalizing critique of reason, threatens to destroy its own foundations. The older Horkheimer does not wish to accept this, though he sees no way out. In his *Notizen* one finds an idea that might have restored to criticism a piece of its self-confidence: "Language, whether it wants to or not, must make a claim to truth" (*N*, 123). And further: "Truth in speech accrues not to the isolated, naked judgment, as if it were printed on a piece of paper, but to the speaker's relationship to the world as it is expressed in judgment, focused on this place and referring to a specific object" (*N*, 172/*DD*, 209). But then Horkheimer was too much the negative philosopher of history, too much the radical critic of reason, to be able to discover a glimmer of reason in everyday communicative practices. As if to avert that thought, he once said: "Today speech is vapid and those who do not want to listen are not really so very wrong. . . . Speech is outdated and so is the kind of action that once resulted from it" (*N*, 26f./*DD*, 129–30).

The late philosophy is governed by a dilemma: *Dialectic of Enlightenment* cannot be the last word, but it bars the way back to the materialism of the 1930s. That it is not to be the last word is certainly not only due to internal reasons. To them must be added at least two external reasons.

After his return to Germany, Horkheimer rebuilt the Institute for Social Research; he set in motion a broadly conceived group experiment and generally promoted the resuscitation of empirical social research on the level of the research techniques meanwhile developed in the United States. This renewed connection with established academic pursuits could not readily be reconciled with the convictions set out in *Dialectic of Enlightenment*. In his works on the critique of positivism, Adorno essentially defended his old position; Horkheimer evaded the problem, unless it was to promote an ethically motivated sociology of marginal groups, albeit uncoupled from social theory as much as possible: "All that comes from theory may only lead to harm" (*N*, 87).

Another problem presented itself on the level of politics. Horkheimer had reached a more positive attitude toward the political form of Western democracies and the life-style of Western civilization than the careful formulation in the 1968 Preface suggests: "To judge the so-called free world by its own concept of itself, to take a critical attitude toward it and yet stand by its ideas . . . is the right and duty of every thinking person" (*KT*, I:xiii/*CT*, ix). Intuitively, Horkheimer entrusted a rational potential to developed capitalist societies that he had long despaired of in theory. Adorno, in turn, in his analysis of "late capitalism," held fast to ideas that dovetailed with the framework of a negativistic philosophy of history. Horkheimer did not find the strength to revise this position again in the light of his altered political experiences; rather, he reached back to the contrasting model of liberal capitalism. Of course, as earlier, Horkheimer saw the limits of bourgeois culture in the fact that self-consciousness, autonomy, and the dignity of the individual had hardened into a cold, atomized isolation rather than unfolding into the emancipation of all. But the older Horkheimer was not only highly conventional in his cultural criticism; he became conservative generally. He now believed that freedom and humanity are bourgeois in their essence: "The freedom of all humanity is that of the bourgeois *[Bürger]* who can develop his capacities. The founders of modern socialism did not reflect on the fact that these capacities themselves belong to the bourgeois mode of production" (*N*, 153).

Yet this affirmative attitude toward the institutions of the Western world, with which Horkheimer rebelled against the inescapability of a totalitarianism that obliterates all traits of individuality and freedom, nevertheless has another, less conspicuous dimension. The sense of life expressed in his late, aphoristic philosophy perhaps best explains its author's inability to bring his splintering insights together once again into a convincing picture of a fractured social reality. Despite all the civic honors accorded him, the Horkheimer who returned from emigration never felt at home in a country he felt might relapse into barbarism at any time. For the rest of his life, this country remained foreign to him. At the end of 1960 he wrote:

In the Germany of 1960, the National Socialist past has undergone a "mastering." . . . It is really about time to rebel against the ostracizing of one's behaviour by foreigners. But one is already strong enough to afford to censure the past oneself, almost as if of one's own accord. . . . How much more justified we here will be, once all that has been settled, in taking on those who triumphed back in 1945, when Germany lay prostrate: taking on the arrogant peoples of the West, who in their folly struck down the Germans and allied themselves with the Russians, against whom they now already so desperately need us; taking on certain individuals, emigrés, Jews, and dubious characters who since then have once more been throwing their weight around, without having heard the whistling of the bombs, without having shared our misery and disgrace. . . . For the time being we will have collective guilt and friendship with Israel, but one day that must end. Soon we will close that chapter. (N, 146f.)

Although the shameless reactions to Bitburg seem to have confirmed these fears,[22] we need not simply accept Horkheimer's words as truth. Yet they do express a truth with which Horkheimer lived in the Federal Republic of Germany, and in view of which, left solitary, he entrusted the continuation of his twice-broken theory to his journal.

Translated by Kenneth Baynes and John McCole

Notes

Horkheimer's texts are cited and English translations, where available, are cross-referenced according to the following key (in some cases the translations have been modified):

N = *Notizen 1950 bis 1969 und Dämmerung: Notizen in Deutschland* (Frankfurt, 1974); *DD* = *Dawn and Decline: Notes, 1926–1931 and 1950–1969* (New York, 1978) (contains selections from *Notizen* and *Dämmerung*).

KT = *Kritische Theorie. Eine Dokumentation*, vols. I, II (Frankfurt, 1968); *CT* = *Critical Theory: Selected Essays* (New York, 1972).

DA = *Dialektik der Aufklärung. Philosophische Fragmente* (Frankfurt, 1969); *DE* = *Dialectic of Enlightenment* (New York, 1972).

"AS" = "Autoritärer Staat," in *Gesammelte Schriften* (Frankfurt, 1987), 5:293–319; "AuthSt" = "The Authoritarian State," in Andrew Arato and Eike Gebhardt, eds., *The Essential Frankfurt School Reader* (New York, 1982), 95–117.

"VS" = "Vernunft und Selbsterhaltung," in *Gesammelte Schriften* 5:320–50; "EndR" = "The End of Reason," in Arato and Gebhardt, eds., *The Essential Frankfurt School Reader*, 26–48.

Jürgen Habermas

1. Hauke Brunkhorst, chapter 4 in this book. cf. Michael Korthals, "Die kritische Gesellschaftstheorie des frühen Horkheimers," *Zeitschrift für Sozialphilosophie* 14:315ff.

2. [Translators' note: *Notizen 1950 bis 1969 und Dämmerung: Notizen in Deutschland* (Frankfurt, 1974), also published in Horkheimer, *Gesammelte Schriften* (Frankfurt, 1991), 6:187–425, with the dates corrected to 1949–1969. See the note on citations and cross-references above.]

3. See, for example, the appeal "For an Association of the Clearsighted." *N*, 107/*DD*, 166.

4. Helmut Dubiel, *Theory and Politics: Studies in the Development of Critical Theory* (Cambridge, 1985).

5. Rolf Wiggershaus, *Die Frankfurter Schule* (Munich, 1986), demonstrates that this step, which in hindsight seems compelling, was initially accompanied by different expectations. In the following I rely upon my Afterword to the new edition of *Dialektik der Aufklärung* (Frankfurt, 1986).

6. [Translators' note: The original German title of this essay was "Reason and Self-Preservation" (*"Vernunft und Selbsterhaltung"*); see the note on citations and cross-references, above.]

7. [Translators' note: "Walter Benjamin zum Gedächtnis" (unpublished hectographed manuscript, 1942).]

8. Helmut Dubiel and Alfons Söllner, eds., *Wirtschaft, Recht und Staat im Nationalsozialismus* (Frankfurt, 1981).

9. See Wolfgang Bonß and Norbert Schindler, "Kritische Theorie als interdisziplinärer Materialismus," and Martin Jay, "Positive und negative Totalität: Adornos Alternativentwurf zur interdisziplinären Forschung," both in Wolfgang Bonß and Axel Honneth, eds., *Sozialforschung als Kritik* (Frankfurt, 1982). [Editors' note: See chapter 5 of this book for a different verison of Bonß's essay.]

10. "Die Aktualität der Philosophie" in Adorno, *Gesammelte Schriften*, vol. 1: *Philosophische Frühschriften* (Frankfurt, 1973), 325ff./"The Actuality of Philosophy," *Telos* 31 (1977): 113–42; "Die Idee der Naturgeschichte," in *Gesammelte Schriften*, 1:345ff. In *Negative Dialectics* Adorno himself remarks that the chapter "World History and Natural History" develops themes from the early essay on the idea of natural history.

11. Adorno, "Die Aktualität der Philosophie," 334/ "The Actuality of Philosophy," 126.

12. "The spirit of this kind of unrelenting theory would be able to turn even pitiless progress to its own end." *DA*, 48/*DE*, 42.

13. "[The antiauthoritarian tendency of Enlightenment] still communicates (though, of course, only in subterranean channels) with that utopia in the concept of reason." *DA*, 100/*DE*, 93.

14. "Enlightenment which is in possession of itself and becoming a force can break through the limits of the Enlightenment." *DA*, 217/*DE*, 208. "The fact that de Sade did not leave it to the Enlightenment's opponents to make it take fright at its own nature makes his work a spur to its redemption." *DA*, 126/*DE*, 117.

Remarks on the Development of Horkheimer's Work

15. "The possibility of a self-critique of reason presupposes, first, that the antagonism of reason and nature is in an acute and catastrophic phase, and, second, that at this state of complete alienation the idea of truth is still accessible." *Eclipse of Reason* (Oxford, 1947), 177. [Editors' note: See also chapter 15 in this book.]

16. Ibid.

17. Axel Honneth has pointed out to me that this motif also appears in Horkheimer, especially in the period of his reorientation. See Horkheimer, "Art and Mass Culture," *Zeitschrift für Sozialforschung* 9 (1941): 290ff./*CT*, 273–90. Nevertheless, it never became a constitutive force in his thought.

18. See Albrecht Wellmer, "Wahrheit, Schein, Versöhnung. Adornos ästhetische Rettung der Modernität" in Wellmer, *Zur Dialektik von Moderne und Postmoderne* (Frankfurt, 1985), 9–47.

19. Jürgen Habermas, *The Theory of Communicative Action,* (Boston, 1984), 1:366ff.; on the status of "negative dialectics" in Adorno's late philosophy, see the contrasting interpretation of Michael Theunissen, "Negativität bei Adorno," in Ludwig von Friedeburg and Jürgen Habermas, eds., *Adorno-Konferenz* (Frankfurt, 1983), 41ff.; Herbert Schnädelbach, "Dialektik der Vernunftkritik," in ibid., 66ff.

20. See Horkheimer, *KT,* II:viiff.

21. Horkheimer's late philosophy has been convincingly portrayed by Alfred Schmidt, "Einleitung" to Horkheimer, *Notizen 1950–1969 und Dämmerung: Notizen in Deutschland* (Frankfurt, 1974), xlff.; see the abridged English translation in chapter 2 in this book.

22. Jürgen Habermas, "Entsorgung der Vergangenheit," in *Die neue Unübersichtlichkeit* (Frankfurt, 1985). English translation: "Defusing the Past," in Geoffrey Hartman, ed., *Bitburg in Moral and Political Perspective* (Bloomington, Ind., 1986).

4

Dialectical Positivism of Happiness: Max Horkheimer's Materialist Deconstruction of Philosophy

Hauke Brunkhorst

As a philosopher, Max Horkheimer today stands in the shadow of Theodor W. Adorno, yet he is the actual founder of the Frankfurt School—not Adorno, and not Marcuse, whose articles in Horkheimer's *Zeitschrift für Sozialforschung* could hardly be said to lay less weight on the philosophical scales than those of its editor. Without the intellectual figure of Horkheimer, the historical existence of the Frankfurt School would be unthinkable. Since Kuhn at the latest, we have come to expect that the heads and fathers of schools provide something like a paradigm, an exemplary, school-forming scientific achievement; but none is to be found in Horkheimer's work. True, the works Horkheimer published between 1930 and 1940 do have a programmatic force. They give direction and orientation to the research done in the Frankfurt circle, the Institute for Social Research, and the *Zeitschrift*. But a towering paradigmatic achievement, of the kind to belabor generations of critical social scientists with riddles, can scarcely be found concealed behind the programmatic cornerstones set out by the 1931 inaugural lecture, "The Present Situation of Social Philosophy and the Tasks of an Institute for Social Research," or the classic 1937 text, "Traditional and Critical Theory." Anyone who expects to find the fundamental philosophical concept of critical theory there is bound to be disappointed.[1] The exemplary work that stands out above the entire current of undogmatic Marxism in this century, from the early Frankfurt School through Habermas, had already appeared in 1923: Georg Lukács' collection of essays, "History and Class Consciousness." As I have shown elsewhere, critical theory's horizon of problems—the founding of a nonpositivist Marxism somewhere between Hegel and Marx, on the one hand, and a sociological reconstruction of the theory of alienation as a Weberian Marxist theory of rationalization on the other—was prefigured there.[2] From that point, lines of development lead to the issue of the normative foundations of historical materialism, as well as to the problem of instrumental, functionalist reason.

Yet the operationalizing of the paradigm as a program of critical social research, its coalescence into a philosophical, social-scientific school that meanwhile forms a tradition of its own, remains the decisive intellectual merit of Horkheimer. He, not Lukács, was the first to lead Marxism unambiguously into conjunction with the research programs of the social sciences, and in doing so, he was following an originally philosophical impulse.

Too glaring, however, is the inconsistency of his articles to inspire the philosophical idea once more with systematic force. Too clear from the start are the contradictions of his thought, which can no longer be resolved dialectically, to make it a promising candidate for a social-scientific paradigm. By no means does this escape Horkheimer's notice. Consequently, he drives his philosophical experiments toward overt aporias. No longer does he wish to be a philosopher with a truly philosophical claim to totality; he is an extreme positivist, influenced by empirio-criticism, whose narrow-gauge, small-time ontology knows only sensory stimuli and individual things. And yet he wants to remain a dialectician after all, holding fast to the being of the singular universal in the figure of true universal interests—only to ensnare himself, by his unconditional negation of the unconditional, in the aporia of absolutely renouncing the absolute.

Horkheimer's attacks on the philosophical tradition's fundamentalism and on its subject-object dualism move within the broad currents of post-Hegelian thought. But Horkheimer has given up the search for a philosophical way out of the crisis of philosophy. Instead, his materialism seeks out aporias and does not wish to break out of them at all. Yet Horkheimer does not stop short at deconstructivism. His way out is the needle's eye of social research, through which all philosophy that wishes to survive must henceforth pass. It is the idea of a social-scientific transformation of philosophy.

The philosophical import of Horkheimer's early works shows itself only in his dual role in the genesis of what was later called the Frankfurt School. Horkheimer is an author of the *Zeitschrift für Sozialfor-schung* and simultaneously director of the institute, and thus editor of the *Zeitschrift*. On the level of a philosophy attributable to him as an individual author, he remained eclectic and inconsistent in the 1930s. Yet if we leave the level of a history of events in individual thought and aggregate the data of the history of science on the level of a structural history of the objective spirit of research programs, then hopeless aporias suddenly become productive contradictions and eclecticism sheds its arbitrariness. From now on, it finds itself subject to the stern judgment of science, which teaches us to see through metaphysics and exposes its fallibilistic, hypothetical status as the relentless grind of everyday science separates the metaphysical chaff from the kernels whose philosophical force henceforth unfolds in the context of research programs in the individual disciplines—and only there.

Horkheimer's philosophical intuitions revolve around such projects as materialism as empirical research and scientific disenchantment; materialism as an individualistic, utilitarian ethic of happiness or, complementarily, of the solidarity of all life in the face of universal suffering; dialectics as a method of mediating and transcending contradiction; and dialectics as the negation of the prevailing order, an insight of unabridged reason. But philosophically, the systematic nexus of these projects has long since collapsed. Under the burden of proving the truth of his metaphysical ideas, the author as philosopher breaks down, only to reappear immediately in the rejuvenated role of the organizer of a social science research program, in order to redistribute the burden of proof, grown too heavy for the old philosopher, onto the many shoulders of the individual disciplines he had always despised.

In the following pages, the "author as philosopher" appears in the first four sections. Once the tragedy of the philosopher is over, however, all's well that ends well after all: the organizer of research programs inherits a weak dialectical force from philosophy, the blasting charge of a critical project in the grey-on-grey of everyday scientific positivity.

First let us turn to the prelude—to Horkheimer's philosophical point of departure. The finitude and worldliness of human life, the brute fact of the privation and misery suffered by "far and away the greatest part of humanity,"[3] of their hopes and longings, and the claim to worldly happiness of "individuals who are, in all seriousness, transitory":[4] these things imprinted themselves so decisively upon Hork-heimer's thinking in the 1930s that he even defended the "finite quantities" of mathematics against the idealistic affront of "deriving them from the infinitely small by means of the infinitesimal calculus." In the mathematical natural sciences' tendency to make "the wretched world which the scholar sets eyes on ever more expressible in the form of differential equations" and thereby to efface any trace of sensually experienceable reality, Horkheimer recognizes the clutch of Western metaphysics, which is in league with domination: to idealize and transfigure the empirical lifeworld, grounding it in an "eternal lo-gos,"[5] in "eternal ideas"[6] beyond this world and its "earthly possibili-ties."[7]

That is Horkheimer's central argument against the idealistic meta-physics of philosophers from Plato to Hegel: they stand in "the service of transfiguration,"[8] because they believe they must ground "the mis-ery of the present" and the "material privation" of the "earthly order"[9]—in short, empirical reality—in an "overarching" "second reality."[10] In view of the irredeemably affirmative alliance between "optimistic metaphysics" and "social pessimism,"[11] Horkheimer sometimes finds it difficult to hold fast to his own program of mate-rialistically preserving the truth content of idealism and metaphysics, of taking up the inheritance of philosophical reason in the materialis-tic context of a theory of society, of reconstructing traditional theory as critical theory.[12] Metaphysics stands convicted of the crime of transfiguration, which can no more be atoned and made amends for than the misery and suffering of the past.

That distinguishes Horkheimer from Adorno and Marcuse. If the thinking of the latter, the most affirmative among the philosophers of negativity, always moved within the spell cast by the idealistic concept of reason, so for Adorno, in even the most radical negation of an enlightenment that has been leveled out by identity philosophy, phi-losophy could only be a question of redeeming the moment of truth in precisely that enlightenment and its rationality. Marcuse's and Adorno's relationship to philosophy—the one more exoteric and con-ventional, the other esoteric—was, however indirectly, that of an in-ternal transformation. Adorno and Marcuse remained philosophers throughout their lives. Compared with them, however, Horkheimer was an antiphilosopher in the most productive phase of his life.

As a complement to the intraphilosophical destruction of metaphysics, whether in its hermeneutic-existential ontological or language-analytical forms, Horkheimer as antiphilosopher developed, in proximity to Nietzsche, a third version: the ideology-critical.

The systematic motive that connects Horkheimer's radicalized ideology critique with Heidegger, Gilbert Ryle, and Wittgenstein is the critique of the dualism of philosophical thinking. Again and again, he polemicizes against the "demotion of the known world to a mere exterior,"[13] the "Cartesian isolation of intellectual substance from all spatial reality,"[14] "the splitting of the world into two mutually independent realms,"[15] the "dualism of thought and being, understanding and perception,"[16] and protests "against the assumption of an absolute, trans-historical subject."[17] The paradigm of traditional theory is the "scientific method" of axiomatic-deductive reasoning,[18] which remains "alive throughout the pursuit of the specialized sciences":[19] "Traditional theory and reality belong to two distinct and separate provinces. . . . Theory remains in the realm of contemplation. Philosophers have frequently made something absolute out of this aspect of theory and, under the title of 'logos' or 'spirit,' have deified the subject of these intellectual activities. It appears in their systems as the creator of the world."[20] Above all, however, Cartesian rationalism disregarded the historically mediated selectivity of our knowledge, the conditionality of "spirit," and failed to take account of its interwovenness with an opaque background "cast in shadows," with a "world" that is not conscious and transparent: the primacy of "material existence," of "praxis," the "lifeworld," the "unconscious" and "preconscious." "The rationalistic separation of the human being into two independent halves, body and mind, had removed the entirety of unconscious and half-conscious psychic processes from scientific theory."[21] Ultimately, therefore, Horkheimer can denounce Cartesian dualism—the "notion of knowing the supposedly unconditional and thereby of being unconditional oneself"[22]—ideology-critically as "a narcissistic projection of one's own temporally conditioned ego onto eternity."[23] For constructing an "unconditional order,"[24] an eternal and absolute truth, an "ultimate, absolutely valid knowledge"[25] means "intellectually eternalizing the earthly conditions underlying it." This "transfiguring function"[26] "reveals" the "indwelling inhumanity" of philosophy.[27]

In the following, I first elucidate the fundamental conceptual scheme of Horkheimer's antiphilosophy: the transition from "idealism" to "traditional theory" and from "materialism" to "critical theory". Critical theory, for Horkheimer, has the form of an "existential judgment." As existential judgment, this theory is supposed to unfold a force at once critical and theoretical. In reality, the synthetic force of existential judgment is due to an equivocation in the concept of existence that Horkheimer ambiguously employs in such a way that the "critical" and "theoretical" dimensions of the meaning of "existential judgment" can break asunder; critique and theory can no longer be mediated. The grounds for the weakness of this mediation lie in Horkheimer's materialistic deconstruction of the philosophical concepts of reason and reasoning. From the very beginning, Horkheimer quite consciously forgoes any discursive justification of critique, the "critical attitude," or the practice of "changing conditions." The deconstruction of transcendental theories of constitution is not succeeded by a materialistic theory of knowledge or constitution; instead, in place of the philosophy of consciousness there appears the overtly aporetic figure of thought of a dialectical positivism. Yet Horkheimer's antiphilosophy opens up a perspective this side of deconstruction, a perspective of which he availed himself as director of the Institute for Social Research, as editor of the *Zeitschrift*, as a social philosopher, and as a diagnostician of his times: the perspective of a social-scientific transformation of philosophy.

Idealism and Traditional Theory

At first, Horkheimer uses the terms *metaphysics* and *idealism* (and occasionally *philosophy of consciousness*) synonymously. The most precise internal differentiation of this complex concept, which spans the entire history of philosophy, is to be found in his 1934 essay, "The Rationalism Dispute in Current Philosophy."[28] Here, "idealism" is internally articulated into a two-sided, interlocking, complementary relationship.

First of all, within the framework of enlightenment (rationalism in the broad sense), rationalism (in the strict sense) and empiricism relate to one another as complementarily opposed functional equivalents, for classical empiricism, like rationalism, rests on a dualism of thought and being, mind and body, interior and exterior, subject and object.

This idealistic enlightenment, which Horkheimer sharply distinguishes from the materialist version, is in turn complementary to counterenlightenment. Idealistic enlightenment is rationalistic, whereas counterenlightenment is irrationalistic, and Horkheimer always defends liberal rationalism against the authoritarian irrationalism of the twentieth century, against the antiscientism, anti-intellectualism, and anti-individualism of the present, against "crude invectives against thought" as well as "warnings about its deadening effects." Horkheimer disposes of such categorial errors of *Lebensphilosophie*, which bemoans the destruction and disintegration of naturally grown forms of life by thought, with a semantic critique: "In reality, reason can only destroy untruth. The proposition that correct thinking destroys its object is self-contradictory. The truth or untruth of many general statements of belief principally eludes verification; but this also voids them of sense, for every proposition makes a truth claim, and every truth is grounded in knowledge."[29] Irrationalism relapses "behind liberalism." "As opposed to irrationalism, materialism attempts to overcome the one-sidedness of analytical thought without discarding it."[30] Of course, that does nothing to alter the structural interchangeability of rationalism and irrationalism. Irrationalism may have the advantage over rationalism (in the broad sense) of the "correct view that the understanding draws on something other than itself."[31] In this respect, it "correctly ascertains the bankruptcy of rationalism," but it "draws the wrong consequences":[32] it does away with rationalism's neglect of the "unconscious," only to idolize it.[33] That is precisely what constitutes the structural identity of idealistic enlightenment and counterenlightenment. In place of the absolute subject, eternal ideas, and the autonomous ego, counterenlightenment sets up timeless collective notions such as nation and community or a "determination of the human essence . . . that spans the night of primaeval history and the end of humankind."[34] Rationalistic and irrationalistic idealism ultimately converge in the motif of serving up "a deeper meaning to existence," a "metaphysical constitution of meaning,"[35] of giving ultimate "security" and certainty, of "grounding action" in an "absolute imperative" or "fixed, essential insight."[36] "Thus both rationalism and irrationalism render services to transfiguration."[37]

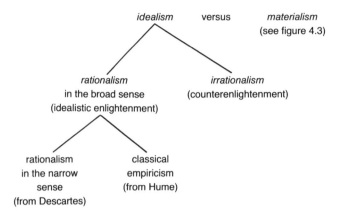

Figure 4.1
Theory Schema 1934 (idealistic wing)

Figure 4.1 illustrates the idealistic wing of Horkheimer's first investigative schema for the history of philosophy.

In the 1937 essay "Traditional and Critical Theory," the term *idealism* (or *metaphysics*) is replaced by the concept of traditional theory.[38] Like idealism, it includes the Cartesian philosophy (rationalism in the narrow sense and classical empiricism) but is no longer applied to the irrationalist currents of the nineteenth and twentieth centuries, such as *Lebensphilosophie* and neoromanticism. In exchange, reaching beyond the term *idealism,* Horkheimer explicitly implicates the contemporary empirical, specialized, or individual sciences, which now fall under the Cartesian paradigm in one particular respect: in their empirical-analytical one-sidedness. That leads to a marked shifting of accents in the relationship between critical theory and the positivism of the sciences of experience, to the disadvantage of the latter and in favor of a sharper, more precise version of the critique of positivism. From now on, positivism is identifiable as Cartesian-organized scientism; the critique of positivism is concretized as a critique of scientism. From the beginning Horkheimer's radically antifundamentalist position was directed against the residual Cartesian strain in neopositivism, for all his affinity to the latter:[39] against the attempt to anchor deductively schematized science, as a neutral language of observation, in an absolutely secure foundation. It is no accident that the few rough, intuitive sketches of his own critical research program that

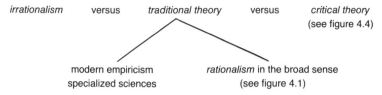

Figure 4.2
Theory Schema 1937 (traditional middle)

Horkheimer occasionally slips into his essays move him toward Popper, and even more so into the proximity of the postempiricist theory of science that stems from Kuhn and Quine: "Not the accretion of facts and theories, but the leap with which dominant categories are recast characterizes the stages of science. What precedes such recasting, of course, is the progressive revision of individual knowledge, which necessarily takes place with reference to uppermost systematic principles that provide the standard of correction. The revolutionizing of fundamental categories, which this only serves to prepare, then raises knowledge as such to a higher level and affects its entire structure."[40]

Figure 4.2 depicts the traditional wing of the second investigative schema for the history of theory.

Materialism and Critical Theory

Yet insofar as the modern, empirical sciences unreservedly accept the primacy of experience, their own conditionality and that of their objects, and the insuperable contingency of empirical reality, they belong within the intellectual lineage of materialism, materialistic enlightenment, and critical theory. The pragmatic concept of scientific "testing" includes, for all its one-sidedness, one of the indispensable motifs of the "materialistic way of thinking": "its critical stance toward the assumption of a transcendent, trans-human truth which, not being fundamentally accessible to experience and praxis, is reserved for revelation and the insight of a select few; this makes it a weapon against mysticism of every sort."[41] And as "Traditional and Critical Theory" says of positivism, "The watchword of keeping to the facts and renouncing illusions of any sort still preserves, even today, a kind of reaction against the alliance between oppression and metaphysics."[42]

In many respects, Horkheimer's "materialism" is extremely nominalistic, even though he does not wish to be a metaphysical nominalist and defends universal interests. He is not concerned with defending a philosophical principle or tenet or with grounding absolute goals within an ultimate horizon of meaning. Materialism is "disenchantment" in Max Weber's sense:

Insofar as the metaphysical schools conceive of the unconditional not as being but as law-giving, as activity, or even as the quintessence of free acts, they also exact respect for the meaning of those acts, an adaptation of empirical human life to the intelligible ground of personality to which philosophy penetrates. However, the underlying reality is regarded as normative not merely where the religious origins of the dependence relationship are still preserved in the form of the precept, but also in all cases where the accord between individual existence and its ground as discovered by metaphysics is regarded as valuable. For them, too, the being to which metaphysics gives "the emphatic name of an actual existence" contains the rule for beings who dispose over themselves. The materialistic thesis excludes such inferences by its very nature. The principle it designates as actuality is not suited to provide norms. The material world is, in itself, senseless; no maxims for the shaping of life follow from its qualities.[43]

Materialist science may be useful to humanity, but it establishes no higher goal. It is disenchantment; it destroys meaning.[44] It "provides no models, maxims, or directives for an authentic life, but only the means to it and is therefore . . . theory."[45] Materialism "replaces the justification of action" with "explanation."[46] It is an "impossible task" to "justify ways of acting with mere philosophy. . . . There is no eternal realm of values. . . . Materialism finds no authority that transcends human beings and distinguishes between helpfulness and profit-seeking, goodness and cruelty, greed and self-sacrifice. Logic, too, remains mute; it accords no precedence to moral convictions." Morality "cannot be substantiated, neither by intuition nor by argument. Rather, it represents a psychic disposition. To describe this . . . is the business of psychology."[47] Here one must read precisely. What Horkheimer—undoubtedly a positivistic skeptic—doubts about the susceptibility of practical questions to truth is not the rational capability of finite human beings to distinguish between good and evil but the grounding of this distinction in a metaphysical "authority that transcends human beings." As a rule, however, Horkheimer—like the positivists—identifies the discursive justification of norms with an absolute, metaphysical justification of them. But that is not the decisive point. Horkheimer's true concern is the idea of the worldliness and finitude of human life. Again and again, therefore, he defends the idea of a general interest, which nonetheless rests on no authority beyond actual interests and needs, beyond human beings' earthly claims to happiness. And Horkheimer rejects only transhuman reason, not that of finite individuals: "They alone have reason."[48] The limits of this reason are empirical limits. The most general fundamental principles of the materialists—constitution-theoretical, even ontological-sounding theses such as that "all that exists is material"—have a merely hypothetical status, dependent on fallible "experience": "They contain the emptiest, most general extract of their experience, but by no means a law for their actions."[49]

The manifold, wide-ranging, unsystematic, and never quite consistent variations in meaning that Horkheimer draws together into the concept of materialism range from a quasi-ontological, materialistic monism, through the strongly accented meaning of a "positive science of experience" and "historicity," to the "idealism ... of the strata struggling against domination," who measure existing conditions against the concept inherent in them and subject them to immanent critique.[50] The guiding thread that leads through this language game is certainly the motif of worldliness and finitude. Nonetheless, one can identify at least four central aspects that go beyond this philosophical motif polemically employed against philosophy. Together, they outline something like a materialist paradigm.

First materialism is praxis oriented toward change: the practical orientation of action toward the "situation of the ruled," toward the "misery of the present" and the "economic causes of material need,"[51] the "changing" of "conditions," "critical behavior." It pursues a "practical interest" that is empirically given and not to be further justified.[52] Preserved in this interest are the "interests of humanity" and the "needs of the generality," that is, the striving of human beings "for happiness."[53] Materialism seeks to overcome the 'metaphysical' opposition between "freedom" and "happiness." Its practical interest leads to a negative morality, which indicts not metaphysical "forgetting of being" but the "piece of immorality" to be found in the "forgetfulness" of the old philosophy—"the indifference toward worldly struggles"[54]—and to a materialistic minimal morality of "compassion" and "politics." The former is the legacy of Schopenhauer in Horkheimer: "solidarity with suffering human beings."[55] "We see human beings not as subjects of their fate, but as objects of blind occurrences of nature, and the response of moral feeling to this is compassion." Temporally, this outlasts any historically "determinate form" of "economic mode," and spatially it encompasses all living organisms: "The solidarity of humanity is part of the solidarity of life as such. . . . Animals are in need of humans. . . . Human traits may bear a particular stamp, but the affinity of human happiness and misery with the life of animals is evident."[56] Politics, which is anchored in the solidarity of life, should produce—in the classical sense of politics—the "happiness of the generality." The goal of politics is, through "struggle" (meaning class struggle), to "improve the lot of the generality," "to actualize" the "content," which must be historically concretized in any given case, of the universalistic "ideas of the bourgeoisie": of "freedom, equality, and justice."[57]

Second, "materialism" is epistemic materialism in the philosophically restricted sense that it is concerned with the de facto limits of reason and will, the empirical and historical preconditions of a rationally organized society. Materialism is the "equation of the subject of knowledge with the finite human being."[58] What "constitutes" itself in "historical action" is always only a "real subject."[59] One of this subject's empirical limits is the irreversibility of past suffering: "Past suffering is irreparable."[60] Thus the guilt of philosophy, which transfigures, is also irreversible! The other limit is the historicity of real subjects. Entirely in the sense of historicism, the contingent historical horizon of the "respective concrete situation of the actor" is an insuperable given for them.[61] Everything is historically conditioned. Nor is that meant as transcendental philosophy: it is only a refutable supposition, which has taken its leave of philosophy. Therefore—and this is the third aspect—Horkheimer's materialism is essentially methodological materialism. It has a decidedly scientistic streak. It accepts the distinction between "is" and "ought." Fallibilistic and oriented toward the sciences of experience, this materialism seeks to expose its

own hopes to disillusionment. Along with Dilthey, it regards metaphysics as a mere hypothesis. It is a resolute attempt at a transformation of philosophy into science but not simply in order to have the
specialized disciplines step into the place of philosophy. Methodological materialism takes the primacy of experience as its point of departure. As with Popper, the real world is "the world of our experiential
reality."[62] What distinguishes Horkheimer from Popper and from all
of modern, language-analytical philosophy is that he overlooks the
methodological role of language. The core of his polemic against the
Vienna Circle's neopositivism is the sensualist, empiricist objection to
reducing real sensory experience to mere experiential propositions,
the so-called protocol sentences.[63]

Finally, materialism is a heuristic principle: the principle of a dialectical method. Hegel's method was materialistic; idealism was only
the content of his philosophy. All materialism must do is to give the
"idealist concept of reason" a "materialist content."[64] Horkheimer needs
"dialectics":

1. In order to ground a research program of sublating philosophy
and science.

2. In order to escape the pitfalls of historical relativism, radical skepticism about reason, or a relapse into metaphysical materialism; to
secure, at least through dialectical rhetoric, the lines of retreat; to be
able to make a stand, at least declaratively, on behalf of reason against
the one-sidedness of positivism and analytical understanding.

3. In order to preserve mediation as a figure of thought against the
irrationalism of the times, with its false celebration of immediacy. Critique thus proceeds from relationships of complementarity such as
those between rationalism and irrationalism, or rationalism (in the
narrow sense) and empiricism, or positivism and existentialism, between the fetishism of "immediate, primal, theory-free circumstances" and "spiritualism and occultism" in Comte and Bergson.
Indeed, the critique of *Lebensphilosophie*'s intuitionism in general pursues the figure of thought of mediation.[65] Horkheimer defines the
normative vanishing point of his own materialism, the idea of happiness, as the mediation of the unmediated: "happiness" is "pleasure"
that is mediated by "that which . . . gives pleasure."[66] Happiness, as
Marcuse later put it, is "estrangement" "in the genuine sense."[67]

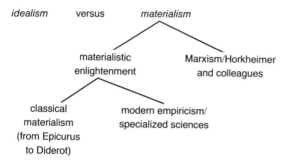

Figure 4.3
Theory Schema 1934 (materialistic wing)

This final aspect makes it clear that Horkheimer's "materialism," like that of critical theory as a whole, is an individualistic materialism: socialism would break the domination of the whole over the parts, "its elements"; the whole would "come under the control of its elements, namely, the human beings who live in it." The lifting of estrangement, to be sure, can never come to rest in an absolute mediation. That, too, is a limit of which individualistic materialism remains aware: the parts, "despite this control, will . . . continue to be dominated by the whole to a certain degree, because that which they create must have a retroactive effect on them. That is self-evident; it is a statement that holds for all living processes"[68]—a motif that recurs in Habermas's early, Marxist Schelling-reception and in the construction of the sociological systems concept in his middle works.[69]

The forerunners of materialism are the ancient pre-Socratic philosophers and the French Enlightenment.[70] The expression itself, like the term *critical theory*, refers directly to Marx's theory and to the Frankfurt School's own theoretical position within the context of Marxism. Until 1937, this position was called "materialism"; after 1937, "critical theory."[71] The materialist wing of the first investigative schema for the history of philosophy (or theory) is depicted in figure 4.3.

The change in terminology signals a shift in meaning similar to that involved in the change from "idealism" to "traditional theory." Alongside the critique of positivism/scientism, which is articulated more firmly from 1937 on, the expression *critical theory* announces a first, if half hearted, approach to versions of the historical materialist philos-

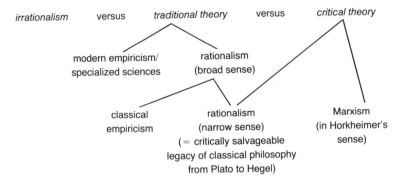

Figure 4.4
Theory Schema 1937

ophy of history such as that of the early Lukács. Nevertheless, for Horkheimer the fleeting, never really consequential assimilation of critical theory and proletarian class consciousness (in Lukács's sense) was only the point of entry into the negative philosophy of history of instrumental reason he developed together with Adorno in the 1940s— a path that, for him, was to end in a negative metaphysics.[72] How firmly Horkheimer still kept his distance from the traditions of the philosophy of consciousness and history in the programmatic text on "Traditional and Critical Theory" is illuminated by the fact that only Marcuse's emphatically calling attention to the essay's deficient grounding induced Horkheimer to revise his position in a text first published together with Marcuse's essay under the title "Philosophy and Critical Theory" in the *Zeitschrift,* and later as a "Postscript" to "Traditional and Critical Theory."[73]

The investigative schema in figure 4.4, which will be explained in more detail in the following section, completes the irrational/traditional/critical trichotomy of figure 4.2 on the critical wing. This complete theory schema of 1937, with its integration of philosophical rationalism and its alliance of critical and traditional theory against the irrationalism dominant in the fascist present, shows clear affinities to a work that arose around the same time, completely independent of Horkheimer: Georg Lukács's *The Destruction of Reason.* The only difference is that for Horkheimer the alliance of traditional and critical theory does not go so far as to reduce the trichotomy to a dichotomy of rationalism/irrationalism, whereby critical and traditional theory would be united, under the aegis of rationalism, into a popular front of sorts.

Critical Theory as "Existential Judgment"

Marcuse had recognized the philosophical weakness of the programmatic text of 1937. What corresponds to an ideology critique that is still radical and totalizing, that seeks to avoid all transfiguring abstraction and believes the sinister power of transfiguration to be at work in every abstraction and every form of rational justification, is a practical decisionism of critique. As a countermove to the "Cartesian view" of method,[74] Horkheimer rejects the "universal concepts" of traditional theory[75] and their "general, hypothetical form"[76] in order to project critical theory as "the unfolding of a single existential judgment."[77] *Existence* is thereby used with a double meaning.

The first meaning is in the sense of Heidegger's "facticity *[Faktizität]*":[78] the existence of human life, which is grounded in the mode of execution characteristic of human action and confronts us with the decision whether to lead an authentic (genuine) or inauthentic (nongenuine) life. For Horkheimer, "genuine life" means "critical activity." It exists: "there is a mode of human activity" he believes can be singled out "as 'critical.' "[79] Only insofar as critical theory overcomes the philosophical dualism of thought and being, theory and practice within itself can it, as critical activity, be a "forward-driving element" in historical "development"[80] and appear "as a stimulating factor for change within it."[81] Whereas within the framework of traditional theory action is bound by "mechanism," corresponding to what Heidegger calls "fallenness" to the ontology of "what is present at hand," in "conscious critical behavior" the "deeds" "of humankind" "flow" "from its decisions." The transition from "mechanism" to "decision" transforms "blind" into "meaningful necessity,"[82] which owes to the "experience *[Erlebnis]* of one's own activity and exertion," to the "existence of a will in the subject of cognition."[83] "Critical behavior" stands in a "conscious connection with historical praxis."[84] "Temporality" and "historicity" leave their imprint on "the existential judgment incorporated into history." Truth is "related to the present situation" at all times. But that does not establish a new, relativistic metaphysics: "No one can make himself into any other subject than that of the historical moment. To speak of the constancy or mutability of truth is only meaningful, strictly speaking, in a *polemical* context. It is directed against the assumption of an absolute, transhistorical subject or the possibility of exchanging subjects, as if one could lift oneself out of the present moment and really transfer oneself into any other at will."[85] Critical theory, as critical behavior, bears the "hope for a fundamental improvement of human existence":[86] "The future of humanity hangs today . . . on the existence of critical behavior."[87] That which makes critical theory into critique and distinguishes it, as critical, from traditional theory is the existence of critical behavior.

Nonetheless—and here Horkheimer distanced himself from Heidegger, whose *Being and Time* he had still cited with unqualified approval in 1934—critical behavior incorporates within itself "elements of traditional theories and of this declining culture in general."[88] That leads us to the second meaning of *existence* in the concept of "existential judgment." Here Horkheimer employs the term *existence* in the sense of Heidegger's "factuality *[Tatsächlichkeit]* of the *factum brutum* of something present-at-hand."[89] In view of the development of the forces of production, there exists today the objective possibility of a "rationally organized . . . society."[90] "Critical theory declares: things do not have to be as they are; humans can change being, the conditions are now at hand."[91] That is the actual theoretical achievement of critical theory: to explain the possibility of a rational society—an explanatory feat that critical behavior alone could never accomplish. As opposed to Heidegger's "existential possibility,"[92] the possibility that "anticipatorily resolute" critical behavior, like revolutionary praxis, "seizes" or "misses"[93] the breakthrough to an authentic life[94] (entirely in Heidegger's sense) is not a timeless *existentiale*; it is a plain, contingent, historical possibility—an empirical possibility. It exists; it is there in the sense of "presence at hand." If it is not structurally available,[95] then there is no possibility of seizing hold of genuine existence—an objection Marcuse had already raised against the philosophy of existence in 1933. "The decisive question," which existentialism no longer poses, is "whether certain situtations that are purely 'accidental' with respect to existence do not already, as such, destroy the essence of a genuine existence, annulling its freedom or reducing that freedom to an empty illusion. All the talk about historicity remains abstract and non-committal so long as the very concrete 'material' situation in which the philosophizing existence in fact lives has not been accentuated, so long as the possibilities and actualities of genuinely existing have not been considered from the perspective of the structure it in fact has"[96]—whereby "in fact" is to be understood not in the sense of Heidegger's (genuine) "facticity *[Faktizität]*" but rather in the sense of his (positively available) "factuality *[Tatsächlichkeit]*." That corresponds exactly to Horkheimer's utterly unheroic realism. It keeps a clear distance from the heroism of the "lost cause," which, in *Being and Time,* once again culminates in a transfiguring pathos of the "mute" "call of conscience" and the "anticipatory resoluteness" of "Being towards death"[97]—in that prefascist semantics that associates "hearkening" *[Horchen],* "hearing" *[Hören],* and "thraldom" *[Hörigkeit]* in order to meet with "the creaking wagon, the motorcycle, . . . the column on the march, the north wind, the woodpecker tapping, the fire crackling" in "the kind of Being of the hearing which understands."[98] For Horkheimer, the conditions for the possibility of an authentic life are empirical conditions. Horkheimer's antiphilosophy no longer seeks a philosophical way out of the crisis of the philosophy of consciousness. Of course, that has considerable systematic consequences: inquiry into and explanation of better possibilities become subject to the division of labor, the task of a part of traditional theories—the empirical sciences, particularly social research.

Critical behavior can have recourse to the work of the empirical sciences in a purely technical sense; it can make use of them as means. The goals of critical behavior are not legitimated by the empirical sciences, with their demonstration of available possibilities as such. In the double sense of "existential judgment," the differentiation of the "critical" from the "theoretical" dimension of the meaning of "existence," the link between theory and critique remains external to critique. In the programmatic text of 1937, the concept of critical theory reproduces the undialectical division of labor between practical existentialism and scientific positivism that critical theory later repeatedly criticized; only in its explanatory and theoretical form, not in its practical and critical bearing, does Horkheimer's critical theory join up internally with the logic of traditional theory. That has disastrous consequences, above all for the relationship of critical theory to the specialized disciplines. No way leads back from the empirical sciences to the concept of critique.

Marcuse was the first to point out the philosophical dilemma: the deficient grounding of critique in a decisionistically abridged version of "critical activity." He pleaded for an appropriation and recasting of philosophy's indispensable legacy: only the concept of reason—the "sole category through which philosophical thinking maintains its connection to the fate of humanity"[99]—can divest critical behavior of its naturalness and demonstrate the interest in the "changing" of "conditions" to be a universal interest.[100] Horkheimer responded positively to this objection and corrected the relationship of critical and traditional theory in his Postscript to his programmatic text.

The concurrence of critical theory's concept of production with that of "constitutive activity" in German idealism is now suddenly emphasized.[101] "Critical theory" seeks to "preserve" not only the "legacy" of German idealism but "that of philosophy as such." Horkheimer no longer calls on the materialistic pre-Socratics, Epicurus, and Democritus as witnesses for a "rational organization of human activity" and the "emancipation of humanity from enslaving conditions," but rather, of all things, "Greek philosophy . . . at its height under Plato and Aristotle."[102] From now on, the moment of truth latent in transfiguring appearances themselves is to transform and transcend transfiguration into critique dialectically and provide the rational justification for a higher "organizational principle" of society:[103] "The self-contemplation of reason, which in ancient philosophy constituted the highest stage of happiness, has in modern thought been turned into the materialist concept of a free, self-determining society."[104] Whereas in the programmatic text Horkheimer had still apodictically declared that consciousness of the opposition between objective possibility and miserable reality stems "not from the imagination but from experience,"[105] "Philosophy and Critical Theory" states that "the goal of a rational society, which admittedly seems to be preserved today only in the imagination, is actually inherent in every person."[106]

Yet the correction of the relationship between critical and traditional theory concerns only the relationship of critical theory to the rationalistic and idealistic part of critical theory, the part involving the philosophy of consciousness. The joint title of Horkheimer's and

Marcuse's supplementary reflections—"Philosophy and Critical Theory"—already betrays this. The corrective excludes the empirical sciences as a possible critical instance. Through its one-sidedness in favor
of the philosophy of consciousness, the compensation for the deficient justification of critical theory ends up by widening the gap between critical theory and empirical science, between philosophical
critique and scientific theory building. After this break, there is no
plausible philosophical model, oriented to the present level of development in "analytical thought," for the original idea of a critical theory—of "materialism" as overcoming the "one-sidedness of analytical
thought."[107] The path to a *Dialectic of Enlightenment,* a philosophy of
history that takes leave of the empirical sciences, now lies open.

Before the deconstruction of philosophy and the sciences could be
made unequivocal, and thus immunized, in the closed figure of a negative philosophy of history, Horkheimer developed the equivocal and
aporetic idea of a consequentially materialistic deconstruction of philosophy. The programmatic text of 1937 was the first attempt at a
systematic resolution of the inconsistencies of his earlier materialism,
an attempt that failed with the dilemma in the construction of the
existential judgment. The experiment thus foundered on the aporia
of this very materialism itself: the aporia of a dialectical positivism,
from whose perspective every attempt—even the negative—at philosophical unequivocality and systematization must appear to work "in
the service of transfiguration."

Dialectical Positivism of Happiness

The dialectical positivism of happiness, in Horkheimer's language,
is "a state of affairs upon which judgment has been passed *[eine beur-
teilte Tatsächlichkeit]."*[108] That is, it is a state of affairs normatively anchored in the inescapable fact of the human striving "for . . . happiness."
"That all human beings strive for happiness" is something that materialism must "acknowledge as a natural state of affairs that needs no
justification." And he refuses "to make a distinction between happiness and pleasure" simply "because the gratification of desires, unlike
the substantiation of 'higher motives,' is said to require excusing or
justification."[109]

Humanity's universal longing for happiness and fulfillment is something ultimate for critical theory: any "rational justification of an action" can, "in the final instance, refer only to the happiness of human beings; a government that dispensed with showing that its acts have this sense for those who are ruled would be mere despotism."[110] Horkheimer sees the ultimate cause for the unhappiness of the whole in the ascetic negation of individual claims to happiness.[111] "In all previous forms of society, the abundance of goods produced for human enjoyment at any given stage went to the immediate benefit of only a small group of people. . . . *But from the beginning a striving to extend the same enjoyment to the majority has been astir in the depths;* however much the organization of classes has suited material purposes, in the end all its forms have proved inadequate [emphasis added]."[112] Horkheimer seems to want to anchor the objectivity and universality, the rationality of the claim to happiness, naturalistically—a path that Marcuse was in fact later to take in his interpretation of Freud.[113]

Unlike in classical hedonism or modern utilitarianism, the "fact" of the desire for happiness is characterized by a peculiarly normative force, which in turn is supposed to lead beyond mere factuality after all, grounding the rational identity of society in the "uniting of happiness and duty," of "freedom" and "happiness,"[114] and ultimately in the mediation between happiness and "correct knowledge."[115] And Horkheimer must impose precisely this task on dialectics: dialectics is to unravel the aporetic entanglement of the factual and the normative. "Reason, which is contained in the very name of rationalism, operates today in theory, whose method was developed by rationalism itself under the title of dialectics."[116]

And yet Horkheimer, true to the deconstructive intentions of his radicalized ideology critique, remains deliberately aporetic. In the end, he must reckon with an unresolved aporia, a contradiction no dialectic can reconcile. Otherwise the dialectical judgment of positivity would also fall victim to transfiguration: "Confronted with the persisting contradictions of human existence, and with the impotence of individuals in the face of conditions they themselves have created, the Hegelian solution appears as a private assertion, the philosopher's personal truce with the world."[117] If critical theory is a *"state of affairs upon which judgment has been passed,"* then it cannot and may not transcend that state of affairs and seek to overtake it conceptually; it can do so only at the cost of transfiguration. Horkheimer's materialism deconstructs any and all attempts to construct an "unconditional order intellectually."[118] Contingent factuality itself is critical theory's own unconditional: "the materialistic way of thinking's unconditional renunciation of any ideal possibility of harmony."[119] It is an unconditional that negates itself.

In view of the positivistic consequences of this deconstruction, the only thing that still does point beyond "mere factuality"[120] is a weak dialectical force. It is the antiutopian Horkheimer's rationalistic complement to that "weak messianic force" Benjamin's surrealistic messianism wishes to evoke. A weak dialectical force is supposed to redeem factuality from that same false consciousness that caused the domination of the whole over the parts to petrify into reification in the first place. A consciousness of factuality that has learned to dispense with transfiguration entirely might just be able to disengage the individual egoistic and destructive drives in human nature from that ascetic recasting and supercharging that first transformed them into social destructive forces.

In the light of this weak dialectical force, happiness could appear in its true, unfalsified positivity. On this point Horkheimer and Nietzsche concur: " 'The judge is a sublimated executioner,' says Nietzsche. If that is true, then the facts of the case would look somewhat different if the judge were to become truly conscious of the executioner in him."[121] Only if the factuality of egoism were "neither covered up, nor made little of, nor indicted" could it become "enjoyment, happiness of the highest order, in which even the gratification of cruel impulses is included."[122] If even the "despised instinctual impulses" were to be raised "to consciousness without rejecting or depreciating them," then they might lose "their demonic force." "By ceasing to act 'in the name' of God, 'in the name' of justice, ethics, honor, or the nation, the will to cause suffering loses, by recognizing itself as such, the frightful power it exercises as long as it remains hidden from its bearer because it is denied on ideological grounds."[123] Only this side of transfiguration would compassion, or suffering along (*Mitleid*)—the fundamental Schopenhauerian motif in Horkheimer's thought—become happiness, a mediated pleasure in something: "In Aristotle's aesthetics, the viewing of suffering in tragedy brings plea-

sure. Humanity becomes purer by allowing this drive—the pleasure
in compassion, suffering along—to be gratified." But of course: "Ca-
tharsis through play watching *[Schauspiel]*, through play in general,
presupposes a transformed humanity."[124]

Critical Theory as a Weak Dialectical Force in the Business of Science

What Horkheimer expects from the shattering of ideological appearances is not the sudden arrival of the absolutely new, the shock that
changes the world at a blow—neither the birth of a new humanity,
nor the coming of the messiah, nor the rule of the unconscious, the
dream, and the imagination. Unlike the anarchistic visions of a radicalized ideology critique, Horkheimer's destruction of transfiguring
appearances remains peculiarly rationalistic: a vision of consciousness
unfalsified by ideology, knowledge of things as they are without illusions. That separates Horkheimer from Nietzsche, from the surreal-
ists, and from Benjamin. But it also separates him from the classical
figure of ideology critique, which still needed the transfiguring appearance itself in order to strengthen ideology's immanent moment
of truth against its own affirmative transfiguration. Horkheimer's dialectical positivism, unlike the ideology critique Marcuse developed in
the 1930s, is not an immanent critique of ideology. For Horkheimer,
dialectics comes in only after the destruction of illusions: in the self-
knowledge without reservations that redeems even cruel instinctual
impulses and naked egoism from their blind naturalness, precisely by
breaking with all illusions.

There is a difficulty, of course: where is the dialectical alternative
to the false evocation of an original immediacy, the correct consciousness that redeems factuality from its naturalness to come from, if not
from the true appearance of false transfiguration? Horkheimer's idea
of a dialectical mediation of the immediate, as he himself admits,
"presupposes a transformed humanity"—the realization of utopia. The
resolution of the aporias of dialectical positivism remains utopian in
Horkheimer. An attempt to substantiate philosophically the implied
utopian perspective—whether through speculative anthropology, as
in Marcuse's *Eros and Civilization,* or a metascientific theory of communication, as in Habermas's *Knowledge and Human Interests*—was not

even ventured by Horkheimer. And later, when Marcuse's book appeared, he emphatically rejected making any such attempt.

And yet precisely Horkheimer's deconstructivism opens up an entirely different perspective, a perspective this side of the utopian horizon. The weak dialectical force that is supposed to distinguish dialectical positivism from mere positivism is clearly too frail to support strategies of philosophical justification. The paradox of an unconditional that negates itself is suitable only for polemical purposes. But if dialectics is too weak for a reconstruction of philosophy, then it may be just weak enough to support the research program of a social-scientifically transformed Marxism. The philosophical weakness of dialectical positivism then becomes the scientific strength of philosophy: critical theory becomes the sublation of critique in theory, of philosophy in science. Only the antiphilosophy of the radically secular materialist Horkheimer could clear the way for the philosophical idea of reason turned fallible—that is, for a social-scientific transformation of philosophy.

Seen purely in terms of the logic of science, therefore, the path Horkheimer set out on with his research program[125] is not so different from that taken by Talcott Parsons, whose first, great works were published at the same time. Both Parsons and Horkheimer distanced themselves from philosophy enough to anchor the philosophical impulse that supports their work this side of philosophy, in the social sciences. And an anticipation of the difference betweeen earlier (Horkheimer) and later (Habermas) critical theory is already inherent in the remaining (structural) difference (aside from the substantive one) between Parsons and Horkheimer. For the director of early critical theory's research program, social philosophy is a heuristic investigative schema, a programmatic frame of orientation for empirical investigations, and a summarizing presentation of the results of the individual sciences. Critical theory, in this sense, is "a social philosophy with an accompanying empirical research program."[126] In Parsons, the connection of philosophy and science is closer; the philosophical impulse is absorbed without remainder in the categorial framework, the general theory of action, the axiomatic A-G-I-L schema,[127] and finally in the "telic system." Horkheimer's early program is unambiguously contextualistic; the later program of critical theory, which postulates a similarly close connection between philosophy and science to that found in Parsons, strengthens the philosophical impulse systematically—as opposed to Parsons—in order to justify the more pronounced critical intentions of social theory. Habermas is therefore forced to make very strong universalistic assumptions; his program is quasi-transcendental.[128] The contextualistic research program has the disadvantage that social-philosophical reflections, being relatively nonbinding and arbitrary, are always in danger of remaining vaguely or inscrutably connected to empirical research—as, for example, in modern philosophical anthropology. The universalistic research program has the disadvantage of its stronger premises: it could quickly turn out to be an overly bold hypothesis. The advantage of contextualism is that it continues to work even when the stronger, and therefore more cogent and binding, program of the "transcendentalists," or universalists, has long since broken down in the tough business of everyday research.

No matter how one assesses the advantages and disadvantages of contextualistic and "transcendental" (more precisely, universalistic) research programs for operationalizing the idea of a critical theory,[129] in all cases, the philosophical idea—the solidarity of all suffering beings and the worldly happiness of all individuals (Horkheimer), the generalization of values (Parsons), or communicative reconciliation (Habermas)—is estranged from the context of philosophy enough to suit the coarser, less subtly self-reflected, less sophisticated and consistent systematic structures of empirical research programs. Only if the philosophical impulse proves itself in the everday problem solving of the individual sciences is it strong enough to redeem the legacy of philosophy that is thought to lie, obscure and forgotten, in the shadowy paradigmatic background of the empirical sciences.

"Materialism," Horkheimer wrote in 1933, "calls for the unification of philosophy and science." A weak dialectical force can unfold philosophy in the sciences only as a "hypothesis," as fallible reason: "Many idealist systems . . . contain . . . valuable material knowledge which represents an important element in scientific progress, despite the metaphysical intentions of their authors. Dialectics itself is idealist in origin. Many schemata of modern metaphysics are of the highest importance as models for judging present-day humanity—as 'hypotheses,' as Dilthey calls the systems of the past."[130] The hypothetical attitude toward ultimate principles and general ideas corresponds to a fallibilism of practical hopes that recalls the closing of Freud's *The Future of an Illusion:* materialist knowledge "turns all its energies, even the most despairing, toward this world, and in so doing it exposes the only belief it allows—hope in the worldly possibilities of humanity— to disappointment."[131] This hope rests on the particular empirical conjecture that "bourgeois commerce and egoism have also bred their negation: individualistic altruism,"[132] and it draws its peculiar dialectical force from that general hypothesis of ideology criticism in which Horkheimer anticipates the idea of communicative reconciliation: "Many a psychic fetter under which people suffer today bursts open when the telling word resounds, and does so because this word can also overcome the forceful isolation of human beings from one another peculiar to the current era. This power inheres in truth, although truth not only renounces all ideological consolation, but endeavors to destroy it."[133]

Translated by John McCole

Notes

Horkheimer's texts are cited and English translations, where available, are cross-referenced according to the following key (in some cases, the translations have been modified):

BPSS = *Between Philosophy and Social Science: Selected Early Writings* (Cambridge, 1993).

"Rationalismusstreit" = "Zum Rationalismusstreit in der gegenwärtigen Philosophie," *Zeitschrift für Sozialforschung* [= *ZfS*] 3 (1934); "The Rationalism Dispute in Current Philosophy," in *BPSS.*

"Traditionelle" = "Traditionelle und kritische Theorie," *ZfS* 6 (1937); "Traditional and Critical Theory," in Horkheimer, *Critical Theory: Selected Essays* [= *CT*] (New York, 1972).

"Metaphysik" = "Materialismus und Metaphysik," *ZfS* 2 (1933); "Materialism and Metaphysics," in *CT.*

"Moral" = "Materialismus und Moral," *ZfS* 2 (1933); "Materialism and Morality," in Horkheimer, *BPSS.*

"Philosophie" = "Philosophie und kritische Theorie," *ZfS* 6 (1937); "Postscript," in *CT.*

"Problem" = "Zum Problem der Wahrheit," *ZfS* 4 (1935); "The Problem of Truth," in *BPSS.*

"Bemerkungen" = "Bemerkungen zur philosophischen Anthropologie," *ZfS* 4 (1935); "Remarks on Philosophical Anthropology," in *BPSS.*

"Angriff" = "Der neueste Angriff auf die Metaphysik," *ZfS* 6 (1937); "The Latest Attack on Metaphysics," in *CT.*

"Egoismus" = "Egoismus und Freiheitsbewegung (Zur Anthropologie des bürgerlichen Zeitalters)," *ZfS* 5 (1936); "Egoism and the Freedom Movement: On the Anthropology of the Bourgeois Era," in *BPSS*.

1. This is the case in Rüdiger Bubner, "Was ist kritische Theorie?" in *Theorie-Diskussion, Hermeneutik und Ideologiekritik* (Frankfurt am Main, 1971), 210 ff.

2. Hauke Brunkhorst, "Paradigmakern und Theoriendynamik der Kritischen Theorie der Gesellschaft," in *Soziale Welt* 1 (1983): 22ff.

3. "Rationalismusstreit," 50/*BPSS*.

4. Ibid., 46/*BPSS*.

5. "Traditionelle und kritische Theorie," 254/*CT*, 198.

6. "Rationalismusstreit," 47/*BPSS*.

7. Ibid./*BPSS*.

8. Ibid., 48/*BPSS*.

9. "Metaphysik," 14f./*CT*, 24.

10. "Rationalismusstreit," 46/*BPSS*.

11. Ibid.

12. Helmut Dubiel, *Wissenschaftsorganisation und politische Erfahrung. Studien zur frühen Kritischen Theorie* (Frankfurt am Main, 1978). English: *Theory and Politics: Studies in the Development of Critical Theory* (Cambridge, 1985); Wolfgang Bonß and Norbert Schindler, "Kritische Theorie als interdisziplinärer Materialismus," in Bonß and Axel Honneth, eds., *Sozialforschung als Kritik* (Frankfurt am Main, 1982); Hauke Brunkhorst, "Paradigmakern und Theoriendynamik der Kritischen Theorie," in *Soziale Welt* 1 (1983).

13. "Metaphysik," 26/*CT*, 38.

14. "Rationalismusstreit," 50/*BPSS*.

15. Ibid., 1/*BPSS*.

16. "Traditionelle," 253, 282/*CT*, 197, 231.

17. Ibid., 290/*CT*, 240.

18. Ibid., 246f./*CT*, 189.

19. Horkheimer in Horkheimer and Herbert Marcuse, "Philosophie," 625/*CT*, 244.

20. "Traditionelle," 292 (from the English-language summary of the essay published with the original text in *ZfS*).

21. "Rationalismusstreit," 33/*BPSS*.

22. "Problem," 356/*BPSS*.

Hauke Brunkhorst

23. "Rationalismusstreit," 47/*BPSS*.

24. "Metaphysik," 32/*CT*, 45.

25. "Problem," 330/*BPSS*.

26. Ibid., 332/*BPSS*.

27. Ibid., 333/*BPSS*.

28. "Rationalismusstreit," 1ff./*BPSS*.

29. Ibid., 13, 16f./*BPSS*.

30. Ibid., 36, 30/*BPSS*.

31. Ibid., 45/*BPSS*.

32. Ibid., 50/*BPSS*.

33. Ibid., 34/*BPSS*.

34. "Bemerkungen," 10/*BPSS*.

35. Ibid., 4/*BPSS*.

36. Ibid., 6f./*BPSS*.

37. Horkheimer, "Rationalismusstreit," 48/*BPSS*. In order to underscore the complementary relationship between rationalism and irrationalism, Horkheimer twice cites Heidegger's assertion, in *Being and Time*, that "irrationalism, as the counterpart of rationalism, merely sees askew what rationalism is blind to." Heidegger, *Sein und Zeit* (Tübingen, 1977), 136. English: *Being and Time*, trans. John Macquarrie and Edward Robinson (New York, 1962), 175, translation modified. Cf. "Rationalismusstreit," 16, 50/*BPSS*.

38. "Traditionelle," 245ff./*CT*, 188.

39. On the early Horkheimer's latent positivism, cf. Michael Korthals, "Die kritische Gesellschaftstheorie des frühen Horkheimer," manuscript (Nijmegen, 1983). Korthals gives a clear account of this positivism, which was based on empiriocriticism and emphatically directed against Lukács's philosophy of history. More than by positivism, of course, Horkheimer was shaped by the historicist critique of reason. Nevertheless, as Dubiel and others have shown, Hegel's dialectical method played a constitutive role in the research program of critical theory from the beginning.

40. "Rationalismusstreit," 49/*BPSS*.

41. "Problem," 343/*BPSS*.

42. "Traditionelle," 283f./*CT*, 232.

43. "Metaphysik," 8f./*CT*, 18f. [Editors' note: The final three sentences of this passage were omitted in the translation that appears in *Critical Theory*.]

44. Ibid., 22, 29/*CT*, 33, 42.

45. Ibid., 9/*CT*, 19.

46. Ibid., 13, 21/*CT*, 23, 32.

47. "Moral," 180f./*BPSS*.

48. Ibid., 177/*BPSS*.

49. "Metaphysik," 9f./*CT*, 19.

50. Ibid., 12/*CT*, 22.

51. Ibid., 12, 14f./*CT*, 22.

52. "Moral," 180/*BPSS*.

53. "Metaphysik," 32f./*CT*, 44f.

54. "Moral," 179f., 173f./*BPSS*.

55. "Metaphysik," 32/*CT*, 44.

56. "Moral," 183f./*BPSS*.

57. Ibid., 184f./*BPSS*.

58. "Metaphysik," 25/*CT*, 36–37.

59. "Moral," 168/*BPSS*.

60. "Metaphysik," 16, and many other places.

61. Ibid., 10, 15, 20, 22, 25, 26, 30, 31, and many other places.

62. Karl R. Popper, *Logik der Forschung* (Tübingen, 1971), 13.

63. "Angriff," 4ff./*BPSS*.

64. "Traditionelle," 292/*CT*, 242; cf. also "Rationalismusstreit," 51/*BPSS*.

65. "Metaphysik," 28/*CT*, 40.

66. Ibid., 32/*CT*, 44.

67. Herbert Marcuse, *Psychoanalyse und Politik* (Frankfurt am Main, 1968), 11.

68. "Rationalismusstreit," 37f./*BPSS*.

69. Cf. Jürgen Habermas, "Dialektischer Idealismus im Übergang zum Materialismus," in Habermas, *Theorie und Praxis*, 3d ed. (Neuwied, 1969), 108ff.

70. Horkheimer, "Anthropologie," 7/*BPSS*. In the same essay, Horkheimer also calls materialism simply "enlightened thinking," 18/*BPSS*.

Hauke Brunkhorst

71. Cf. Dubiel, *Wissenschaftsorganisation und politische Erfahrung,* 122.

72. On the development of critical theory's research program from the original transformation of the philosophy of history of class consciousness (Lukács) into an empirical social psychology of workers' consciousness (Fromm, Horkheimer), by means of a step-by-step falsification of the social-psychological hypotheses, through the possible and current class consciousness of the proletariat in the thesis of the integration of the proletariat, to the final transformation into a negative philosophy of history of instrumental reason, cf. Dubiel, *Theory and Politics;* Brunkhorst, "Paradigmakern."

73. Horkheimer and Marcuse, "Philosophie und kritische Theorie," *ZfS,* 6, 625ff.; Horkheimer, "Nachtrag" in Horkheimer, *Kritische Theorie: Eine Dokumentation* (Frankfurt am Main, 1968), II:192ff. For Marcuse's contribution, see Herbert Marcuse, "Philosophy and Critical Theory," in *Negations: Essays in Critical Theory* (Boston, 1968).

74. "Traditionelle," 265/*CT,* 211.

75. Ibid., 276/*CT,* 224.

76. Ibid., 278/*CT,* 226.

77. Ibid., 279/*CT,* 227.

78. Cf. Heidegger, *Sein und Zeit,* 56, 135/*Being and Time,* 82, 173. [Editors' note: We have followed Macquarrie and Robinson' s translation in rendering *Faktizität* as "facticity" and *Tatsächlichkeit* as "factuality."]

79. "Traditionelle," 261/*CT,* 206.

80. Ibid., 268/*CT,* 214.

81. Ibid., 269/*CT,* 227.

82. Ibid., 281/*CT,* 229.

83. Ibid., 282/*CT,* 230.

84. Ibid., 284–85/*CT,* 233–34.

85. Ibid., 289–90/*CT,* 239–40.

86. Ibid., 284/*CT,* 233.

87. Ibid., 292/*CT,* 242.

88. "Traditionelle," 292/*CT,* 242.

89. Heidegger, *Sein und Zeit,* 135/*Being and Time,* 174.

90. "Traditionelle," 267/*CT,* 213.

91. Ibid., 279, n. 1/*CT,* 227.

92. Heidegger, *Sein und Zeit,* 38, 143/*Being and Time,* 63, 183.

93. Ibid., 12, 260ff., 305ff./*Being and Time*, 32f., 304ff., 352ff.

94. Cf. also Georg Lohmann, "Authentisches und verdinglichtes Leben," in *Philosophische Rundschau* 3/4 (1983), 253ff.

95. This concept of "structural possibility," which is derived from Hegel, still involves critical intentions in Jürgen Habermas's *Theory of Communicative Action:* "The theory of rationalization makes it possible to frame counterfactual questions that would, of course . . . not be accessible *for us* who pursue such a theoretical strategy if we were not able to find heuristic support in the *internal* development of the cultural systems of action—science, law, morality, and art—and if we did not *know* in an exemplary way how the *possibilities* of expanding cognitive-instrumental, moral-practical, and aesthetic-expressive knowledge—possibilities that are grounded *in abstracto* through the modern understanding of the world, that is, in terms of a developmental logic—can look *in concreto.*" Habermas, *The Theory of Communicative Action* (Boston, 1984), 1:220. Of course, in the transition from Horkheimer to Habermas, the emphasis shifts from the rational potential of the relations of production to those of communication; see Brunkhorst, "Paradigmakern," 46, as well as Brunkhorst, "Kommunikative Vernunft und rächende Gewalt," in *Sozialwissenschaftliche Literatur Rundschau* 8/9 (Neuwied, 1983), 7ff.

96. Marcuse, "Philosophie des Scheiterns," in H. Sauer, ed., *Karl Jaspers in der Diskussion* (Munich, 1973), 131.

97. Heidegger, *Sein und Zeit*, 267ff./*Being and Time*, 312ff.

98. Ibid., 163/206–7.

99. Marcuse in Horkheimer and Marcuse, "Philosophie," 632.

100. "Metaphysik," 13/*CT*, 22–23.

101. "Philosophie," 625f./*CT*, 244f.

102. Ibid., 626/*CT*, 245f.

103. Ibid., 629/*CT*, 249.

104. Ibid., 628/*CT*, 248.

105. "Traditionelle," 266. [Editors' note: This sentence appeared in the original published version of the essay in 1937. However, it was deleted in the 1968 collection *Kritische Theorie*, and therefore does not appear in the published English translation of the essay in *Critical Theory*. Variations between the two versions are indicated in the notes to the text in Horkheimer, *Gesammelte Schriften*, vol. 4.]

106. "Philosophie," 630/*CT*, 251.

107. "Rationalismusstreit," 30/*BPSS*.

108. "Traditionelle," 271/*CT*, 217.

109. "Metaphysik," 31f./*CT*, 44–45.

110. "Rationalismusstreit," 36/*BPSS*.

111. Ibid., 43/*BPSS*; " Egoismus," 161ff./*BPSS*.

112. "Traditionelle," 266/*CT*, 212.

113. Marcuse, *Triebstruktur und Gesellschaft* (Frankfurt am Main, 1965). English: *Eros and Civilization* (Boston, 1955).

114. "Moral," 173/*BPSS*.

115. Marcuse, "Zur Kritik des Hedonismus," in Marcuse, *Schriften* 3 (Frankfurt am main, 1979), 284f.

116. "Rationalismusstreit," 51/*BPSS*.

117. "Traditionelle," 259/*CT*, 204.

118. "Metaphysik," 32/*CT*, 45.

119. "Rationalismusstreit," 47/*BPSS*.

120. "Traditionelle," 264/*CT*, 209.

121. "Egoismus," 229/*BPSS*.

122. Ibid.

123. Ibid., 230/*BPSS*.

124. Ibid., 231/*BPSS*.

125. Dubiel, *Wissenschaftsorganisation und politische Erfahrung*, 122f.

126. Raymond Geuss, *Die Idee einer kritischen Theorie* (Königstein, 1983), 111. English: *The Idea of a Critical Theory: Habermas and the Frankfurt School* (Cambridge, 1981).

127. [Editors' note: Parsons introduced the A-G-I-L schema in his later work as a model of societal interchange in the four dimensions of adaptation (A), goal attainment (G), integration (I), and pattern maintenance or "latency" (L). See Talcott Parsons, with Robert F. Bales and Edward A. Shils, *Working Papers in the Theory of Action* (New York, 1953), chaps. 3, 5.]

128. For an explanation of the term *quasi-transcendental*, see Brunkhorst, "Kommunikative Vernunft und rächende Gewalt," in *Sozialwissenschaftliche Literatur Rundschau* 8/9 (Neuwied, 1983), 13ff.

129. Cf. Geuss, *Die Idee einer kritischen Theorie*, 82ff.

130. "Metaphysik," 22f./*CT*, 34.

131. "Rationalismusstreit," 47/*BPSS*.

132. "Anthropologie," 22/*BPSS*.

133. "Rationalismusstreit," 49f./*BPSS*.

5

The Program of Interdisciplinary Research and the Beginnings of Critical Theory

Wolfgang Bonß

Although it has often been declared dead, the critical theory of the 1930s and 1940s exhibits an astonishing ability to survive. If at times it has appeared to be only of historical interest,[1] today there are more and more who directly or indirectly link their work to the intentions of its social-scientific program. The best-known recent example is Jürgen Habermas, who has described "early critical theory" as an important approach to explaining "those pathologies of modernity that other approaches pass right by for methodological reasons."[2] For Habermas, what "remains instructive" above all is the "interdisciplinary research program," which in his eyes offers greater intellectual stimulus for a critical theory of society than the later theses on the "dialectic of enlightenment" and the concept of "instrumental reason."[3] Nevertheless, Habermas himself concedes that this is only a "conjecture" whose validity may well be contested.[4]

This is precisely the starting point for this chapter. It attempts to explicate the interdisciplinary program of early critical theory from three perspectives. The first step is to reconstruct the basic arguments and underlying concepts formulated by Horkheimer in his reflections on the possibilities and limits of scientific knowledge. Here I will show that the precondition of critical theory in the early 1930s is a specific critique of the contemporary social sciences, in both their "bourgeois" and "materialist" versions. Second, according to these analyses, not only the bourgeois (or idealist) paradigm but also the materialist version of science exhibits specific aporias, which are different but not independent. A critical theory, Horkheimer concludes, must reflect these aporias and try to avoid them by developing a new form of organizing scientific work. The concept of "interdisciplinary materialism" represents an attempt to do so by combining social philosophy with social research from this "organizational" perspective. In conclusion, I will discuss the problems and shortcomings inherent in Horkheimer's early project. My thesis is that the revision of interdisciplinary materialism toward the end of the 1930s was by no means due to changing circumstances alone. Contrary to what is often claimed (by Habermas as well), it points to epistemological weaknesses whose articulation appears particularly important at a time when the reactualization of critical theory could easily lead to the construction of a myth.

The Critique of Science as Basis and Justification for Critical Theory

From its beginnings, the basic concern of critical theory was to "determine the social role of science."[5] This can be demonstrated particularly clearly with reference to the *Zeitschrift für Sozialforschung*, where empirical analyses and (meta)theoretical reflections were always closely related to one another. That the latter were accorded decisive significance was evident even in the first issue, which was to have been introduced with a piece by Horkheimer, "Science and Society." Due to his illness, this essay was never written, and "Notes on Science and the Crisis" was published in its place. These notes are of great importance for the conception of interdisciplinary materialism; they contain in highly condensed form the basic propositions of early critical theory's interpretation of science, propositions that were elaborated in Horkheimer's later essays. From a systematic perspective, these basic propositions present three theses on (1) the relation of science to society, (2) the relation of science to truth, and (3) the crisis tendencies of science.

1. Science, according to Horkheimer's first thesis, is always related to society in two ways. On the one hand, it is a socially conditioned structure; its development obeys the imperatives of "importance for [social] life" and the form in which it appears "itself changes as part of the social process" ("Bemerkungen," 1/*CT*, 3). On the other hand, as

"a productive power and a means of production," science also transforms society since it expands the power of human control and provides the intellectual preconditions for a growing domination of outer and inner nature.

2. Insofar as the usefulness of science is not identical with its validity, scientific knowledge is only incompletely explained by its relation to society. Horkheimer therefore supplements the first proposition with the thesis of the truth relatedness of science, which is also spelled out in two directions. That science cannot be reduced to its relation to society is shown, first, by the universalizability of scientific knowledge, since its "truth holds even for those who oppose it, ignore it, or declare it unimportant" ("Wahrheit," 239/"Truth," 423). On the other hand, its relation to truth also implies a certain autonomy; despite its social conditioning, "it is not for social interests to decide what is or is not true; rather, the criteria for truth have developed in connection with progress at the theoretical level" ("Bemerkungen," 1/*CT*, 3).

3. From the viewpoint of its relation to society as well as its relation to truth, science presents the potential for progress in knowledge. However, its realization depends on social conditions that can hinder or encourage it. According to Horkheimer's third thesis, in advanced capitalism those elements inhibiting progress achieve more and more importance, necessarily resulting in an external and internal crisis. From the perspective of its relation to society, scientific knowledge "shares the fate of other productive forces and means of production: its application is sharply disproportionate to its level of development and to the real needs of humankind" ("Bemerkungen," 2/*CT*, 4). These external hindrances carry over into an immanent "limitation on science evident . . . in its content and form, its subject matter and method" ("Bemerkungen," 7/*CT*, 9), resulting in a far-reaching crisis in its relation to truth.

These theses make it clear that for early critical theory, science represents a unity, encompassing both facts and theory. Facts are facts only in the context of theoretical interpretations, and the further development of theories depends on empirical investigation. As a unity of theoretical and empirical work, science is not only a cognitive but also a social context, and its development can be described as a "double," social-cognitive structure. Science appears as an externally conditioned and internally secured system for the development of knowledge that increasingly impedes itself—not, to be sure, in the sense of a "dialectic of enlightenment" but due to the sharpening contradictions of the capitalist organization of society.

This argument was spelled out more closely through various historical and systematic analyses of the evolution of modern science in which Horkheimer went on to distinguish between a bourgeois and a materialist line of development. Bourgeois and materialist science were conceived in this context as two social-cognitive structures that can be clearly distinguished from one another but not in such a way that one is clearly superior. Rather, embedded in the general dynamic of social development, they included both merits and the potential for crises. These divergent features would have to be precisely articulated in order to create the basis for developing a comprehensive scientific program, one capable of providing a starting point for overcoming society's self-imposed impediments to the progress of knowledge.

If we first consider the bourgeois line of development, we find, according to Horkheimer, a systematic history of decline, beginning with epoch-making progress in knowledge and ending with a growing contradiction between science as a productive power and capitalist relations of production. The epochal achievement of bourgeois thought consists in the emancipation of knowledge from traditional, feudal conditions and in the formation of new structures of perception; bourgeois society no longer accepts the world as God given, but recognizes it as something produced and capable of being produced. This change is most evident in modern natural science, which aims at "increasing the knowledge of nature and achieving new powers of control over man and nature" ("Metaphysik," 14/*CT,* 24). And with respect to inner nature, one can also see, since the development of early bourgeois law, a gradual "liberation . . . from the comprehensive unity of the Middle Ages" ("Metaphysik," 167/*CT,* 91), culminating in the rational philosophy of the eighteenth century and, in particular, in the notion of constitutive reason. With this notion, the knowing subject acquires for the first time "consciousness of itself as an independent being" (ibid.) that posits the world from out of itself and claims to ground social objectivity rationally.

Although the self-thematization of society founded on rational philosophy played a decisive role in the struggle against absolutism, its arguments, developed in this context, cannot explain the social order: "The manner in which each individual contributes to the workings of the entire society through his labor, and is at the same time influenced by it, remains completely obscure" ("Metaphysik," 167/*CT*, 91). For just this reason it is also "idealistic": the entire social fabric appears as a subjective-moral order, not as one codetermined by structures independent of the subject. This view, typical of the Enlightenment, begins to falter as the institutionalization of bourgeois society progresses. The process of institutionalization makes it emphatically clear that social relations get established behind the backs of the subjects without conforming to the idea of their rational constitution.

As is well known, within philosophy, this idea was interpreted as "division *[Entzweiung]*" and, at the same time, universalized.[6] Corresponding to this figure of thought, familiar since early romanticism, social objectivity no longer appears as the result of the subjects' own rational action but rather confronts them as quasi-natural, external coercion. As for the structure of the social production of knowledge, this means a momentous separation of these spheres that persists even if the division of subject and object is conceived as something produced, as it is for Hegel. Given this condition, the world of social objects takes on, in reflective consciousness, a life of its own and increasingly attracts scientific interest. This trend forms the basis for the emergence of the "positive," specialized sciences that enjoyed such an undreamed-of boom in the nineteenth century.

Horkheimer leaves open the specifics of how this change in the production of knowledge is to be conceived. But as the later essays show ("Wahrheit," 326ff./"Truth," 412ff.; "Traditionelle," 255ff./*CT*, 199ff.), he assumes a functional parallelism between social and scientific development. The external condition for the positivizing of science lies in the universalization of a mode of social perception in which the reality of the world of social objects is measured according to criteria of utilization, exploitation, and administration. Within science this structural change takes the form of an intensive occupation with the logic peculiar to specific object-domains; these are investigated "without presuppositions," that is, independent of their place in the social totality, however this may be constituted. This epistemological perspective makes possible an expansion of research according to an ambiguous dynamic. On the one hand, reified structures, independent of the subject, can be articulated in great detail; on the other hand, the fiction of a "presuppositionless" analysis of social reality leads to an uncritical reproduction of the dominant principles of utilization, exploitation, and administration. The very impulse that initiates progress in the specialized sciences thus makes them narrow-minded and renders them blind to their own social constraints.

The limitation of research to the logic of external forms points, for Horkheimer, to shortcomings that at first go unnoticed but eventually grow into a "crisis" as the contradictions of capitalist society become acute. With the accumulation of isolated knowledge of details, the specialized disciplines fail to face "the problem of the social process as a whole," which in effect seems unreal, although it "dominates reality through deepening crises and social conflicts" ("Bemerkungen," 3/ CT, 5). The quantitative expansion of knowledge comes into contradiction with the qualitative need for a rational analysis of society. This manifests itself in deficits in the organization of science as well as in epistemological aporias.

With respect to the organization of science, first to be noticed is the "chaotic specialization" ("Lage," 40) of the individual disciplines that leads to a "neglect of the dynamic relationships between the separate object-domains" ("Bemerkungen," 4/CT, 6). Knowledge expands, but no deepening of knowledge results. Particular and specialized analyses, which do not permit assertions concerning society as a whole and together constitute only an irrational picture of reality, emerge in place of a systematic analysis of the social totality of humanity and nature.

Still clearer is the shift from an external to an "internal crisis" in the epistemological "narrowing" of scientific rationality, which takes the form of a conflict between "empirical science" and "speculative social philosophy" ("Bemerkungen," 4/CT, 6). Horkheimer addressed this opposition in terms of a polarization between positivism and metaphysics. Justified concerns underlie both forms of knowledge: the true core of the positivism of the individual sciences lies in its insistence on deciphering social being as a positive, functional nexus, that of metaphysics in its fundamental inquiry "into the 'whither' of human existence" ("AbG," 70/BPSS). But the historical bifurcation and absolutizing of both modes of knowledge turn their legitimate concerns into ideology. Since they confront one another as closed conceptions of science, bolstered by comprehensive worldviews, the conclusion is warranted that one is dealing with "two different phases of a single philosophy that downgrades natural knowledge" ("Metaphysik," 28/ *CT*, 40). As complementary elements of a negative developmental logic, they systematically paralyze the investigation of the total social process.

In contrast to the later models of critical theory, in the early 1930s the aporias in epistemology and the organization of science are not explained as the result of an unalterable "dialectic of enlightenment." For Horkheimer the causes lay in social relations and the organization of science, with the result that "the prevailing practice of science . . . is outdated in its form" ("Metaphysik," 23/*CT*, 34). Against this "outdated" form stand the materialist analyses; as an alternative to bourgeois science, the materialist paradigm also offers the fundamental point of departure for overcoming the aporias. This becomes evident, however, only if the concept of "materialism" is not too narrowly conceived. Or, in a formulation counter to the contemporary orthodoxy, materialism means more than "such definitive statements as that 'everything real is material' " ("Metaphysik," 9/*CT*, 19). As an alternative conception of science, it refers to a cognitive and social learning process that goes beyond the principle of returning to material states of affairs. It begins with the achievements of the bourgeois sciences, transcends them, and leads to a more comprehensive form of constituting and appropriating reality.

This emphatic characterization should not be misunderstood. As the history of materialism reveals, its characteristic form of constitution and appropriation has not been without crises of its own. For Horkheimer, an adequate concept of materialism emerges only if it is developed historically. As the precursor and point of departure for the materialist paradigm, he first takes up the "materialism of the early bourgeoisie" ("Metaphysik," 23/*CT*, 33), which emerged in the natural law doctrines of the sixteenth century and in the oft-cited "Copernican revolution." The methods of observation proposed by Copernicus, Galileo, and Newton may have represented a crude materialism, conceiving the world as a purely mechanical nexus of material states. But its separation from theological ties made possible for the first time a consciously productive treatment of outer nature. Precisely here, for Horkheimer, lay a decisive moment, for materialism first becomes possible on the basis of the idea of a rational domination of nature, and the "idea that we may have already passed the optimum level of technological productivity" is foreign to it ("Metaphysik," 16/*CT*, 26–27).

Such confidence in the positive possibilities of the development of productive forces may seem almost naive today. But in contrast to contemporary cultural pessimism à la Spengler, it is completely understandable, and the idea of the rational domination of nature retains its sense if conceived in noninstrumental terms as the possibility of a rational alterability of the world. One might well dispute whether this interpretation was actually Horkheimer's during the early 1930s. In favor of such a reading, however, is the fact that he also accorded the assumption of a potential and, in principle, rational alterability the status of a fundamental epistemological principle. According to Horkheimer, materialist thought is distinguished by its fundamentally open structure; it refers to a "concept of knowledge as a nonindependent process which can be defined only in the context of the dynamic of society" ("Metaphysik," 19/*CT*, 30). It leads neither to absolute truth nor to ultimate, definitive statements but rather stands in a "dialectical" relationship with social development.

For Horkheimer, "dialectics" constitutes the ultimately decisive key to characterizing the open-endedness of materialist knowledge. He distinguishes two stages in the development of the dialectical conception of knowledge. According to his interpretation, the first is found in Hegel who, in *The Phenomenology of Spirit,* worked out the processual character of scientific knowledge. Here truth is not an ontological condition but is realized only in the movement of thought as knowledge of the conditioned character of all isolated contents and in their progressive transformation:

Recognition of the conditional character of every isolated view and rejection of its absolute claim to truth does not destroy this conditional knowledge; rather, it is incorporated into the system of truth at any given time as a conditional, one-sided, and isolated view. Through nothing but this continuous delimitation and correction of partial truths, the process itself evolves its proper content as knowledge of limited insights in their limits and connection. ("Wahrheit," 328/"Truth," 414)

Nevertheless, Hegel himself undermines his own processual approach, since he conceives of an immediate identity of being and concept and "posits his system as absolute" ("Metaphysik," 21/*CT*, 32), so that in the end, social truth becomes an emanation of absolute Spirit. Here lies the point of departure for the second development, in Feuerbach, Marx, and Engels, through which dialectical thought becomes materialistic and, according to the well-known formula, "stands Hegel on his feet": "When Feuerbach, Marx, and Engels freed the dialectic from its idealist form, materialism achieved an awareness of the ever changing but irreducible tension between its own teaching and reality, and acquired in the process its own conception of knowledge" ("Metaphysik," 23/*CT*, 32). Just as the mysteries of theory find their solution in social praxis and a scientific understanding of it,[7] so the truth-claim of Hegelian philosophy is first realized for Marx in the analysis of the political economy of capitalism, which carries out its own material negation. The critique of ideology applied to idealistic philosophy becomes identical with its sublation *(Aufhebung)* in the critique of political economy as the "anatomy of bourgeois society."[8] In Horkheimer's eyes, with this sublation understood as both "appropriation" and "critique," Marx formulates a "unification of philosophy and science" ("Metaphysik," 25/*CT*, 34) that brings with it a "major transformation of the supporting concepts" and "raises knowledge in general to a higher level" ("Rationalismusstreit," 49/*BPSS*). With the replacement of the spiritual principles of idealism by the real principles of social evolution, grounded in the economy, a "turn from taphysics to scientific theory" ("Geschichte," 132/*BPSS*) is achieved. As a consequence, a new relationship arises between the material and ideal, normative and descriptive moments: the contradictions of real being become the conditions for its transformation.

For Horkheimer, as for Lukács, the subject and addressee of these experiences of contradiction is the proletariat,[9] and Marxist theory, as the self-thematization of this class, appears as fundamentally "postbourgeois." This is true from the scientific as well as the political point of view; as "a formulation of historical experience that corresponds to the current state of knowledge" ("Geschichte," 133/*BPSS*), the critique of political economy provides the intellectual conditions for overcoming the social "misery of our times" ("Metaphysik," 14/*CT*, 24) without defining praxis in an authoritarian fashion. Rather, its productivity lies precisely in its openness and in the knowledge "of the irresolvable difference between concept and reality" ("Wahrheit," 345/"Truth," 438). It refers to an experience of contradiction whose truth is considered in scientific discourse and decided in social praxis. Aware of this, it guides social praxis without being able to replace it.

From these characteristics, it also follows that Marxist theory can hardly be reduced to a cognitively or strategically "fixed" explanatory model; if it serves "as a universal method of construction in place of concrete investigations" ("Geschichte," 132/*BPSS*), then it transforms itself into a "closed, dogmatic metaphysics," which seems just as suspect of being an ideology as its bourgeois counterparts. On the other hand, the critique of political economy remains a valid model if, in a historically reflective attitude, it is applied to itself and developed further. The "laws" of social development worked out by Marx do not represent laws in the sense of the natural sciences, which obtain independently of the subject (cf. "Voraussage," 409ff.); rather, they represent a set of overarching structural and functional relationships whose concrete form must constantly be worked out and justified anew according to a given context of social issues.

In materialist theory after Marx, however, this demand was repressed rather than fulfilled—a repression that increased in tandem with the integration of the working class into the bourgeois structure of domination. This development, which became increasingly clear after 1918, not only called into question the unity of theory and praxis; it also affected the scientific claims of the materialist paradigm, which had not anticipated the absence or failure of revolution. Horkheimer's sharpest formulation of this problem was his note, "The Impotence of the German Working Class," in which he emphatically distinguished between a crisis of materialist praxis and a theoretical deficit connected with it. The practical crisis, that is, the stagnation of the workers' movement, was explained in terms of the developmental dynamic of capitalism, which had destroyed the unity of the proletariat: "In our time, the gulf between the employed and those who only work sporadically or not at all is as wide as that between the entire working class and the lumpenproletariat at an earlier period. . . . Work and misery no longer come together, people no longer experience both. . . . But the employed worker is no longer typical of those who most urgently need change" (*Dämmerung*, 282–83/*DD*, 61–62). Only the unemployed still have an interest in socialism, but they lack "the capacities for education and organization, the class consciousness, and the dependability of those who are more or less integrated into the capitalist enterprise" (*Dämmerung*, 282–83/*DD*, 61–62). By contrast, the employed, who directly experience the contradictions of capitalist production (and, according to Lukács, should be the first to recognize them), are uninterested since they fear the threat of unemployment. Out of this necessarily arises a "division between the two revolutionary elements: the direct interest in socialism and clear theoretical consciousness are found on different sides of the proletariat" (*Dämmerung*, 283/*DD*, 62), which then paralyze one another: "The capitalist process of production has thus driven a wedge between the interest in socialism and the human qualities necessary to its implementation. . . . In contemporary Germany, it expresses itself through the existence of two workers' parties and the wavering of sizable segments of the unemployed between the Communist and the National Socialist parties. It dooms the workers to practical impotence" (*Dämmerung*, 283–84/*DD*, 62–63).

According to Horkheimer, these oppositions between the unemployed and the employed, interests and consciousness, radicalism and reformism also result in a massive internal crisis of materialism, which shows itself in a false connection to theory and in gaps in research and theory construction. The unity of philosophical intention and scientific precision that Marx achieved apparently falls apart since the "two elements of the dialectical method—factual knowledge and clarity concerning fundamentals" (*Dämmerung*, 285/*DD*, 64) are isolated, fragmented, and often unintelligibly opposed to one another: "There are those who recognize existing society as bad, but they lack the knowledge to prepare the revolution practically and theoretically. The others might be able to produce that knowledge but lack the fundamental experience of the urgent need for change" (*Dämmerung*, 285–86/*DD*, 65). What emerges is thus a dilemma comparable to the opposition between positivism and metaphysics, which finds an immediate reflection in the various segments of the workers' movement. Whereas the Communists make materialism into a dogma, limited to a "mere repetition of slogans" (*Dämmerung*, 283/*DD*, 63), the Social Democrats have lost their "grasp of all theoretical elements" (*Dämmerung*, 284/*DD*, 63). They lapse into a positivistic, domesticated analysis of praxis and reject the possibility of radical change. Conceptually blind revolutionary rhetoric and an equally blind accommodation to poor conditions negatively supplement one another, just as do positivism and metaphysics, hindering both a real explanation of the crisis of the workers' movement and practical steps to overcome it.

The Construction of Interdisciplinary Materialism

What is surprising in the diagnosis I have sketched is undoubtedly the similarity in the symptoms of crisis, which is quite significant for Horkheimer's further argument. Insofar as the contradictions between the theory and the practice of the labor movement were seen to parallel those between positivism and metaphysics, it might be possible to link their reconstructions and to develop a comprehensive solution that could be formulated in either bourgeois or materialist terms, as needed.[10] In order to work out the structure as well as the problems of this proposal, it is useful briefly to recall once more the aporias of both paradigms.

With respect to materialism, Horkheimer points first and foremost to the theory-praxis problem as posed by the experience of a missed revolution and a split in the working class. Thus, the central aporia is the contradiction between the revolutionary claim and the partial integration of the proletariat. Insofar as this development remains unrecognized within the labor movement, a second complex of problems arises: the phenomenon of theoretical gaps that, according to Horkheimer, result in either a dogmatization or dissolution of materialism, calling into question its scientific character.

The aporias of the bourgeois line of development are described not as a problem of praxis but as an immanent narrowing of the rationality of knowledge. This appears, on the one hand, as an epistemological problem: with the "division" of reason, the dimensions of factual knowledge and reflexive, theoretical knowledge are separated from one another and become independent, contrasting modes of knowledge. Horkheimer also sees this dissociation carried over into a crisis in the organization of science, which results in both a separation of philosophy from science and an apparently haphazard differentiation of specialized disciplines.

The connection of these separate arguments now results in a skillfully balanced translation of the materialist paradigm into the perspective of the bourgeois line of development. This process proceeds in two steps that refer to a gradual withdrawal into the immanence of scientific experience. First, in view of the absence of a revolutionary labor movement, the proletariat is redefined not as the subject but as the addressee of theory, and the theory-praxis dilemma is transformed into the problem of a theory of society that encompasses factual and theoretical knowledge. The reformulation of the concept of materialism thus appears uncoupled from the dimension of praxis mediating between fact-oriented science and reflection-oriented "philosophy." Then, on this foundation, the crisis of Marxism appears in an altered form, as a problem of inadequate explanations; it is interpreted as the result of deficient theoretical and empirical distinctions and, at the same time, translated into a question of scientific organization, since these theoretical gaps can, according to Horkheimer, be closed only through an interdisciplinary extension (or differentiation) of the materialist paradigm.

The drawing of a parallel between the aporias (theory-praxis dilemma/separation of factual and theoretical knowledge) thus leads to a connection between the subordinate complexes of problems (theoretical gaps/deficits in the organization of science), and out of this transformation the concept of "interdisciplinary materialism" as a programmatic guideline is developed. The justification of the program results from the redefinitions at the first level. Its formulation, by contrast, begins on the second level, that is, from a perspective strictly immanent to science, and proceeds in three separate steps. The point of departure is the thesis of theoretical gaps, which is explicated both descriptively and prescriptively. Building upon this, the decision for interdisciplinary differentiation (or extension) of the materialist paradigm is spelled out more precisely, and the goals and methods of the disciplines involved are justified. The third step is a metatheoretical extension of the argument: the interdisciplinary choice is framed in an analysis of the connection between "social philosophy" and disciplinary "social research" and developed so as to make it suitable for concrete research.

The claim about Marxism's theoretical gaps produced not only arguments concerning the organization of science but substantive starting points for research as well. Here the vigorous critique of the orthodox base-superstructure model should be noted, a model whose shortcomings, for Horkheimer, lay not so much in theory as in its empirical consequences. The revolutionary transformations Marx predicted occurred only in Russia, where they were least to be expected according to his own assertions.[11] In advanced capitalist societies such as Great Britain, the United States, or Germany, a potential for stabilization was evident, despite deepening economic crises. Moreover, developments such as the emergence of fascism in the Weimar Republic pointed to unexpected, regressive developments in the social superstructure. For precisely these reasons, it was necessary to rethink "the view that cultural disorder is connected with economic relationships" ("Bemerkungen," 6/CT, 9). On the side of the economy, what had to be considered above all were "the pressures tending toward the planned regulation of the economy" ("Vorwort," III), which gained importance with the transition to monopoly capitalism.[12] Along with this, the apparent decline in class consciousness, the growing role of conservative and reactionary attitudes, and the obviously retarding influence of cultural traditions would have to be elucidated. As Horkheimer stated in his inaugural address as director of the Institute for Social Research, against this background the substantive work of interdisciplinary materialism should center on one question, "that is, on the question of the connection between the economic life of society, the psychological development of the individual, and the transformations of the cultural spheres in a strict sense, to which belong not only the 'intellectual' matters of science, art, and religion, but also law, morality, fashion, public opinion, sport, leisure, lifestyle, and so on" ("Lage," 43). This formulation already makes clear the Frankfurt circle's strong "fixation on the superstructure." They were less interested in the internal transformations of the economic structure than in extra-economic processes, whose social determination (in accordance with the Marxist distinction between the essence and appearance of capitalist relations) was to be investigated as well as their intrinsic logic of development. For Horkheimer, making good on this claim was less a theoretical problem than a problem of the organization of science. Psychological, cultural, and historical arguments must be employed alongside economic arguments, since the autonomy and nonsynchronic character of the extra-economic processes could no longer be understood through further refinements in economic explanation:

Rather, it is a question . . . of organizing investigations on the basis of current philosophical issues, investigations in which philosophers, sociologists, political economists, historians, and psychologists join together in ongoing working groups and do in common. . . . what proper researchers have always done— namely, to pursue philosophical questions directed at the big picture with the most refined scientific methods; to reformulate and sharpen these questions in the course of the work; to devise new methods; and yet not lose sight of the larger context. ("Lage," 41/*BPSS*)

With this emphasis, the problem of materialist theory construction shifted to reintegrating the individual disciplines, which were to be dealt with from a social-theoretical standpoint in order to make them compatible with the materialist paradigm. The elements of the interdisciplinary extension arose out of the explanatory deficits, which also established their hierarchical arrangement. According to Horkheimer, social psychology was to provide the principal contribution to explaining the "powerlessness of the working class" and, in view of the "lost revolution," to advance to the position of a second basic discipline, alongside economics: "The economic appears as comprehensive and primary, but knowledge of conditionedness in detail, the working out of the mediating processes themselves, and thus also comprehension of the results depend upon psychological work . . . , since the present is characterized more by the unknown effect of economic relations upon the whole form of life than by conscious economic motives" ("Geschichte," 140–41/*BPSS*).

The task of clarifying the nonsynchronic relation between base and superstructure falls to social psychology conceived as an (individualistic) "psychology of the unconscious" ("Geschichte," 135/*BPSS*).[13] From this key position, it prestructured the order and orientation of the other disciplines, which, therefore, were seen in almost functional terms. The cultural disciplines as represented in the Institute by Adorno's sociology of music and Löwenthal's sociology of literature are noteworthy in this respect.[14] According to Horkheimer, within the interdisciplinary context, their task consisted of analyzing the production of economically generated and social-psychologically mediated cultural objectivations, in order to supplement the "subjective" (or psychological) side of the superstructure with a grasp of its "objective" (or sociological) structures.

This claim remained selective in more than one respect. For instance, transindividual social structures could not be comprehended on the basis of individual psychology's presuppositions, a defect that ultimately indicates a critical "sociological deficit."[15] Moreover, both programatically and factually, the emphasis lay on problems of the "sociocultural system," whereas the second major sphere of the "objective" superstructure, the political system, was neglected. Of course, the Institute included highly competent specialists such as Otto Kirchheimer and Franz Neumann, but Horkheimer did not feel compelled to accord political sociology or political science an independent status within the program.[16] In contrast to history, these were not even mentioned in listings of the various components of interdisciplinary materialism. On this point, Horkheimer clearly remained dependent on traditional Marxism, which had dealt with the realm of politics but did not regard it as an independent entity.

Nevertheless, his concept went beyond orthodox materialism just as it went beyond those conceptions of interdisciplinary social analysis developed by contemporary sociology from Weber to Tönnies.[17] In contrast to the "bourgeois" models, Horkheimer's concept of interdisciplinary research was explicitly grounded in social theory, and overcoming the chaotic specialization ("Lage," 40/*BPSS*) of the individual disciplines seemed possible only to the extent that they were opened up to a historically sensitive, materialist approach. Horkheimer described the linkage and the social-theoretical turn given to the partial results of the disciplines more precisely as a process of coordinating research strategy that consists of three elements: social philosophy, social research, and the theory of the course of history. By this view, the starting point for social theory is social philosophy, which, as a differentiated, materialistic critique, formulates the "theoretical intention oriented to what is universal and 'essential'" ("Lage," 41/*BPSS*). It does this in the form of general assumptions about the structure and development of the social totality. According to Horkheimer, such assumptions cannot initially claim scientific objectivity, although they are not at all particularistic or subjectivistic. Rather, they appear with a claim to universalizability based upon prescientific experience. This claim can be scientifically reformulated to the extent that the assumptions are successfully tested at the level of economics, social psychology, or the cultural sciences.[18] The "prescientific" status of social philosophy already indicates the importance of social research. Its task is to transform the "big questions" ("Lage," 41/*BPSS*) into the standards of the individual disciplines and treat them comprehensively with the available methodological tools. Work in the individual sciences results in a transformation and securing of the universalizable concepts of social philosophy, which acquire a new form through their objectivation in the sciences and receive a deeper grounding. What Horkheimer calls the "theory of the historical course of the present epoch" ("Vorwort," III) can then arise from the collaborative effort of social philosophy and social research, that is, an analysis that summarizes the various dimensions of capitalistic relations. This analysis synthesizes scientific and philosophical claims to objectivity in such a way that the whole social process becomes visible as a "concrete totality."

The Revival of Interdisciplinary Materialism—and Its Limits

Horkheimer's argument as a whole comes down to three points that comprise the constructive logic of the program. The starting point lies in the thesis that science is a social-cognitive structure, that is, one that is relative to both society and truth; science enters a crisis to the extent that these two defining moments come into conflict with one another. The elaboration of this thesis proceeds through a historical-systematic reconstruction of two types of science, the bourgeois and the materialist paradigms, whose differing courses of development lead to the formation of their own aporias. Finally, from the analysis and reciprocal translation of these aporias, Horkheimer derives the program of interdisciplinary materialism, conceived in terms that encompass the paradigms; this program is meant to reintegrate the moments relating to truth and to society. The interconnection of these three steps becomes more visible when they are graphically represented (figure 5.1).

By comparison with other contemporary assessments of the possibility of critical social analysis, this line of argument is both refined and ambitious. Unlike orthodox Marxism, Horkheimer does not treat discussions about science and crisis as a problem limited to "bourgeois science," and unlike the sociology of knowledge,[19] he does not abandon social-theoretical claims and settle for an epistemological relativism that makes reduced truth-claims. Rather, the interdisciplinary model was to make possible a productive handling of aporias that, according to Horkheimer, cannot be overcome but can be managed

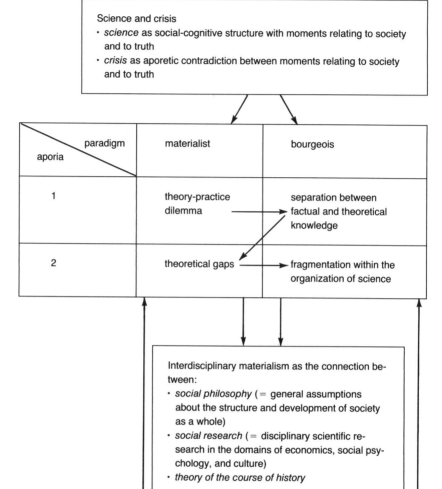

Figure 5.1

through the organization of science. Precisely here lay his decisive, innovative achievement. This accomplishment is all the more impressive if one bears in mind that the social sciences were still insufficiently differentiated from the domains of philosophy, jurisprudence, and public administration in the German-speaking world in the early 1930s.

With this shift to the organization of science and the redefinition of substantive problems as procedural ones, Horkheimer anticipates developmental trends whose systematic formulation first became possible with the methodological turn constitutive of today's versions of critical theory (Habermas, Wellmer).[20] Such anticipatory moments have formed the basis for ascribing to interdisciplinary materialism a "very timely and relevant potential, as yet unrealized in the history of science,"[21] a potential to be made good on in the present—a claim that Habermas has adopted. Of course, both Habermas and others have pointed out that early critical theory was concerned with an "interpretation of Marx's work under conditions that belong irretrievably to the past," an interpretation that as such can hardly be simply revived.[22] But this reservation is generally intended less systematically than historically and can even serve to strengthen claims for its contemporary significance; the fact that the interdisciplinary program encountered obstacles to its realization in practical research, and thus was silently abandoned at the end of the 1930s, is traced not to systematic weaknesses but to "historical contingencies."[23] The implicit thesis is that if these "historical contingencies" are overcome, a direct reactivation is possible.

With respect to the epistemological structure of interdisciplinary materialism, however, such an assessment is too limited, and it seems significant that attempts at reactivating it, like that of Habermas, invoke Horkheimer more rhetorically than substantively. That Horkheimer's program remained bound to those fronts on which it toiled can be seen first of all in a frequently overlooked "rupture" between the critique of science and the proposed solution to it. This rupture becomes more apparent in figure 5.1. However plausible the individual elements of interdisciplinary materialism (social philosophy, social research, theory of the course of history) may be at first sight, their selection and ordering are only indirectly connected to the preceding critique of science. The directional arrows between the individual steps in the argument make it clear that the transformation of the aporias in the central, "theoretical" (or foundational) section of the diagram is not continued below in the presentation of the scientific program of interdisciplinary materialism. Nor is this unclarity simply an artifact of the figure, since it does not disappear if one attempts, as Helmut Dubiel has, to spell out the logic of the interdisciplinary program more precisely.[24] Horkheimer's concept can be interpreted from this perspective as a reformulation of Marx's view of the relation between "research" and "presentation,"[25] but this does not begin to explain how the interdisciplinary production of knowledge can lead to a solution of those aporias that, according to Horkheimer's own analysis, originated after or apart from Marx's own work.

The fact that the trio of social philosophy, social research, and the theory of the course of history was not as well thought through as it appears also shows itself at other points, such as the frequently used metaphor of "interdisciplinary" research. The notion of interdisciplinary research is generally defined as an "ongoing working group" of various scientists that arises "on the basis of current philosophical issues" ("Lage," 41/*BPSS*) and almost automatically transforms the conditions of knowledge. Insofar as the representatives of the various disciplines join together in a problem-oriented team "and do in common . . . what proper researchers have always done" (ibid.), they transcend the fragmentation of science and contribute to overcoming the opposition between positivism and metaphysics. The emphatic formulation of this thesis may at first seem to carry conviction, but upon sober consideration it can be conceded only limited validity. Apart from the shared set of problems, in Horkheimer's conception the work of the disciplines remains unchanged. In the end, the interdisciplinary claim amounts to no more than an external formula for integration, a view that is certainly vulnerable to objections. This is all the more true since the magic words *interdisciplinary research* have lost much of their critical connotation. It has long since become fashionable in political science to immunize oneself against criticism by invoking an interdisciplinary orientation. In light of such experiences, an unarticulated trust in the procedural-transformative dynamic of interdisciplinary "working groups" seems both naive and distorting, for the envisioned qualitative changes do not result automatically. Rather, these changes can be realized only by going beyond the mere collaborative work of various specialized disciplines to interact in a way that transforms the disciplines themselves.

With his "naive" understanding of interdisciplinary research, Horkheimer also falls short of the level on which his own critique of science operates. If his argument is taken seriously, one must assume that, along with the breakdown of the connection once posited between philosophy and science, the forms of scientific-rational appropriation developed within the context of the Enlightenment concept of reason are also brought into question. The crisis of science thus also means a crisis of its methods, and overcoming the aporias Horkheimer described correspondingly presupposes the development of an alternative methodology. However, this issue is never raised; from a methodological point of view, Horkheimer's conception remains largely conventional. He was, of course, well aware of the selectivity of the work within the individual disciplines, but he hardly took into account that this selectivity is conditioned by the way the disciplines constitute their objects and is continually reproduced at the methodological level. Instead, Horkheimer called for social research to go on applying the "most refined scientific methods" ("Lage," 41/*BPSS*) as if they were value neutral and would be given a critical turn ex post through their integration with social philosophy.

From today's point of view, such a conception seems more than problematic. It also indicates decisive weaknesses in the program as a whole. Quite apart from the fact that the reformulation of materialism was achieved at the cost of separating materialist critique (= social philosophy) from material analysis (= social research), this conception amounts to a tacit upgrading of social philosophy that is both unclear and ambiguous. To be sure, Horkheimer believes that after Marx philosophy as material theory can no longer be justified, but in his eyes it was not thereby overcome or, as in the case of Habermas, reduced to the status of an inquiry concerned with justification. Instead, philosophy appears as a loose bundle of convictions drawn from the philosophy of history—the normative remains of the critique of political economy, which functions as a kind of "court of final appeal." It is hardly surprising that this "court" remained remarkably vague, apart from a few associative references to historical materialism, since even then Horkheimer's conception amounted to a history of the decline of philosophy. But at the programmatic level, he did not draw the consequences. Despite his own postulates Horkheimer was in no position to think through the concept of philosophy in a post-Hegelian form, nor could he imagine an autonomous development of social research.

From this perspective, Adorno was more consistent. His "The Actuality of Philosophy" (1931) at times suggests an alternative model for the program of interdisciplinary materialism.[26] Adorno interpreted the crisis of science and philosophy as a transformation of the conditions of the possibility of knowledge. He assumed that after the breakdown of the Enlightenment's concept of reason, knowledge can only be produced negatively. To the extent that the universalization of the commodity form eliminates the potential of social life to oppose the existing structures, "only history now vouches for the images of our lives."[27] They appear only in traces, splinters, and fragments, and deciphering them requires a concept of "preserving traces" that goes beyond the "most refined scientific methods" in Horkheimer's sense and points to a different form of scientific appropriation.[28]

Of course, one may argue whether Adorno's version of the concept of "preserving traces" can be reconciled at all with the program of an interdisciplinary social science, but it can hardly be contested that his argument took Horkheimer's critique of science more seriously and even radicalized it. As Susan Buck-Morss has shown, on this point Adorno stood much closer to the "dialectic of enlightenment" than to the concept of "interdisciplinary materialism,"[29] and precisely this emphasis was probably what hindered his line of thought from achieving more influence on the development of early critical theory. For Horkheimer at the beginning of the 1930s, there could be no question of anticipating the "dialectic of enlightenment." Like Adorno, he saw an increasing trend toward irrationalism but did not interpret these symptoms of a crisis as an irreversible destruction of reason. Rather, they appeared as a temporary, socially conditioned regression that was to be illuminated by the positive, specialized sciences. And the integration of these sciences, in turn, was understood to be fundamentally rational, inasmuch as the "detour" of analyzing the regression would uncover the possibility of bringing about a realization of reason.

This perspective resulted in a selective perception of the individual disciplines. Notice was taken only of what appeared to be useful for the envisioned explanatory goal. Of interest was less their internal logic (including their respective social-theoretical merits and deficits) than their suitability for being integrated into a theory of the "lost revolution." The unclarities and ambiguities this involved can be seen particularly clearly in the case of the economy, which ultimately appears in two different forms. On the one hand, it constitutes an indispensable, fundamental concept of social theory; on the other hand, according to the interdisciplinary program, it must be identifiable as an individual scientific discipline. In the work of the Institute, these two aspects were carefully separated from one another and assigned their own jurisdictions. Thus, the social-theoretical implications of political economy, such as the formulations on class and revolution, were integrated into the basic assumptions of Horkheimer's social philosophy. On the other hand, in the domain of social research, Pollock worked at developing a conventional, positive economics with a functionalist stamp, in which economic processes were conceived as isolated functional complexes apart from all political connotations.[30] Consequently, the reception of political economy remained ambivalent. Although it constituted a basic element in the theoretical framework as well as the self-conception of the Frankfurt circle, the unpolitical economic functionalism represented by Pollock implicitly ran counter to this self-conception, though none of the members reflected on this contradiction at the time.

The selectivity and the functionalist bias in the analyses of the individual disciplines are also discernable in social psychology, which was to research the psychic processing of economically induced behavioral imperatives and their transformation into specific cultural meanings. Such an explanation of "ideology as arising from the interaction between the apparatus of psychic drives and socio-economic conditions"[31] seemed indispensable in view of the increasing discrepancy between the "objective" economic situation and the "subjective" readiness for action, but the explanation never went beyond precisely this discrepancy. The constitutional issue of the conditions of possibility of proletarian class consciousness was not discussed, nor were concealed counterstructural attitudes systematically inquired into. What remained was an analysis of the functional character of consciousness for an oppressive economic base and its one-dimensional channeling into authoritarian patterns of thought and behavior, a theme that governed the empirical work of the 1930s as well as the 1940s.[32]

Upon considering the problematic points already outlined above—the "break" between the critique of science and the scientific program, the "naive" conception of interdisciplinary research, the lack of methodological reflection, the ambiguous concept of philosophy, the functionalist bias and selectivity of the individual disciplines—it becomes clear that the "capsizing" of interdisciplinary materialism, which first became visible in Horkheimer's treatment of the relationship between traditional and critical theory, was neither accidental nor historically contingent. Given these weaknesses, the program—whose epistemological inconsistencies should be noted above all—could hardly have resolved the crisis of science, quite apart from the traumatic experiences of fascism and emigration. The interdisciplinary conception remains relevant, for it attempted to comprehend the course of society as a crisis-ridden nexus of various dimensions that today are still usually described in isolation as different social systems. But the mediation of these systems, and thus the social totality, cannot be adequately grasped in the manner Horkheimer proposed. A direct connection with early critical theory does not seem promising. It would be better to learn from the shortcomings of interdisciplinary materialism and to inquire into epistemologically more adequate means for mastering the fundamental aporias, which remain in force. Critical theory is an open-ended project whose solutions must continually be confronted "with the state of awareness in which we find ourselves."[33]

Translated by Kenneth Baynes and John McCole

Notes

Horkheimer's texts are cited and English translations, where available, are cross-referenced according to the following key (in some cases the translations have been modified):

BPSS = *Between Philosophy and Social Science: Selected Early Writings* (Cambridge, 1993).

"AbG" = "Anfänge der bürgerlichen Geschichtsphilosophie" (Stuttgart, 1930); "Origins of the Bourgeois Philosophy of History," in *BPSS*.

"Lage" = "Die gegenwärtige Lage der Sozialphilosophie und die Aufgaben eines Instituts für Sozialforschung," in *Sozialphilosophische Studien* (Frankfurt, 1972), 33ff.; "The Present Situation of Social Philosophy and the Tasks of an Institute for Social Research," in *BPSS*.

"Vorwort" = "Vorwort," *Zeitschrift für Sozialforschung* [= *ZfS*] 1 (1932): 1ff.

"Bemerkungen" = "Bemerkungen über Wissenschaft und Krise," *ZfS* 1 (1932): 1ff.; "Notes on Science and the Crisis," in *Critical Theory: Selected Essays* [= *CT*] (New York, 1972).

"Geschichte" = "Geschichte und Psychologie," *ZfS* 1 (1932): 125ff./"History and Psychology," in *BPSS*.

"Metaphysik" = "Materialismus und Metaphysik," *ZfS* 2 (1933): 1ff.; "Materialism and Metaphysics," in *CT*.

"Moral" = "Materialismus und Moral," *ZfS* 2 (1933): 161ff.; "Materialism and Morality," in *BPSS*.

"Rationalismusstreit" = "Zum Rationalismusstreit in der gegenwärtigen Philosophie," *ZfS* 3 (1934): 1ff.; "The Rationalism Dispute in Current Philosophy," in *BPSS*.

"Voraussage" = "Zum Problem der Voraussage in den Sozialwissenschaften," *ZfS* 2 (1933): 407ff.

Dämmerung = *Dämmerung. Notizen in Deutschland*, in *Notizen 1950 bis 1969 und Dämmerung. Notizen in Deutschland* (Frankfurt, 1974); *DD* = *Dawn and Decline: Notes 1926–1931 and 1950–1969* (New York, 1978). (Contains only selections from *Dämmerung*.)

"Wahrheit" = "Zum Begriff der Wahrheit," *ZfS* 4 (1935): 321ff.; "Truth" = "On the Problem of Truth," in Andrew Arato and Eike Gebhardt, eds., *The Essential Frankfurt School Reader* (New York, 1982).

"Traditionelle" = "Traditionelle und kritische Theorie," *ZfS* 6 (1937): 245ff.; "Traditional and Critical Theory," in *CT*.

1. Martin Jay, *The Dialectical Imagination: A History of the Frankfurt School and the Institute of Social Research, 1923–1950* (Boston, 1973).

2. Jürgen Habermas, *Theorie des kommunikativen Handelns* (Frankfurt, 1981), 2:554/*Theory of Communicative Action* [= *TCA*] (Boston, 1987), 2:378.

3. Ibid., 562/*TCA*, 2:383; 1:489ff./*TCA*, 1:366ff.

4. Ibid., 2:562/*TCA*, 2:383.

5. Alfred Schmidt, "Die kritische Theorie. Denkmotive von Horkheimer, Adorno und Marcuse. Referate gehalten auf der Tagung am 23. Juni 1973 in Bad-Boll" (unpublished manuscript, n. d.), 2.

6. Joachim Ritter, *Hegel und die französiche Revolution* (Frankfurt, 1972), 7ff. English translation: *Hegel and the French Revolution* (Cambridge, 1982).

7. Karl Marx and Friedrich Engels, *Werke 1845–1846* (*Marx-Engels Werke*, vol. 3) (Berlin/DDR, 1969), 7.

8. Karl Marx and Friedrich Engels, *Werke 1859–1860* (*Marx-Engels Werke*, vol. 13) (Berlin/DDR, 1969), 8.

9. On Lukács's thesis of the speculative identity of proletarian class consciousness and social theory in *History and Class Consciousness*, see Lukács, *Geschichte und Klassen-*

bewußtsein (Neuwied/Berlin, 1968), esp. 342ff.; see also Martin Jay, "Positive und negative Totalität. Adornos Alternativenwurf zur interdisziplinären Forschung," in Wolfgang Bonß and Axel Honneth, eds., *Sozialforschung als Kritik* (Frankfurt, 1982), 69f. English translation: "Positive and Negative Totalities: Implicit Tensions in Critical Theory's Vision of Interdisciplinary Research," in Jay, *Permanent Exiles: Essays on the Intellectual Migration from Germany to America* (New York, 1985). Helmut Dubiel, *Wissenschaftsorganisation und politische Erfahrung. Studien zur frühen Kritschen Theorie* (Frankfurt, 1978), 39ff. English translation: *Theory and Politics: Studies in the Development of Critical Theory* (Cambridge, 1985).

10. Thus, Horkheimer employed an exclusively "bourgeois" terminology in his inaugural address as director of the Institute (1931), whereas in the aphorisms of *Dämmerung* (1926–1931) he used primarily materialist language. In most of his essays, however, these paradigms appear alongside one another, resulting in the well-known "Aesopian language" whose ambiguity was as significant for early critical theory as it was for its reception by the student movement.

11. From this perspective, it is perhaps not surprising that the revolutionary transformation in Russia did not succeed but was perverted and collapsed.

12. See chapter 9 in this book.

13. See Erich Fromm, "Über Methode und Aufgabe einer analytischen Sozialpsychologie," in *ZfS* 1 (1932): 28ff. English translation: "The Method and Function of an Analytical Social Psychology," in Andrew Arato and Eike Gebhardt, eds., *The Essential Frankfurt School Reader* (New York, 1982), 477ff.; Wolfgang Bonß, "Psychoanalyse als Wissenschaft und Kritik," in Wolfgang Bonß and Axel Honneth, eds., *Sozialforschung als Kritik. Zum sozialwissenschaftlichen Potential der Kritischen Theorie* (Frankfurt, 1982): 367ff.

14. T. W. Adorno, "Zur gesellschaftlichen Lage der Musik," *ZfS* 1 (1932): 103ff., 356ff.; Leo Löwenthal, "Zur gesellschaftlichen Lage der Literatur," in *ZfS* 1 (1932): 85ff.

15. See Axel Honneth, "Max Horkheimer's Original Program: The Sociological Deficit of Critical Theory," chapter 8 in this book.

16. See Alfons Söllner, *Geschichte und Herrschaft: Studien zur materialistischen Sozialwissenschaft 1929–1942* (Frankfurt, 1979), 165ff.

17. See Susanna Schad, *Empirical Social Research in Weimar Germany* (Paris/Den Haag, 1972), 76ff., and Rainer M. Lepsius, ed., *Soziologie in Deutschland und Österreich 1918–1945. Materialien zur Entwicklung, Emigration und Wirkungsgeschichte* (Köln/Opladen, 1982).

18. Viewed in this way, moreover, Horkheimer's concept of social philosophy shows parallels to that of Weber, who in his essay " 'Objectivity' in Social Science and Social Policy" characterized social philosophy as a system of "speculative value judgements" that are to be emphatically distinguished from social research. Max Weber, " 'Objectivity' in Social Science and Social Policy," in *The Methodology of the Social Sciences* (New York, 1949), 49ff.

19. See, for instance, Karl Mannheim, *Ideology and Utopia* (New York, 1954).

20. The trend toward method is especially true of Habermas (e.g., *Zur Logik der Sozialwissenschaften* [Frankfurt, 1967]), who also made the remarkable comment, on the occasion of Adorno's death, that now Adorno's "theoretical veil" would no longer conceal

the "methodological skeleton" of critical social theory. See C. Grossner, *Verfall der Philosophie* (Reinbek bei Hamburg, 1971), 15.

21. Söllner, *Geschichte und Herrschaft,* 220.

22. Schmidt, "Die Kritische Theorie—Denkmotive von Horkheimer, Adorno und Marcuse," 1.

23. Dubiel, *Wissenschaftsorganisation und politische Erfahrung,* 206.

24. Ibid., 170ff.

25. Ibid.

26. See Jay, "Positive and Negative Totalities."

27. Adorno, "Die Aktualität der Philosophie," in Adorno, *Gesammelte Schriften* (Frankfurt, 1973), 1:325. English translation: "The Actuality of Philosophy," *Telos* 31 (1977).

28. On the concept of "preserving traces" in general, see Carlo Ginzburg, "Spurensicherung: Der Jäger entziffert die Fährte, Sherlock Holmes nimmt die Lupe, Freud liest Morelli—Die Wissenschaft auf der Suche nach sich selbst," *Freibeuter,* 3, no. 4 (1980): 11ff. For an attempt to interpret Adorno's project in this way, see Wolfgang Bonß, "Empirie als Dechiffrierung von Wirklichkeit. Zur Methodologie bei Adorno," in Ludwig von Friedeburg and Jürgen Habermas, eds., *Adorno-Konferenz* (Frankfurt, 1983), 204ff.

29. Susan Buck-Morss, *The Origin of Negative Dialectics: Theodor W. Adorno, Walter Benjamin, and the Frankfurt Institute* (New York/London, 1977).

30. On the problem of the social-theoretical "neutrality" of Pollock's economics, see chapter 9 in this book.

31. Fromm, "Über Methode und Aufgabe einer analytischen Sozialpsychologie," 54/ "Method and Function of an Analytical Social Psychology," 496.

32. Wolfgang Bonß, *Die Einübung des Tatsachenblicks. Zur Struktur und Veränderung empirischer Sozialforschung* (Frankfurt, 1982), 167ff.

33. T. W. Adorno, *Philosophische Terminologie* (Frankfurt, 1973), 1:69.

6

The Idea of a Critical Theory and Its Relation to Philosophy

Thomas McCarthy

The remarks that follow are offered with an eye to current debates about the posttranscendental critique of reason. Their focus, however, is the program for a critical social theory advanced by Max Horkheimer at the Institute for Social Research in the early 1930s.[1] From the perspective adopted here, that program has the virtue of developing by transforming both aspects of Kant's critique of reason, the assurance of reason's "lawful claims" as well as the dismissal of "groundless pretensions."[2] In contrast to exclusively deconstructionist approaches, it allows for a critical reconstruction of Enlightenment conceptions of reason and the rational subject, a kind of determinate negation in which they are recast in sociohistorical forms rather than simply dismantled. This has the advantage of linking the philosophical critique of reason to modes of inquiry developed in history and the human sciences to deal reflectively with the same domains of thought and action. It is in this spirit that Horkheimer, in his inaugural lecture as director of the institute, characterized critical theory as an "ongoing dialectical interpenetration" of philosophy and empirical research, a form of "philosophically oriented social inquiry."[3]

I

Early in the 1930s Max Horkheimer found himself in an intellectual milieu similar to the contemporary situation in philosophy in one respect: it was marked by a sharp swing away from previously dominant forms of neo-Kantianism and toward pronounced forms of antirationalism. In his 1934 discussion, The Rationalism Dispute in Current Philosophy," Horkheimer endorsed without reservation the historicist view that "there is no final picture of either the essence or the appearance of reality. The very idea of a supernatural subject who could comprehend it is madness. . . . It is the human being who thinks, not the Ego or Reason. . . . [And that] is not something abstract, such as the human essence, but always human beings living in a particular historical epoch." [4] It is just this embeddedness in historical life that rationalists ignored when they projected worldviews untainted by "any trace of the societal beings that produced them, rather as if they were pure mirrors of an eternal order." [5] On the other hand, Horkheimer warned, none of this warranted a swing to the opposite, antirationalist extremes represented in his day by *Lebensphilosophie* and existentialism. To hypostatize Life or Existence was not to escape metaphysical thinking but only to turn in the old set of fundamental categories for a new one. Critical theory required more than the simple invocation of concrete-sounding, but no less essentialistic, determinations of this sort. It called for a continuation-through-transformation of the critique of reason, a materialist account of its nature, conditions, and limits. If the subject of knowledge and action could no longer be viewed as solitary, disengaged, and disembodied and if the structures of reason could no longer be viewed as timeless, necessary, and unconditioned, then the transformation called for carried the critique of reason in the direction of sociohistorical inquiry.

At the same time, Horkheimer repeatedly urged that this project not be viewed reductionistically. In particular, he was careful to distinguish it from the increasingly influential sociology of knowledge being developed at the time by Karl Mannheim, and with good reason: his critical social theory shared with Mannheim's sociology of knowledge a recognition of the socially conditioned character of human thought. He wished, however, to hold fast to a strong distinction between true and false consciousness and thus to avoid the relativistic implications of Mannheim's approach. Although traditional philosophy's radical dichotomy between the ideal and the real could no longer be upheld, it was not necessary to retreat to a relativism of socially conditioned perspectives. What was needed was a new concept of truth that, while renouncing every God's-eye view, retained the dichotomy between the true and the false, albeit in a more modest, suitably human form.

Thus, in his 1930 review of Mannheim's *Ideology and Utopia,* Horkheimer argued that the historically conditioned character of thought is not per se incompatible with truth. Only against the background of traditional ontological-theological conceptions of eternal, unchanging truth did that seem to be the case.[6] But there was no need of any absolute guarantee to distinguish meaningfully between truth and error. Rather, what was required was a concept of truth consistent with our finitude, our historicity, the dependence of thought on changing social conditions. On such a concept, failure to measure up to absolute, unconditioned standards was irrelevant. To regard this failure as leading directly to relativism was just another version of the "God is dead, everything is permitted" fallacy of disappointed expectations. As Horkheimer put it: "That all our thoughts, true and false, depend on conditions that can change . . . in no way affects the validity of science. It is not clear to me why the fact of *Seinsgebundenheit* [being historically conditioned] should affect the truth of a judgment—why shouldn't insight be just as *seinsgebunden* as error?"[7] In the first instance, the challenge was to deontologize, detranscendentalize the notion of truth.

In his 1935 essay "On the Problem of Truth," Horkheimer attempted to do just that.[8] He argued against the equation of fallibility with relativity. To grant that there is no final and conclusive theory of reality of which we are capable is not to abandon the distinction between truth and error. We make this distinction in relation to the "available means of knowledge."[9] The claim that a belief is true must stand the test of experience and practice in the present. Knowing that we are fallible, that what stands the test today may well fail to do so tomorrow or in the next century, does not prevent us, or even exempt us, from making and defending claims to truth here and now. The abstract recognition that all our beliefs are open to correction does not make a rationally warranted belief any less warranted or any less rational.

A few years later, in 1939, having emigrated to New York, Horkheimer published in the journal of the transplanted Institute for Social Research an essay, "The Social Function of Philosophy." He stressed the ways in which philosophy did not fit neatly into the system of specialized sciences. From the time of Socrates, he wrote, it has taken on "the unpleasant task of throwing the light of consciousness upon even those human relations and modes of response which have become so deeply rooted that they seem natural, immutable, and eternal." [10] Given this interest in questioning what is normally taken for granted, in probing behind established modes of thought and action, it is no wonder, Horkheimer went on, that philosophical discussions "are so much more radical and unconciliatory than discussions in the sciences. Unlike other pursuits, philosophy does not have a field of action marked out for it within the given." [11] Rather, its function is to keep us from losing ourselves "in those ideas and activities which the existing order of society instills into its members," [12] to help us to understand what we are doing in the interest of enabling us consciously to shape our lives. In short, philosophy is critical enlightenment, an ongoing "attempt to bring reason into the world." [13] On the other hand, Horkheimer was fully aware that this sort of radical, practically oriented reflection on reason and its realizations could no longer be carried out in the manner of classical philosophy. There is, he argued, no way of comprehending the structures of reason that does not involve sociohistorical inquiry. And if the actualization of reason is to be more than a pious wish, philosophical utopias will have to be replaced by empirically based accounts of "concrete relations and tendencies that can lead to an improvement of human life." [14] For that reason too, the critical mission of philosophy had to be continued in the medium of social research.

From this standpoint, Horkheimer judged Mannheim's sociology of knowledge to be practically, no less than theoretically, wrongheaded. Treating styles, methods, and systems of thought merely as the expression of specific social situations promoted a skeptical deflation of philosophical notions of reason rather than their refraction in the denser medium of empirical research. "The attitude taken to philosophical ideas does not comprise objective testing and practical application, but a more or less complicated correlation to a social group. [This] merely repeats the skeptical view we have already criticized. It is not calculated to explain the social function of philosophy, but rather to perform one itself—namely, to discourage thought from its practical tendency of pointing to the future." [15] This had been a major theme of Horkheimer's earlier essays as well. In "On the Problem of Truth," for instance, he had written: "Since the recognition of the truth of particular ideas disappears behind the display of conditions, the coordination with historical unities, this impartial relativism reveals itself as the friend of what exists at any given time. . . . What is coming into being needs conscious decision in its struggle, while the limitation to mere understanding and contemplation serves what is already in existence." [16]

Thus, while Horkheimer joined with the dominant forms of anti-rationalism in calling for an investigation of the real conditions of thought, he distanced himself from them in refusing to celebrate the newly minted hypostatizations of History, Society, Life, or Existence.[17] What the critics of rationalism failed to appreciate, he argued, is that the turn to the psychological, social, and historical roots of thought did not herald the end of reason but was the latest and most radical phase in its ongoing self-critique. The "detachment" they announced from the subject-centered categories "originally absolutized by bourgeois liberal thought" usually went hand in hand with a methodological indifference to questions of validity.[18] In certain varieties of historicism, for instance, this took the form of an aestheticized tour through the *musée imaginaire* of the past, with the aim of understanding everything rather than taking sides. The claims to validity of past systems of thought were not taken seriously and rationally evaluated. Instead, critique was replaced by "reverential empathy and description." [19] What concerned Horkheimer about the methodological replacement of *sachliche Prüfung*, or critical examination, with detached contemplation was the skepticism it generated with respect to the basic normative ideas of truth, justice, freedom, responsibility, and the like. While the hegemonic forms of these ideas were all too often distorted, the aim of the materialist critique of reason was not to discard them altogether but to unmask the specific distortions and render them unserviceable for the justification of injustice and oppression: "Whenever in history nations or classes have secured their continued existence not only with cold steel but with moral, metaphysical, and religious ideas, these ideas were in the end exposed to attack from those being dominated. A struggle against the cultural supports of social conditions usually introduces and accompanies political rebellion. . . . For this reason, devaluation of the specific ideas through which a despised state of affairs is grounded, supported, and transfigured is as old as these struggles themselves." [20]

At that time Horkheimer had particular reason to worry about the abstract negation of the conceptual repertoire of rationalist individualism in favor of its binary opposites—history and tradition, community and culture. This sort of simple inversion, combined with skepticism about any strong claims to validity, fostered and justified passivity in the midst of an increasingly irrational and dangerous world. The individual was pictured as thoroughly submerged in the social whole, and the historical movement of the whole as governed by sub- or suprapersonal forces beyond the reach of reason. The idea of rationally influencing the shape of social life by attempting to put the insights of historical, social, and cultural studies into effect appeared ridiculously naive, overcome, dépassé. As Horkheimer pointed out, the peculiar reflexivity of thought about individual and social life is such that thinking something is so can help make it so. The kind of insight into the depths of existence and the shallowness of enlightenment at which German philosophy excelled was only too effective in nourishing cynical and accommodative attitudes toward a world in the process of going mad. [21]

II

In the context of contemporary critical theory, left-Hegelian formulas of "realizing reason" and promoting "a rational organization of society" have a disagreeably totalizing ring to them. Much in the early Horkheimer bears criticism on this score: his tendency to conceptualize society as at least potentially a unified subject with a unified will and hence to marginalize considerations of social, cultural, and political pluralism; his overreliance on Marxian political economy, particularly class analysis, in identifying the causes and conditions of injustice in existing social orders; his subscription to a philosophy of history or "grand metanarrative" that underplayed the roles of contingency, locality, and identity in struggles against oppression. These and other related weaknesses in Horkheimer's conception of critical theory have been spelled out repeatedly, even by theorists working within the Frankfurt School tradition. Because I am not concerned here with offering an overall assessment of his work, I shall focus on aspects of it that are of interest for contemporary debates by virtue of either lending support to or calling into question widely held views.

Given the widespread opposition to global accounts of reason and rationalization of any sort, it may be well to ask why this type of approach deserves to be considered at all. The complicated confluence of neo-Nietzschean and neo-Heideggerian thought with the concerns of new social movements has channeled intellectual energies increasingly into modes of social and cultural criticism more suited to a highly variegated "politics of identity." Feminist, minority, and Third World liberation theorists have, for understandable reasons, been highly critical of universalizing and globalizing approaches. And even social movements with prima facie universalist interests in peace, antinuclear, and environmental issues have often found the rhetoric of antirationalism more to their purposes than that of critical rationalism. Whatever the special demands of the different political situations, however, there is a case to be made against any totalization of the classical critique of reason and for its continuation in the medium of sociocultural studies. The facts that contextualist and perspectivalist accounts of rationality invariably fall into the self-referential or "performative" contradiction of having implicitly to presuppose what they want explicitly to deny, that the politics of otherness and difference makes sense only on the assumption of the very universalist values— freedom, justice, equality, respect, tolerance, dignity—that they seek to deconstruct, and that reported escapes into global ironizing are given the lie in every situation of personal or political exigency suggest that it is important to attempt the latter. Add to these the fact that deconstructionist thinkers have not balanced their jeremiads against "technoscience" with any even halfway convincing account of what Kant called the "lawful claims" of scientific and technological reasoning, and the suggestion becomes an admonition. It becomes an imperative if we consider further that any "politics of positionality," if it is not to be pursued by each group at the expense of others, will have to be guided by considerations of justice that will have to be justified to individuals and groups who, though not occupying the same position, are yet all supposed to feel bound by them.

These factors might still be outweighed by the welter of objections deconstructionists have raised against "logocentrism" if it were really a matter of having to choose between the universal and the particular.

This is the grand either-or structuring of postmodern rhetoric: either one is for the totality, necessity, authority, and homogeneity of the universal, or one rejects it in the name of the fragmentary, contingent, spontaneous, and heterogeneous particular. This neat opposition has been so often criticized that one can only marvel at its continued robustness—all the more so in light of the generally acknowledged need for the multiplicity of new social movements to forge some common ground. It is not enough merely to point to some common enemy such as, for example, global capitalism. This not only invites a correspondingly global account of the socioeconomic field in which all positions are located but also raises questions about the conceptual resources available for framing any such general account. One response has been to oppose what is pictured as traditional deductivism with a new kind of inductivism: let the different groups each work out the specifics of its own situation and then "generalize" through an expanding network of strategic affiliations and alliances with others.[22] This approach, however, soon runs up against problems analogous to those encountered by purely inductivist approaches in science. The very terms in which any particular is represented derive from some general understanding, however tacit. Parts selected and characterized from different points of view will not of themselves add up to a coherent whole. On the contrary, it is only when particular accounts are already informed by shared concepts, assumptions, values, criteria, and the like that they can be understood as belonging to the same universe of discourse. This is not to say that the general should always determine the particular any more than the converse. The relation between constructing general accounts and analyzing particular situations is best viewed as one of reciprocal influence and mutual coherence rather than one-way determination in either direction.

The dialectical relation between the universal and the particular, where each informs and is informed by the other, is an old story, which seems recently to have been forgotten. It entails that no generalizing approach to the critique of reason should serve as a closed framework for concrete studies or as the unimpeachable "tribunal" that Kant thought it to be. If the end of foundationalism means anything, it means at least the permanent openness of any proposed universal frame to deconstructive and reconstructive impulses from what Adorno called the "nonidentical." On the other hand, it is folly to suppose that social and cultural studies can get along without general conceptions of reason and rationalization. The interpretive and evaluative frameworks that invariably, albeit often tacitly, inform the ways in which sociocultural phenomena are selected, described, ordered, analyzed, appraised, and explained, typically include categories and assumptions tailored to grasping the "rationalization" of modern society. And these are usually of philosophical provenance, for the simple reason that modern philosophy has centered around the critique of reason. This is obvious in the work of classical social theorists like Marx, Durkheim, and Weber no less than in that of contemporary deconstructionist critics like Foucault, Derrida, and Rorty.[23] Accordingly, the presumption underlying my remarks here is that some general, "philosophical" level of analysis of ideas of reason, rationality, truth, objectivity, subjectivity, autonomy, and so forth is still of fundamental importance for critical social and cultural inquiry. This is, of course, not to say that it is the only significant mode of inquiry, or that it could replace more contextually specific modes, or that it is itself unaffected by the results of the latter.[24] The hope is that many of the objectionable features of the classical critique of reason can be overcome by deabsolutizing ideas of reason through stressing their relations to social practice and building deconstructive concerns into reconstructive endeavors from the start.

With this in mind, let us turn to Horkheimer's programmatic contrast between "Traditional and Critical Theory" and situate his approach in relation to views now current among critical theorists.[25] The axis on which the contrast turns is the reflexivity—in both its primary senses—of social inquiry. Horkheimer repeatedly insists both upon the fact that social researchers are themselves engaged in socially situated forms of social action and upon the importance of bringing this to conscious awareness and thinking through its implications. The social sciences, in modeling themselves after the natural sciences, attempted to position themselves centrally in an industrial society increasingly dependent on monitoring and managing key socioeconomic variables. By promoting a positivistic image of themselves as just telling it like it is, they could claim to offer a view from nowhere with all of its rights and privileges; other approaches thereby became marginalized as prescientific, ideological, self-interested, or the like. One of the first tasks of critical theory is to challenge the privileged "nonposition" of social-scientific knowledge by analyzing the modes of its production, the role it plays in society, the interests it serves, and the historical processes through which it came to power.

Leaving aside the details of Horkheimer's analysis, which reflects in key respects the Marxian political-economic framework he took over, it is important for contemporary discussions to note that he did not regard the deconstruction of allegedly disembodied social knowledge as entailing the delegitimation of empirical social research as such. On the contrary, processing and deploying vast bodies of "factual" knowledge is a requirement of any developed society. The need to produce knowledge useful for social reproduction within an established social framework would not disappear with organized capitalism (205). The problem arises from its absolutization, "as though it were grounded in the nature of knowledge as such or justified in some other ahistorical way" (194). And the solution is to recognize the sorts of interests that such knowledge serves in the present society, as well as the place it might occupy in a better society, and by thus "locating" it to leave ample space for other interests and other types of knowledge.

Unlike "traditional" theory, then, critical social theory takes as topics of investigation the reflexivity of social research, the division of labor—including scientific and scholarly labor—in which it is carried on, and its social functions—that is, it studies "what theory means in human life" (197). It reflects, in particular, on the contexts of its own genesis and application, that is, on its own embeddedness in the social matrix out of which it arises and within which it will find its uses. Unlike contemporary deconstructionists, however, Horkheimer does not understand this as prohibiting all but "local" knowledge. Rather, he seeks to locate both traditional and critical research within a broad account of contemporary society, which, he wants to claim, is more adequate than any of its competitors. I shall have more to say about that below. For now it will be worthwhile to explore a bit further the distinctive sense in which sociocultural knowledge is reflexive knowledge, for that is the key to its differences from natural science.

While the goals and directions of research in the natural sciences are less and less a purely intrascientific matter, in the social sciences the events, structures, and processes that influence the agenda of research also belong to the subject matter of research (195–96). More generally, social inquiry is a moment of the very process of social reproduction it aims to comprehend. The social world is produced and reproduced in and through the social actions of social actors, including the activities of agents engaged in analyzing it. This peculiar reflexivity has a number of implications. For one thing, it suggests a social constructionist view of social reality, which positivism completely misses with its passive, perceptual models of subject-object relations (200). For another, it means that the social subjects of knowledge are shaped by the same historical forces that shape their objects of knowledge; for them to understand something of the latter is also to understand something of themselves. Finally, it means that in some sense the topics and resources of social inquiry are the same: the social world is itself constructed in part by the very ideas that researchers employ to understand it (200–1). This is true, in particular, of the types of social research carried on within established social structures, for example, in studying business and administration. The domain of objects investigated is in some measure reproduced by activities according to the very notions used to comprehend it (202). Thus, what C. Wright Mills would later call "bureaucratic" social science could largely restrict itself to processing data with conceptual resources that were themselves operative in the very production of the phenomena being studied.

Critical social theory breaks with that type of approach by, among other things, taking the reflexivity of social inquiry explicitly into account. This entails a challenge to the traditional dichotomies between genesis and justification, justification and application, fact and value, and so forth, which were used to rope off a "neutral" field for social research (208). Critical theory is concerned precisely with the historical and social genesis of the facts it examines and with the social contexts in which its results will have their effects. It stresses that social research is itself a form of social interaction in which the objects of knowledge are potentially subjects of the very same knowledge, and thus that it is willy-nilly a potential factor in changing social relations. Consciously taking up this reflexive relation to social practice, critical social theory expressly aims at becoming a factor in social change by becoming part of the self-consciousness of oppressed social groups. It does not consider the purposes it serves to be external to the context of inquiry.

Through a social-practical reformulation of certain Kantian ideas, Horkheimer could argue that the moral-political orientation of critical social inquiry was not arbitrary but inherently rational. In the framework of the philosophy of consciousness, Kant had argued that reason was at bottom a capacity not for speculation but for freedom. Once we turn our attention from consciousness to culture and society, the privileged status that Western philosophy has generally accorded to knowledge and representation becomes even less plausible. In fact, if knowledge itself is understood to be a social product, the traditional oppositions between theory and practice, fact and value, and the like break down, for there are practical dimensions to any social activity, theorizing included. Translated into social-theoretical terms, the primacy of practical reason means, according to Horkheimer, that an interest in "reasonable conditions of life" is intrinsic to the exercise of our rational capacities. We shall have an opportunity below to consider how he connects this with an interest in a just organization of society.[26] At present it is important to note that this practical concern enters into the very construction of a critical theory and is at work in the research processes informed by the theory. It is, in fact, what lends consistency and coherency to a tradition of thought that accepts the ongoing necessity of adapting its concepts, theories, techniques, and the like to an ever-changing reality. "To strive for a state of affairs in which there will be no exploitation or oppression . . . is not to bring it to pass. The transmission of critical theory in as rigorous a fashion as possible is a condition of its historical success. That transmission does not, however, take place via established practices and fixed procedures but via an interest in social change. This interest is aroused ever anew by prevailing injustices, but it must be shaped and guided by the theory and in turn react back upon it" (241).

One can, and Horkheimer sometimes does, formulate the practical interest that guides and shapes critical theory in "pragmatic" terms of striving to reduce suffering and promote happiness. In this formulation, the moral-political ideas that give expression to that interest function only regulatively, not constitutively; that is, they serve to guide and evaluate thought and action but not to represent realized or realizable states of affairs. But too often Horkheimer formulates that interest in terms of the holistic representations with which the Marxist tradition abounds. Thus, he readily translates "reasonable conditions of life" into a "rational organization of society" in which an "all-embracing subject" does away with "the opposition between the individual's purposefulness, spontaneity, and rationality, and the processes and relations of social labor on which society is built" (210). The idealist conception of freedom as self-conscious self-determination is thereby projected onto a unified macrosubject of which individuals are harmonious moments. It is against just such "totalizing" representations that postmodernist thinkers have launched their most telling attacks. But there is no need to construe the sociocultural embodiment of practical reason in those terms. Thus, Habermas, who uses a similar figure of thought, criticizes this construal as a residue of the "philosophy of consciousness" in Hegelian-Marxist thought and focuses instead on the conditions and procedures of democratic pluralism. But here I want to consider again another matter: the usefulness of grand narratives and big pictures.

Sociocultural critique is best thought of as a polymorphic, multilayered, and multidimensional enterprise. Not all critical work need be or can be done in the same way or at the same level of specificity or generality. Moreover, determining for what purposes and in what contexts different groups occupy the same or different "positions" inevitably involves pragmatic considerations. There is no objective reason why, for certain purposes and in certain contexts, a more universal "we" should not be appropriate. It could be useful, for instance, in attacking the cultural supports of a general order of domination from which numerous groups suffer or in analyzing the expanding global networks of symbolic and material interchange. Critics who appeal to one notion or another of encapsulated forms of life to deny that in some important respects we are all living in the same situation are simply themselves living in the past. We do not have first to create a global space; that is already being done, and at breakneck speed.[27] To understand this process better, we have to go beyond local cultural studies and try to understand the internationalization of politics and economics, science and technology, information and communication that now affects the inside of every local culture.

Cultural criticism is not the self-sufficient, self-enclosed undertaking its more textualistically inclined practitioners sometimes make it appear to be. For obvious reasons, critics located in the humanities tend to foreground the sorts of phenomena they have been trained to identify and analyze and to move everything else to the background. We can use only the tools at our disposal, but that need not prevent us from recognizing that such phenomena are embedded in a broader social matrix and from acknowledging the interdependence of "textual" studies with social and cultural studies of various other sorts. One of the broadest goals of a genuinely multidisciplinary research practice would be a "critical theory of the present," that is, a general view of contemporary society and its problems and prospects. That is what Horkheimer referred to as a "comprehensive existential judgment," which he delivered in classical Marxist terms (227). Writing in the midst of profound socioeconomic changes, however, he added an important qualifier: owing to the continuous transformation of its object, this is a judgment with an ineliminable historical dimension (239). Thus, critical theory has to be understood as an ongoing attempt to "reflect a living totality" (237), an ever-renewed effort to comprehend contemporary society from a practically interested point of view. "It is not a metaphysics of history but rather a changing picture of the world that develops in connection with practical efforts to improve it . . . [and that] offers no clear prognosis for historical development." [28] To be sure, Horkheimer himself was convinced that this object would remain essentially the same so long as capitalism was the dominant social formation, and thus that the "essential content" of Marxist political economy would remain valid through all the necessary adaptations and adjustments (238–40). But there is no need to take this position to see the value of situating local cultural practices within a larger field of relationships. It is, in fact, not difficult to show that antiholistic critics usually rely on some general view of contemporary society, its tensions, and its tendencies in conceiving and carrying out their specific interventions. Because these big pictures are seldom openly avowed, they do not get properly scrutinized and thus function largely as sets of unexamined assumptions. To many, this is preferable, it seems, to running the risks of totalizing thought. But those are not the only alternatives. Critical theorists can develop and deploy practically interested, theoretically informed, general accounts in a fallibilistic and open manner, that is, without claiming closure. The point, here too, is to view big pictures and grand narratives as ongoing accomplishments. They are never finished but have to be constructed, deconstructed, and reconstructed in ever-changing circumstances. If such global accounts are going to play a role in any case, it is better to put them up for discussion from the start.

Locating particular practices in a larger field is one way of gaining distance from them, of not leaving the final word about their significance to participants and their traditions. Critical theorists of very different stripes agree in seeing a need for some such "outsider's" perspective to get beyond shared meanings and their hermeneutic retrieval. Foucault's way of creating distance from the practices we live in, for instance, is to display their "lowly origins" in contingent historical circumstances, to dispel their appearance of self-evident givenness by treating them as the outcome of multiple relations of force. The Frankfurt School approach is also based on a rejection of what Marx characterized as the specific "German ideology" of understanding ideas solely in terms of other ideas. Its guiding principle is that the full significance of ideas can be grasped only by viewing them in the context of the social practices in which they figure and by studying the genesis, structures, and functions of those practices. And its underlying intention is to transform our self-understanding in ways that affect how we live. Gaining a critical perspective on what is normally taken for granted—for instance, by showing that the genesis of what has heretofore seemed universal and necessary involves contingent relations of force and an arbitrary closing off of alternatives, or that what parades as fair and impartial actually helps to maintain unjustifiable imbalances in social benefits and burdens—can affect the way we act. Ideas and beliefs, values and norms, standards and procedures formerly accepted as purely and simply rational may come to be seen as in the service of particular interests, and this may undermine the authority that derives from their presumed rationality. Whether this is so, and the extent to which it is so, are not matters of conceptual necessity or theoretical inference but of contingent historical conditions. The practical significance of critical insight varies with the circumstances.

While critical social theory does not take participants' views of their practices as the last word in interpreting and assessing them, it differs from exclusively deconstructionist approaches in taking them seriously, in seeking to engage them in the very process of gaining distance from them. In a word, it treats them dialectically. In particular, the dialectical critique of reason does not abstractly negate ideas of reason but seeks critically to appropriate them and to enlist them in the struggle for a better world. Thus, in an essay entitled "Philosophy and Critical Theory," published in the *Zeitschrift für Sozialforschung* in the same year as Horkheimer's "Traditional and Critical Theory," Herbert Marcuse stressed that idealist and individualist conceptions of reason and rational practice were not mere ideology, for they established reason as a critical instance: "The individual was to examine and judge everything given," and this meant that "the concept of reason contained the concept of freedom as well. For such examination and judgment would be meaningless if human beings were not free to act in accordance with their insights." [29] From his perspective, it was precisely the situation-transcendent import of ideas of reason—a red flag to strict deconstructionists—that was their saving grace. Critical theory "opposes making reality into a criterion. . . . When truth cannot be realized within the established order, it always appears to the latter as mere utopia. This transcendence speaks not against, but for, its truth. The utopian element was long the only progressive element in philosophy." [30] This interest in the "truth content" of ideas, Marcuse went on, distinguishes critical theory from the type of strictly contextualist approach of the sociology of knowledge. Research that considers only "the dependent and limited nature of consciousness" betrays critical theory's "interest in the liberation of human beings." That interest "binds it to certain ancient truths"—"universal propositions whose progressive impetus derives precisely from their universality . . . for they claim that everyone . . . should be rational, free, and happy." In a society that "gives the lie to all these universals . . . adherence to universality is more important than its philosophical destruction." [31] The tension between an established social order and the ideas of reason it relies on is just the point at which dialectical critique drives its wedge.

In the same vein, Horkheimer urged critical theorists not to surrender such ideas to the regressive forces who used them to justify their privileged positions and betrayed them whenever it was in their interest to do so. They should, instead, critically reappropriate them for progressive purposes: "The battle cries of the Enlightenment and of the French Revolution are valid now more than ever. The dialectical critique of the world borne along by them consists precisely in showing that they have retained rather than lost their actuality. . . . Politics should not abandon those demands, but realize them . . . not, however, by clinging in utopian fashion to historically conditioned definitions of them, but in accordance with their meaning. The content of these ideas is not eternal but subject to historical change . . . because the human impulses that demand something better take [historically] different forms." [32]

The context-transcendence of ideas of reason harbors not only a utopian but also a subversive potential, for claims to unconditional validity are permanently exposed to criticism from all sides. Understood in this way, they point in the opposite direction from those metaphysical representations that occupy deconstructionist critics—toward an ongoing critique of dogmatism, bias, and self-deception in their many forms. The tension between the real and the ideal that their context-transcendent import builds into the constructions of social life marks a normative surplus of meaning that critical theorists can draw upon in seeking to transcend and transform the limits of their situations. In short, the dialectical critique of reason is "internal" rather than "total."

One might well ask whether the latter option is available to deconstructionists, for we are always and inescapably participants in social life, before, during, and after any critical studies in which we might engage. There is no extramundane standpoint from which we can set our social world as a whole at a distance. It is thus not surprising that would-be total critics of Western "logocentrism" invariably rely on the same idealizing presuppositions regarding meaning, reference, truth, logic, and so forth that they seek to undercut and that the radical critics of modern rationalism continually draw on assumptions specific to the modern worldview, such as the disenchantment of the world and the possibility of reflectively questioning inherited beliefs and values, gaining critical distance from traditional roles and norms, and challenging ascribed individual and group identities. Nor is it surprising that the values that underlie their criticisms typically include a host of distinctively modern orientations toward pluralism, diversity, tolerance, human dignity, equal respect, and the like. Accordingly, there must be an "analytical" as well as a "dialectical" side to any critique of reason, for it will be important to identify and analyze those presuppositions to which participants in the discourse of modernity have either no alternative at all or none they would care to defend.

Thomas McCarthy

III

In a "Postscript" to Marcuse's "Philosophy and Critical Theory," Horkheimer endorsed the idea that critical social theory could be understood as inheriting philosophy's concern with the life of reason.[33] Its defining insight, he agreed, is that the possibility of giving reasonable form to individual existence depends upon the possibility of instituting reasonable conditions of social life, and thus that philosophy's concern with the life of reason has to be continued at the level of social theory. Like Marcuse, Horkheimer characterized the object of the practical interest guiding critical social inquiry as a "free, self-determining society," which he went on to specify in terms of "real agreement" in a "real democracy," whose overriding aim is "the happiness of all individuals" in a "world that satisfies the needs and powers of human beings."[34] Or, as he elsewhere put it, "concern for the abolition of injustice . . . is the materialist content of the idealist concept of reason."[35] This general strategy of linking a deindividualized conception of practical reason to the theory of justice is familiar today in the versions of neo-Kantianism developed by Rawls, Habermas, and others. A bridge from the 1930s discussion to the contemporary discussions can be constructed from elements of Horkheimer's critique of Kantian ethics in a 1933 essay, "Materialism and Morality."[36]

Horkheimer stressed that morality and moral theory in their current senses are historical phenomena that have to be understood in historical terms. On his account, their characteristic opposition between duty and interest, the universal and the particular, is an expression of the tension in capitalist society between the possessive individualism required to thrive in a market economy and a concern for the general welfare that, invisible-hand notions notwithstanding, is ill served by market mechanisms. Against the background of the inequitable distribution of misery and happiness, burdens and pleasures, poverty and wealth that have resulted from capitalist development, the move from traditional ethics to rationalist moralities of the Kantian type can be seen as shifting the burden of deep-seated social tensions to the site of the individual conscience. It is the isolated moral subject who must struggle to overcome the opposition between self-interest and the general interest, precisely by renouncing the former in the name of the latter. The spiritualized universalism that commands in the moral domain is just the other face of the narrow egoism that reigns in the marketplace. It is, Horkheimer argues, just this transposition of sociostructural problems into the inner lives of individuals that is the ideological function of morality, for there is no possibility of reducing the tension between individual goods and the common good through the moral intentions of individual agents acting within the given institutional framework. A social-structural problem requires a social-structural response, which Horkheimer characterizes generally as the effective incorporation of individuals into collective decision-making processes.

To say that modern moral theory in its paradigmatic Kantian form is a contingent historical construction that has to be understood genealogically is, for Horkheimer, not to say that it is merely ideology or false consciousness and should therefore be dismantled without remainder. It possesses a truth content as well, which it is the task of his dialectical critique to free from its ideological trappings, transform, and retain in a more adequate conception of the relation between the universal and the particular. The idea of their reconciliation that Kant elaborated under the title of "the highest good" and set as the goal for a moral politics could not, as he evidently saw, be even approximately realized within the existing order of society. In projecting its realization into the noumenal beyond, he gave distorted expression to the truth that morality impels us to transcend the social order that gave birth to it, an order in tension with the very idea of practical reason to which it appeals for justification. It is precisely the utopian element in Kant's idea of a perfected order in which the conflict between self-interest and the general interest is overcome that dialectical critique takes as the point of transition to its reconstructive movement.

Horkheimer never discussed at any length the institutions and procedures that might effectively allow individuals to have a voice in the collective decision-making processes that were to replace the blind operation of market forces. He was much more concerned with recentering the eudaemonistic element of ethics that had been marginalized in moral theory. But he repeatedly insisted that the ideals of freedom, justice, and equality not be surrendered to the regressive forces that had expropriated them to justify unnecessary suffering. Rather, they were to be reclaimed and deployed in the struggle against the causes of human misery. "Dialectical critique [is] borne along by them. . . . [They] are nothing but the isolated traits of a rational society as anticipated in morality. Politics should not abandon these demands but realize them." [37] But first they had to be freed from their moralistic confines by shifting theoretical attention away from private efforts by isolated individuals to subdue unruly inclinations and toward collective efforts by social groups to transform unjust relations. Though guided by universal ideals, the public politics that was thus to reclaim center stage from private morality could not cling to unchanging formulations of them. Their content was "not eternal but subject to historical change; they took different forms in different historical circumstances." [38] That is, the concrete meaning or content of abstract ideas and principles had to be continuously reinscribed into ever changing contexts. This general commitment to political and social ideals that are universal in import but require ongoing recontextualization is common to most critical social theorists. But another element in Horkheimer's *Aufhebung* of Kantian morality distinguishes his position strongly from the one later elaborated by Habermas: he replaces Kant's "fact of pure reason" with an "ungrounded feeling" of compassion for suffering humankind.

Morality, he wrote, "admits of no grounding, neither through intuition nor through argument. Rather, it represents a frame of mind. To describe the latter, to make comprehensible its personal conditions and the mechanisms for transmitting it from generation to generation is the business of psychology." [39] At its center, Horkheimer ventured, is a moral feeling or sentiment *(Gefühl)* directed toward all persons as potential members of a happy human race, to their needs and capacities, to the alleviation of their suffering and the development of their powers. To this moral sentiment "it appears that all living beings have a claim to happiness, for which it asks no justification or grounds." [40] The specific form this sentiment takes in our day, "when the poverty of humanity cries out in such contradiction to its potential wealth," is sympathy or compassion *(Mitleid)*. [41] It expresses itself in a "solidarity" with the wretched of the earth that motivates the critical theorist to pursue a politics aimed at realizing universal ideals while transforming them. [42]

Notwithstanding the attractions of this way of avoiding problems of "grounding," [43] Horkheimer's account creates as many problems as it solves. Granted that feelings of indignation, compassion, love, solidarity, and the like neither need nor admit of philosophical grounding in pure practical reason, the issue remains whether they are susceptible to rational criticism and justification in any sense. The fact that questions such as: Sympathy with whom? Solidarity with which side? Indignation at what? can be, are, and should be repeatedly raised and critically considered suggest that the sharp split between irrational feelings and rational discourse is another untenable opposition that has to be broken down. To drop the idea of pure rational motivation is not to deny that motives can be elaborated, criticized, defended, and shaped by reasons, particularly when these are presented in the context of communicative exchanges with other agents moved by similar or different motives. Moreover, as Horkheimer himself is at pains to insist, psychic dispositions have to be viewed in relation to established social and cultural patterns. It is in this vein, for instance, that he explains the consciousness of a pure rational ought, the feeling of being bound by absolute commands, as a sublime form of internalized social compulsion. Thus, he cannot treat the psychic disposition he calls moral feeling as an independent variable prior to and unaffected by social relations. Why should we accord such special status to a feeling for the feelings of all other human beings or an interest in the generalizability of interests? Are they and the corresponding universalist ideals any more than mere curiosities of particular historical cultures?

One source of these problems is Horkheimer's jump from the absence of pure rational—that is, nonempirical—motivations for morality to the absence of any rational justification of its basic commands. A related source is the tendency he has to equate rational justification with ultimate grounding of some sort. Because we cannot have the latter, we must do without the former as well. If, however, Horkheimer had introduced into his discussion of morality the nonfoundationalist sense of rational justification he appealed to in his discussion of truth, this connection could not have been sustained. He analyzed the validation of truth claims in terms of demonstrating their rational acceptability, not absolutely but with respect to "the available means of knowledge" and in the fallibilistic awareness that these might well change. Had he adopted a similar approach to justice claims, he could have avoided the pitfall of equating rational warrants with a priori foundations, and thus the necessity of choosing between reasons and feelings. He was, of course, not the last to fall into that crowded pit.

Adopting a more pragmatic approach to moral justification also would have fit quite well with Horkheimer's historical account, in connection with his analysis of modern ideologies, of how the appeal to generally acceptable reasons comes to play an ever greater role in legitimating social orders. With the disappearance of value-imbued cosmologies, the privatization of religion, and the growing disenchantment of the world, it is increasingly the only form of justification available. As a result, it becomes more and more difficult to convince exploited and oppressed groups that they deserve their suffering and that their tormentors deserve whatever degrees of power, privilege, and wealth they happen to enjoy. The early modern ideologies that once accomplished this improbable task have been and continue to be relentlessly shredded with the sharp tools of criticism. This increasingly leaves contemporary societies with very little else to appeal to in legitimating their laws, institutions, and policies than the free and reasoned agreement of their members. But is this state of affairs anything more than an arbitrary outcome of contingent historical processes? What, in particular, does it have to do with practical reason?

Once we get beyond the Hobbesian-Cartesian paradigm of the solitary subject as the proper framework for analyzing the structures of thought and action, once we acknowledge their intrinsically social character, agreements freely arrived at on the basis of considering reasons pro and con come to be central to the conception of rationality in theory and in practice. This has been argued in respect to truth claims from Pierce to Putnam and Habermas and in respect to justice claims from Mead to Rawls and Habermas. Whatever problems there may be with specific proposals, it is becoming increasingly difficult to think of plausible alternatives to one form or another of communicative rationality. If some such approach to practical reason could be sustained, then the gap that Horkheimer saw between ungroundable feelings of compassion and rational justification of universal ideals would not be as unbridgeable as it seemed. One could then argue both in a neo-Kantian vein that democratic forms of decision making best accord with the communicative structure of practical reason and in a neo-Aristotelian or neo-Hegelian vein that the dispositions of character and motivation needed to sustain democratic institutions and practices can be reliably reproduced only in certain types of sociocultural settings. It is just this sort of dual-track program that Habermas has attempted to develop in his theory of communicative action.

Notes

1. I shall not consider the quite different version of critical theory, more Nietzschean in spirit, propounded by Horkheimer and Adorno in the 1940s, particularly in their *Dialectic of Enlightenment,* trans. John Cumming (New York, 1972). In the case of Horkheimer, the changes took place gradually, after the National Socialists came to power and the Institute was moved first to Geneva and then to New York. They are already evident in his 1937 essay, "Traditional and Critical Theory," trans. Matthew J. O'Connell, in Max Horkheimer, *Critical Theory* (New York, 1972), 188–243, and in his 1939 piece, "The Social Function of Philosophy," also in *Critical Theory,* 253–72, both of which I shall discuss below but without noting the shifts that are underway. In general, I shall not be attempting to present a balanced interpretation of the early Horkheimer but merely developing a few points that strike me as especially relevant to contemporary debates in and about critical theory.

2. Immanuel Kant, *Critique of Pure Reason,* trans. Norman Kemp Smith (New York, 1961), 9.

3. Max Horkheimer, "The State of Contemporary Social Philosophy and the Tasks of an Institute for Social Research," trans. Peter Wagner, in Stephan Bronner and Douglas Kellner, eds., *Critical Theory and Society* (New York, 1989), 31, 36, and in *Between Philosophy and Social Science: Selected Early Writings* (Cambridge, 1993), *BPSS* hereafter. Translation altered. Henceforth, existing translations will be altered as required for consistency or accuracy, without special note of the fact.

4. Max Horkheimer, "Zum Rationalismustreit in der gegenwärtigen Philosophie," in Horkheimer, *Kritische Theorie* (Frankfurt, 1968), 1:145/*BPSS.*

5. Ibid., 149.

6. Max Horkheimer, "Ein neuer Ideologiebegriff?" in V. Meja and N. Stehr, eds., *Der Streit um die Wissenssoziologie* (Frankfurt, 1982), 2:485/*BPSS.*

7. Ibid., 485–86.

8. Max Horkheimer, "On the Problem of Truth," in Andrew Arato and Eike Gebhardt, eds., *The Essential Frankfurt School Reader* (New York, 1978), 407–43.

9. Ibid., 421.

10. "The Social Function of Philosophy," 257.

11. Ibid., 261.

12. Ibid., 265.

13. Ibid., 268.

14. Ibid., 269.

15. Ibid., 264.

16. "On the Problem of Truth," 418.

17. "Zum Rationalismusstreit," 150.

18. Max Horkheimer, "Materialism and Metaphysics," in *Critical Theory*, 11–12.

19. Ibid., 13.

20. "Ein neuer Ideologiebegriff?" 487.

21. "Zum Rationalismusstreit," 158ff.

22. Something along these lines is suggested, for example, by Ernesto Laclau and Chantal Mouffe in their *Hegemony and Socialist Strategy* (London, 1985).

23. I argued this for the last three in part I of *Ideals and Illusions: On Reconstruction and Deconstruction in Contemporary Critical Theory* (Cambridge, Mass., 1991), 11–123.

24. It goes without saying that "philosophical" critique carried on as a form of sociocultural analysis will not be as directly related to political practice—as timely, situation specific, action oriented, and so forth—as less academic forms of cultural politics or even as some other academic forms of cultural criticism. Dealing as it does with the most general, abstract, and thus situation-nonspecific of our cultural resources, its analyses will not be tailored to any given, particular audience—which is not to say that it is aimed at no audience—nor, typically, will the impact of its results be restricted to one particular discipline—which is not to say that it floats free of all disciplinary settings. The continuation-cum-transformation of the universalist mode of discourse characteristic of traditional philosophy is, all aseverations to the contrary notwithstanding, quite evident in the work of such contemporary practitioners of philosophically oriented cultural criticism as Derrida, Foucault, Habermas, and Rorty. Their work also makes clear that this level of analysis can be pursued without renewing the theoretically and practically objectionable claims of traditional philosophy to be *the* voice of reason, truth, and justice.

25. See note 1. Page references to this essay appear in parentheses in the text.

26. On 213 he says that this interest is "immanent in human labor." I shall not be pursuing that line of thought, however, but the one developed earlier in his 1933 essay, "Materialism and Morality," trans. Frederick Hunter and John Torpey, *Telos* 69 (1986):85–118 and reprinted in Horkheimer, *Between Philosophy and Social Science* (Cambridge, Mass., 1993).

27. George Marcus and Michael Fischer stress this point in regard to interpretative anthropology in *Anthropology as Cultural Critique* (Chicago, 1986).

28. "Materialism and Morality," 114.

29. Herbert Marcuse, "Philosophy and Critical Theory," trans. Jeremy J. Shapiro, in *Negations* (Boston, 1968), 136.

30. Ibid., 143.

31. Ibid., 152–53.

32. "Materialism and Morality," 108.

33. Max Horkheimer, "Postscript," in *Critical Theory*, 244–52.

34. Ibid., 248–50.

35. "Traditional and Critical Theory," 242.

36. See note 32. See also chapter 11 in this book.

37. "Materialism and Morality," 108.

38. Ibid.

39. Ibid., 104.

40. Ibid., 106.

41. Ibid.

42. Ibid., 107.

43. Compare Richard Rorty's rejection of any sort of grounding for morality beyond compassion for and solidarity with those who suffer, in *Contingency, Irony, and Solidarity* (Cambridge, 1989), and my critique in *Ideals and Illusions*, 35–42.

7

Stranded at the Crossroads of Dehumanization: John Desmond Bernal and Max Horkheimer

Wolf Schäfer

We know only a single science, the science of history. One can look at history from two sides and divide it into the history of nature and the history of men. The two sides are, however, inseparable; the history of nature and the history of men are dependent on each other so long as men exist. The history of nature, called natural science, does not concern us here; but we will have to examine the history of men, since almost the whole ideology amounts either to a distorted conception of this history or to a complete abstraction from it.

Karl Marx and Friedrich Engels, The German Ideology, *1845–1846*[1]

Science is much too important to be left to the scientists.
James B. Conant, after World War II[2]

The time has come for Karl Marx and Friedrich Engels to be quoted like Friedrich Schiller or Johann Wolfgang Goethe, names of famous German writers who sound familiar but are not read by the masses. Anyone who refers to them now may just want to show off an Old World education or may indeed have a genuine interest—a literary, historical, or philosophical reason. The withering away of Soviet-type state socialism has helped Marx and Engels to become true classics at last, if we can define true classics as sources that invite continuous interpretation and reinterpretation, so that even seasoned readers can return to the same text and always learn more from it.

To welcome the incorporation of the works of Marx and Engels into the library of immortal texts is perhaps not inappropriate in a volume on Max Horkheimer, the doyen of critical theory. Horkheimer and his close associates read Marx and Engels with subtle minds and not with reverential awe and brains turned off. They quoted Engels, Marx, Kant, Freud, and Weber in a scholarly and not an ideological manner. They felt free to question the role of the working class in the twentieth century, the dogmatization of class struggle and economic substructure.[3] In addition, the Horkheimer school of critical theory emigrated to New York and not to Moscow and returned to West and not to East Germany. It valued economic and intellectual independence as well as individual liberty and satisfaction. It was orthodox in the legacy of Marx, the scholar, but not in the dreadful tradition of oppressive Marxism. Today, Frankfurt School critical theorists are firm defenders of liberal democracy and civil society.

I intend to problematize a blind spot and not to dwell on what is admirable in the academic field of critical thought running from Marx to Horkheimer, Habermas, and beyond. While critical theory was creative and rather effective in building small, interdisciplinary bridges joining philosophy, psychoanalysis, and social psychology and in connecting economics, sociology, literature, and music, it failed to overcome the bigger and more important divide between the social and natural sciences, modern technology and humanistic philosophy. I propose to critique critical theory for restricting its research program to the humanities and social sciences—a shortcoming similar to that of Karl Mannheim's rival theory of knowledge, which exempted physics, mathematics, and logic from sociological inquiry.[4]

The two quotations at the head of this chapter may be read as defining the historico-theoretical context of my critique. They mark important steps toward our understanding of the social function of technoscience in 1845 and 1945, respectively. At one end rise Marx and Engels. When they developed their materialistic theory of history in *The German Ideology*, they stressed the mutual interdependence—as long as humans exist—of the history of nature and of humans; they emphasized that natural and social history are but two sides of one history. The tantalizing lines made a powerful statement in favor of perceiving history as an inseparable history of nature and society. Yet the passage concluded by bracketing the history of nature; once again, the natural side of history was snuffed out—if we follow this quotation to the close. But the fact that the passage was deleted[5] by the authors seems to indicate that they themselves felt that it does not make much materialistic sense to consider ideology as an issue only in the "history of men."

At the other end stands the Yankee scientist and Harvard president, James Bryant Conant, who flatly declared in 1945 that one can no longer have an adequate understanding of human history, at least modern human history, without an adequate understanding of the natural sciences.[6] Conant had been deeply impressed by his intimate and privileged encounter with natural science at war, an experience of fundamental change shrouded in secrecy. He had concluded that a democratic society cannot afford to entrust science to the experts, that modern technoscience is much too big and too fateful to be handled by insiders only, and that it is dangerous if nonscientists are forced by ignorance to regard the technological offspring of scientific work as the output of an alien culture. He began to tackle the received illiteracy regarding the scientific-technical side of history and to use his elevated position to institutionalize educational remedies.[7]

Conant's discontent was timely and acute. By now, both the reality of technoscience and public ignorance about it had reached critical proportions. But the issue of widespread unfamiliarity with the hard core of modern culture did not come to the fore until the late 1950s and early 1960s. It was then universally recognized as the problem of the "two cultures." This, however, was unintentionally achieved by the English scientist and novelist Charles Percy Snow. His Rede Lecture delivered in 1959, "The Two Cultures and the Scientific Revolution,"[8] drew attention, heightened by a nasty attack,[9] and prompted a lively international debate about the state of science in modern culture.[10]

I will proceed from two basic assumptions. First, Marx and Engels were right about the two sides of human history. Second, neglecting either half of history, the social or the natural, is to distort one side or the other—and therefore the understanding of the whole. Theoretically, critical Marxian social theory had connected the two sides of history since 1845, but practically it kept ignoring the culture of the natural sciences. Thus, the bracketing of natural science and the human history of nature in *The German Ideology* constituted an ur-failing that was repeated over and over again, from Marx to Horkheimer, Habermas, and beyond. But what is true for the locals on one side of the cultural equation is also true for the folks who work the other side. Most practitioners of natural science are comparatively illiterate when it comes to understanding philosophy, the humanities, and the social sciences. This mutual unfamiliarity with the respective other side of history prevents the actors on both sides from adequately addressing historical issues. A case in point is "dehumanization," a far-reaching technodream on one side and radical technocritique on the other. These two versions of a half-truth are presented by local actors on the split screen of the two cultures, here by the scientist John Desmond Bernal (1901–1971) and the philosopher Max Horkheimer (1895–1973).

The setting for a comparative biographical experiment is perfect. There is no record of a historical encounter: they never met and almost certainly did not know about each other. Outside this book, no reference to Bernal can be found in the literature about Horkheimer, and vice versa.[11] This provides an ideal opportunity to demonstrate that it makes sense to mention Bernal and Horkheimer in one breath and on the same page. Indeed, I will go further and argue that the high probability of finding complementary figures like Bernal and Horkheimer disconnected and uncompared in our memory, history, and intellectual life is a symptom of the very cultural schism and bifurcated history that has been the object of serious educational, political, and social concern since Conant and Snow.[12]

Bernal and Horkheimer: each can be taken to embody one of the two cultures. Horkheimer is at home on the side of the world of words, our traditional humanistic culture, which is oriented toward the interpretation, creation, and transmission of great texts; Bernal represents the world of laboratories, our natural science culture, which creates great machines and is programmed to explain, manipulate, and transform nature. These two halves of culture, separated for quite some time, do not have much in common beyond reciprocal prejudices. Thus, the philosopher's deep thought is so much "hot air"[13] to the scientist, and the scientist's confidence in the future—the expectation of "more jam tomorrow"—is greeted by his critic as artificially sweetened "human emptiness."[14]

Since the end of World War II and with the spread of public knowledge about the role of technoscience in the secret research and development projects of the warring states, countless discussions have taken place on the dangers, as well as the prospects, of modern science and technology. Most participants in the discussion share the conviction that a rational orientation of scientific-technological progress would be beneficial for all humankind, yet a generally accepted solution has never been found. Attempts at certain junctures to steer the progress of modern science and technology in the "right" direction have regularly failed. Of course, the inability to reach consensus about choosing the right way has more than one cause. I submit, however, that it is not insignificant that the discussants of this problem generally occupy separate continents of culture, lead different intellectual lives, and do not speak the same language.

Comparing the technodream of the crystallographer Bernal with the technocritique of the social philosopher Horkheimer demonstrates this cultural apartheid and shows that the split of the two cultures touches even those minds that we rightfully consider original, independent, and outstanding. Even the most exceptional brain is biased toward the culture it is nurtured by. Its thinking may span many social and political boundaries but not necessarily the main cultural break. Neither Bernal nor Horkheimer stands above the two cultures; rather, each man is rooted in his domain and affected by its current state. Horkheimer's remarkable pessimism pays tribute to a declining literary-philosophical culture and Bernal's astonishing optimism to a rising natural-scientific and technological one. The philosopher and the scientist interpret the world differently not only due to their own subjective inclinations but also in accordance with assumptions taken for granted in each of the two cultures. This is all the more the case because the usual variations in social origin, political inclinations, and professional careers are not particularly significant in the case of Bernal and Horkheimer. Both men came from relatively well-to-do families, both committed themselves as students to Marx and socialism, and both attained stable academic positions when still young.

Bernal was born on an estate in Ireland. His friend C. P. Snow remarked: "To anyone interested in social niceties, Bernal was by birth an Irish Catholic gentleman who had an upper class English education and spoke all his life with the accent of a privileged Englishman."[15] The Bernal family, however, is presumably of Sephardic descent. An apothecary Bernal participated in 1502 in Columbus's third expedition to North America; an Abraham Nunez Bernal was burned at the stake in 1654 in Cordoba; a brother escaped via Holland to England; his descendants adopted the Catholic faith in Ireland.[16] The ten-year-old John Desmond was sent to a Jesuit boys' boarding school in England and remained "always a man of faith,"[17] be it Catholic or Communist.

Horkheimer was born in a villa in Stuttgart. His father, Moses Horkheimer, was a successful textile industrialist in Württemberg. The elder Horkheimer viewed his religion as a private matter and resisted leaving Germany until 1938–1939: "My family has been living here longer than that of Herr Hitler," he informed his son, who had emigrated to the United States.[18] Max Horkheimer became an American citizen. He is one of the few German Jewish intellectuals who returned to his native land after the collapse of the Third Reich. Horkheimer resumed the professorial chair he was forced to leave in 1933 and rebuilt the Institute for Social Research. In 1951, he was elected president of the University of Frankfurt, "the first Jew in the history of the German university."[19]

Bernal's and Horkheimer's political orientation is similar until the mid-1930s only. Horkheimer established contact with left-wing student groups during his undergraduate years, criticized the reformist line of Wilhelmine as well as Weimar Social Democracy, and followed with "a beating heart" the Soviet effort to overcome the "frightening social injustice" of the capitalist world.[20] But Horkheimer never joined a party and, beginning with the Moscow trials, increasingly lost faith in orthodox Marxism and the Bolshevik experiment. In 1969 he explained: "I recognize in Marx, but certainly not in his followers, a great thinker, but not so great that one would place him before Kant or Hegel."[21]

Bernal joined two left-wing parties, the large British Labour party and the small Communist party of Great Britain. In 1923 he left the latter but only for tactical reasons.[22] In reality Bernal never gave up his lifelong affiliation with the Communist party or his unwavering and repeatedly expressed trust in the historical mission of the Soviet Union and its "great leader." In 1953, after Stalin's death, Bernal praised the Soviet dictator as "the greatest figure of contemporary history" and, in addition to this generous overstatement, as a "great scientist."[23]

Bernal and Horkheimer both enjoyed early success in the academy, irrespective of their less than conventional political views. Horkheimer received Frankfurt's chair in social philosophy, at the age of thirty-five, and became director of the Institute for Social Research, replacing the ailing Carl Grünberg. Bernal, in 1927, at the age of twenty-six, was the first lecturer in structural crystallography in Cambridge's Department of Mineralogy under Professor Arthur Hutchinson;[24] in 1937 he was elected a fellow of the Royal Society at the age of thirty-six, and received the professorship of physics at Birkbeck College in London, succeeding Patrick M. S. Blackett, who moved to Manchester. Bernal and Horkheimer were not satisfied with success in their academic fields alone. They rose above professional confines and broke through disciplinary fences; they reflected upon human history at large and looked into the crystal ball to tell the future of humanity. And what did the philosopher and the scientist see? Two worlds that were worlds apart.

II

All this world is heavy with the promise of greater things, and a day will come, one day in the unending succession of days, when beings, beings who are now latent in our thoughts and hidden in our loins, shall stand upon this earth as one stands upon a footstool, and shall laugh and reach out their hands amid the stars.

H. G. Wells, 1902[25]

Mankind as a whole, given peace, plenty and freedom, might well be content to let alone the fanatical but useful people who chose to distort their bodies or blow themselves into space; and if, at some time, the magnitude of the changes made them aware that something important and terrifying had happened, it would then be too late for them to do anything about it. Even if a wave of primitive obscurantism then swept the world clear of the heresy of science, science would already be on its way to the stars.

John Desmond Bernal, 1929[26]

Bernal's first book bears a biblical title: *The World, the Flesh and the Devil.* The subtitle marks it as an *Enquiry into the Future of the Three Enemies of the Rational Soul.* It was published in 1929 and republished forty years later, in 1969, with a Foreword to the second edition in which the author confesses great attachment to it and writes: "It contains many of the seeds of ideas which I have been elaborating throughout my scientific life."[27] There is no reason to believe otherwise. Bernal's early study of the future is not only a serious and rather influential piece of science fiction, it is also a window that opens onto the Bernalian mindscape. *The World, the Flesh and the Devil* contains the essential Bernal. Everything Bernal produced thereafter, including *The Social Function of Science* (1939), and everything Bernal was known, noted, or notorious for, has roots in the rational dream of his first book. He wished this dream to come true and never had second thoughts about it.

Bernal attempted to examine the future objectively. Being the first Cambridge lecturer in structural crystallography, he looked into the crystal ball scientifically, to be sure. The introductory chapter of his endeavor in prediction is about the methods of and tools for a "science of the future." To predict future states of the universe scientifically, Bernal tried to put his desire for one future or another aside, excluding as far as possible illusions and mystical anticipations.[28] He enlisted history, the physical sciences, and psychology as aids and applied Lyell's leading principle in creating scientific geology in the nineteenth century, namely that "the state of the present and the forces operating in it contain implicitly the future state and point the way to its interpretation."[29] But since the future of the entire universe would go beyond the limits of a small book—and probably even a huge one—Bernal restricted the scope of his essay to the future of human activities.

The World, the Flesh and the Devil covers three fields of human action where further progress is likely. Bernal's three areas of interest are defined in terms of "three kinds of struggle."[30] First is the war on the battlefield of the world, which stands for the struggle with the "unintelligent forces of nature." Second is the war on the battlefield of the flesh, which represents the struggle with the human body, "its health and disease"; and finally comes the war on the battlefield of the devil, which signifies the struggle with our "desires and fears."[31] Thus, Bernal moves aggressively from the outer world through the human body toward the inner world of the mind. Yet the human mind is just an intermediate stage, a stopover or a footstool, to use Wells's word, in the evolutionary voyage of conquest from the low life on planet earth to a much higher life among the stars.

Bernal's entryway into the future is physics or the Baconian mastery of nonliving matter and energy. In starting with physics Bernal takes the first modern science as his guide, assuming that it will set the pattern for a successful mastery of living matter through molecular biology and, eventually, of thinking matter through a hard psychological science. This is why in 1969 he not only hails rocketry, the laser, and the electronic computer as triumphs of physics but also the revelation of the molecular structure of DNA as "the greatest discovery in all modern science."[32] Self-critical discomfort is expressed only about his earlier use of Freudian psychology.[33]

In 1929, Bernal made two predictions concerning the physical world. He anticipated a revolution in materials science and a higher level of civilization—the emancipation of intelligent life from the surface of this globe through space travel and colonization "beyond the bounds of the solar system."[34] With regard to the study of materials, Bernal correctly predicted the step from analysis to synthesis, that is, the production of materials "which are not merely modifications of what nature has given us . . . , but are made to specifications of a molecular architecture."[35] He foretold an age of designer materials for all kinds of uses, "a world incomparably more efficient and richer." His prophecy included "the production of food under controlled conditions, biochemical and ultimately chemical." Carried away by this prospect, he complacently announced that synthetic food would, for the first time, rank gastronomy with the other arts.[36]

Envisaging the emancipatory conquest of the solar system and the sidereal universe, Bernal embraced the idea of building "a permanent home for men in space." He pictured hollow globes, "ten miles or so in diameter . . . made out of the substance of one or more smaller asteroids, rings of Saturn or other planetary detritus."[37] They would orbit the sun, receive energy through a hard yet thin and transparent skin, contain a life-sustaining atmosphere, and harbor up to thirty thousand inhabitants. The development, growth, and reproduction of these globes would be the main task of humans in space. Bernal imagined the day when the majority of human beings will populate such structures. Their life in these globes is beyond conflict and passion, functions like a well-oiled mechanism, and has "no more need for government than . . . a modern hotel." The settlers of Bernal's future are altered human beings who are completely rational and not interested in "diversity of scene, of animals and plants and historical associations."[38] They behave like dispassionate natural scientists, or, more correctly, natural scientists are Bernal's model for the evolution of humankind into a new species tailored for life in hollow, ungoverned globes.

> Already the scientist is more immersed in his work and concentrates more on relations with his colleagues than on the immediate life of his neighbourhood. On the other hand, present aesthetic tendencies verge towards the abstract and do not demand so much inspiration from untouched nature. What has made a small town . . . a narrow sphere of interest has been on the one hand its isolation, and on the other hand the fact that the majority of its inhabitants are at so low a level of culture as to prevent any considerable intellectual interchange within its boundaries. Neither limitation holds for the globes, and the case of ancient Athens is enough to show that small size alone does not prevent cultural activity.[39]

The chapter about the world concludes with a couple of presumptions that drive Bernal's space program. Bernal affirms that modern man will not stop "until he has roamed over and colonized most of the sidereal universe" and declares that "the stars cannot be allowed to continue in their old way, but will be turned into efficient heat engines."[40] Hence, homo faber will be the all-powerful master of the universe, putting an end to the cosmic waste of energy and transforming the stars into public utilities.

If the stars cannot be allowed to continue in their old way, the flesh cannot be permitted to stay constant and unchanged either. To quote Bernal again: "Man himself must actively interfere in his own making and interfere in a highly unnatural manner."[41] Bernal is not interested in simply making the best of the existing species by indirect methods. He has little patience with the "eugenists and apostles of healthy life" who aim only at optimizing what nature has produced by chance. Bernal wants to overcome the Darwinian blindness of nature and "short-circuit" evolution.[42] Interested in a "radical alteration" of the human body, he wants to construct homo super-sapiens by using direct methods. His praise of the discovery of the double helix in 1969 reflects his joy over a big leap toward genetic engineering he had already conceived in 1929 as "physiological chemistry."[43]

It is never easy to predict exactly how the future will come about, so Bernal presented a fable of how the flesh will change. "Sooner or later," he suggests, "some eminent physiologist will have his neck broken in a super-civilized accident" and "will then be forced to decide whether to abandon his body or his life." Bernal's solution to this seemingly unpleasant dilemma leaves no room for ambiguity: "After all it is brain that counts."[44] The moral is clear: the body can go, the brain must stay. To think is to be alive.

Bernal sketches the human transformation in three stages from normal to new. In stage 1 "man will have anything from sixty to a hundred and twenty years of larval, unspecialized existence—surely enough to satisfy the advocates of the natural life. In this stage he . . . can occupy his time . . . in dancing, poetry and love-making. . . . Then he will leave the body whose potentialities he should have sufficiently explored."[45] Stage 2 is "a complicated and rather unpleasant process" of combining the existing body with "new sensory organs" and "motor services," the fine details of which I leave to the reader of *The World, the Flesh and the Devil*. Second-stage man is "a completely effective, mentally directed mechanism" who would be "physically plastic in a way quite transcending the capacities of untransformed humanity."[46] In stage 3, the new man finally emerges, "a strange, monstrous and inhuman creature" for the uninitiated.[47] According to Bernal, this dehumanized creature is "mechanized for scientific rather than aesthetic purposes":

Instead of the present body structure we should have the whole framework of some very rigid material, probably not metal but one of the new fibrous substances. In shape it might well be rather a short cylinder. Inside the cylinder, and supported very carefully to prevent shock, is the brain with its nerve connections, immersed in a liquid of the nature of cerebro-spinal fluid, kept circulating over it at a uniform temperature. The brain and nerve cells are kept supplied with fresh oxygenated blood and drained of de-oxygenated blood through their arteries and veins which connect outside the cylinder to the artificial heart-lung digestive system—an elaborate, automatic contrivance.[48]

The brain-case specimen of man has "guaranteed continuous awareness." It is connected with all sorts of devices, immediate sense and motor organs as well as self-repairing mechanisms, and numerous other new extensions that "only belong in a loose sense to any particular person." Bernal contemplates the linking together of individual brain-cases, thus making possible compound brains and minds. Compound

men, in turn, open the way to a "more perfect and economic transference of thought . . . necessary in the co-operative thinking of the future," to the postponement of death "for three hundred or perhaps a
thousand years," and to a "state of ecstasy" in which "feeling would
truly communicate itself." Bernal refers to his brain creatures appropriately as "angels." They control the stars and all life in the universe
and have left our bodies of mere flesh far behind.[49] "Finally, consciousness itself may end or vanish in a humanity that has become
completely etherialized, losing the close-knit organism, becoming masses
of atoms in space communicating by radiation, and ultimately perhaps resolving itself entirely into light."[50]

After this heady stuff, the chapter on the devil addresses the acute
state of bewilderment Bernal expects his reader to have reached by
this point. Bernal admits that he too felt some "real distaste . . . , especially in relation to the bodily changes."[51] Such uncomfortable feelings, he explains, are the work of the devil. The devil does not want
us to "abandon the world and subdue the flesh."[52]

Bernal's devil sits at the crossroads into the future of humanity,
causing our fears and affecting our desires. The spirit of evil recom-
mends the road of the flesh, not the way of the rational soul. Yet the
horizon is open, for either a future ruled by the devil or a future *al
gusto* Bernal. The devil's alternative is said to lead to the "end of the
scientific age,"[53] at times predicted by Bertrand Russell, Aldous Huxley, D. H. Lawrence, and others. Bernal, however, claims that his alternative leads to a "sound intellectual humanity."[54] If the fleshly
minded win, that is, if those under the sway of the evil spirit win,
progress will be abandoned in favor of "an idyllic Melanesian existence."[55] If the "crop of perverted individuals capable of more than
average performance"[56] wins—a humble way of saying: if scientists
like Bernal determine the future—humanity will develop further by
dehumanization.

Original in Bernal's use of the devil is not the established alternative
between progress and standstill but his idea of progress as dependent
upon "the evolution of human desire."[57] Bernal takes the Freudian
concept of sublimation and suppression of basic instincts and asks:
What is the long-term significance of the transformation of our carnal
energies into more refined activities? Will intellectual refinement remain a kind of perversion, or does it indicate a line of progress? His

answer turns Freud's three-layered spatial structure of id, ego, and superego into a historical tendency, unfolding in time, and leading from the primitive id over the realistic ego up to the truly upwardly mobile superego that reaches out for the stars by leaving the animal body behind. He therefore calls on "applied psychology . . . to bring . . . the ideals of the superego in line with external reality."[58]

The World, the Flesh and the Devil does not predict the outcome of the struggle between the rational soul and its enemies with certainty. Bernal hopes for a victory of science but does not preclude that the "emotional reactions of the mass . . . hostile to all mechanism" might prevail in what he calls the "war of the machines."[59] In fact, he introduces another interesting possibility: "the development of a dimorphism in humanity in which the conflict between the humanizers and the mechanizers will be solved not by the victory of one or the other but by the splitting of the human race."[60]

Why should humanity progress as a whole? asks Bernal. After all, "more fish remain in the sea than ever came out of it."[61] If the masses should choose not to advance their own dehumanization, the species could still "divide definitely into a progressive and unprogressive part."[62] This might happen quite secretly, muses Bernal in 1929. For instance, the new nations—the United States, China, or the Soviet Union—could allow the scientists, technicians, and experts to move gradually from advisory to governing status; or a future Soviet state, "freed from the danger of capitalist attack," could make its scientific institutions the government; or big scientific corporations could become "almost independent states and be enabled to undertake their largest experiments without consulting the outside world—a world which would be less and less able to judge what the experiments were about."[63] So, one way or another, the human world might become a world of dupes, ruled by Cartesian scientists (instead of Platonic philosophers). The earthlings will live in permanent now-time and, having left the design of the future to their rational guardians, "the balance which is now against the splitting of mankind might well turn, almost imperceptibly, in the opposite direction."[64]

But there is reason to cheer up. In the brave new world to come, humanists and scientists will be united in relentless care for the masses. Bernal imagined a planet without science and technology assessment, a world that travels through space as a happy human zoo, "a zoo so intelligently managed that its inhabitants are not aware that they are there merely for the purposes of observation and experiment." That prospect, concluded the author of *The World, the Flesh and the Devil*, "should please both sides: it should satisfy the scientists in their aspirations towards further knowledge and further experience, and the humanists in their looking for the good life on earth."[65]

III

Thinking objectifies itself to become an automatic, self-activating process, an impersonation of the machine that it produces itself so that ultimately the machine can replace it.

Max Horkheimer and Theodor W. Adorno, Dialectic of Enlightenment, *1947*[66]

Like any existing creed, science can be used to serve the most diabolical social forces, and scientism is no less narrow-minded than militant religion.

Max Horkheimer, Eclipse of Reason, *1947*[67]

Dehumanization was a key issue for Horkheimer as for Bernal, but unlike Bernal, Horkheimer did not use the term in order to propagate a new man. In *Eclipse of Reason,* a book based in part on public lectures delivered at Columbia University in the spring of 1944, Horkheimer said: "Advance in technical facilities for enlightenment is accompanied by a process of dehumanization. Thus progress threatens to nullify the very goal it is supposed to realize—the idea of man."[68] For Horkheimer, *dehumanization* signifies an abhorrent tendency and can have only negative meaning. However, Bernal used the same word in a strictly positive sense. At one point he remarked in *The World, the Flesh and the Devil:* "The great necessity for production either of food or other articles of consumption will disappear rapidly with the progress of dehumanization."[69] For Bernal, dehumanization is a desirable development, fostered by technoscience. It denotes an avenue of concrete advancement beyond any traditional idea and current physical reality of *homo sapiens sapiens.* It leads, after all, to the angels of the future, a posthuman species of disembodied master brains, a neural network of thinking machines with pure consciousness and complete power over the universe.

The difference between Horkheimer's and Bernal's understanding of dehumanization is fundamental, yet this difference was not a given; it emerged as a consequence of a radical paradigm change in Horkheimer's philosophy of history. There are two Horkheimers at the very least, Horkheimer I and Horkheimer II. Horkheimer I, the young Horkheimer of the 1930s, was a fairly orthodox Marxist philosopher who had learned his materialist lesson and repeated it as well as anyone else, Bernal included. This lesson told the world that "the application of all intellectual and physical means for the mastery of nature is hindered because in the prevailing circumstances these means are entrusted to special, mutually opposed interests."[70] Horkheimer I did not criticize the mastery of nature (as the later Horkheimer would do with a vengeance); in fact, he affirmed that it is the only "function of knowledge which will continue to be necessary even in a future society."[71] In other words, present class society with its antagonism between capital and labor hampers the domination of nature by hindering the full bloom of science and technology; a classless society will unleash the powers of science and technology and achieve complete human mastery of nature.

This was the official science-at-the-crossroads position that was propagated during the First Five Year Plan (1929–1933) by such fine and tragic Soviet sages as Nikolai Bukharin and Boris Hessen.[72] They communicated their reading of history in 1931 to the Second International Congress for the History of Science in London very effectively.[73] Of course, they reached only the converted, Bernal among them. Not only in England but everywhere else, left-wing intellectuals who cared to think about science, technology, and society sported a sanguine view about the great promise of a future socialist science. Looking back at those cheerful days before World War II, when the advancement of socialism and the development of technoscience were still in harmony, Joseph Needham, the eminent scholar of Chinese culture and science, Christian socialist and honorary Taoist, remembered the pattern: "All my friends and fellow-writers believed that applied science was essentially beneficial to mankind; and our objection to capitalism was that it prevented this process taking place."[74] By the war's end, this inexperienced optimism had suffered some sobering blows. Since then, people everywhere and on all sides of the political spectrum have lost their naiveté and begun to question the good-naturedness of straight technoscientific progress. Horkheimer was among the first to rethink the rosy prewar expectations of his generation and change course radically.

Horkheimer II, the mature Horkheimer, emerged in the early 1940s as a disenchanted social philosopher, both a socialist intellectual haunted by the thought that Stalinism might represent the future of fascism and a critical theorist ever more drawn to Schopenhauer's skeptical and gloomy humanism. Critical theory, which had once meant to lead the individual to a rational and transformative social praxis, away from theory for theory's sake, was now informed by a pessimistic attitude that required "utter hopelessness" to retain a glimmer of hope.[75] It shifted to a notion of philosophy in which the attainment of truth was still not possible without a critical activity, but this "critical activity"— originally a code word for revolutionary praxis that had "society itself for its object"[76] —had become self-critical and dystopian.

Horkheimer's turn to a pessimistic disposition was certainly in tune with the unique negative achievements of the twentieth century: concentration camps, genocides, atom bombs, untold misery, and countless deaths by ceaseless hunger and war. I do not think, therefore, that Horkheimer II has to be defended against accusations of lack of high hopes, upper-middle-class decadence, sagging academic output, or whatever the charges of his critics may be. If despair about the advancement of human and animal suffering is an acceptable reason, Horkheimer had sufficient cause to abandon the certitudes of his youth and the aim of improving the world on paper and in theory. What he wrote about Schopenhauer's philosophy characterizes his own mature thinking: it is "ill-suited to education for efficiency, even academic efficiency."[77] Horkheimer II had lost all previous faith in the future of human history, including his earlier belief in the intrinsic benevolence of the technoscientific mastery of nature.

The reversal of premises came to the fore in 1942, in the final issue of Horkheimer's journal, in an article appropriately entitled "The End of Reason." Here, Horkheimer argued that "through reason man frees himself of the fetters of nature. This liberation, however, does not entitle man to dominate nature (as the philosophers held) but to comprehend it."[78] In one sentence, the technoscientific side of the project of modernity from Bacon and Descartes to Wells, Haldane, and Bernal was declared illegitimate, and Marx, who had announced in his eleventh thesis on Feuerbach that interpretive comprehension of the world is no longer asked for,[79] was turned downside up on his head. Now the critical theorist attacks occidental reason and instrumental rationality and finds the project of enlightenment "totalitarian."[80] Horkheimer developed this new "comprehensive philosophical theory"[81] about Western history together with Theodor W. Adorno in two major texts, the five Columbia lectures on "Society and Reason," which became *Eclipse of Reason,* and the brilliant *Dialectic of Enlightenment,* which was dedicated and presented in manuscript form to Friedrich Pollock on his fiftieth birthday, May 1944.[82]

In order to appreciate the depth of this philosophical change, one must realize the uncomfortable intellectual proximity of Horkheimer II and Adorno to a thinker with truly adverse political intuitions— Martin Heidegger, who had always been critical of the enlightenment project and Western instrumental rationality. Adorno and Heidegger entertained similar hopes as to the redemptive power of art; Heidegger and Horkheimer II decoded the technological rise of the West as a symptom of its essential decline; and all three believed that the fatal technoscientific will to power was set in motion long before actual technoscience, in ancient Greece, by occidental metaphysics or some other creative mishap.[83] Horkheimer II, Adorno, and Heidegger view the global technoscientific civilization with fundamental objections and comparable discontent.

Nothing but the mystical power of the true word was left for Horkheimer II after the fall from orthodox grace. He no longer viewed historical progress as an advancement to a better world but as a rapid movement toward cultural barbarism and the self-destruction of humanity. He was convinced that "domination of nature involves domination of man"[84] and could not believe that the main contradiction of industrial modernity—a powerful mastery of nature on the one hand and a manifest weakness in coping with social problems on the other— could ever be resolved without curing the "disease of reason" emanating from the "deepest layers of civilization."[85] If humanity wanted to cure this disease, it would have to eradicate "man's urge to dominate nature."[86] But this was an unlikely cure. Revolutionary subjects and progress toward a society without domination and exploitation, planned technoscience, and rational mastery of nature—the Marxian elements of early critical theory had fallen in ruins beyond repair. The only reasonable remnant of reason was the desperate ability to cry murder, "the faculty of calling things by their name."[87]

Once it was the endeavor of art, literature, and philosophy to express the meaning of things and of life, to be the voice of all that is dumb, to endow nature with an organ for making known her sufferings, or, we might say, to call reality by its rightful name. Today nature's tongue is taken away. Once it was thought that each utterance, word, cry, or gesture had an intrinsic meaning; today it is merely an occurrence.[88]

At this point, I think, it is safe to say that all and any intellectual commonality between Bernal and Horkheimer—Horkheimer II, to be sure—lies in the fact that each formulated the other's antithesis. What began as an ideologically compatible development matured into a divergence at the crossroads of dehumanization. The philosopher and the scientist encounter a rapidly changing world and view the future of humans in ways as different and opposed as can be. Bernal fears too little dehumanization, and Horkheimer already sees too much of it; the same goes for technoscience, material progress, mastery of nature, and so on. Where does this total opposition spring from? And what shall we make of it?

Bernal's technodream hardened during World War II. Its author played a decisive role in the British war effort; he had a "good war" and even saw an anticipation of scientific socialism in the efficient wartime coordination of the capitalist societies.[89] Horkheimer was less lucky. Faced with the anti-Semitic legislation of the Third Reich, he moved himself and his Institute out of harm's way in 1933 and, in due course, experienced the formidable combination of exile, culture shock, and war, however cushioned by financial security. His turn from a positive to a negative philosophy of Western civilization was strongly influenced by the experience of extreme historical stress; we have to take that into account. But this is not an essay in the social determination of individual ideas (a notoriously inconclusive enterprise), so we do not have to base our biographical experiment on the external context of Horkheimer II. The main interest here is comparative—an attempt to show that Bernal and Horkheimer had different resources of thought, were drawing from unlike heaps of cultural capital, were not rooted in the same soil. The crystallographer's dream was fed by the minerals of science and technology, the artificial manure of homo faber; the critique of the critical theorist was nourished by layers of theology, philosophy, and literature, the humus of humanists.

The fact that Bernal and Horkheimer construct incompatible theories about dehumanization is less relevant than the fact that neither commands the cultural resources of the other. Both men are predominantly schooled, experienced, and fully literate in either one or the other of two distinct and absorbing cultures. Separate pools of cultural resources are accessed when Bernal and Horkheimer think. They work with dissimilar cognitive maps and divergent frames of reference and reach into different traditions and toolboxes. Bernal applies the cultural resources of technoscience when he propagates the fission of the human race into earthbound humanists and star-trekking scientists. He takes the wedge that has already split Western culture and drives it into the species itself. He labors for progressive dehumanization, at least of an avant-garde, and assumes the creation of a new superspecies on a voluntary basis or by covert action. Horkheimer II is as free as Bernal. He uses the rich resources of his cultural domain to write about the "decline of the individual."[90] His critical voice is tinged with the undertones of a conservative *Kulturkritik*. When he looks at the "tremendous technological progress that promises to revolutionize the conditions of human existence,"[91] he observes the "liquidation" of the [male] subject[92] and notes the instrumental rationality of the engineer:

It is true that the engineer, perhaps the symbol of this age, is not so exclusively bent on profitmaking as the industrialist or the merchant. Because his function is more directly connected with the requirements of the production job itself, his commands bear the mark of greater objectivity. His subordinates recognize that at least some of his orders are in the nature of things and therefore rational in a universal sense. But at bottom this rationality, too, pertains to domination, not reason. The engineer is not interested in understanding things for their own sake or for the sake of insight, but in accordance with their being fitted into a scheme, no matter how alien to their own inner structure; this holds for living beings as well as for inanimate things. The engineer's mind is that of industrialism in its streamlined form. His purposeful rule would make men an agglomeration of instruments without a purpose of their own.[93]

Indeed, a Bernalist would say, our new man is an agglomeration of instruments with electronic devices "for detecting wireless frequencies, eyes for infra-red, ultraviolet and X-rays, ears for supersonics, detectors of high and low temperatures, of electrical potential and current, and chemical organs of many kinds."[94] The technoscientific domination of nature is neither embarrassing nor metaphorical for a Bernalist. He aims at the domination of human nature, and not human nature in a metaphysical sense; he wants to "subdue the flesh" to improve the very physical nature of the human animal. Whenever Horkheimer comes close to realizing that, he misses the point. For him, the symptoms of dehumanization assault the metaphysical idea of a human being and not its physical nature. Dehumanization is physical for Bernal and metaphysical for Horkheimer. A "gulf of mutual incomprehension"[95] divides scientist and philosopher. Bernal and Horkheimer are prisoners of their respective cultures, however innocent or guilty as the case may be. They are stranded at the crossroads of dehumanization and not in a good position to guide us.

Conclusion

Horkheimer II has many rare and valuable things to offer but not a secure standpoint for claims to truth, if such a firm footing exists. "It must be observed," wrote the disenchanted Horkheimer in *Eclipse of Reason,*

that the division of all human truth into science and humanities is itself a social product that was hypostatized by the organization of the universities and ultimately by some philosophical schools, particularly those of Rickert and Max Weber. The so-called practical world has no place for truth, and therefore splits it to conform it to its own image: the physical sciences are endowed with so-called objectivity, but emptied of human content; the humanities preserve the human content, but only as ideology, at the expense of truth.[96]

If one could regard this statement itself as true and as not being warped by ideology, then the professional fractalization of truth could be cured and made whole and healthy again by a new social product, perhaps by reorganizing the universities and our intellectual life according to the gospel of some holistic philosophical school. False objectivity and true ideology could be overcome; truths without human content could be rehumanized; and truths with untruthful human content could be corrected. But the view of Horkheimer II cannot be true since it was produced inside the humanities—those branches of learning that "preserve the human content ... as ideology." Horkheimer must situate his own thinking in this ideological context. We may as well conclude, therefore, that Horkheimer II fell victim to his own deconstruction of occidental reason—that he is part of the problem and not of the solution.

The same holds true for Bernal. His nonchalance in considering secret dehumanization is unacceptable. We may feel tempted to apply Horkheimer's critique of positivism—"narrow-minded scientism"—to Bernal's overall attitude. This judgment might reflect what we may think about Bernal's advocacy of a scooped-out and souped-up braincase species, but it might also deflect our attention from the reality content of his technodream. Bernal's vision of our future merits full attention, serious discussion, and careful assessment. We are still at the crossroads of dehumanization, in fact more so with the ongoing, rapid advancement of genetic engineering, computer science, and nanotechnologies.[97] Modern technoscience is already very powerful and yet still in *its* infancy; it will not exempt our physical nature from its critical activity. Hence we cannot afford to leave the future of the human species to the Bernalists.

But neither early, middle, nor current critical theory has paid, or is paying, enough attention to the sciences and technologies that feed into and shape the natural half of human history. The dreams, fantasies, and projects of our technoscientific culture thrive with very little or no internal technocritique that is not purely technical; our most eloquent technocritics are often crudely antitechnological; and relevant academic fields, like the professional history and sociology of science and technology, care more about their own problems and research fronts than about society at the crossroads into the future.

Our universities could request and encourage cross-cultural trade between the Bernals and Horkheimers on campus; scholars in social studies of science and technology could function as intermediaries between the scientific and humanistic cultures; humanists could gain some technoscientific literacy; scientists could combine objective research methods with subjective human compassion; and critical theorists could look at both sides of human history. But our knowledge system promotes selective cultural ignorance. We have poor cross-cultural communications among the camps of technoscience, social science, and postmodern humanities. These cultural divisions provide native thinkers richly, but solely, with local cultural resources and, worse, imbue them with fundamentalist tendencies resulting in scientism, relativism, defeatism, or some other overdoing. We are stranded on the cultural islands of our civilization, not a good position when it comes to problems that require a multi- and not a monocultural response.

This chapter has not looked for a solution to unrelated technodreams and technocritiques about dehumanization. It should be clear, however, that neither the challenge of dehumanization nor the autistic structure of the two major intellectual subcultures is a one-dimensional problem. These are problems in need of an enlightened multicultural[98] response. But this response is not forthcoming. Our intellectual compartmentalization is deeply entrenched. It would be helpful, therefore, to know our cultural limits. And just for that reason we have to research the cultural division of cognitive labor, do more comparative cultural work, and have historians of consciousness take stock of the different cultural resources utilized in highly skilled and learned brains.

Notes

Part of this chapter was delivered in August 1989 as a public lecture at the XVIIIth International Congress of History of Science, Hamburg-Munich, in a symposium commemorating the fiftieth anniversary of the publication of Bernal's *Social Function of Science* (1939).

1. Marx and Engels (1976:28f., note). The *German Ideology* was abandoned "to the gnawing criticism of the mice" (i.e., never published during the lifetime of Marx and Engels); it came out for the first time in full in 1932. The quoted passage was crossed out by the authors in the manuscript, and is often omitted in paperback editions. The original German reads: "Wir kennen nur eine einzige Wissenschaft, die Wissenschaft der Geschichte. Die Geschichte kann von zwei Seiten aus betrachtet, in die Geschichte der Natur und die Geschichte der Menschen abgeteilt werden. Beide Seiten sind indes nicht zu trennen; solange Menschen existieren, bedingen sich Geschichte der Natur und Geschichte der Menschen gegenseitig. Die Geschichte der Natur, die sogenannte Naturwissenschaft, geht uns hier nicht an; auf die Geschichte der Menschen werden wir indes einzugehen haben, da fast die ganze Ideologie sich entweder auf eine verdrehte Auffassung dieser Geschichte oder auf eine gänzliche Abstraktion von ihr reduziert" (Marx and Engels 1959:18, note).

2. This is from a talk Conant gave in Germany in 1953 (Conant 1953:16). The German original reads: "Die Naturwissenschaft ist viel zu wichtig, als daβ man sie den Natur-

wissenschaftlern überlassen könnte." Conant was a Harvard chemist who became the twenty-third president of Harvard University (1933–1953) and High Commissioner (1953–1955) and U.S. ambassador (1955–1957) to West Germany. As chairman of the National Defense Research Committee (NDRC) between 1941 and 1945, he was in charge of the American atomic bomb project. In the fall of 1945 (in his Terry Lectures at Yale University) he argued: "We need a widespread understanding of science in this country, for only thus can science be assimilated into our secular cultural pattern. When that has been achieved, we shall be one step nearer the goal which we now desire so earnestly, a unified, coherent culture suitable for our American democracy in this new age of machines and experts" (Conant 1947:3).

3. Thus inviting numerous attacks from all varieties of more conventional, and sometimes vulgar, Marxisms, namely Leninism, Stalinism, Trotskyism, Lukácsism, and Althusserianism. Cf. Held (1980:353ff.). Martin Jay (1973:296) went so far as to say that "in the end, the institute presented a revision of Marxism so substantial that it forfeited the right to be included among its many offshoots." However, I think that future rereadings of Marx and Engels might well be inspired by the renegade works of critical theory and not by the dead horses of dogmatic Marxism.

4. The young Horkheimer criticized Mannheim's sociology of knowledge as a sophisticated and, therefore, dangerous revision of Marx's main point (that the world needs to be changed and not only interpreted); see his extensive review of Mannheim's *Ideology and Utopia* (Horkheimer 1930). Mannheim exempts physics, mathematics, and formal logic when he says: "The existential determination of thought may be regarded as a demonstrated fact in those realms of thought in which we can show . . . that the process of knowing does not actually develop historically in accordance with immanent laws, that it does not follow only from the 'nature of things' or from 'pure logical possibilities,' and that it is not driven by an 'inner dialectic' " (Mannheim 1936:239f.). For a strong position in favor of the sociologizing of all sorts of thought, see David Bloor (1973).

5. See note 1 above.

6. Conant, who spent his childhood in Dorchester, would have been the ideal educator for Henry Adams, his fellow Bostonian from Quincy, who had tried so hard at the turn of the century to learn the lesson of technoscientific modernity. See Adams (1973) and Conant (1970).

7. Conant inaugurated a series of new "general education courses" for all Harvard undergraduates. He designed, and taught for many years, one of these courses himself. In it, students of the social sciences and humanities were to develop an understanding of the specific research methods of the experimental sciences and the explosive growth of scientific research "as an organized activity of society."

8. Cf. Snow (1971).

9. The critic Frank Raymond Leavis, the "Himmler of literature" as he was subsequently called, savaged Snow in 1962. Cf. Leavis (1962).

10. For bibliographical references see Boytinck (1980).

11. One English study of Bernal, however, mentions the critique of instrumental rationality in connection with Marcuse and Habermas but not Horkheimer. Cf. Rose and Rose (1981:285): "The reborn radical science movement of the late 1960s was to criticize not so much the inadequacy of support for science under capital, but the science

itself, which had become revealed as oppressive and anti-human. It was not the ortho-dox Marxists but the Frankfurt school's (especially Marcuse's, and later Habermas's) critique of instrumental rationality which was to inform its challenge to capital and to capital's science."

12. Talk about the two cultures has been around for over one hundred years. It began in the 1880s, at the latest, as a well-tempered exchange between two Victorian gentle-men, with Thomas Henry Huxley arguing for a science-based education and Matthew Arnold defending humanistic *Bildung*. It peaked in the 1960s with the ill-tempered Leavis-Snow controversy. Today, it is a lukewarm issue put on the back burner of uni-versity presses. But there, removed from questions of public interest, it has become fashionable to go *Beyond the Two Cultures,* as the title of a recent book suggests. Cf. Slade and Lee (1990). However, I am convinced neither that we have progressed beyond the divide of the two cultures, nor that today's professional work—the literary analysis of scientific discourses, scrutiny of scientific texts, interpretation of scientific tropes and metaphors—cares about the problem that 99 percent of the workers in the fields of modern technoscience are not affected by the subtle operations of, say, the Society for Literature and Science (founded in 1985) or any other such meritorious academic en-terprise. We have gotten accustomed to the two cultures (or three, if one adds the social sciences, especially sociology, to the humanities and the natural sciences). Cf. Lepenies (1988) and Mazlish (1989). Intellectual compartmentalization has become a fact of pro-fessionalization, and we have lost the sensitivity to feel the weight of our ignorance. Thus, the old problem of the two cultures is still around and still unsolved.

13. Cf. Snow (1956:413): "As Rutherford said cheerfully to Samuel Alexander: 'When you think of all the years you've been talking about those things, Alexander, and what does it all add up to? *Hot air,* nothing but *hot air.*' " Snow continues by aiming at the main philosophical current of the 1950s: "That is what contemporary scientists would say. They regard it as a major intellectual virtue, to know what not to think about. They might touch their hats to linguistic analysis, as a relatively honourable way of wasting time; not so to existentialism."

14. Cf. Leavis (1962:302, 303) "And this, for me, evokes that total vision which makes Snow's 'social hope' unintoxicating to many of us—the vision of our imminent tomor-row in today's America: the energy, the triumphant technology, the productivity, the high standard of living and the life-impoverishment—the human emptiness; emptiness and boredom craving alcohol—of one kind or another."

15. Cf. Snow (1978:16).

16. Cf. Hodgkin (1980:17).

17. Snow (1978:17). John Desmond, the schoolboy, was an Irish nationalist as well as a fervent Catholic. At his local school in Ireland he conceived that he "would use science and apply it to war to liberate Ireland." Later, in his first English school, he started "a fraternity of Perpetual Adoration of the Sacred Heart." Cf. Hodgkin (1980:21).

18. Cf. Gumnior and Ringguth (1973:11), Wiggershaus (1986:56, 292). In all three places the dates are different: fall 1939, summer 1939, and 1938, respectively.

19. Gumnior and Ringguth (1973:94).

20. Ibid., 33.

21. Ibid., 122f.

Stranded at the Crossroads of Dehumanization

22. See Werskey (1978:166): "In 'losing' his party card, he was of course free to operate in public as an 'independent' intellectual of Marxist persuasion." Cf., however,
Goldsmith (1980:31): "He lost his CP card in 1933 or 1934, and never rejoined." Goldsmith, a science writer, was denied access to the Bernal papers in Cambridge, but this
did not prevent him from writing a rather disappointing and superficial biography of
Bernal. See Robert Young's critical essay review of Goldsmith's book in *Radical Science
Journal* 10 (1980): 85–94.

23. Cf. Bernal (1953:133).

24. Cf. Hutchinson's account of Bernal's job interview in Snow (1964:22f.).

25. Wells in a lecture, "The Discovery of the Future," at the Royal Institution, London,
January 24, 1902. Cf. Wells (1924:389).

26. Bernal (1969:75).

27. Ibid., v.

28. Cf. ibid., 4.

29. Ibid., 5f.

30. Compare Bernal's line—"Man is occupied and has been persistently occupied since
his separate evolution, with three kinds of struggle" (ibid., 10)—with the *Manifesto of
the Communist Party*—"The history of all previous society is the history of class struggles"—and mark the division of the two cultures: Bernal struggles with nature; Marx
and Engels fight with society.

31. Cf. ibid.

32. Ibid., vi.

33. Cf. ibid.: "The section in the book on the Devil remains the most important but,
looking at it now, I find it is expressed too much in Freudian terms which are likely to
be superseded." Bernal expects that the soft science part of his approach will become a
hard science, too.

34. Ibid., 27.

35. Ibid., 12.

36. Cf. ibid., 14.

37. Cf. ibid., 18f.

38. Cf. ibid., 25.

39. Ibid., 26.

40. Cf. ibid., 28.

41. Ibid., 30.

42. Cf. ibid., 32.

43. Ibid., 31.

44. Cf. ibid., 34: "After all it is brain that counts, and to have a brain suffused by fresh and correctly prescribed blood is to be alive—to think."

45. Ibid., 36.

46. Ibid., 37.

47. Cf. ibid., 41.

48. Ibid., 38.

49. Cf. ibid., 39–45.

50. Ibid., 47. A word on Bernal's sources of inspiration might not be out of place here. There is, of course, a religious background on the one hand—the Christian tradition that loves to leave the world, the flesh, and the devil behind. John Donne, for instance, wrote in one of his "divine" poems: "gluttonous death will instantly unjoynt / My body, and soule, and I shall sleepe a space, / But my'ever-waking part shall see that face, / Whose feare already shakes my every joynt: / Then, as my soule, to'heaven her first seate, takes flight, / And earth-borne body, in the earth shall dwell, / So, fall my sinnes, that all may have their right, / To where they'are bred, and would presse me, to hell. / Impute me righteous, thus purg'd of evill, / For thus I leave the world, the flesh, and devill" (Donne 1978:7; commentary, p. 67: "the final line of the sonnet recalls the renunciations which precede the administration of baptism in the book of Common Prayer"). And, on the other hand, there is the scientific tradition of heretic dreams about the physical world. One thinks of Johannes Kepler, who wrote *Somnium*, the first Copernican science-fiction novel featuring a voyage to the moon, and of Giordano Bruno, who was killed by the Inquisition because he had strayed too early and too far from the politically correct Aristotelian cosmology: "Henceforth I spread confident wings to space; / I fear no bar rier of crystal or of glass; / I cleave the heavens and soar to the infinite. / And while I rise from my own globe to others / And penetrate ever further through the eternal field, / That which others saw from afar, I leave far behind me" (Singer 1950:249). One also thinks of the more contemporary H. G. Wells as an important influence in Bernal's vision of the future, and of the Webbs and G. B. Shaw. But above all, one is reminded of the paper that was read to the Cambridge Heretics in 1923 by J. B. S. Haldane. Haldane, who was convinced "that science is vastly more stimulating to the imagination than are the classics," is quoted in Bernal's first book on pages 30 and 36. As if to give Bernal a signal, Haldane had argued: "We must regard science then from three points of view. First it is the free activity of man's divine faculties of reason and imagination. Secondly it is the answer of the few to the demands of the many for wealth, comfort and victory, . . . gifts which it will grant only in exchange for peace, security and stagnation. Finally it is man's gradual conquest, first of space and time, then of matter as such, then of his own body and those of other living beings, and finally the subjugation of the dark and evil elements in his own soul" (Haldane 1924:29, 81f.).

51. Bernal (1969:58).

52. Ibid., 48.

53. Ibid., 52.

Stranded at the Crossroads of Dehumanization

54. Ibid., 57.

55. Ibid., 56.

56. Ibid., 53.

57. Ibid., 55.

58. Ibid., 57.

59. Cf. ibid., 59.

60. Ibid., 60. The ideas of Bernal's rich and radical essay fell on fertile ground in many scientists' minds. Freeman Dyson, for instance, the eminent theoretical physicist at the Princeton Institute for Advanced Study, took care of the cosmic dimension of genetic engineering, including the splitting of the human race into many species. Cf. Dyson (1979:225–38). Being interested in the conflicting traditions of technodreams and technocritiques I have compared Dyson with Hans Jonas (Schäfer 1989a).

61. Bernal (1969:71).

62. Ibid., 72.

63. Ibid., 78.

64. Ibid., 79.

65. Ibid., 80.

66. Horkheimer and Adorno (1972:25).

67. Horkheimer (1992:71).

68. Ibid., vi.

69. Bernal (1969:64).

70. Cf. "Traditional and Critical Theory," in Horkheimer (1972:213).

71. Ibid., 240.

72. Cf. Schäfer (1988), and for a more detailed version of this article, with notes and references, Schäfer (1989b).

73. Cf. *Science at the Cross Roads* (1971).

74. Needham (1986:iv).

75. Cf. Horkheimer (1967:68f.): "Without thinking about truth and thereby of what it guarantees, there can be no knowledge of its opposite, of the abandonment of mankind, for whose sake true philosophy is critical and pessimistic—there cannot even be sorrow, without which there is no happiness." The article's last sentence reads like a variation on Tertullian's *credo, quia absurdum:* "There are few ideas that the world today needs more than Schopenhauer's—ideas which in the face of utter hopelessness, because they confront it, know more than any others of hope" (ibid., 71).

Wolf Schäfer

76. Cf. Horkheimer (1972:206, 207): "The critical attitude of which we are speaking is wholly distrustful of the rules of conduct with which society as presently constituted provides each of its members. The separation between individual and society in virtue of which the individual accepts as natural the limits prescribed for his activity is relativized in critical theory. The latter considers the overall framework which is conditioned by the blind interaction of individual activities (that is, the existent division of labor and the class distinctions) to be a function which originates in human action and therefore is a possible object of planful decision and rational determination of goals."

77. Horkheimer (1967:56).

78. Horkheimer (1941:387). The title page of volume 9, no. 3, of *Studies in Philosophy and Social Science* gives 1941 as the year of publication, yet the copyright is from 1942 and Horkheimer's preface to number 3, which contains the quoted article, is dated "March 1942."

79. Because "the point is to change it" (Marx and Engels 1976:5).

80. Horkheimer and Adorno (1972:6).

81. Cf. Horkheimer (1992:vii): "These lectures were designed to present in epitome some aspects of a comprehensive philosophical theory developed by the writer during the last few years in association with Theodor W. Adorno."

82. The manuscript was mimeographed a few months later in five hundred copies as a publication of the Institute for Social Research, entitled *Philosophical Fragments*.

83. Cf. Heidegger (1977); for a recent study of Heidegger's views on technology and productionist metaphysics, see Zimmerman (1990) (unfortunately with poor knowledge about the origin and theoretical development of the older Frankfurt school tradition; cf. ibid., 217f.).

84. Horkheimer (1992:93).

85. Ibid., 176.

86. Ibid.

87. Horkheimer (1941:387).

88. Horkheimer (1992:101).

89. Cf. Werskey (1978:273f.).

90. Horkheimer (1992:128–61).

91. Ibid., 151.

92. Cf. ibid., 93: "The total transformation of each and every realm of being into a field of means leads to the liquidation of the subject who is supposed to use them. This gives modern industrialist society its nihilistic aspect. Subjectivization, which exalts the subject, also dooms him." Why "him" and not "it"? Because the human subject has a male character for Horkheimer and Adorno. Cf. Horkheimer and Adorno (1972:33): "Men had to do fearful things to themselves before the self, the identical, purpo-

sive, and virile nature of man, was formed, and something of that recurs in every childhood."

93. Horkheimer (1992:151).

94. Bernal (1969:35).

95. Snow (1971:15).

96. Horkheimer (1992:75).

97. Nanotechnology is the ultimate small technology; it is meant to reach complete control over the structure of matter, atom by atom. Cf. Drexler (1990). Marvin Minsky writes in the Foreword to Drexler's book, p. vii: "Nanotechnology could have more effect on our material existence than those last two great inventions in that domain— the replacement of sticks and stones by metals and cements and the harnessing of electricity."

98. The term *multicultural* is used here in a cognitive and not an ethnic sense.

References

Adams, Henry (1973). *The education of Henry Adams: An autobiography*. New edition by Ernest Samuels. Boston: Houghton Mifflin.

Bernal, John Desmond (1953). Stalin as scientist. *Modern Quarterly*, 8(3): 133–42.

————— (1969). *The world, the flesh and the devil: An enquiry into the future of the three enemies of the rational soul* (1st ed. 1929). Foreword to the 2d ed. by J. D. Bernal, 1968. Bloomington and London: Indiana University Press.

Bloor, David (1973). Wittgenstein and Mannheim on the sociology of mathematics. *Studies in History and Philosophy of Science* 4: 173–91.

Boytinck, Paul (1980). *C. P. Snow: A reference guide*. Boston: G. K. Hall.

Conant, James Bryant (1947). *On understanding science: An historical approach*. New Haven: Yale University Press.

————— (1953). Staatsbürger und Wissenschaftler. *Arbeitsgemeinschaft für Forschung des Landes Nordrhein-Westfalen: Geisteswissenschaften*, 17: 15–21.

————— (1970). *My several lives: Memoirs of a social inventor*. New York: Harper & Row.

Donne, John (1978). *The divine poems* (1st ed. 1952). Edited with introduction and commentary by Helen Gardner. Oxford: Clarendon Press.

Drexler, K. Eric (1990). *Engines of creation* (1st ed. 1986). Foreword by Marvin Minsky. London: Fourth Estate.

Dyson, Freeman J. (1979). *Disturbing the universe*. New York: Basic Books.

Goldsmith, Maurice (1980). *Sage: A life of J. D. Bernal*. London: Hutchinson.

Gumnior, Helmut, and Ringguth, Rudolf (1973). *Max Horkheimer in Selbstzeugnissen und Bilddokumenten.* Reinbek bei Hamburg: Rowohlt.

Haldane, J. B. S. (1924). *Daedalus or science and the future.* New York: E. P. Dutton & Co.

Heidegger, Martin (1977). *The question concerning technology and other essays.* Translated and with an introduction by W. Lovitt. New York: Harper & Row.

Held, David (1980). *Introduction to critical theory: Horkheimer to Habermas.* Berkeley and Los Angeles: University of California Press.

Hodgkin, Dorothy M. Crowfoot (1980). John Desmond Bernal. *Biographical Memoirs of Fellows of the Royal Society* 26:17–84.

Horkheimer, Max (1930). Ein neuer Ideologiebegriff? *Archiv für die Geschichte des Sozialismus und der Arbeiterbewegung* 15: 33–56.

—— (1941). The end of reason. *Studies in Philosophy and Social Science* 9(3): 366–88.

—— (1967). Schopenhauer today. In K. H. Wolff and B. Moore, eds., *The critical spirit: Essays in honor of Herbert Marcuse,* 55–71. Boston: Beacon Press.

—— (1972). *Critical theory: Selected essays.* New York: Herder and Herder.

—— (1992). *Eclipse of reason* (1st ed. 1947). New York: Continuum.

Horkheimer, Max, and Adorno, Theodor W. (1972). *Dialectic of enlightenment* (1st. ed. 1947). New York: Herder and Herder.

Jay, Martin (1973). *The dialectical imagination: A history of the Frankfurt school and the Institute of Social Research, 1923–1950.* Boston: Little, Brown.

Leavis, F. R. (1962, March 9). The significance of C. P. Snow. *Spectator,* 297–303.

Lepenies, Wolf (1988). *Between literature and science: The rise of sociology* (1st German ed. 1985). Cambridge and Paris: Cambridge University Press and Maison des Sciences de l'Homme.

Mannheim, Karl (1936). *Ideology and utopia: An introduction to the sociology of knowledge* (1st. German ed. Bonn: 1929). Preface by Louis Wirth. London: Routledge & Kegan Paul.

Marx, Karl, and Engels, Friedrich (1959). *Werke.* Vol. 3: *Thesen über Feuerbach; Die deutsche Ideologie.* Berlin: Dietz Verlag.

—— (1976). *Collected Works.* Vol. 5: *Theses on Feuerbach; The German Ideology.* New York: International Publishers.

Mazlish, Bruce (1989). *A new science: The breakdown of connections and the birth of sociology.* New York and Oxford: Oxford University Press.

Needham, Joseph (1986). *Time: The refreshing river* (1st ed. 1943). Reprint with Preface to New Edition. Nottingham: Spokesman.

Rose, Hilary, and Rose, Steven (1981). The two Bernals: Revolutionary and revisionist in science. *Fundamenta Scientiae* 2(3/4): 267–86.

Schäfer, Wolf (1988). Boris Hessen and the politics of the sociology of science. *Thesis Eleven* 21: 103–16.

——— (1989a). Die Büchse der Pandora. Über Hans Jonas, Technik, Ethik und die Träume der Vernunft. *Merkur. Deutsche Zeitschrift für europäisches Denken* 43: 292–304.

——— (1989b). Äussere Umstände des Externalismus. Über Boris Hessen und das Projekt einer Geschichte der Wissenschaftsforschungs-Geschichte. In H. Poser und C. Burrichter, eds., *Die geschichtliche Perspektive in den Disziplinen der Wissenschaftsforschung*, 7–46. Berlin: Technische Universität. TUB-Dokumentation Kongresse und Tagungen, Heft 39.

Science at the cross roads: Papers presented to the international congress of the history of science and technology held in London from June 29th to July 3rd, 1931, by the delegates of the U.S.S.R (1st ed. 1931) (1971). With a new foreword by Joseph Needham and a new introduction by Paul Gary Werskey. London: Frank Cass & Co.

Singer, Dorothea Waley (1950). *Giordano Bruno: His life and thought. With annotated translation of his work "On the infinite universe and worlds."* New York: Henry Schuman.

Slade, Joseph W., and Lee, Judith Yaross, eds. (1990). *Beyond the two cultures: Essays on science, technology, and literature*. Ames: Iowa State University Press.

Snow, Charles Percy (1956, October 6). The two cultures. *New Statesman and Nation*, 413–14.

——— (1964). J. D. Bernal, a personal portrait. In M. Goldsmith and A. Mackay, eds., *Society and Science*, 19–29. New York: Simon and Schuster.

——— (1971). *Public affairs*. New York: Charles Scribner's Sons. (Contains: Prologue. The two cultures and the scientific revolution, 1959. The two cultures: A second look, 1963. The case of Leavis and the serious case, 1970. Science and government, 1960. Appendix to 'science and government', 1962. The moral un-neutrality of science, 1960. The state of siege, 1968. Epilogue.)

——— (1978). Bernal, John Desmond. *Dictionary of Scientific Biography*, 15, Supplement I, 16–20.

Wells, H. G. (1924). The discovery of the future. In *The works of H. G. Wells. Atlantic Edition*, 4: 357–89. New York: Charles Scribner's Sons.

Werskey, Gary (1978). *The visible college*. London: Allen Lane. (Reprinted with foreword by Robert M. Young and new preface by G. Werskey, London: 1988.)

Wiggershaus, Rolf (1986). *Die Frankfurter Schule: Geschichte, Theoretische Entwicklung, Politische Bedeutung*. Munich: Carl Hanser.

Zimmerman, Michael E. (1990). *Heidegger's confrontation with modernity: Technology, politics, art*. Bloomington: Indiana University Press.

II

**Reason, Domination, and the Fate of
Emancipation in Horkheimer's Mature Work**

8

Max Horkheimer and the Sociological Deficit of Critical Theory

Axel Honneth

Critical theory originated more than fifty years ago under the intellectual authority of an individual yet as the work of a group of scholars and scientists. It made its first appearance in Max Horkheimer's inaugural address as director of the Institute for Social Research and in subsequent years was developed in his contributions to the *Zeitschrift für Sozialforschung*. Since then, it has been for many the paradigm of a social theory in which the intention of a philosophically guided diagnosis of the times is combined with an empirically grounded social analysis. In this chapter, I reexamine this conception in order to avoid an all-too-uncritical acceptance of Horkheimer's program of critical theory. From the very beginning, critical theory was shaped by a peculiar inability to analyze society. It failed to treat that sphere of the social that constitutes the particular object of sociology. The difficulties that Horkheimer encountered in his attempt to ground a critical social theory are rooted in a philosophy of history that conceptually reduces the process of social development to the dimension of the domination of nature. As a result of this narrow model of history, Horkheimer was forced to exclude the whole spectrum of everyday social action from the object domain of the interdisciplinary social research he attempted to develop in his programmatic essays.

I

In his essay "Traditional and Critical Theory," which appeared in the sixth year of publication of the *Zeitschrift für Sozialforschung* (1937),

Horkheimer attempted to sum up the theoretical claim and the political position of a critical theory of society.[1] His essay, written in exile in America, formulates the self-understanding of the Institute for Social Research during the 1930s. Horkheimer's aim is to expose the practical roots of the modern conception of science in order to be able to ground critical theory, as the self-conscious expression of processes of social and political emancipation, in the practical context that is made visible.

Horkheimer takes up the modern (or what he calls "traditional") model of science in connection with Descartes' reflection on method. According to this model, the task of scientific theories consists in the collection of deductively acquired statements that are hypothetically applied to empirically observable reality. The explanatory value of theory increases to the extent that the experimentally controlled observation of reality confirms individual statements within a logically consistent set of statements. The truth of a scientific theory is identical with the prognostic explanatory force of its body of statements. Horkheimer is not interested in the corrections to and modifications of this ideal of a unified science developed by post-Cartesian philosophy of science. The difference between deductive and inductive acquisition of general statements, in terms of which the classical schools of epistemology can be distinguished, or even the difference between experimental and phenomenological observations of reality, which distinguishes developments in the philosophy of science up to Horkheimer's own time, are secondary for him. He is interested much more in the basic model according to which the modern age envisions the relationship between scientific theory and reality. According to Horkheimer, the distinctive feature of traditional theory is defined by the following characterization of this relationship: "There is always, on the one hand, the conceptually formulated knowledge and, on the other, the facts to be subsumed under it. Such a subsumption or establishing of a relation between the simple perception or verification of a fact and the conceptual structure of our knowing is called its theoretical explanation."[2]

The merely external application of a set of statements (however they are acquired) to a natural process or to a historical event should make possible the explanation of the empirical state of affairs insofar as it becomes part of a series of propositions. In this way, as more and more segments of reality are caught in the net of hypothetical statements, natural and social processes as a whole can finally be theoretically predicted and controlled. Horkheimer sees in this function of traditionally conceived theories (that is, in their capacity to predict, control, and finally direct real processes) the constitutive context of modern science: "The manipulation of physical nature and specific economic and social mechanisms demand alike the amassing of a body of knowledge such as is applied in an ordered set of hypotheses." [3] The function of control that is presupposed by a scientific theory that seeks to explain and predict empirical states of affairs within a general set of statements betrays its origins: It is part of the practical process of reproduction in which the human species preserves its life through increasing control over its natural environment and its own social world. Horkheimer implicitly relies upon an assumption drawn from the philosophy of history for an explanation of how the achievements of social labor have made possible the emancipatory process that has freed the human world from the oppressive power of nature and produced a civilization that dominates nature and increasingly expands in relation to it. But—and this is the perspective in which Horkheimer is interested—traditional theory does not recognize its own constitutive context. Although it is "a factor in the conservation and continuous renewal of the existing state of affairs," [4] it has fictively cut itself off from all social processes of production: Reflecting a significant misunderstanding, traditional theory views itself as "pure" theory. As a result, Horkheimer, in a manner reminiscent of the early Marx, can ascertain not only how its specific object but also how the type and manner of its contact with reality is shaped by the prevailing condition of the forces of social production, that is, by the accumulated effects of the control over natural and social processes:

The objects we perceive in our surroundings—cities, villages, fields, and woods—bear the mark of having been worked on by man. It is not only in clothing and appearance, in outward form and emotional make-up that men are the product of history. Even the way they see and hear is inseparable from the social life-process as it has evolved over the millennia. The facts which our senses present to us are socially preformed in two ways: through the historical character of the object perceived and through the historical character of the perceiving organ. [5]

The knowing subject and the object known are mutually determined from the beginning by the social process of the cultivation of nature, the product of which is the history of the species as a whole.

However, the self-deception in which modern science considers itself free from all ties, even to this labor process, is clarified further by reference to a second assumption derived from the philosophy of history and more or less arbitrarily introduced into his essay: The production of social life has itself not yet been understood in the history of the species as the synthesizing, cooperative achievement of all laboring subjects. Of course, the process of production sketched out, oriented to the domination of nature, has so far brought about historical progress, but the acting subjects have not recognized their common constitutive accomplishments. This lack of awareness is simply continued in the self-understanding of traditional theory. Just as the human species is unaware of its historically constitutive productive activity, so modern science is unaware of the historically constitutive context to which it belongs as a result of all its cognitive achievements.

In order to illustrate this line of thought, Horkheimer draws an analogy between the still-unconscious synthesizing accomplishments of labor already achieved by the human species throughout history and the synthetic achievements of the transcendental ego in Kant's epistemology. This analogy admittedly also reveals for the first time the idealist fiction to which Horkheimer's construction of a unified species-subject leads: [6]

The internal difficulties in the supreme concepts of Kantian philosophy, especially the ego of transcendental subjectivity, pure or original apperception, and consciousness-in-itself, show the depth and honesty of his thinking. The two-sidedness of these Kantian concepts, that is, their supreme unity and purposefulness, on the one hand, and their obscurity, unknownness, and impenetrability, on the other, reflects exactly the contradiction-filled form of human activity in the modern period. The collaboration of men in society is the mode of existence reason urges upon them, and so they do apply their powers and thus confirm their own rationality. But at the same time their work and its results are alienated from them, and the whole process, with all its waste of labor-power and human life, and with its wars and all its senseless wretchedness, seems to be an unchangeable force of nature, a fate behind man's control. In Kant's theoretical philosophy, in his analysis of knowledge, this contradiction is preserved. [7]

Horkheimer uses Kant's epistemological model to clarify the construction derived from the philosophy of history: Just as Kant traces the world of objects of possible experience back to the structurally given capacities of a transcendental subject, so the social world is regarded as the still-unconscious product of human cultivation of nature. The transcendental manner of speaking called for by this materialistic reading of Kant's epistemology requires a singular subject, employed by Horkheimer, in order to characterize the human accomplishments of labor lumped together as "the" activity of the species. Horkheimer must assign to it all the ordering accomplishments that Kant ascribed to the transcendental ego. Thus, as a singular subject of history, the human species always already produces the social world, and does so in a continuously better way. However, it remains unaware of its constitution up to the present time. This lack of awareness on the part of the species is the ultimate cause of the catastrophic blindness of the present course of history. Modern science is itself still an unconscious moment of this perpetually productive yet blind self-preservation. The materialistic interpretation first clarifies traditional theory in this situation by tracing it back to the labor process from which it grew and to which it remains methodologically tied. Along the path of this interpretation, traditional theory finally recovers its "positive social function," [8] the rational domination of nature.

Horkheimer attempts to explain the self-misunderstanding of traditional theory in terms of this interpretive framework, derived from the philosophy of history, which unambiguously ascribes to the historical expansion of productive forces, to the rational means for dominating nature, an emancipatory potential, one virtually guaranteeing progress. His sketch, which seems to be derived directly from the "model of the estrangement of labor" that lies at the basis of Marx's early critique of capitalism, [9] treats the civilizing process of history as the process of a progressive perfection of the human domination of nature. The species is separated from the enjoyment of its power only as a result of its own lack of historical understanding. It is this interpretation of the contradiction between productive forces and productive relations that now governs Horkheimer's attempt to provide a foundation for a critical theory of society: The productive forces are seen as an emancipatory potential whose unplanned organization in capitalism is regarded only as the expression of human self-deception.

Horkheimer can initially derive the first feature of a critical theory without any difficulties *ex negativo,* that is, by avoiding the basic errors of traditional theory. Whereas traditional theory, insofar as it believes it can ground its methods through criteria immanent to knowledge alone, is separated from its own practical origin, critical theory is continuously conscious of its constitutive context. The self-knowledge with which the materialistic interpretation must first encounter traditional theory, so to speak, from without, is the first task and the deepest principle of critical theory: More or less repeating Karl Korsch's formula that historical materialism must always be applied to itself, in this essay Horkheimer states that "the influence of social development on the structure of the theory is part of the theory's doctrinal content." [10] But how can Horkheimer now define with greater conceptual precision the practical context to which critical theory is constitutively related if its starting point in the philosophy of history still reduces all social practice to the productive activity of the human species? The reply to this question reveals a first ambivalence, forced upon Horkheimer by his philosophy of history, in his solution to the claims made by a critical theory of society.

On the one hand, Horkheimer is simply being consistent when he traces critical theory back to the same mode of activity of the human species from which traditional theory is also supposed to proceed, though against its own self-understanding. Both types of theory would in the same way be dependent forms of expression of the civilizing process of the domination of nature. However, critical theory also introduces a knowledge that goes beyond given reality and is informed about the immanent evolutionary potential of the productive forces. Horkheimer is closest to this interpretation when he speaks of a tendency toward the "maintenance, increase, and development of human life" inherent in the labor process. [11] Critical theory is thus itself the awareness of this immanent evolutionary direction:

Now, inasmuch as every individual in modern times has been required to make his own the purposes of society as a whole and to recognize these in society, there is the possibility that men would become aware of and concentrate their attention upon the path which the social work process has taken without any definite theory behind it, as a result of disparate forces interacting, and with the despair of the masses acting as a decisive factor at major turning points. Thought does not spin such a possibility out of itself but rather becomes aware of its own proper function. [12]

Within the conceptual framework of the philosophy of history proposed by Horkheimer this line of thought is, at first glance, conclusive: If the process of human history as a whole can be understood as a process of the gradual perfection of the domination of nature, then every society whose organizational form retards or does not fully exhaust the possibilities of freedom represents a condition of only partially realized reason. Corresponding to complete reason, which would be "identical with the domination of outer and inner nature" through free decision,[13] is a knowledge that is able to clarify the potential of the productive forces to explode the present because it is inherent in the progressive development of the human domination of nature. In this sense Horkheimer speaks of "the idea of a rational organization of society that meets the needs of all . . . and is inherent in labor." [14] However, the logic of this argument still leaves unclear how a critical theory so tailored (that is, as an intellectual extension of a second-order labor process) should be of a methodologically different structure, namely one that ought to be able to carry out a critique of the existing society. If Horkheimer is correct in tracing traditional theory back to the cognitive achievements introduced by the activity of labor, then the knowledge furnished by this type of theory is primarily suited only for the explanation and prediction of empirical processes. It does not contain the reflective moment that would be necessary to call into question the range that an existing social order grants to the development of productive forces. This methodological gap also cannot provide a higher-order knowledge, a knowledge about the direction of the domination of nature through science. A theory that consciously refers back to the process of social labor and has as its object the immanent developmental logic of the accomplishments of social labor rather than the actual processes of nature could, of course, fictively project this developmental course into the future, but it could not then use it as a criterion for a critique of social life. For the latter such a theory would still require knowledge derived from a philosophy of history, which must in fact lie at the basis of Horkheimer's own argument, in order to criticize a society in terms of its development-inhibiting organization of labor. Horkheimer himself obviously sees the contradiction to which this interpretation of the constitutive social conditions would lead: "An activity that, oriented to this emancipation, aims at an alteration of society as a whole might well be of service in theoretical work carried on within reality as presently ordered. But it lacks the pragmatic character that results from traditional thought as a socially useful professional activity." [15]

Traditional thought represents an intellectually objectified form of knowledge, collected in the historical process of the domination of nature. It possesses a practical character because it solves scientific problems, resulting from the reproduction of an existing organization of production, through the schema of a set of propositions which permit only the explanation and prediction of real natural processes. Just as theories of this sort arise from the practical conflict between humans and nature, so they again flow back into the process of the social domination of nature as knowledge of optimal control. Even a higher level of reflection upon the same practical origin, which makes conscious the immanent developmental dynamic of the process of social labor, cannot escape this framework of application. The consequence of Horkheimer's argument is that theory can only yield a technical knowledge that at best anticipates the future conditions of application of more developed productive forces, but does not permit a critique of its present mode of organization. The scientific perfection of the domination of nature does not itself lead to the "rational decision" that, in assigning the emancipatory potential of the productive forces to the conscious control of the producers, breaks through human self-deception.

At this point, alongside this first inadequate version, Horkheimer introduces another interpretation of the constitutive social conditions of critical theory. In this version, critical theory is not an immanent component of the developmental process of human labor but a theoretical expression of a prescientific "critical activity." This type of activity is not "pragmatic," like the activity of labor contained in the process of the self-preservation of society, but is critically related, in a distanced way, to the whole context of social life:

We must go on now to add that there is a human activity which has society itself for its object. The aim of this activity is not simply to eliminate one or another abuse, for it regards such abuses as necessarily connected with the way in which the social structure is organized. Although it itself emerges from the social structure, its purpose is not, either in its conscious intention or in its objective significance, the better functioning of any element in the structure. On the contrary, it is suspicious of the very categories of better, useful, appropriate, productive, and valuable, as these are understood in the present order, and refuses to take them as nonscientific presuppositions with which it has had nothing to do.[16]

This line of thought now leads Horkheimer not only to a different formulation of the constitutive social conditions of critical theory but also to an elaboration of its second theoretical feature. Initially this set of considerations presents a kind of human activity that has not nature but "society itself" as its object. It is concerned not with an extension of the domination of nature to social life as social control but with an activity that goes beyond the societally established functional system. Horkheimer quite obviously has in mind a kind of practical, socially transformative activity to which critical theory is itself connected. Of course, this argument, which makes direct reference to a dimension of social struggle, has no systematic place in the framework of the philosophy of history that Horkheimer has presupposed thus far: So long as this framework reduces the course of human history to the quasi-natural developmental process of the domination of nature, there is no conceptual possibility for a different form of social praxis which aims not at constantly expanding productive self-preservation but at a new mode of organizing societal self-preservation. With this Horkheimer repeats a conceptual dilemma of the early Marx. From the perspective of both epistemology and the philosophy of history, Marx's "Theses on Feuerbach," with their vague, general concept of "praxis," treat the history of the species as a nature-transforming, productive activity without thereby securing a place in the conceptual framework for the concept of "practical-critical activity" which in the same text clearly denotes a politically emancipatory, revolutionary activity.[17] But the line of thought that Horkheimer opens up with the concept of "critical activity" becomes clearer when it is developed to the point where the second methodological feature of a critical social theory is worked out.

Horkheimer pursues the methodological delineation of critical from traditional theory by attempting to define the different ways in which the two types of theory respectively relate the knowing subject to the object of investigation. In nature-transforming activity, of which traditional theory is the theoretically objectified form of expression, the acting subject relates to a natural event that represents a praxis-independent reality. To be sure, humans manipulatively intervene in this natural process, but only in a way that makes use of a lawfulness that transcends the subject. At the level of scientific theory, the experiment represents this nature-transforming activity. Like the acting subject, in the scientific experiment which produces artificial processes of natural reaction for the purpose of "visual instruction," the knowing subject relates to a reality that also remains unchanged by experimental intervention. Thus, in the case of traditional theory, scientific knowledge is external to the object of investigation. Of course, the relation between the knower and the known must change as soon as it is a matter of a critical theory of society. Horkheimer now shows that since critical theory has "society itself" as its object, "critical activity," whose intellectually objectified expression it is, is itself part of the reality investigated. Thus, in critical theory, subject and object are not externally opposed to one another in the same way as in traditional theories. [18]

Horkheimer firmly retains and develops this second interpretation, which understands critical social theory as the scientific objectification of a practical-critical activity. Theory is no longer only the intellectual product of an extra-theoretical transformative praxis; in addition, it continuously has a voice in directing it. From this Horkheimer now draws a conclusion: Only because critical theory constantly influences in an action-guiding manner the same social praxis through which it is known to have been produced is it a practically transformative moment in the social reality it investigates. The altered relation of subject and object denotes a second methodological feature of critical theory. Henceforth, it is no longer only knowledge of the practical conditions of its own origin; at the same time, it is the controlled application of an action-guiding knowledge to present political praxis. Since theory attempts both to make conscious its constitutive historical conditions and to anticipate its political context of application, it is potentially, as Horkheimer still describes it in 1937 using the language of the left-Hegelian Marxism of the 1920s, the "self-awareness of the subjects of a great historical transformation." [19] This formulation, which unambiguously grounds critical theory in a dimension of social struggle rather than in the societal domination of nature, dramatically reveals the disparity between its epistemological characterization and the philosophy of history that underlies it. In his analysis of the constitutive conditions of critical theory Horkheimer invokes a concept of social praxis that is more comprehensive than that permitted by his conception of the philosophy of history. At the level of the philosophy of history, the formation and the evolution of human societies are traced back to the process of the human domination of nature. The appropriation of nature represents that dimension in which human history moves along a line of increasing material abundance. The natural character of this progress is initially overcome in the historical moment in which the species first recognizes itself in its productive activity. However, in his second version, at the level of the methodological self-reflection of critical theory, Horkheimer is concerned with a dimension of practical-critical activity. The socio-cultural development moves within the orbit of both social production and social struggle. To be sure, this struggle is mediated by the economic development of productive forces, since the "protest" directing it, as Horkheimer unclearly puts it, arises from an "economic mechanism."[20] On the other hand, the structure of action which lies at the basis of social struggle is of a different kind than that of the nature-appropriating activity of labor.

Whereas in social labor the human species preserves and expands its social life in proportion to the practical conquest of natural processes, critical activity calls into question precisely the existing mode of organization of this process of societal self-preservation. An objective, pregiven power of nature corresponds to the activity of labor. Humanity is emancipated from it through a technical knowledge which assembles the practical results of this goal-directed manipulation of natural events. By contrast, the historicity of a socially established productive relation corresponds to practical-critical activity. This relation is connected with force and oppression so long as the "material and ideological power operates to maintain privileges."[21] A critical knowledge that has as its goal the "intensification of the struggle"[22] liberates humanity from this social power relation. If social labor derives its incentive from an objective pressure for survival, the incentives for practical-critical activity grow out of the subjective experience of a "prevailing injustice"[23] which is structurally connected to a given distribution of social labor among social classes. For this reason, Horkheimer ascribes the nature-transforming labor that guarantees socio-cultural survival in general to the human species as a whole, as a transcendental subject that has become actual, whereas he ascribes the critical praxis of social struggle only to social groups that are excluded from the privilege of the appropriation of social wealth.

The restriction of the subject of critical activity to individual groups or classes indicates that social conflict—in contrast to the cultivation of nature objectively attained by the species—is embedded in a process of the experientially mediated interpretation of the historical situation. Only a framework of action in which the activity of the subject is prompted not by a single, common perspective united by the force of self-preservation but rather by varying perspectives shaped by experience can explain why Horkheimer allows only groups, as bearers of action, to correspond to practical-critical activity. In this dimension of social practice, namely social conflict, particular interpretations of reality, which are the forms of expression of conflicting constellations of interests, emerge in opposition to one another in order to struggle over the justness of an organization of social production. Therefore, Horkheimer understands critical theory's practical framework of application as the process of a dialogically mediated interpretation of social reality in the light of injustice experienced by the oppressed class:

If, however, the theoretician and his specific object are seen as forming a dynamic unity with the oppressed class, so that his presentation of societal contradictions is not merely an expression of the concrete historical situation but is also a force within it to stimulate change, then his real function emerges. The course of the conflict between the advanced sectors of the class and the individuals who speak out the truth concerning it, as well as of the conflict between the most advanced sectors with their theoreticians and the rest of the class, is to be understood as a process of interaction in which awareness comes to flower along with its liberating but also its aggressive forces which incite while also requiring discipline. [24]

Horkheimer did not further clarify the specific structure of the social practice characterized by the phrase "critical activity." To be sure, the idea of a dialogically mediated application of critical social theory opens up the insight into the interpretive dependence upon social experiences. But Horkheimer does not make use of this for a conceptually broadened demarcation of the category of "critical activity" in contrast to the category of "social labor." At the theoretical level the concept of practical-critical activity remains peculiarly undefined. To the contrary, at the level of his basic assumptions concerning the philosophy of history, Horkheimer omitted completely the dimension of a critique of everyday life in which theory is known to be located since that theory participates in the cooperative process of an interpretation of the present in the interest of overcoming suffered injustice. This conceptual reductionism prevents Horkheimer from grasping the practical dimensions of social conflict and struggle as such. Despite his epistemological definition of critical theory, he does not seriously treat the dimensions of action present in social struggle as an autonomous sphere of social reproduction. But, for that reason, Horkheimer gives up the possibility of considering sufficiently the interpretive organization of social reality. The result is, as will be shown, a sociological deficit in the interdisciplinary social science that Horkheimer views as the solution offered by the program of a critical social theory.

II

The lack of political orientation that seemed to confront the institute in the 1930s may have contributed to the conceptual ambivalence of Horkheimer's arguments. In this case, concrete uncertainty about the practical application of theory would have hindered an adequate consideration of the dimension of social struggle from the perspective of the philosophy of history. The realm of critical activity would have been completely excluded from the conceptual framework of historical interpretation because the theory of society is unsure of its role at the present historical moment. In fact, a political confusion, which could well be the source of such a precipitous generalization, characterizes Horkheimer's political writings from this period: On the one hand, there is no doubt that under the conditions of capitalism a critical theory of society aimed at political praxis must look for its addressees only among the social class of the wage laborer, the proletariat. For reasons connected with the social structure, only this group is open to theoretical enlightenment and ready for political revolution. On the other hand, in these writings, as a result of the experiences of the National Socialists' seizure of power and of Stalinism, the doubt has increased about whether, under the conditions of postliberal capitalism, the proletariat still bears the potential for transformation resulting from its experience of oppression and crisis, as the Marxist concept of revolution assumes.[25] A major portion of the theoretical construction and social research of the institute during the 1930s was an attempt to provide an empirical answer to the problem expressed in this tension. Its guiding motif is formed by the question, "What psychic mechanisms have come about that enable the tension between the social classes to remain latent, even though it borders on conflict as a result of the economic situation?"[26] The program of an interdisciplinary social science, outlined by Horkheimer at the beginning of the 1930s, is tailored to the investigation of this phenomenon.

In his 1931 inaugural lecture, "The Present Situation of Social Philosophy and the Tasks of an Institute for Social Research," Horkheimer already makes it clear that a critical theory of society that accepts the difficult project of reflecting upon its social origins as well as upon the political possibilities for its realization can fulfill its task only within an interdisciplinary context. The model he presents for this task is that of a "continuous dialectical interpenetration and development of philosophical theory and particular scientific practice."[27] Horkheimer has in mind a critical theory that analyzes the structural conditions and consequences of capitalist crises through a constant interaction between philosophical diagnoses of the present and research projects within the particular sciences. "History and Psychology," an essay published the same year in the *Zeitschrift*, attempts to expand and concretize this roughly sketched theoretical program. The paradigm derived from the philosophy of history, which will later provide the framework for the methodological approach of critical theory, is found here in the form of a materialist reinterpretation of Hegel's philosophy of history. It provides an interpretive background for the task of integrating the individual scientific disciplines into a theoretical structure appropriate to the subject matter. According to Horkheimer, the materialist interpretation of history is indebted to Hegel's concept of history since it includes the idea of a context of action that goes beyond the intentions of individual agents. Nevertheless, it is also opposed to it since it traces the course of human history back to the development of the human domination of nature rather than to the unfolding of absolute Spirit. It is this idea, critically directed against Hegel, that now ushers in the idea of a process of social labor that shapes socio-cultural progress, an idea characteristic of the early Horkheimer: "The knowledge of actual relations dethrones Spirit as an autonomous power shaping history and puts in its place, as the motor of history, the dialectic between the various human forces that arise as a result of the conflict with nature and the antiquated forms of society. . . . According to it [the economic interpretation of history—A.H.], the maintenance and renewal of social life forces its own specific arrangement of social classes on humanity." [28] Horkheimer makes basic a process of the development of productive forces which, with each new level of the technical domination of nature, also produces a new level in the social organization of production. The dimension of social struggle which, as the constitutive ground of critical theory, will later assume such a divided role in the epistemological essay is nevertheless still completely absent from this concept of social evolution. The domination of nature, self-preservation solely through the processes of social labor, is the only dimension in which sociocultural progress takes place. Horkheimer explicitly equates the "life process of a society" with the "conflict with nature." [29] This conceptually limited model of history, a decisive component of Horkheimer's early critical theory, forms the theoretical base upon which he erects the edifice of an interdisciplinary social science. Political economy is then the individual science that assumes the uncontested role of the fundamental discipline within the social sciences. Only economic concepts grasp the objective structure of the process of social life, since the history of civilization is disclosed as the process of a gradual development of productive forces freed from the fetters of outmoded productive relations: "If history is divided according to the various ways that the life process of human society is realized, then it is not psychological but economic categories that are historically fundamental." [30] As a result of this argument, Horkheimer can identify the central concepts of Marx's analysis of capital as the social-scientific concepts which express the capitalist form of the species-historical process of the domination of nature.

Of course, Horkheimer is aware that the economic theory of capitalism, which is supposed to form the backbone of interdisciplinary social science, must, so to speak, shift historically along with its object of investigation. Critical theory, if it wants to be an expression of an actual historical situation, must impartially comprehend the internal structural change that the capitalist system has undergone since its liberal era. Thus, for Horkheimer during the 1930s, the task of economics consisted in investigating the tendency of capitalism, as a result of the process of concentration, to move toward planned economic organization. Friedrich Pollock was at the institute at this time to assist in this project.[31] The legal and political work of Franz Neumann and Otto Kirchheimer, which had as its object the judicial and political "mediatization" of the capitalist crisis dynamic, are also relevant here.[32] Horkheimer viewed the postliberal phase of capitalism as a mode of production in which the planning organ of an economic power elite replaced the steering medium of the market and the "monopolist" of the planned economy replaced the "manufacturer" of the liberal period.[33] However, it is largely thematized as an economic structure whose internal psychic dynamics were to be explained by the second discipline of interdisciplinary social science: psychology.

The argument with which Horkheimer presents psychology as a discipline complementing economic theory sounds familiar. It reflects the theoretical consensus that formed the common background of the "Freudian left" (Marcuse) in the 1920s and the 1930s in its efforts to integrate historical materialism and psychoanalytic theory.[34] Horkheimer turns against a sociological overburdening of the explanatory model presupposed in economic theory. A theory of society that reasons from the level of the motives of action hypothetically assumed by economic theory to the level of actual action implicitly relies upon a trivial psychology, indebted to utilitarian thought, that only recognizes "economic egoism" as a motive in social action. All the psychic motives that operate in a context of social action other than the purposive-rational pursuit of private interests are bypassed in an economic theory arbitrarily elevated to a psychology. In the place of such a trivial psychology, based on the rationalistic model of action in utilitarianism, a psychology that begins with the malleability and displaceability of human instincts should be developed. We can theoretically explain the modes of action of those social groups that participate in social repression against their own rational interest only if we consider that the needs motivating a subject not only exhibit extraordinary variation but also, under pressures of frustration, are forcibly deferred to compensatory goals. Therefore, a critical theory of society that investigates the causes of the latency of the class conflict it predicts must rely upon a psychology that has abandoned the theoretical presupposition of the purposive-rational motivation of all human action:

In any event, human action does not simply arise from the psychic strivings for self-preservation, nor simply from immediate sexual drives, but also, for example, from needs related to participation in aggressive forces, to recognition and confirmation of their own person, to concealment in a collectivity, and other movements affecting drives. Modern psychology (Freud) has shown how such claims are distinguished from hunger in that the latter demand a direct and continual satisfaction, while the former can be deferred, altered and made accessible to imaginary satisfaction.[35]

The psychological concept offered to analyze the social integration of the subject into a self-contradictory mode of production must be so constituted that it permits the instinctual life of humans to be viewed as an initially plastic, instinctual process that is shaped by societal demands upon action and constantly prepared for psychically constructed substitutes. It then becomes clear why the experience of social dependency and oppression is, so to speak, blocked and repressed by "an instinctual motor that falsifies consciousness" before it can become "knowledge."[36] The cognitive disclosure of a social reality which the ego would repair if it perceived injustice is thwarted by a dynamic process of denial and repression that substitutes perceived impotence with the imaginary experience of personal or collective power. Projection and identification are the psychological means that make this phantastical inversion possible.

It is this dualism of a knowledge adjusted to reality and an irrational instinctual process that marks the point at which Horkheimer introduces psychology into the interdisciplinary structure of critical social research. The capitalist domination of nature, in which there is a striking discrepancy between the developmental state and the mode of organization, is joined to a process of individual socialization that adjusts the instinctual potential of the subject to prevailing relations of oppression. This takes place in a process of instinctual dynamics that, by diverting socially undesirable needs to goals secured through domination, force the subject unconsciously into a constant misapprehension of reality that undermines the accomplishments of rational knowledge. Consequently, the economic reproduction of the capitalist system of domination rests upon the fluid basis of this constantly recurring instinctual process: It is, Horkheimer writes, "The historically developed psychic properties or set of drives that determines whether outmoded relations between productive elements are to be maintained and, with them, the social structure built upon them." [37] Therefore, within an interdisciplinary social science that empirically investigates the capitalist situation of crisis, economics requires a psychological theory that analyzes the socialization process of individual drives through which a social system that controls nature is integrated into the socially accepted unity of a life process. Psychoanalysis offers the theoretical paradigm that, according to Horkheimer, has the explanatory capacity to solve this problem. Its basic idea, the structuring of libidinal energies through the child's interaction with his parents, thus provides the second theoretical model that emerges as a complement to the basic mode of social labor derived from the philosophy of history.

Horkheimer assumes the version of psychoanalysis found in Erich Fromm's analytic social psychology. Within the intellectual circle of the Institute for Social Research, Fromm was entrusted with the task of working out a psychology that could be linked to economics without any fissure. His proposal thus conforms to the idea that led Horkheimer to include psychology within interdisciplinary social research: "Neither the external power apparatus nor rational interests would suffice to guarantee the functioning of the society, if the libidinal strivings of the people were not involved. They serve as the 'cement,' as it were, without which the society could not hold together, and which contributes to the production of important social ideologies in every cultural sphere." [38] Fromm links together two concepts arising from different sources in order to analyze the process of socialization that forces libidinal energies into the behavioral system required by society. [39] First, like other Marxist psychoanalysts of his time, he begins with the assumption that the institutional demands raised by the capitalist system of social labor are conveyed to the adolescent by the parents. The family is thus the social medium in which the socio-economic imperatives for behavior are preserved and passed on in a socially effective manner. Second, from an interpretation of Freud's psychoanalytic personality theory, mediated via the lectures of Karl Abraham, he derives the idea that the personality structure of an individual consists in stabilized behavioral traits on the level of psychosexual development. Individual character is a bundle of firmly bound impulses taken from early childhood eroticism. Taken together, these concepts yield the basic categories of Fromm's social psychology: Parental rearing practices that reflect the external force of society within the family fix the psychosexual development of the child at the level appropriate to the socially required system of behavior. In contrast to this, the instinctual elements that strive to go beyond the forms of expression valued in the family are either repressed or sublimated—the libidinal strivings of the adolescent subject are incorporated into the societally desired frameworks of action.

When he speaks of psychology as a subdiscipline of a critical social theory, Horkheimer has in mind Fromm's social psychology. In his essays from the early 1930s Fromm developed his theory with reference to class-specific personality structures, a model he later replaced with a class-transcending notion of the sadomasochistic character in the institute's *Studies on Authority and the Family*.[40] Insofar as Horkheimer does not make any conceptual revisions, he must inevitably adopt the weaknesses of Fromm's earlier model. Fromm lets the basic concepts of a psychoanalytic personality theory mesh directly with the basic concepts of an economic theory of society; the dimension of *social action*, the concrete reality of which gradually forms individual instinctual potential, is, so to speak, crushed between these two conceptual frameworks. The family, which represents the whole communicative context of society in Fromm's conceptual framework, appears as the mere function of an all-encompassing economic process: The functional imperatives of the capitalist economy are simply reflected as behavioral constraints within familial interaction. Within the structure of these systemic demands, shaped by the parent's rearing practices, the libidinal strivings of the adolescent apparently develop without friction. The closed functionalism into which this model falls is the hidden core of Fromm's social psychology. As Helmut Dahmer states, it moves in the direction of a "theory of total socialization,"[41] since, in opposition to the systemic forces of the economy, it does not grant a libidinal surplus to individual needs or any autonomy to social action.

Horkheimer seems to be aware of this. As if to guard against the economic reductionism that would characterize a social theory short-circuited by a combination of Fromm's social psychology and Pollock's analysis of capitalism, Horkheimer inserts a third dimension of social reproduction between the realm of the socialization of individual instincts and the encroaching system of social labor—namely, culture.

The concept of "culture" apparently represents the conceptual means with which he hopes to resist the danger of leading critical social theory astray into a latent functionalism through the theoretical merger of political economy and psychoanalysis alone. Nevertheless, the enigmatic significance and ambivalent place this concept acquires within the idea of interdisciplinary social science is the price of the conceptual reductionism of Horkheimer's own philosophy of history.

On the one hand, Horkheimer deals with a sphere of cultural action that extends beyond the socially differentiated subsystems of aesthetic or intellectual production and includes the realm of symbolic expressions and social interactions. In his inaugural address as director of the institute he begins with the assumption that culture is a third dimension of social reproduction which, together with the system of social labor and the socialization of individual instincts, interdisciplinary social science must consider if it wants to analyze the integration of the functional imperatives of the economy into the always-fragile unity of social life. Critical social theory thus rests upon the three bases of economic, psychological, and cultural disciplines:

Not simply within social philosophy narrowly conceived, but rather within the circles of sociology as well as within those of philosophy in general, discussions about society have gradually crystallized around a question that is not simply of contemporary significance, but is at the same time the contemporary formulation of the oldest and most important philosophical problems, namely, the question of the relationship between the economic life of society, the psychic development of the individual and the changes within the cultural sphere in the narrower sense (to which belong not only the so-called intellectual content of science and religion, but also law, ethics, fashion, public opinion, sport, leisure, life-style, etc.). The intention of investigating the relationships between these three processes is nothing more than a formulation, appropriate to the state of our knowledge and methods, of the ancient question of the connection between particular existence and universal reason, reality and idea, life and Spirit, only now related to a new set of problems.[42]

The category of culture invoked here, which also recalls the use of the concept now adopted in Germany from British cultural history and working-class sociology,[43] denotes a field of social action in which social groups create common values, objectify them in the institutions of everyday life, and hand them down in the form of symbolic utterances. The dimension of social reproduction that Horkheimer thus seems to aim at with the help of such a concept of culture is one in which cognitive as well as normative self-interpretations are produced and secured within the medium of social action. These patterns of value orientation, produced within specific groups and communicatively reinforced, mediate between the system of social labor and the formation of individual motives, since within them the economic constraints upon action are reinterpreted within the context of everyday practices and thereby accumulated in a socially effective manner. The natural potential of human drives and the socially independent forces of economic reproduction are refracted by the foundation of everyday interpretive accomplishments in which subjects reciprocally secure social meanings and values. Through the filter of these collective norms of action that are fixed in the group-specific interpretations of "law" and "morality" and that are symbolically represented in the habitualized forms of "fashion" and "lifestyle," the constraints upon action pre-given from above and the action motives repressed from within first become effective in subjects socialized in a life situation. The "cement" of a society, which, in Horkheimer's words, "artificially holds together the parts tending toward independence," [44] consists in the culturally produced and continuously renewed action orientations in which social groups have interpretively disclosed their own individual needs as well as the tasks required of them under the conditions of the class-specific division of labor. However, Horkheimer does not draw this conclusion. Rather, even before he becomes aware of the action-theoretic logic of his own use of the concept, his use of the category of culture reverts back to a traditional line of thought that no longer refers to a specific domain of social action but rather refers to a realm of socially generalized institutions of socialization. Within the conceptual framework that lies at the basis of Horkheimer's program of an interdisciplinary social science, this second concept of "culture" is instructive:

The process of production influences men not only in the immediate contemporary form in which they themselves experience it in their work, but also in the form in which it has been incorporated into relatively stable institutions which are slow to change, such as family, school, church, institutions of worship, etc. To understand why a society functions in a certain way, why it is unstable or dissolves, therefore demands a knowledge of the contemporary psychic makeup of men in various social groups. This in turn requires a knowledge of how their character has been formed in interaction with all the shaping cultural forces of the time. [45]

It is the system of reference and not only the conceptual range that has shifted in the context of this argument. Here Horkheimer deals with a series of cultural institutions that mediate between the behavioral requirements of social production and the subject through the stably institutionalized processes of education and acculturation. Parental rearing practices, school curricula, and religious rituals are media that affect all social classes and continuously reflect the behavioral constraints of the economic system back upon the individual psyche, albeit indirectly and in a fragmented manner. In one such use the concept of culture approximates the central Marxist notion of the "cultural superstructure," despite the fact that Horkheimer emphasizes the peculiar inner dynamics of cultural institutions more strongly than his predecessors. [46] Namely, the referential system decisive here restricts the concept of culture to permanently fixed institutions that are apparently removed from the everyday course of action. Not the cooperative production of normative patterns of orientation, i.e., cultural action, but rather the socializing function of formative institutions, the institutions of culture, provides the real paradigm toward which Horkheimer's second concept of culture is oriented.

Horkheimer has quietly transformed the action-theoretic concept of culture that he apparently has in view in his inaugural address into the institution-theoretic concept of the "cultural apparatus." [47] Culture now appears between the system of social labor and malleable human instincts in the obstinate form of organized learning processes that anchor the behavioral expectations required by the economy as libidinally charged goals of action in the individual psyche. In almost all the texts that Horkheimer published in the *Zeitschrift* during the 1930s this concept of the cultural institution has replaced the action-theoretic concept. In this way the conceptual reductionism of his philosophy of history is secured within Horkheimer's theory of social science. At the conceptual level he cannot pursue further the notion of cultural action, since the basic model of his philosophy of history leaves no room for another type of social action alongside the societal cultivation of nature.

Only an institution-theoretic concept of culture that attempts to get hold of the socially integrative function of education and religious institutions is compatible with a view of history that limits the development of civilization to the gradual expansion and refinement of human capacities for labor. In this process an institutionalized structure of cultural agencies undertakes the function of generating at the societal level the action motivations required by the social organization of labor and of ideologically supporting the established distribution of privileges. The institutions of culture are thus stabilizing factors, reaching through individual instincts, in the species-historical process of the social domination of nature. However, within this model of history Horkheimer can no more entertain a concept of cultural action that designates the cooperative activity of producing and securing group-specific action orientations than he can the epistemological concept of critical activity, since both are conceptually ruled out by referring all human action to labor. With both concepts Horkheimer strives for more than he is able to achieve at the level of a philosophy of history. Between the Marxist model of social labor and the psychoanalytic model of the socialization of individual instincts there is no third theoretical model available in connection with which he could conceptually develop the structure of cultural action or social struggle. This is the reason why Horkheimer is finally compelled to leave unutilized the action-theoretic concept of culture just as he did the concept of critical activity, although he introduced both of them.

If we follow the implicit suggestions of Horkheimer's early writings, social struggle is the conflictual counterpart to cultural action. In their everyday action, members of a social group have harmonized their class-conditioned interests and their specific needs within relatively stable value orientations and interpretive patterns that enable them, without losing their psychic identity, to participate actively in the institutionalized structures of a social order. Within the horizon of such cultural systems of action, which have acquired a certain permanence in traditional forms of interaction and symbolic orders, class-specific burdens appear reduced to a biographically bearable degree and individual drives appear integrated into a calculable organization of needs. A group-specific horizon of orientation, which is supposed to fulfill both tasks, is, of course, extremely fragile since it must be renewed and confirmed constantly by group members. Unexpected events and information previously unknown interrupt the reproduction of established orientations and endanger the disrupted normative structure of a social group. Critical activity is then the directed process of a cooperative testing and problematizing of interpretations worked out within the group. This process is set off by experiences, that have not yet been interpretively integrated and that put in a new light the previously accepted extent of social burdens and libidinal renunciations. The disruption of culturally secured everyday action forces the group member to correct and expand the traditional horizon of orientation in the face of unmasked reality. Critical activity is thus also the reflexive continuation of an everyday communication shaken in its self-understanding. On this basis, social struggle can be conceived as the cooperative organization of this everyday critique: It would be the attempt by social groups, forced by the conditions of the class-specific division of labor and excessive burdens, to realize within the normative structures of social life the norms of action acquired in the repeated experience of suffered injustice. However, since he does not know how to decipher the normal case of everyday action, Horkheimer must leave this paradigm of critical activity theoretically undefined. The force of his basic model of the philosophy of history is so strong that he cannot help but compress culturally guided everyday action and the critical-practical activity of social groups into a conceptual framework limited to social labor and the socialization of individual instincts. It is not the social actions of societal members but an institutionalized ring of cultural agencies that mediates between the economic imperative of societal self-preservation and the complementary task of the socialization of individual needs.

As a result of this conceptual inconsistency, Horkheimer screens the whole spectrum of everyday social action out of the object domain of interdisciplinary social science. In contrast to the sociological task of investigating social reality with reference to group-specific background experiences and the cooperative process of creating social patterns of orientation, he seems to be locked within the programmatic structure of critical social research. Neither the familiar cultural communication within social groups nor the everyday clash between cultural action orientations of social groups is taken seriously as an object of social-scientific research. Within the interdisciplinary structure of Horkheimer's critical social theory, sociology thus assumes the marginal position of an auxiliary science. Since it does not possess an independent theoretical model, it is simply pushed aside in favor of political economy or psychoanalysis when the cultural stabilization of the economic process or the social mediation of need formation are themes of investigation. However, Horkheimer is not concerned with providing a conceptual foundation for sociology. The action-theoretic programs in which Max Weber, on the one hand, and George Mead, on the other, attempt to give sociology the form of an autonomous science are foreign to him. Therefore, like Fromm—the functionalistic consequences of whose concept he hoped to correct through the construction of a theory of culture—he must finally be satisfied with a critical social theory that combines political economy and psychoanalysis. When he wants to analyze the process through which a system of dominating nature is integrated with the culturally accepted unity of social life, Horkheimer is thrown back to the dualism of a knowledge adapted to reality and irrational instincts. A tremendous gulf remains between rational insights into reality and libidinally induced misunderstandings of reality, so that only empirical information concerning the mechanism of social integration can be obtained. This is the fundamental consideration behind the institute's research project on authority and the family, directed by Horkheimer, on the latent readiness of the German people for fascism.

The entire edifice of interdisciplinary social science that Horkheimer attempted to sketch out during the 1930s rests upon the disciplines of economics and psychoanalysis alone. Within it a theory of culture is simply the failed attempt at a systematic consideration of social action. But the theory of culture actually applied in the work of the institute is based not upon a theory of action or upon a theory of institutions, but rather upon a third version of the concept of culture. At this point, in a (so to speak) second step of reduction, the traditionalist concept of culture, limited to aesthetic products, once again prevails over the use Horkheimer had originally made of this concept. Leo Löwenthal and Theodor Adorno, who within the division of labor in the institute were responsible for the sector of cultural theory, made use of this limited perspective in their research into cultural events. The goal of their research was the ideological-critical deciphering of the social content of the work of art. A materialist sociology of literature and music emerges in the place that, in Horkheimer's program of an interdisciplinary social science, should have been assumed by a theory of culture whose task was to analyze the social mediation of processes of economic development and human instincts. Within the quiet transformation of the concept of culture from one based on a theory of action to one restricted to institutions, and finally to one articulated aesthetically, the change of perspective in the philosophy of history is already announced—namely, the change critical theory undergoes at the end of the 1930s in the work of Adorno.

Translated by Kenneth Baynes

Notes

Horkheimer's texts are cited and English translations, where available, are cross-referenced according to the following key (in some cases, the translations have been modified):

> *BPSS* = *Between Philosophy and Social Science: Selected Early Writings* (Cambridge, 1993).
> TCT = "Traditional and Critical Theory," in *Critical Theory* (New York, 1972).
> AF = "Authority and Family," in *Critical Theory* (New York, 1972).

1. TCT, 188–243

2. TCT, 193.

3. TCT, 194.

4. TCT, 196.

5. TCT, 200.

6. On the following, compare J. P. Arnason, *Von Marcuse zu Marx* (Neuwied and Berlin, 1971), 79ff.; Michael Theunissen, *Gesellschaft und Geschichte* (Berlin, 1969), 14ff.

7. TCT, 203–4. In his "Notes" from the 1950s and the 1960s, Horkheimer once again reiterated this line of thought in a virtually structuralist version that abolishes the human species as the unified subject of synthetic achievements and replaces it with a subjectless process of structuring (see "A Kantian Sociology," in *Dawn and Decline*).

8. TCT, 205.

9. Compare Ernst Michael Lange, *Das Prinzip "Arbeit"* (Frankfurt, 1980).

10. TCT, 238.

11. TCT, 212.

12. TCT, 212.

13. Max Horkheimer, "Zum Problem der Voraussage in den Sozialwissenschaften," in *Kritische Theorie,* volume 1 (Frankfurt, 1968), 117.

14. TCT, 213.

15. TCT, 208.

16. TCT, 206–7.

17. Compare Karl Marx, "Theses on Feuerbach," in *Marx: The Early Writings.*

18. TCT, 229.

19. TCT, 231 [translation modified]. On the understanding of theory within critical Marxism of the 1920s, compare Furio Cerutti, "Hegel, Lukács, Korsch. Zum dialektischen Selbstverständnis des kritischen Marxismus," in *Aktualität und Folgen der Philosophie Hegels,* ed. O. Negt (Frankfurt, 1970), 195ff.

20. TCT, 229.

21. TCT, 219.

22. TCT, 219.

23. TCT, 241.

24. TCT, 215.

25. See Helmut Dubiel, *Theory and Politics: Studies on the Development of Critical Theory* (Cambridge: MIT Press, 1984).

26. Max Horkheimer, "Geschichte und Psychologie," *Zeitschrift für Sozialforschung* (Munich, 1980), volume 1, 125ff./*BPSS.*

27. Max Horkheimer, "Die gegenwärtige Lage der Sozialphilosophie und die Aufgaben eines Instituts für Sozialforschung," in *Sozialphilosophische Studien,* ed. Werner Brede (Frankfurt, 1972), 40/*BPSS.*

28. Horkheimer, "Geschichte und Psychologie," 131ff./*BPSS.*

29. Ibid., 133/*BPSS.*

30. Ibid.

31. Compare Friedrich Pollock, *Stadien des Kapitalismus,* ed. Helmut Dubiel (Munich, 1975).

32. Compare Alfons Söllner, *Geschichte und Herrschaft. Studien zur materialistischen Sozialwissenschaft, 1929–1942* (Frankfurt, 1979), chapter 3.

33. TCT, 238.

34. Compare Helmut Dahmer, *Libido und Gesellschaft. Studien über Freud und die Freudsche Linke* (Frankfurt, 1973), chapter III.2.

35. Horkheimer, "Geschichte und Psychologie," 139/*BPSS.*

36. Ibid., 135/*BPSS.*

Axel Honneth

37. AF, 54–55.

38. Erich Fromm, "The Method and Function of an Analytic Social Psychology," in *The Crisis of Psychoanalysis* (Fawcett, 1970), 158 [originally published in *Zeitschrift*, vol. 1, 1932].

39. In addition to the essay cited in the previous note, see especially Fromm's "Psychoanalytic Characterology and Its Relevance for Social Psychology," in *The Crisis of Psychoanalysis* [originally published in *Zeitschrift*, vol. 1, 1932].

40. Compare Erich Fromm, "Sozialpsychologischer Teil," in *Studien über Autorität und Familie*, ed. M. Horkheimer (Paris, 1936), 77ff.

41. Helmut Dahmer, "Notizen zur antifaschistischen Sozialpsychologie," *Arbeiterbewegung, Theorie und Geschichte*, Jahrbuch 4 (Frankfurt, 1976), 66ff.

42. Horkheimer, "Die gegenwärtige Lage der Sozialphilosophie und die Aufgaben eines Instituts für Sozialforschung," 43/*BPSS*.

43. Compare *Family and Inheritance: Rural Society in Western Europe: 1200–1800*, ed. E. P. Thompson, J. Goody, and J. Thirsk (Cambridge University Press, 1976); Raymond Williams, *Keywords: A Vocabulary of Culture and Society* (Oxford University Press, 1985). An earlier essay by Fritz Sack, which worked out the conceptual significance of such a concept of culture in relation to research on American subculture and which has remained largely unnoticed, is "Die Idee der Subkultur: Eine Berührung zwischen Anthropologie und Soziologie," *Kölner Zeitschrift für Soziologie und Sozialpsychologie* 23 (1971), 261ff.

44. AF, 54.

45. AF, 54.

46. "But if past and present coercion plays its part even in the sublimest movements of the human psyche, yet the psyche itself, like all the mediating institutions such as family, school, and church which form the psyche, has its own laws." (AF, 57.)

47. AF, 59.

9

Critical Theory and Political Economy

Moishe Postone and Barbara Brick

Max Horkheimer's thought was of central significance in the elaboration and transformation of critical theory in the 1930s and 1940s. Horkheimer, together with Adorno, Löwenthal, Marcuse, Pollock, and others associated with the Institute for Social Research, sought to formulate a fundamental social critique adequate to the changed conditions of twentieth-century capitalism.[1] In the process of conceptualizing those changes, these theorists developed a critique of instrumental reason and of the domination of nature, a critique of culture and ideology, and a critique of political domination. They did so on the basis of a sophisticated appropriation of Marx's theory as a critical and self-reflexive analysis of the intrinsic interrelatedness of the social, economic, political, and cultural dimensions of life in capitalism. Their investigations provided the basis for a rich and powerful critical theory of postliberal capitalism. Yet, in the course of its development, critical theory encountered serious theoretical difficulties and dilemmas. These became manifest in a pessimistic theoretical turn taken in the late 1930s, whereby postliberal capitalism came to be viewed as a completely administered, one-dimensional society.

In this chapter, we elucidate the problems entailed by the pessimistic turn of critical theory and argue that they are rooted in, and indicate the limits of, some of its theoretical presuppositions. That is, although such pessimism is certainly understandable with reference to critical theory's historical context—the failure of revolution in the West, the development of Stalinism, the victory of National Socialism, and, later, the character of postwar capitalism—it is not fully explainable in those terms. The pessimism became intrinsic to the theory itself; it resulted from the fundamental assumptions constituting the framework within which those major historical developments were analyzed.[2] Critical theory recognized the significance of the changed morphology of postliberal capitalism and examined it incisively. It interpreted postliberal capitalism, however, as a social totality that no longer possessed an intrinsic structural contradiction and, hence, intrinsic historical dynamic out of which the possibility of a new social formation could emerge.[3] The pessimism of critical theory thus concerned the immanent historical possibility that capitalism be superseded, and not only the probability that this occur.[4] This pessimistic turn rendered problematic the basis of the critical social theory itself.

We shall analyze the basic assumptions of this pessimism by investigating the development of Max Horkheimer's notion of critical theory in light of the political-economic analysis of postliberal capitalism developed by Friedrich Pollock. By clarifying the political-economic dimension of critical theory and indicating its intrinsic relation to the social, political, and epistemological dimensions of that theoretical approach, we intend to illuminate an important dimension of its pessimistic turn and uncover the limits of its underlying presuppositions. In this way, we hope to contribute to the reconstruction of a contemporary social critique that could incorporate many of the insights of critical theory while overcoming its basic theoretical limitations.

Friedrich Pollock and "The Primacy of the Political"

Friedrich Pollock's analysis of the transformation of capitalism associated with the rise and development of the interventionist state played an important role in the pessimistic turn of Max Horkheimer's critical theory of society. Pollock developed that analysis in the early 1930s, together with Gerhard Meyer and Kurt Mandelbaum, and extended it in the course of the following decade. The Great Depression, the resultant increasingly active role played by the state in the socioeconomic sphere, as well as the Soviet experience with planning, led Pollock to conclude that the political sphere had superseded the economic as the locus of economic regulation and the articulation of social problems. He characterized this shift as the primacy of the political over the economic.[5] This notion, which has since become widespread, implies that the Marxian critique of political economy had been valid for the period of laissez-faire capitalism but has since become anachronistic as a result of the repoliticization of society in postliberal capitalism.[6]

Such a position may appear to be a self-evident consequence of the transformation of capitalism in the twentieth century. It is, however, based upon a set of questionable assumptions that lead to serious theoretical problems in analyzing postliberal capitalism. We do not question Pollock's basic insight that the development of the interventionist state entailed far-reaching economic, social, and political consequences. Our concern is to examine critically the theoretical framework within which he analyzed those changes.

Pollock's analysis of the fundamental causes of the Great Depression and its possible historical results presupposed some basic assumptions of what we will call traditional Marxism. We are not using this term to delineate a specific historical tendency in Marxism but to characterize generally all analyses of capitalism that view its essential social relations in terms of private ownership of the means of production and a market economy. Within this general interpretation, the fundamental categories of Marx's critique, such as those of value, commodity, surplus value, and capital, are understood essentially as categories of the market and of the private expropriation of the social surplus.[7] The basic contradiction of capitalism is considered to be between these relations and the developed forces of production, interpreted as the industrial mode of production. The unfolding of this contradiction gives rise to the historical possibility of socialism, which is conceptualized as collective ownership of the means of production and economic planning.

Pollock sought to get beyond this traditional interpretation in attempting to analyze the transformation of twentieth-century capitalism, yet he retained some of its basic assumptions. The combination of these two moments was constitutive of the pessimism of critical theory.

Pollock's analysis developed in two, increasingly pessimistic, phases. In two essays written in 1932–1933,[8] Pollock characterized the course of capitalist development in terms of an increasing contradiction between the forces of production, interpreted in the traditional fashion, and private appropriation mediated socially by the "self-regulating" market.[9] This growing contradiction gave rise to a series of economic crises culminating in the Great Depression, marking the end of the era of free market or liberal capitalism.[10] There could be no return to a laissez-faire economy, according to Pollock.[11] Nevertheless, a new social form that could resolve the difficulties of the older one had developed within the latter; the development of free market capitalism had given rise to the possibility of a centrally planned economy.[12] Yet—and here is the decisive turning point—that need not be socialism. Pollock maintained that a laissez-faire economy and capitalism were not necessarily identical and that the economic situation could be stabilized through massive and ongoing state intervention.[13] Instead of identifying socialism with planning, Pollock distinguished between a capitalist planned economy based on private ownership of the means of production and, hence, existing within the framework of class society, and a socialist planned economy marked by social ownership of the means of production within the social framework of a classless society.[14] He maintained that a capitalist planned economy, rather than socialism, would be the most likely result of the Great Depression.[15] In both cases the free market economy would be replaced by state regulation. At this stage of Pollock's thought, the difference between capitalism and socialism in an age of planning had become reduced to that between private and social ownership of the means of production. However, even the determination of capitalism in terms of private property had begun to be ambiguous in these essays.[16] It was effectively abandoned in Pollock's essays of 1941, in which the theory of the primacy of the political was fully developed.

In these essays—"State Capitalism" and "Is National Socialism a New Order?"[17]—Pollock characterized the newly emergent order as state capitalism. He set up a contrast between totalitarian and democratic state capitalism as the two primary ideal types of this new social order.[18] Within the totalitarian form, the state is in the hands of a new ruling stratum, an amalgamation of leading bureaucrats in business, state, and party.[19] In the democratic form, it is controlled by the people. Pollock's analysis concentrated on the totalitarian state capitalist form. When stripped of those aspects specific to totalitarianism, his examination of the fundamental change in the relation of state to civil society can be seen as constituting the political-economic dimension of a general critical theory of postliberal capitalism, which was developed more fully by Horkheimer, Marcuse, and Adorno.[20]

The central characteristic of the state capitalist order, according to Pollock, is the supersession of the economic sphere by the political. Balancing production and distribution has become a function of the state rather than of the market.[21] Although a market, a price system, and wages may remain in existence, they no longer serve to regulate the economic process.[22] Moreover, even if the legal institution of private property is retained, its economic functions have been effectively abolished.[23] Consequently, for all practical purposes, economic "laws" no longer are operative.[24] No autonomous, self-moving economic sphere exists in state capitalism. Problems of administration, therefore, have replaced those of the process of exchange.[25]

This transition, according to Pollock, has broad social implications. He maintained that all social relations under liberal capitalism are determined by the market; people and classes confront one another in the public sphere as quasi-autonomous agents. In spite of the inefficiencies and injustices of the system, the rules governing the public sphere are mutually binding. Such an impersonal legal realm is constitutive for the separation of the public and private spheres and, by implication, for the formation of the bourgeois individual.[26] Under state capitalism the state becomes the determinant of all spheres of social life.[27] Market relations are replaced by those of a command hierarchy in which a one-sided technical rationality reigns in the place of law. The impetus to work is effected by political terror or by psychic manipulation.[28] Individuals and groups, no longer autonomous, are subordinated to the whole, whereby persons are treated as means, because of their productivity, rather than as ends in themselves.

Both the market and private property—that is, the basic capitalist social relations (traditionally understood)—have been effectively abolished in state capitalism, according to Pollock. Nevertheless, the social, political, and cultural consequences of that abolition have not necessarily been emancipatory. Expressing this view in Marxian categorial terms, Pollock claimed that production in state capitalism is no longer commodity production but is for use. Yet the latter determination did not guarantee that production served "the needs of free humans in an harmonious society."[29] Given Pollock's analysis of the nonemancipatory character of state capitalism and his claim that a return to liberal capitalism was impossible, the problem became whether state capitalism could be superseded by socialism.[30] That possibility could no longer be considered immanent to the present society, as emerging from the unfolding of an intrinsic contradiction driven by a self-moving economy, since the economy had become totally manageable, according to Pollock.[31] He attempted to avoid the pessimistic implications of his analysis of state capitalism by sketching the beginnings of a theory of political crises. State capitalism, in Pollock's analysis, arose historically as the solution to the economic ills of liberal capitalism. Hence, the primary tasks of the new social order would be to maintain full employment and enable the forces of production to develop unhindered, while maintaining the basis of the old social structure.[32] Mass unemployment would result in a political crisis of the system. Totalitarian state capitalism, as an extremely antagonistic form, must, additionally, not allow the standard of living to rise appreciably, since such a rise would free people to reflect critically on their situation.[33] Only a permanent war economy, according to Pollock, could achieve these tasks simultaneously. In a peace economy, the system could not maintain itself, despite mass psychological manipulation and terror. A high standard of living could be maintained by democratic state capitalism, but Pollock seemed to view it as an unstable, transitory form: either class differences would assert themselves, pushing development toward totalitarian state capitalism, or democratic control of the state would result in the abolition of the last remnants of class society, thereby leading to socialism.[34]

The prospects of the latter, however, appeared dim, given Pollock's thesis of the manageability of the economy and his awareness that a policy of military "preparedness," which allows for a permanent war economy without war, is a hallmark of the state capitalist era.[35] Pollock's analysis of state capitalism could not ground his hope that democratic state capitalism could be established and developed further in the direction of socialism. His position was fundamentally pessimistic. The overcoming of the new order could not be derived immanently from the system itself but had become dependent on an unlikely "extrinsic" circumstance: world peace.

Assumptions and Dilemmas of Pollock's Thesis

Several aspects of Pollock's analysis are problematic. His examination of liberal capitalism indicated its developmental dynamic and historicity. It showed how the immanent contradiction between its forces and relations of production gave rise to the possibility of an economically planned society as its historical negation. Pollock's analysis of state capitalism, however, was static; it merely described various ideal types. No immanent historical dynamic was indicated out of which the possibility of another social formation could emerge. We must consider why, for Pollock, the stage of capitalism characterized by the "primacy of the economic" is contradictory and dynamic, while that characterized by the "primacy of the political" is not.

We can elucidate this problem by considering Pollock's understanding of the economic sphere. In postulating the primacy of politics over economics, he conceptualized the latter in terms of the quasi-automatic market-mediated coordination of needs and resources.[36] The market is central to Pollock's notion of the economic. His assertion that economic "laws" lose their essential function when the state supersedes the market indicates that, in his view, such laws are rooted only in the market mode of social regulation. The centrality of the market to Pollock's notion of the economic was also indicated by his interpretation of the commodity: a good is a commodity only when circulated by the market; otherwise, it is a use value. This approach implies an interpretation of the Marxian category of value—purportedly the fundamental category of the relations of production in capitalist society—solely in terms of the market. Pollock, in other words, understood the economic sphere and, implicitly, the Marxian categories of the relations of production only in terms of the mode of distribution. He interpreted the contradiction between the forces and relations of production accordingly, as one between industrial production and the bourgeois mode of distribution (the market, private property).[37] This contradiction generated a dynamic that made possible and, indeed, required the supersession of the old relations of production by a new mode of regulation, characterized by planning and by the effective absence of private property.[38] It follows from this interpretation that when the state supplants the market as the agency of distribution, the economic sphere is essentially suspended; a conscious mode of distribution and social regulation replaces the non-conscious, economic mode. In such a situation, according to Pollock, economics as a social science loses the object of its investigation and is replaced by problems of administration.[39] Underlying Pollock's notion of the "primacy of the political" is an understanding of the economic based on the presupposition of the primacy of the mode of distribution.

It should now be clear why state capitalism, within the framework of such an interpretation, possesses no immanent dynamic. The latter implies a logic of development, above and beyond conscious control, which is based on a contradiction intrinsic to the system. According to Pollock's analysis, the market is the source of all nonconscious social structures of necessity and regulation. Accordingly, it must constitute the basis of the so-called laws of motion of the capitalist social formation. Pollock maintained, moreover, that planning alone implies full conscious control and is not limited by any economic laws. It follows, therefore, that the supersession of the market by state planning must signify the end of any blind logic of development. Historical development now is regulated consciously. Furthermore, an understanding of the contradiction between the forces and relations of production as one between distribution and production—that is, in terms of the growing inadequacy of the market and private property to conditions of developed industrial production—implies that a mode of distribution based on planning and the effective abolition of private property is adequate to those conditions. Within the framework of a theory that proceeds from the traditional, distribution-oriented interpretation of the relations of production, a contradiction no longer exists between such new "relations of production" and the industrial mode of production. Hence the Marxian notion of the contradictory character of capitalism becomes relegated implicitly to the period of liberal capitalism. Pollock's notion of the primacy of the political thus refers to an antagonistic society possessing no immanent dynamic pointing toward the possibility of socialism as its historical negation. The pessimism of his theory is rooted in its analysis of postliberal capitalism as an unfree, yet noncontradictory society.

Pollock's analysis reveals the problems with a critique of the social formation that assumes the primacy of the mode of distribution. According to his approach, the development of state capitalism entailed the abolition of the social relations expressed by the Marxian categories of value and the commodity. In Pollock's ideal-typical analysis, value (interpreted as a category of the market) had been superseded and private property had effectively been abolished. The result, Pollock argued, did not necessarily constitute the foundation of the "good society." On the contrary, it could and did lead to forms of greater oppression and tyranny that could no longer be adequately grasped by means of the category of value. Furthermore, according to his interpretation, the overcoming of the market meant that the system of commodity production had been replaced by one of use-value production. Yet that was shown to be an insufficient condition of emancipation; it did not necessarily mean that the "needs of free humans in a harmonious society" were being met. For value and the commodity to be considered critical categories adequate to the capitalist social formation, however, they must sufficiently grasp the core of that contradictory, alienated society, so that their abolition simultaneously implies the social basis of freedom. Pollock's analysis implies that the Marxian categories, when understood only in terms of the mode of distribution, do not adequately grasp the grounds of unfreedom in capitalism. He did not, however, proceed to reconsider the source of those limitations of the categories, the one-sided emphasis on the mode of distribution. Instead he retained that interpretation while implicitly limiting the validity of Marx's categories to liberal capitalism.

Pollock's retention of the assumption of the primacy of distribution, however, gave rise to serious theoretical difficulties in his treatment of state capitalism. His understanding of the economic sphere renders opaque the material conditions underlying the differences between state capitalism and socialism. In Pollock's treatment, the basic economic organization (in the broader sense) of both is the same: central planning and the effective abolition of private property under conditions of developed industrial production. This, however, implies that the difference between a class system and a classless society is not related to fundamental differences in their economic organization but is simply a function of the mode and goal of their administration. No relation exists any longer between social structure and economic organization. Pollock therefore could not ground the continued existence of class in the mode of production or of distribution. Instead, he was compelled to posit a political sphere that not only maintains and reinforces class differences but grounds them. Class relations became reduced to power relations, the source of which remains obscure.

The limitations of Pollock's underlying assumption in adequately grasping the changed morphology of capitalism clearly emerged in his treatment of the capitalist relations of production. The notion itself, as must be emphasized, refers to what characterizes capitalism as capitalism, that is, to the essence of the social formation as such. As we have seen, capitalism—as state capitalism—could exist, according to Pollock, without the market and private property. These, however, are its two essential characteristics as defined by traditional Marxist theory. What, in the absence of those "relations of production," characterizes the new phase of capitalism? The logic of Pollock's interpretation should have led to a fundamental reconsideration: If the market and private property are indeed to be considered as the capitalist relations of production, the ideal-typical postliberal form should not be considered capitalist. On the other hand, characterizing the new form as capitalist, in spite of the (presumed) abolition of those relational structures, implicitly demands a different understanding of the relations of production that are essential to capitalism. Such an approach, in other words, should call into question the identification of the market and private property with the essential relations of production, even for the liberal phase of capitalism. Pollock, however, did not undertake such a reconsideration. Instead he modified the traditional understanding of the relations of production by limiting its validity to the liberal phase of capitalism and postulated its supersession by a political mode of distribution. The result is a new set of theoretical problems and weaknesses that point to the necessity for a more radical reexamination of the traditional theory. If one maintains that the capitalist social formation possesses successively different sets of "relations of production," one necessarily posits a core of that formation that is not fully grasped by any of those sets of relations. This separation of the essence of the formation from all determinate relations of production indicates, however, that the latter have been inadequately determined.

It is therefore not surprising that Pollock was unable to justify adequately his characterization of postliberal society as capitalist. He did speak of the continued importance of profit interests but dealt with the category in an indeterminate fashion, as a subspecies of power.[40]

His treatment of profit was basically empty; it merely emphasized the political character of state capitalism without elucidating its capitalist dimension. The ultimate ground for Pollock's characterization of post-liberal society as state capitalist is that it remains antagonistic, that is, a class society.[41] The term *capitalism*, however, requires a more specific determination than that of class antagonism, for all developed historical forms of society have been antagonistic in the sense that the social surplus is expropriated from its immediate producers and not used for the benefit of all. A notion of state capitalism necessarily implies that what is being regulated politically is capital; it therefore demands a concept of capital. Such considerations, however, are not to be found in Pollock's treatment. What in Pollock's analysis remains the essence—class antagonism—is too historically indeterminate to be of use in the specification of the capitalist social formation.

These weaknesses indicate the inadequacy and limits of Pollock's point of departure: locating the relations of production only in the sphere of distribution. We shall develop the broader cultural and epistemological ramifications of this position when we investigate Horkheimer's approach. Pollock's analysis of the significant transformations associated with the development of postliberal capitalism does contain many important insights. They should, however, be placed on a firmer theoretical basis. A critique of the basic assumptions of the one-sided critique of distribution that characterizes traditional Marxism could provide such a basis. Given the importance of Pollock's analysis for Horkheimer's social theory, such a critique would also call into question the necessary character of critical theory's pessimism.

Critical Theory and Traditional Marxism

As the foregoing arguments suggest, we do not regard as adequate a critique of Pollock that proceeds from the presuppositions of traditional Marxism. Such an approach could reintroduce a dynamic to the analysis by pointing out that market competition and private property have by no means disappeared or lost their functions under state-interventionist capitalism.[42] Indeed, on a less immediately empirical level, the question could be raised whether it would be possible at all for bourgeois capitalism to reach a stage in which all elements of market capitalism are overcome. Nevertheless, reintroducing a dynamic to the analysis of state-interventionist capitalism on the basis of the continued significance of the market and private property does not get at the roots of Pollock's pessimism. It simply avoids the fundamental problems raised when that development is thought through to its end point: the abolition of those "relations of production." The question must then be faced whether that abolition is indeed a sufficient condition for an emancipated society. As we have attempted to show, Pollock's approach, in spite of its frozen character and shaky theoretical foundation, indicates that an interpretation of the relations of production and, hence, value in terms of the sphere of distribution does not sufficiently grasp the core of unfreedom in capitalism. To criticize him from the standpoint of such an interpretation would be to fall beneath the level of the problem as it has emerged in the consideration of Pollock's analysis.[43]

In spite of the difficulties associated with Pollock's ideal-typical approach, it has the unintended heuristic value of allowing a perception of the problematic character of the presuppositions of traditional Marxism. We have characterized that theory in very general terms as one based on the assumption that the capitalist relations of production are to be identified essentially with the market and private property, that is, with the bourgeois mode of distribution. Within this theoretical framework, industrial production arose out of, and eventually came into contradiction with, free-market capitalism. This contradiction gave rise to the historical possibility of centralized planning and the abolition of private property, that is, to the possibility of a just and consciously regulated mode of distribution of the enormous wealth created by industrial production. The development of large-scale industrial production, in other words, is considered essentially as the historical mediation from the capitalist mode of distribution to the possibility of another. The transition to socialism is considered in terms of a transformation of the mode of distribution—not, however, of production itself.

Industrial production is thus understood as a technical process, intrinsically independent of "capitalism." The latter is conceptualized in terms of extrinsic factors: private ownership and exogenous conditions of the valorization of capital within a market economy. Within this basic framework, industrial production based on proletarian labor, once historically constituted, is considered to be independent of, and nonspecific to, capitalism. Socialism thus is imagined as a new mode of political administration and economic regulation of the same industrial mode of production to which capitalism gave rise, as a mode more adequate to industrial production. The ultimate concern of this theory is to provide a historical critique of the mode of distribution. Traditional Marxism, as a theory of production, does not entail a critique of production. On the contrary, production serves as the historical standard of the adequacy of the mode of distribution, as the point of departure for its critique.

This critique of distribution is based on a transhistorical understanding of labor as an activity mediating humans and nature that transforms matter in a goal-directed manner and is a condition of social life. Marx's own mature theory was based on an analysis of the historical specificity and significance of labor in capitalism. This specificity, however, is not recognized in the traditional interpretation. Instead labor, treated in a historically indeterminate way (what Marx critically characterized as "labor"[44]), is posited as the principle of social constitution and the source of wealth in all societies.

The basis of such an interpretation is closer to the assumptions of classical political economy than it is to those of Marx's critique of political economy. It is thus no surprise that Marx's "labor theory of value" is frequently considered to be a more consistent and rigorous version of Ricardo's theory rather than its critique.[45] It is taken to be a theory that demystifies capitalist society by revealing "labor" to be the true source of social wealth. The transhistorical notion of "labor," then, is the basis for a critique of capitalist society that has the form of a one-sided critique of the mode of distribution and locates the essential contradiction of the social formation between production and distribution.

When socialism is considered in terms of a transformation of the mode of distribution into one adequate to industrial production, that adequacy implicitly becomes the condition of general human freedom. Emancipation, in other words, is grounded in "labor." It is realized in a social form where "labor," freed from the fetters of "value" (the market) and "surplus value" (private property), has openly emerged and come to itself as the regulating principle of society.[46] This notion is inseparable from that of socialist revolution as the "coming to itself" of the proletariat. The forms of labor and of production are excluded from the purview of such a historical critique of capitalism.

This traditional framework remained unproblematic only for the strain of traditional Marxism that considered "actually existing socialist societies" to be emancipatory. Its limitations, however, became particularly evident in those positions that shared the traditional assumptions regarding the essence and dynamic of capitalism and attempted to provide a Marxist critique of such "socialist" societies. An understanding of the economic sphere in terms of the mode of distribution alone did not allow for an immanent categorial critique once central planning and the abolition of private property had been realized.[47] In other words, the Marxian categories, when understood within the framework of a one-sided critique of the mode of distribution from the standpoint of "labor," cannot critically grasp the social totality. This, however, became historically evident only when the market lost its central role as the agency of distribution. Our examination of Pollock's analysis revealed that any attempt based on the traditional interpretation to characterize the resultant politically regulated social order as capitalist must remain inconsistent or underdetermined; it also showed that the abolition of the market and private property is an insufficient condition for human emancipation. Pollock's treatment of postliberal capitalism thus inadvertently indicated that the market and private property are not adequate determinations of the most basic social categories of capitalism and, hence, that the traditional Marxist categories are inadequate as critical categories of the capitalist social totality. The abolition of what they express does not constitute the condition of general freedom.

Pollock's analysis also showed that the Marxian notion of contradiction as a hallmark of the capitalist social formation is not identical with the notion of class antagonism. Whereas an antagonistic social form can be static, the notion of contradiction necessarily implies an intrinsic dynamic. By considering state capitalism to be an antagonistic form that does not possess such a dynamic, Pollock's approach drew attention to the problem of social contradiction as one that must be located structurally in a manner that goes beyond considerations of class and ownership. Finally, Pollock's refusal to consider the new form, in its most abstract contours, merely as one that is not yet fully socialist, enabled him to uncover its new, more negative modes of political, social, and cultural domination.

Pollock and the other members of the Frankfurt school did break with traditional Marxism in one decisive respect. One of Pollock's basic insights was that central planning in the effective absence of private property is not, in and of itself, emancipatory, although that form of distribution is adequate to industrial production. This implicitly calls into question the notion that "labor"—in the form of the industrial mode of production, for example, or, on another level, the social totality constituted by labor—is the basis of general human freedom. Yet Pollock's analysis remained too bound to some fundamental presuppositions of traditional Marxism to constitute its adequate critique. Because he adopted its one-sided emphasis on the mode of distribution, Pollock's break with the traditional theory did not really overcome its basic assumptions regarding the nature of labor in capitalism. Instead, he retained the notion of "labor" but implicitly reversed his evaluation of its role. According to Pollock's analysis, the historical dialectic had run its course; "labor" had come to itself. The totality had been realized, but the result was anything but emancipatory. His analysis suggested that this result must therefore be rooted in the character of "labor." Whereas "labor" had been regarded as the locus of freedom, it now implicitly came to be considered a source of unfreedom. This reversal is expressed more explicitly in Horkheimer's works. Both the optimistic and the pessimistic positions we have been examining share an understanding of labor in capitalism as "labor." Pollock retained this notion and continued to locate the contradiction of capitalism conceptually between production and distribution. He therefore concluded that no immanent contradiction exists in state capitalism. His analysis resulted in a conception of an antagonistic and repressive social totality that has become essentially noncontradictory and no longer possesses an immanent dynamic. It is a conception that calls into question the emancipatory role traditionally attributed to "labor" and to the realization of the totality but that ultimately does not get beyond the horizons of the traditional Marxist critique of capitalism.

Max Horkheimer's Pessimistic Turn

Pollock's analysis of the qualitative transformation of capitalist society entailed a transformation of the nature of the critique itself. We shall investigate the broader implications of this transformation and its problematic aspects by analyzing the development of Max Horkheimer's conception of critical theory. Before proceeding with that examination, we must first briefly outline the relation of the notion of contradiction to an immanent social critique. The hallmark of such a critique is self-reflection. Presupposing the social constitution of humans, an immanent social critique must be able to explain the possibility of its own existence. It cannot proceed from a standpoint that, implicitly or explicitly, purports to be outside its social universe. The critique, therefore, can take no normative position extrinsic to that which it investigates (which is the context of the critique itself). Indeed, the very notion of such a standpoint must be regarded as spurious. This means that an immanent critique does not critically judge what "is" from a conceptual position outside of its object—such as a transcendent "ought." Instead it must be able to locate that "ought" as a dimension of its own context, as a possibility that is immanent to the unfolding of the existent society. As self-reflective, the social critique must, additionally, be able to ground its own standpoint by means of the same categories with which it grasps its object. The existent, in other words, must be grasped in its own terms. The nature of the concepts must be related to the nature of their object, when the latter is the social context of the theory itself. Hence, an immanent social analysis can be critical only if it can show that its object, the society of which it is a part, is not unitary and static. The analysis is also historical if it demonstrates that its context possesses an immanent dynamic that points beyond itself to a realizable "ought" that is immanent to the "is" and that serves as the standpoint of the critique. Such a dynamic can either be presupposed, as is the case with transhistorical evolutionary theories that simply posit historical development, or it can be socially explained. An analysis indicating that the fundamental relational structures of the society are contradictory in character provides such a social explanation.

The significance of social contradiction thus goes beyond its more narrow interpretation as the basis of economic crises in capitalism. It should also not be understood simply as the social antagonism between laboring and expropriating classes. Social contradiction refers, rather, to the very structure of a society, to a self-generating "nonidentity" intrinsic to its forms of social relations that do not constitute a stable, unitary whole. Social contradiction is the precondition of an intrinsic historical dynamic, as well as of an immanent social critique.[48]

The adequacy of an immanent social critique is a function of the adequacy of its categories. This means that the fundamental categories of the critique of capitalism must adequately express the particularity of the social formation so that the historical abolition of the formation expressed by the categories gives rise to the social conditions of freedom. If the formation is contradictory, moreover, the categories expressing the forms of social relations must themselves embody the contradiction.

Pollock, as we have seen, analyzed postliberal capitalism as a noncontradictory totality. This analysis was important in the transformation of the immanent critique at the heart of critical theory. That transformation has been characterized in terms of the supersession of the critique of political economy by the critique of politics, the critique of ideology, and the critique of instrumental reason.[49] This shift frequently has been understood as one from a critical analysis of modern society whose focus is restricted to one sphere of social life, to a broader and deeper approach. Yet our discussion suggests that this evaluation must be modified. Pollock's analysis was based on a traditional understanding of Marx's categories, coupled with the recognition that those traditional categories had been rendered inadequate by the development of postliberal capitalism. Nevertheless, because that recognition did not lead to a fundamental reconceptualization of the Marxian categories themselves, the broadening of the social critique of capitalism by critical theory involved a number of serious theoretical difficulties.

It is a mistake, in other words, to consider the differences between the critique of political economy and the critique of instrumental reason, for example, to be simply a matter of the relative importance attributed to particular spheres of social life. As we shall suggest, the centrality of labor to Marx's analysis does not signify that he thought material production as such was the most important aspect of social life. Rather, he considered the peculiarly abstract and directionally dynamic character of capitalist society to be its hallmark, and he maintained that those features could be explained in terms of the historically specific character of labor in that society. A critique of political institutions or of instrumental reason could only be considered to supersede (rather than extend or supplement) Marx's critique of political economy if it also could account for the historical dynamism of the social formation by indicating, for example, a contradiction intrinsic to its object of investigation. This is an exceedingly unlikely proposition, in our opinion. Furthermore, the shift in the focus of critical theory outlined above was related precisely to the assumption that the postliberal social totality was without any intrinsic historical dynamic inasmuch as it had became noncontradictory. That analysis not only resulted in a fundamentally pessimistic position; it also undermined the possibility that critical theory could be consistently self-reflexive as an immanent critique. Moreover, it has proved to be questionable historically.

The transformation of the nature of critique associated with an analysis of state capitalism as a noncontradictory totality can be seen by comparing two essays written by Horkheimer in 1937 and 1940. In his classical essay, "Traditional and Critical Theory," Horkheimer still grounded critical theory in the contradictory character of capitalist society. He proceeded from the assumption that the relation of subject and object is to be understood in terms of the social constitution of both: "In fact, social practice always contains available and applied knowledge. The perceived fact is therefore co-determined by human ideas and concepts even prior to its conscious assimilation by the knowing individual. . . . At the higher stages of civilization, conscious human praxis unconsciously determines not only the subjective side of perception but, to an increasing degree, the object as well."[50] Such an approach implies the historical determinateness of thought and demands that both traditional and critical theory be grounded sociohistorically. Traditional theory, according to Horkheimer, is an expression of the fact that although subject and object are always intrinsically related within a historically constituted totality, that intrinsic relation is not manifest in capitalism. Because the form of social synthesis in that society is mediate and abstract, what is constituted by cooperative human activity is alienated and thus appears as quasi-natural facticity.[51] This is expressed theoretically, for example, by the Cartesian assumption of the essential immutability of the relation of subject, object and theory.[52] Such a hypostatized dualism of thought and being does not, according to Horkheimer, allow traditional theory to think the unity of theory and practice.[53] Moreover, as a result of the form of social synthesis characteristic of capitalism, the various areas of productive activity do not appear related, constituting a whole, but are fragmented and exist in a mediate, apparently contingent relation to one another. An illusion of the independence of each sphere of productive activity is thus elicited, similar to that of the freedom of the individual as economic subject in bourgeois society.[54] Consequently, in traditional theory, scientific and theoretical developments appear to be immanent functions of thought or of independent disciplines and are not understood with reference to real social processes.[55]

Horkheimer asserted that the problem of the adequacy of thought to being must be dealt with in terms of a theory of their constitution by social practice. Kant did begin to develop such an approach, but he did so in an idealist fashion. He claimed that sensuous appearances have already been formed by the transcendental Subject, that is, by rational activity, when they are perceived and consciously evaluated.[56] Horkheimer argued that Kant's concepts have a double character. They express unity and goal-directedness on the one hand, and an opaque and unconscious dimension on the other. This duality is expressive of capitalist society, according to Horkheimer, but not self-consciously so; it corresponds to the "contradictory form of human activity in the modern era": "The cooperation of people in society is the mode of existence of their reason. . . . At the same time, however, this process, along with its results, is alienated from them and appears, with all its waste of labor power and human life, to be . . . an unalterable natural force, a fate beyond human control."[57] Horkheimer grounded this duality in the contradiction between the forces and relations of production. Within the theoretical framework he presents, collective human production constitutes a social whole that potentially is rationally organized. Yet the market-mediated form of social interconnectedness and class domination based on private property impart a fragmented, torn, and irrational form to that social whole.[58] Capitalist society is therefore characterized by blind mechanical developmental necessity and by the utilization of the developed human powers of controlling nature for particular and conflicting interests rather than for the general interest.[59] According to Horkheimer's account, the economic system based upon the commodity form was characterized in its early stages by the notion of the congruence of individual and social happiness. During the period of its emergence and consolidation, that system entailed the unfolding of human powers, the emancipation of the individual, and increasing control over nature. Its dynamic, however, has since given rise to a society that no longer furthers human development but increasingly checks it and drives humanity in the direction of a new barbarism.[60] Within this framework, production is socially totalizing but is alienated, fragmented, and increasingly arrested in its development by the market and private property. Capitalist social development hinders the totality from realizing itself.

This contradiction, according to Horkheimer, constitutes the condition of possibility of critical theory, as well as the object of its investigation. Critical theory does not accept the fragmented aspects of reality as necessary givens but seeks to grasp society as a whole. This necessarily entails a perception of its internal contradictions, of that which fragments the totality and hinders its realization as a rational whole. Grasping the whole thus implies an interest in the supersession of its present form by a rational human condition, rather than in its mere modification.[61] Critical theory thus rejects the acceptance of the given, as well as its utopian critique.[62] It involves an immanent analysis of capitalism in its own terms that, on the basis of the intrinsic contradictions of that society, uncovers the growing discrepancy between what is and what could be.[63]

Social production, reason, and human emancipation are intertwined and provide the standpoint of a historical critique in "Traditional and Critical Theory." The idea of a rational social organization adequate to all of its members—a community of free persons—is, according to Horkheimer, a possibility immanent to human labor.[64] Whereas in the past, the misery of large segments of the producing population may have been in part conditioned by the low level of technical development and, hence, in a sense, was "rational," this is no longer the case. Negative social conditions such as hunger, unemployment, crises, and militarization are based only "on relations, no longer adequate to the present, under which production occurs."[65] Those relations now hinder "the application of all intellectual and physical means for the mastery of nature."[66] General social misery, caused by anachronistic, particularist relations, has become irrational in terms of the potential of the forces of production. Inasmuch as that potential allows for the possibility that rationally planned social regulation and development supplant the blind, market-mediated form characteristic of capitalism, it reveals the latter form to be irrational as well.[67] Finally, on another level, the historical possibility of a rational social organization based on labor also reveals the dichotomous relation of subject and object in the present society to be irrational: "The mysterious correspondence of thought and being, understanding and sensuousness, human needs and their satisfaction in the present, chaotic economy—a correspondence which appears to be accidental in the bourgeois epoch—shall, in the future epoch, become the relation of rational intention and realization."[68]

The immanent dialectical critique outlined by Horkheimer is an epistemologically sophisticated and self-reflexive version of traditional Marxism. The forces of production are identified with the social labor process, which is hindered from realizing its potential by the market and private property. Those relations, according to this approach, fragment and veil the wholeness and connectedness of the social universe constituted by labor. Labor is simply identified by Horkheimer with control over nature. Its mode of organization and application is called into question—but not its form. Thus, whereas for Marx the constitution of the structure of social life in capitalism is a function of labor mediating the relations among people as well as the relations between people and nature, for Horkheimer it is a function of the latter mediation alone, of "labor." The standpoint of his critique of the existing order in the name of reason and justice is provided by "labor" as constitutive of the totality. Horkheimer grounds the possibility of emancipation and the realization of reason in "labor" coming to itself and openly emerging as that which constitutes the social totality. Hence, the object of critique is whatever hinders that open emergence.

This positive view of "labor" and of the totality later gave way, in Horkheimer's thought, to a more negative evaluation of the effects of the domination of nature, once he considered the relations of production to have become adequate to the forces of production. In both cases, he conceptualized the labor process only in terms of the relation of humanity to nature; social relations were conceived to be extrinsic to that process.

The later pessimistic turn in Horkheimer's thought should not be too directly and exclusively related to the failure of proletarian revolution and the defeat of working-class organizations by fascism. Horkheimer wrote "Traditional and Critical Theory" long after the

National Socialist seizure of power. He nevertheless continued to analyze the social formation as essentially contradictory; that is, he continued to develop an immanent critique. Although his evaluation of
the political situation was certainly pessimistic, that pessimism had not
yet acquired a necessary character.

The possibility of critical theory, according to Horkheimer, remained rooted in the contradictions of the present order. As a result
of the setbacks, ideological narrowness, and corruptions of the working class, however, that theory was momentarily being carried by a
small group of persons.[69] This implies that the integration or defeat
of the working class does not, in and of itself, signify that the social
formation is no longer contradictory. In other words, the notion of
contradiction for Horkheimer referred to a deeper structural level
than that of immediate class antagonism. Thus, he claimed that as an
element of social change, critical theory exists as part of a dynamic
unity with the dominated class but is not immediately identical with
that class.[70] If critical theory were to formulate passively the current
feelings and visions of the class, it would, according to Horkheimer,
be structurally no different from the disciplinary sciences.[71] Critical
theory deals with the present in terms of its immanent potential; it
cannot be based on the given alone.[72] Horkheimer's pessimism at this
point was clearly about the probability that a socialist transformation
would occur in the foreseeable future; the possibility of such a transformation remained, in his analysis, immanent to the contradictory
capitalist present.

He did argue that the changed character of capitalism demands
changes in some elements of critical theory, and he proceeded to outline the new possibilities for conscious social domination available to
the small circle of the very powerful as a result of the vastly increased
concentration and centralization of capital. He then argued that this
change was related to a historical tendency for the sphere of culture
to lose its previous position of relative autonomy and become more
directly embedded in the framework of social domination.[73] Horkheimer laid the groundwork here for a critical focus on political domination, ideological manipulation, and the culture industry. However,
he insisted that the basis of the theory remained unchanged inasmuch
as the basic economic structure of society had not changed.[74]

At this point, Horkheimer did not propose that society had changed so fundamentally that the economic sphere had been replaced by the political. On the contrary, he argued that private property and profit still play decisive roles and that people's lives are now even more immediately determined by the economic dimension of social life, whose unchained dynamic gives rise to new developments and misfortunes at an ever-increasing tempo.[75] The shift in the object of investigation of critical theory proposed by Horkheimer, the increased emphasis on conscious domination and manipulation, was tied to the notion that the market no longer played the role it did in liberal capitalism. This shift was not yet bound, however, to the view that the immanent contradiction of the forces and relations of production had been overcome. Horkheimer's critique remained immanent. Its character then changed following the outbreak of World War II. That change was related to the change in theoretical evaluation expressed by Pollock's notion of the primacy of the political.

In his essay "The Authoritarian State," written in 1940, Horkheimer characterized the new social form as "state capitalism . . . the authoritarian state of the present."[76] The position developed here was basically similar to Pollock's, although Horkheimer more explicitly introduced the Soviet Union as the most consistent form of state capitalism and considered fascism to be a mixed form, inasmuch as the surplus value won and distributed under state control is transmitted to industrial magnates and large landowners under the old title of profit.[77] All forms of state capitalism are repressive, exploitative, and antagonistic. Horkheimer predicted that because the market had been overcome, state capitalism would not be subject to economic crises. Nevertheless, he claimed that the form was ultimately transitory rather than stable.[78]

In discussing the possible transitory character of state capitalism, Horkheimer expressed a new, deeply ambiguous attitude toward the emancipatory potential of the forces of production. On the one hand, the essay contains passages in which the forces of production, traditionally understood, are still described as potentially emancipatory. Thus, Horkheimer argued, they are consciously held back as a condition of domination.[79] The increased rationalization and simplification of production, distribution, and administration have rendered

Moishe Postone and Barbara Brick

political domination increasingly irrational. To the extent that the state has become potentially anachronistic, it must become more authoritarian; that is, it must rely to a greater degree on force and the permanent threat of war in order to maintain itself.[80] Horkheimer did foresee a possible collapse of the system, which he grounded in the restriction of productivity by the bureaucracies. He claimed that the utilization of production in the interests of domination rather than to satisfy human needs would result in a crisis. The crisis would not, however, be economic (as was the case in market capitalism) but would be an international political crisis tied to the constant threat of war.[81]

Horkheimer thus continued to speak of the fetters imposed on the forces of production, yet the gap he delineated between what is and what could be the case were it not for those fetters now only highlights the antagonistic and repressive nature of the system. It no longer has the form of an intrinsic contradiction. The international political crisis Horkheimer outlined is not analyzed as a moment of the emergence of the possible determinate negation of the system but is represented as a dangerous outcome that demands its negation. Horkheimer spoke of the collapse of the system but did not indicate its preconditions. Instead, he sought to elucidate those democratic, emancipatory possibilities that are not realized, or are crushed in state capitalism, in the hope that, out of their misery and the threat to their existence, people would oppose the system.

The dominant tendency of the article, moreover, is to maintain that there is, indeed, no contradiction or even necessary disjunction between the developed forces of production (traditionally understood) and authoritarian political domination. On the contrary, Horkheimer now skeptically wrote that although the development of productivity may have increased the possibility of emancipation, it certainly has led to greater repression.[82] The forces of production, freed from the constraints of the market and private property, have not proved to be the source of freedom and a rational social order: "With each bit of realized planning, a bit of repression was originally supposed to become superfluous. Instead, even more repression has emerged through the administration of the plans."[83] The adequacy of a new mode of distribution to the developed forces of production had proved to be negative in its consequences. Horkheimer's statement that "state capitalism at times appears almost as a parody of classless society"[84] implies that repressive state capitalism and emancipatory socialism possess the same "material" basis. It thus indicates the dilemma of traditional Marxist theory on reaching its limits.

Faced with this dilemma, however, Horkheimer did not reconsider the basic determinations of that theory. Instead, he continued to equate the forces of production with the industrial mode of production. He consequently was compelled to change his evaluation of production and to rethink the relationship between history and emancipation. Horkheimer now radically called into question any social uprising based on the development of the forces of production: "The bourgeois upheavals did indeed depend on the ripeness of the situation. Their successes, from the Reformation to the legal revolution of fascism, were tied to the technical and economic achievements that mark the progress of capitalism."[85] The development of production is now evaluated negatively as one that only takes place within, and remains bound to, capitalist civilization. At this point, Horkheimer began to turn to a pessimistic theory of history. Because the laws of historical development, driven by the contradiction between the forces and relations of production, have led only to state capitalism, a revolutionary theory based on that historical development—one that demands that "the first attempts at planning should be reinforced, and distribution made more rational"—could only hasten the transition to the state capitalist form.[86] Horkheimer therefore reconceptualized the relation of emancipation and history by according social revolution two moments: "Revolution brings about what would also happen without spontaneity: the societalization of the means of production, the planned management of production and the unlimited control of nature. And it also brings about what would never happen without resistance and constantly renewed efforts to achieve freedom: *the end of exploitation*."[87]

That Horkheimer accorded these two moments to revolution, however, indicates he had fallen back to a position characterized by an antinomy of necessity and freedom. His view of history had become completely determinist; he now presented it as a fully automatic development in which labor comes to itself—but not as the source of emancipation. Freedom is grounded in a purely voluntarist fashion, as an act of will against history.[88] Horkheimer now assumed, as is indicated by the passage just cited, that the material conditions of life in which freedom for all could be fully achieved are identical to those in which unfreedom for all is realized, that those conditions automatically emerge, and that they are essentially irrelevant to the question of freedom. One does not have to disagree with Horkheimer's proposition that freedom is never achieved automatically to question those assumptions. Bound by a traditional Marxist vision of the material conditions of capitalism and socialism, Horkheimer did not question the presupposition that a publicly planned mode of industrial production in the absence of private property is a sufficient condition for socialism. Nor did he consider whether industrial production itself might not be understood in social terms, as having been molded by the social form of capital. If the latter were the case, the development of another form of production would be no more automatic than the achievement of freedom. Not having undertaken such a reconsideration, Horkheimer no longer considered freedom to be a determinate historical possibility but one that is historically and therefore socially indeterminate: "Critical Theory . . . confronts history with that possibility which is always visible within it. . . . The improvement of the means of production may have improved not only the chances of oppression but also of its elimination. But the consequence that follows from historical materialism today as it did then from Rousseau or the Bible, that is, the insight that 'now or in a hundred years' the horror will come to an end, was always timely."[89]

Whereas this position emphasizes that a greater degree of freedom has always been possible, its historically indeterminate character does not allow for a consideration of the relation among various sociohistorical contexts, different conceptions of freedom, and the sort (rather than degree) of emancipation that can be achieved within a particular context. It does not question, to use one of Horkheimer's examples, whether the sort of freedom that might have been obtained had Münzer and not Luther been successful is comparable to that conceivable today. Horkheimer's notion of history had become indeterminate; it is unclear whether he was referring to the history of capitalism in the passage just quoted or to history as such. This lack of specificity is related to the historically indeterminate notion of labor as the mastery of nature that underlies Horkheimer's earlier one-sided positive attitude toward the development of production, as well as its later negative complement.

In conceptualizing state capitalism as a form in which the contradictions of capitalism had been overcome, Horkheimer came to realize the inadequacy of traditional Marxism as a historical theory of emancipation. At the same time, he remained too bound to its presuppositions to undertake a reconsideration of the Marxian critique of capitalism that would allow for a more adequate historical theory. This dichotomous theoretical position was expressed by the antinomial opposition of emancipation and history and by Horkheimer's departure from his earlier, dialectically self-reflective epistemology. If emancipation is no longer grounded in a determinate historical contradiction, a critical theory with emancipatory intent must also take a step outside history.

Horkheimer's theory of knowledge was based on the assumption that social constitution is a function of "labor," which, in capitalism, is fragmented and hindered from fully unfolding by the relations of production. He now began to consider the contradictions of capitalism to have been no more than the motor of a repressive development, which he expressed categorically with his statement that "the self-movement of the concept of the commodity leads to the concept of state capitalism just as for Hegel the certainty of sense data leads to absolute knowledge."[90] Horkheimer had thus come to realize that a Hegelian dialectic, in which the contradictions of the categories lead to the self-unfolded realization of the Subject as totality (rather than to the abolition of totality), could result only in the affirmation of the existing order. Yet he did not formulate his position in a manner that would go beyond the limits of that order, for example, in terms of Marx's critique of Hegel and Ricardo. Instead Horkheimer reversed his earlier position. "Labor" and the totality earlier had been the standpoint of the critique and the basis of emancipation; they now became the grounds of oppression and unfreedom.

The result was a series of ruptures. Not only did Horkheimer locate emancipation outside history but, to save its possibility, now felt compelled to introduce a disjunction between concept and object: "The identity of the ideal and reality is universal exploitation. . . . The difference between concept and reality—not the concept itself—is the foundation for the possibility of revolutionary praxis."[91] This step was rendered necessary by the conjunction of Horkheimer's continued passion for general human emancipation with his analysis of state capitalism as an order in which the intrinsic contradiction of capitalism had been overcome (although, as we have seen, this analysis was not completely unequivocal in 1940). An immanent social critique presupposes that its object—the social universe that is its context—and, therefore, the categories that grasp that object, are not unidimensional. The notion that the contradiction of capitalism had been overcome implies, however, that the social object has become one-dimensional. Within such a framework, the "ought" no longer is an immanent aspect of a contradictory "is." Hence, the result of an analysis that grasps what is would necessarily be affirmative. Because Horkheimer no longer considered the whole to be intrinsically contradictory, he now posited the difference between concept and actuality in order to allow room for another possible actuality. This position converged in some respects with Adorno's notion of the totality as necessarily affirmative (rather than contradictory and pointing beyond itself even when fully unfolded). In taking this step, Horkheimer weakened the epistemological consistency of his own argument.

As is indicated by his statements on the self-movement of the concept of the commodity and the identity of the ideal and reality, Horkheimer did not suddenly adopt a position that concepts are one thing and reality another. His statements imply, rather, that correspondence between the object and its concepts does exist but that it is affirmative, not critical. Given the fundamental presuppositions of such a position, the concept that presumably no longer fully corresponds to its object cannot be considered to be an exhaustive determination of the concept, if the theory is to retain its self-reflexive character. Horkheimer's position—that the critique is to be grounded outside the concept—necessarily posits indeterminacy as the basis of the critique. Such a position essentially argues that since the totality does not subsume all of life, the possibility of emancipation, however dim, is not extinguished. Yet it cannot point to the possibility of a determinate negation of the existing social order. Relatedly, it has no way of accounting for itself as a determinate possibility and, hence, as an adequate critical theory of its social universe.

Horkheimer's critical theory could have retained its self-reflexive character only if it had embedded the affirmative relation it posited between the concept and its object within another, more encompassing set of categories that would have continued to allow theoretically for the immanent possibility of critique and historical transformation. Horkheimer, however, did not proceed with such a reconsideration, which, on another level, would have entailed a critique of the traditional Marxist categories on the basis of a more essential, "abstract" set of categories. Instead, by positing the nonidentity of the concept and actuality in the interests of preserving the possibility of freedom within a presumed one-dimensional social universe, Horkheimer undercut the possible self-reflexive explanation of his own critique. The disjunction of concept and actuality Horkheimer posited rendered his own position similar to that of traditional theory, which he criticized in 1937: theory is not understood as a part of the social universe in which it exists but is accorded a spurious, independent position. Horkheimer's concept of the disjunction of concept and reality hovers mysteriously above its object. It cannot explain itself.

The epistemological dilemma entailed by this pessimistic turn retrospectively highlights a weakness in Horkheimer's earlier, apparently consistent epistemology. In "Traditional and Critical Theory," the possibility of an all-encompassing social critique, as well as of the overcoming of the capitalist formation, were grounded in the contradictory character of that society. Yet that contradiction was interpreted as one between social "labor" and those relations that fragment its totalistic existence and inhibit its full development. Within this interpretation, such Marxian categories as value and capital grasp those inhibiting social relations—the mode of distribution—and are ultimately extrinsic to "labor" itself. This indicates, however, that within such an interpretation, the concepts of commodity and capital do not really grasp the social totality while expressing its contradictory character. Instead, they grasp only one dimension of that totality, the relations of distribution, which eventually comes to oppose its other dimension, social "labor." In other words, when the Marxian categories are understood only in terms of the market and private property, they are essentially one-dimensional from the very beginning. They grasp only one of the terms of the contradiction. This implies that even in Horkheimer's earlier essay, the critique is external to, rather than grounded in, the categories. It is a critique of the social forms that are expressed by the categories from the standpoint of "labor."

In spite of its apparently dialectical character, then, Horkheimer's earlier critical theory did not succeed in grounding itself as critique in the concept. That would have required recovering the contradictory character of the Marxian categories, an undertaking that would have required reconceptualizing those categories in a manner that would incorporate the historically determinate form of labor as one of their dimensions. Such a reconceptualization, which would formulate more adequately the categories of the commodity and capital, differs fundamentally from any view that treats "labor" in a transhistorical fashion as a quasi-natural social process—as simply a matter of the technical domination of nature by means of the cooperative efforts of humans. Without such a reconsideration, the self-reflexive analysis of capitalism can be critical only if it grounds itself in the contradiction between the categorial forms and "labor" rather than in the categorial forms of commodity and capital themselves.

Horkheimer's traditional Marxist point of departure meant from the very beginning, then, that the adequacy of concept to actuality was implicitly affirmative. That affirmation was, nevertheless, of only one dimension of the totality. Critique was grounded outside the categories, in "labor." Once, given the repressive results of the abolition of the market and private property, "labor" no longer appeared to be the principle of emancipation, the previous weakness of the theory emerged manifestly as a dilemma.

The dilemma, however, illuminates the inadequacy of the point of departure. In discussing Pollock, we argued that the weakness of his attempt to characterize postliberal society as state capitalism reveals that the determination of the essential capitalist relations of production in terms of the market and private property had always been inadequate. By the same token, the weakness of Horkheimer's self-reflexive social theory indicates the inadequacy of a critical theory based on a notion of "labor." Such a theory interprets the relations of production only in terms of those of distribution. Overcoming those relations alone does not, however, signify the overcoming of capital. Rather, it has historically entailed the emergence of a more concrete mode of capital's total existence, mediated by gigantic bureaucratic organizations rather than by liberal forms. A materialist dialectical theory based upon the notion of "labor," then, ultimately is affirmative with regard to the unfolded totality. Such a critique is adequate only to liberal capitalism and only from the standpoint of a historical negation that does not point beyond capital: state capitalism.

Horkheimer became aware of the inadequacy of that theory without, however, reconsidering its assumptions. The result was to reverse, rather than to go beyond, an earlier traditional Marxist position. In 1937, Horkheimer still positively regarded "labor" as that which, in its contradiction to the social relations of capitalism, constitutes the ground for the possibility of critical thought, as well as of emancipation. In 1940 he began to consider the development of production as the progress of domination. In *Dialectic of Enlightenment* and *Eclipse of Reason* (both 1947), Horkheimer's evaluation of the relationship between production and emancipation became more unequivocally negative: "Advance in technical facilities for enlightenment is accompanied by a process of dehumanization."[92] He claimed that the nature of social domination had changed and increasingly had become a function of technocratic or instrumental reason. He grounded such reason, however, in "labor."[93] Production had become the source of unfreedom. Horkheimer did assert that the contemporary decline of the individual and the dominance of instrumental reason should not be attributed to technics or production as such but to the forms of social relations in which they occur.[94] Yet his notion of such forms remained empty. He treated technological development in a historically and socially indeterminate manner, as the domination of nature. Like Pollock, Horkheimer regarded postliberal capitalism as an antagonistic society in which usefulness for the power structure, rather than for the needs of all, is the measure of economic importance.[95] He treated social form in postliberal capitalism reductively, in terms of power relations and the particularistic political practices of the leaders of the economy.[96] Such a notion of social form can be related to technology only extrinsically, in terms of the use to which it is applied; it cannot, however, be intrinsically related to the form of production. Yet a social, as opposed to a technical, explanation of the instrumentalization of the world can be made only on the basis of such an intrinsic relation. Hence, in spite of Horkheimer's disclaimer that the dominance of instrumental reason and the destruction of individuality should be explained in social terms and not be attributed to production as such, it can be maintained that he did indeed associate instrumental reason and "labor."[97]

This association expresses the reversal of an earlier traditional Marxist position and is implied by Pollock's notion of the primacy of the political. Lacking a conception of the specific character of labor in capitalism, critical theory ascribed its consequences to labor as such. The frequently described shift of critical theory from the analysis of political economy to a critique of instrumental reason does not, then, signify that the theorists of the Frankfurt School simply abandoned the former in favor of the latter. Rather, that shift was based on a particular conception of political economy, more specifically, a traditional understanding of Marx's critique of political economy, which then informed the nature of their subsequent critique of instrumental reason.

The possibilities of emancipation in the postliberal universe described by Horkheimer have become very meager. Deprived of the possibility of an immanent historical critique, the task of critical philosophy becomes reduced to uncovering the anti-instrumentalist values sedimented in language—that is, to drawing attention to the gap between the reality and the ideals of the civilization in the hope of inducing greater popular self-awareness.[98] The social critique no longer can delineate the social foundations of an order in which a more humane existence would be possible. The attempt to attribute a determination to language that, if realized, would have emancipatory consequences,[99] is rather weak and cannot veil the fact that the theory has become exhortative.

That exhortative character is not, however, an unfortunate but "necessary" consequence of the transformation of twentieth-century industrial capitalism. It is a function of the assumptions with which that transformation was interpreted. Pollock and Horkheimer were aware of the negative social, political, and cultural consequences of the emergence of the new form of the totality. The bureaucratic and state capitalist character of the postliberal form provided the "practical refutation" of traditional Marxism as a theory of emancipation. Yet because Pollock and Horkheimer retained some basic assumptions of the traditional theory, they were not able to respond to that "refutation" with a more fundamental and adequate critique of capitalism.

The most recent historical transformation of capitalism, which began in the early 1970s, has dramatically manifested the limits of the welfare state in the West (and of the totalistic party state in the East) and can be viewed, in turn, as a sort of practical refutation of the thesis of the primacy of the political. It retrospectively shows that critical theory's analysis of the earlier major transformation of capitalism was too linear and strongly suggests that the totality has indeed remained dialectical.

The critical pessimism so strongly expressed in *Dialectic of Enlightenment* and *Eclipse of Reason* must be understood not only with reference to its historical context. It must also be understood as expressing an awareness of the limits of traditional Marxism in the absence of a fundamental reconstitution of the dialectical critique of what, in spite of its significant transformation, remains a dialectical social totality.

The Marxian Critique

We conclude by briefly outlining the theoretical approach that provides the standpoint of our analysis of critical theory and that points beyond its problematic pessimism.[100] As a response to the theoretical dilemmas of critical theory, it differs from Jürgen Habermas's approach, which attempts to get beyond such pessimism and recover the possibility of social critique by limiting the scope of labor's social significance and supplementing it with the notion of a sphere of social life constituted by communicative action. Habermas's approach, however, presupposes the same traditional conception of "labor" shared by Pollock and Horkheimer. This weakens his attempt to construct an adequate contemporary social critique and raises a new set of theoretical problems that cannot be elaborated within the framework of this chapter.[101]

Another approach would entail reconceptualizing a critical theory of capitalism by calling into question the notion of "labor," which is the fundamental presupposition of traditional Marxism. Marx's critique of political economy itself provides the basis for such a reconceptualization.[102] Marx did not merely criticize the bourgeois mode of distribution as inadequate to industrial production; he formulated a critique of labor and production in capitalism. Far from having adopted and refined Ricardo's labor theory of value, Marx criticized Ricardo for having posited the indeterminate category of "labor" as the source of value without having examined further the historical specificity of commodity-determined labor and of the value form of wealth. In Marx's mature theory, the notion that labor constitutes the social world and is the source of all wealth refers to capitalist or modern society alone, and not to society in general. Moreover, his analysis does not refer to labor as it is generally and transhistorically conceived: a goal-directed social activity that mediates between humans and nature, transforming material in a determinate manner. Rather,

Marx analyzes a peculiar role that labor purportedly plays in capitalist society alone: it mediates a new form of social interdependence—different from forms based on qualitatively specific, overt social relations (such as kinship ties)—that is abstract, quasi-objective, and historically dynamic. In other words, labor in capitalism constitutes a historically specific form of social mediation that is the ultimate social ground of the basic features of modernity. Marx's categories are not extrinsic to labor but critically grasp the consequences of its historically specific role in capitalism. Labor in capitalist society, then, has a dual character. It is both labor as commonly understood and a socially mediating activity. By the same token, its products—commodities—are both labor products and objectified forms of social mediation. Value is the objectification of this historically specific dimension of labor. As such, it is not only a form of wealth but also a form of social mediation.

In his mature critique, Marx analyzed capitalism as a peculiarly dynamic form of social life whose directionally dynamic character is grounded in the dualistic nature of the historically specific forms he analyzed (labor, commodity, process of production, and so forth). He located the contradictory character of the social formation in those dualistic forms, thereby implying that structurally based social contradiction is specific to capitalism. The notion that reality or social relations in general, or both, are essentially contradictory and dialectical appears, in light of this analysis, to be one that can only be metaphysically assumed, not explained.[103] Marx's approach suggests that any theory that posits an intrinsic developmental logic to history as such, whether "dialectical" or evolutionary, projects what is the case for capitalism onto the history of humanity. An approach based on the Marxian critique is therefore able to dispense with evolutionary conceptions of history and with the notion that human social life is based on an ontological principle that "comes into its own" in the course of historical development (for example, "labor" in traditional Marxism or communicative action in Habermas's recent work).[104]

This reinterpretation of Marx's analysis as a critique of the historically specific character of labor in capitalism, rather than as a critique of capitalism from the standpoint of "labor," leads to an understanding of capitalist society very different from that of traditional Marxist interpretations. It does not consider the basic social relations of capi-

talism in terms of the bourgeois mode of distribution alone—that is, in terms of class relations, rooted in property relations and mediated by the market. Instead, it understands the fundamental social relations of capitalism in terms of the quasi-objective mode of social mediation constituted by labor in capitalism. These impersonal and abstract social relations structure capitalist society as a totality. They constitute a historically new, abstract form of domination—a form of abstract necessity and nonconscious regulation—that is not grounded solely in the market and gives rise to the directional dynamic of capitalist society, molding its form of production. Within this framework, capitalism is a historically specific, contradictory, social totality.

This approach shifts the primary focus of the critique of capitalism away from considerations of the mode of distribution to focus on the form of social mediation constitutive of capitalism. It critically analyzes the nature of production, work, and growth in that society in terms of that form of mediation, thereby arguing that those features of modern society are socially, rather than technically, constituted. Relatedly, it grounds the subject-object dualism at the heart of instrumental reason in the form of social mediation constitutive of capitalist society rather than simply in the interactions of humans with nature. This approach locates the fundamental contradiction of capitalism within the sphere of production itself rather than between production and distribution.[105] It thereby points to a critique of the industrial process of production as molded intrinsically by capital and to a reconceptualization of the basic determinations of socialism as the overcoming of proletarian labor, not its realization. More generally, this approach analyzes the totality as contradictory rather than as one-dimensional. Hence, it conceptualizes the overcoming of capitalism in terms of the overcoming of the totality constituted by labor in capitalism—not in terms of the realization of the totality. Finally, because the dualistic categories used to grasp the form of social mediation constitutive of capitalism are able to express its contradictions intrinsically, they allow for a form of critique that is grounded in the concept. According to the approach we have briefly outlined, in other words, the *standpoint* of critique in traditional Marxism is the *object* of critique in Marx's critique of political economy.[106]

Inasmuch as this reinterpretation implies an analysis of capitalism that is not bound to the conditions of nineteenth-century liberal capitalism, and entails a critique of industrial production as capitalist, it could provide the basis for a critical theory able to overcome—the theoretical limits of the Frankfurt school's critical theory while incorporating many of itsinsights.

An analysis of the contradiction of capitalism and its abstract form of domination in terms of the double character of labor in that society suggests, for example, that the supersession of the market by the state does not mean that the basic contradiction of capitalism, as well as all forms of nonconscious social regulation and compulsion, have been overcome. It signifies rather that the mode of distribution has become consciously regulated—subject, however, to the limits imposed by the continued blind necessities, such as that of accumulation, that are rooted in the dialectic of the dualistic structuring forms of capitalism. That is, abstract domination continues to exist even in the absence of private property, so long as social relations remain mediated by labor.[107] The transformation of the contours of the social formation with the supersession of liberal capitalism is significant—in terms of a changed relation of the relations of distribution to those of production, however, not in terms of the supersession of the latter. The term *state capitalism,* which Pollock used but was unable to ground, could be justified to describe a social form in which capitalist relations of production continue to exist but in which bourgeois relations of distribution have been replaced by bureaucratic, political forms of distribution, with all of their political, social, and cultural implications.[108] This, however, is very different from Pollock's thesis of the primacy of the political, which rests on the assumption that the mode of distribution—whether in the form of the "automatic" market or as mediated politically—constitutes the essential core of the social formation.

The retention of the implicit assumption of the primacy of the mode of distribution was at the heart of the fundamental pessimism of the critical theory formulated by Pollock and Horkheimer, and that assumption rests ultimately on a transhistorical concept of "labor." Critical theory's analysis of the social totality as essentially noncontradictory, that is, one-dimensional, although antagonistic and repressive, implies that history has come to a standstill. We have sought to argue that it indicates, instead, the limits of any critical theory resting on the notion of "labor."

Notes

1. An earlier version of this chapter appeared as "Critical Pessimism and the Limits of Traditional Marxism," *Theory and Society*, no. 11 (1982). Revised portions also appear in M. Postone, *Time, Labor and Social Domination: A Reinterpretation of Marx's Critical Theory* (Cambridge, 1993).

2. For an interpretation that more strongly emphasizes the direct effects of historical changes on the development of critical theory, see Helmut Dubiel, *Theory and Politics*, trans. Benjamin Gregg (Cambridge, Mass., 1984).

3. In focusing on the problem of contradiction, we shall be concerned with the question of the social forms constitutive of capitalist society. This level of analysis is not the same as one that focuses on class struggle and the problem of the proletariat as revolutionary subject. We argue that the historical dialectic of capitalism encompasses, but cannot be reduced to, class struggle. A position that maintains that capitalist society no longer possesses an intrinsic contradiction thus goes beyond the claim that the working class has become integrated into that society.

4. Herbert Marcuse represents a partial exception in this regard. He continued to seek an immanent possibility of emancipation even when he viewed postliberal capitalism as a one-dimensional totality. In *Eros and Civilization*, for example, he attempted to locate that possibility by transposing the locus of contradiction to the level of psychic formation. See Herbert Marcuse, *Eros and Civilization* (New York, 1962), 85–95, 137–43.

5. Friedrich Pollock, "Is National Socialism a New Order?" *Studies in Philosophy and Social Science* 9 (1941): 453.

6. Jürgen Habermas, for example, presented a version of this position in "Technology and Science as 'Ideology,' " in *Toward a Rational Society*, trans. Jeremy Shapiro (Boston, 1970), and further developed it in *Legitimation Crisis*, trans. Thomas McCarthy (Boston, 1978).

7. See Paul Sweezy, *The Theory of Capitalist Development* (New York and London, 1968), 52–53; Maurice Dobb, *Political Economy and Capitalism* (London, 1940), 70–71; Ronald Meek, *Studies in the Labour Theory of Value* (London, 1956), 303.

8. Pollock, "Die gegenwärtige Lage des Kapitalismus und die Aussichten einer planwirtschaftlichen Neuordnung," *Zeitschrift für Sozialforschung* (1932), vol. 1, and "Bemerkungen zur Wirtschaftskrise" (1933), vol. 2.

9. Pollock, "Die gegenwärtige Lage," 21.

10. Ibid., 10, 15; "Bemerkungen," 350.

11. "Bemerkungen," 332.

12. "Die gegenwärtige Lage," 19–20.

13. Ibid., 16.

14. Ibid., 18.

15. "Bemerkungen," 350.

16. Ibid., 338, 345–46, 349.

17. Both appeared in *Studies in Philosophy and Social Science* 9 (1941).

18. Pollock, "State Capitalism," *Studies in Philosophy and Social Science* 9 (1941), 200. In 1941, Pollock included the Soviet Union as a state-capitalist society (ibid., 211, n. 1).

19. Ibid., 201.

20. See A. Arato, Introduction, to A. Arato and E. Gebhardt, eds., *The Essential Frankfurt School Reader* (New York, 1978), 3; H. Dubiel, Introduction to *Friedrich Pollock: Stadien des Kapitalismus* (Munich, 1975), 7, 17, 18; G. Marramao, "Political Economy and Critical Theory," *Telos*, no. 24 (Summer 1975): 74–80.

21. "State Capitalism," 201.

22. Ibid., 204; "Is National Socialism," 444.

23. "Is National Socialism," 442; "State Capitalism," 208–9.

24. "State Capitalism," 208–9.

25. Ibid., 217.

26. "Is National Socialism," 443, 447; "State Capitalism," 207.

27. "State Capitalism," 206.

28. "Is National Socialism," 448–49.

29. Ibid., 446.

30. Ibid., 452–55.

31. Ibid., 454; "State Capitalism," 217.

32. "State Capitalism," 203.

33. Ibid., 220.

34. Ibid., 219, 225.

35. Ibid., 220.

36. Ibid., 203; "Is National Socialism," 445ff.

37. For Marx, property relations as well as the market are moments of the mode of distribution. In the *Grundrisse,* he characterized property relations—"the worker's propertylessness and . . . the appropriation of alien labour by capital"—as modes of distribution that, although representing an aspect of the relations of production, do so *"sub specie distributionis."* This implies that the concept of the relations of production is not exhausted by a consideration of the mode of distribution but entails an aspect *"sub specie productionis."* Marx, *Grundrisse,* trans. Martin Nicolaus (London, 1973), 832.

38. Pollock, "Bemerkungen," 345ff.; "Die gegenwärtige Lage," 15.

39. Pollock, "State Capitalism," 217.

40. "State Capitalism," 201, 205, 207.

41. Ibid., 201, 219.

42. This, of course, would not apply to the so-called real existing socialist variants of state capitalism. One weakness of traditional Marxism is that it cannot provide the basis for an adequate critique of such societies.

43. For an example of a sophisticated critique of Pollock that, however, ultimately remains within the bounds of the traditional interpretation, cf. Marramao, "Political Economy."

44. Marx, *Theories of Surplus Value* (Moscow, 1968), 2:164.

45. See Dobb, *Political Economy*, 58; Martin Nicolaus, Introduction to Marx, *Grundrisse*, 46; Paul Walton and Andrew Gamble, *From Alienation to Surplus Value* (London, 1972), 179.

46. See Rudolf Hilferding, "Böhm-Bawerks Marx Kritik," in H. Meixner and M. Turban, eds., *Die Marx-Kritik der österreichischen Schule der Nationalökonomie* (Giessen, 1974), 143; Helmut Reichelt, *Zur logischen Struktur des Kapitalbegriffs bei Karl Marx* (Frankfurt, 1970), 145.

47. For an example of the limitations of an analysis that interprets the categories of value and use-value only in terms of the market, cf. Antonio Carlo's attempt to analyze critically the Soviet Union: "The Socioeconomic Nature of the USSR," *Telos* 21 (Summer 1974). Carlo denied that the Soviet Union was socialist but rejected all attempts to analyze it as state capitalist on the grounds that, in the absence of a market, production was of use-value. He claimed, therefore, that, although production in the Soviet Union had the same form as in capitalism, its working class did not constitute a proletariat. This is an extreme example of the social emptiness of the Marxian categories when interpreted in terms of the mode of distribution alone.

48. Opposing the reality of society to its ideals is frequently considered to constitute an immanent critique, also within the tradition of critical theory. This approach is not the same as that immanent critique presented by Marx in *Capital*, which proceeds from an awareness of the historicity of its object and seeks to explain socially both the ideals and the reality of society. Rather than calling for the realization of a society's ideals, the latter critique attempts to show the contradictory and transitory character of its object while analyzing it in its own terms. The former notion of immanent critique is one that seeks to unmask bourgeois ideologies such as that of equal exchange. Such a theory is essentially exhortative in character. The Marxian analysis includes such unmasking as a moment of a more fundamental theory that seeks to ground particular ideologies and locate them historically.

49. See Arato, Introduction, 12, 19.

50. "Traditional and Critical Theory," in M. Horkheimer, *Critical Theory*, trans. by M. O'Connell and others (New York, 1972), 200–201. [Authors' note: Translation modified. The published translation, unfortunately, is not fully adequate.]

51. Ibid., 199, 204, 207.

52. Ibid., 211.

53. Ibid., 231. Horkheimer is not referring to the unity of theory and practice simply in terms of political activity, but, more fundamentally, on the level of social constitution.

54. "Traditional and Critical Theory," 197.

55. Ibid., 194–95.

56. Ibid., 202.

57. Ibid., 204 [translation modified].

58. Ibid., 201, 207, 217.

59. Ibid., 229, 213.

60. Ibid., 212, 213, 227.

61. Ibid., 207, 217.

62. Ibid., 216.

63. Ibid., 207, 219.

64. Ibid., 213, 217.

65. Ibid., 213 [translation modified].

66. Ibid.

67. Ibid., 208, 219.

68. Ibid., 217 [translation modified].

69. Ibid., 214–15, 241.

70. Ibid., 215.

71. Ibid., 214.

72. Ibid., 219, 220.

73. Ibid., 234–37.

74. Ibid., 234–35.

75. Ibid., 237.

76. "The Authoritarian State," in Arato and Gebhardt, *Essential Frankfurt School Reader*, 196.

77. Ibid., 101–2.

78. Ibid., 97, 109–10.

79. Ibid., 102–3.

80. Ibid., 109–11.

81. Ibid.

82. Ibid., 106–7, 109, 112.

83. Ibid., 112 [translation modified].

84. Ibid., 114 [translation modified].

85. Ibid., 106 [translation modified].

86. Ibid., 107.

87. Ibid. [translation modified].

88. Ibid., 107–8, 117.

89. Ibid., 106 [translation modified].

90. Ibid., 108.

91. Ibid., 108–9.

92. Horkheimer, *Eclipse of Reason* (New York, 1974), vi.

93. Ibid., 21.

94. Ibid., 153.

95. Ibid., 154.

96. Ibid., 156.

97. Ibid., 21, 50, 102.

98. Ibid., 177–82, 186–87.

99. Ibid., 179–80.

100. The reinterpretation of the Marxian critique outlined below is based upon a more extensive reconstruction of that critique in Postone, *Time, Labor and Social Domination.*

101. For an elaboration of some of these points, see M. Postone, "History and Critical Social Theory," *Contemporary Sociology* 19, no. 2 (March 1990).

102. Marx, *Grundrisse*, 157–58.

103. M. Postone and H. Reinicke, "On Nicolaus," *Telos*, no. 22 (Winter 1974–1975): 135–36.

104. See Jürgen Habermas, *The Theory of Communicative Action*, 2 vols., trans. Thomas McCarthy (Boston, 1984).

105. Marx, *Grundrisse*, 704ff.

106. To the degree that this reversal is considered historically, it cannot, of course, be explained exegetically, that is, by arguing that Marx's writings were not properly interpreted in the Marxist tradition. In our opinion, a historical explanation should include a consideration of the transformation of the theory as a result of its appropriation by working-class movements in their struggle to constitute themselves, achieve social recognition, and effect social and political change. The historical question on the agenda was of the formation and consolidation of the class and could hardly have been that of its self-abolition and of the labor it does. The notion of the self-realization of the proletariat, based on a positive attitude toward "labor" as the source of social wealth, was an image adequate to that historical context, which was projected forward in the future as a determination of socialism. That notion, however, necessarily implies the developed existence of capital, not its abolition. By the same token, a historical explanation would also have to locate the reading outlined in this chapter.

107. The notion of abstract domination is used by in Habermas in *Legitimation Crisis* to refer to class domination that is not manifest but is veiled by the nonpolitical form of exchange (52). The existence of this form of domination, according to Habermas, grounded Marx's attempt to grasp the crisis-prone development of the social system by means of an economic analysis of the laws of motion of capital. With the repoliticization of the social system in postliberal capitalism, domination once again becomes overt; the validity of Marx's attempt is therefore limited to liberal capitalism (52–53). Like Pollock, Habermas identifies the law of value with the self-regulating market and grounds domination in class structure. According to the interpretation presented here, however, class domination does not remain the ultimate ground of social domination but itself becomes a function of a superordinate, "abstract" form of domination. Domination in capitalism is ultimately grounded not in the dominating class but in the compulsions exerted by the alienated forms of social relations (value, capital). Those forms can neither be grasped adequately in terms of the market nor, as quasi-independent forms that exist outside and opposed to individuals and classes, can they be understood only in terms of concrete social relations.

108. Although such a transformation would not affect the basic temporal determination of the value form, it would entail a significant change in the manner in which that form prevails. While the market does not play a central role in Marx's analysis of the relations of production in volume 1 of *Capital,* competition is important in volume 3, for example, as the means by which an average rate of profit is established. It is at this level that the emergence of state capitalism demands a revision of Marx's critical analysis.

10

The Long Friendship: Theoretical Differences between Horkheimer and Adorno

Stefan Breuer

That critical theory is not a unity has long been known. The differences between early critical theory and Horkheimer's and Adorno's work from *Dialectic of Enlightenment* onward have recently been stressed once again by Jürgen Habermas in his *Theory of Communicative Action*. Less well known is the fact that alongside this *rupture épistemologique* there are further, fundamental differences in the approaches of the most important representatives of critical theory—differences not only between the so-called inner circle and the other members of the Institute for Social Research but also within the inner circle itself, in particular between Horkheimer and Adorno. This is not to say that such differences were played out consciously, or that they placed their collaboration in question. *Dialectic of Enlightenment* is the product of a theoretical alliance that presupposes a far-reaching agreement on certain fundamental principles. Nonetheless, the discourse between Horkheimer and Adorno goes beyond this agreement. They concurred only in certain areas, whereas in others they pursued divergent, sometimes contrary goals.

I

The conception of critical theory that Horkheimer formulated in his inaugural lecture of 1931 appears, at first sight, to be a remarkable advance over both orthodox historical materialism and the philosophical attempts to revive dialectics undertaken by Lukács and Korsch in the early 1920s.[1] In this address, Horkheimer criticized empiricism and factual research fragmented into individual questions. But he was at least equally emphatic in criticizing the hypostatization of philosophy pervasive in Western Marxism at the time. Whereas Lukács had declared that the validity of the dialectical method would not be impaired even if research were to disprove every one of Marx's individual theses, Horkheimer emphatically rejected any such strategy of immunization. All those totalities by which the great totality—the subject-object—is determined are, in his view, "abstractions utterly devoid of meaning and by no means, for instance, souls of reality,"[2] so long, at least, as they are understood to be immediate certainties rather than tasks for research. By contrast with Lukács, who transforms the Hegelian category of totality into a method dissociated from the matter at hand, in effect treating it as a value relationship as Rickert did, Horkheimer renews the young Marx's demand for a demystifying critical theory guided by historical and empirical material, one that does not transfigure reality by depicting it as reason in existence. Instead of conceiving totality as something open to insight at any time through the choice of a particular method, the task is to combine philosophical theory with the practice of the individual disciplines in such a way that they interpenetrate and enrich one another. Thus, Horkheimer considers it to be the institute's crucial task "to organize studies, based on current philosophical formulations of the problems, that unite philosophers, sociologists, political economists, historians, and psychologists in ongoing research groups" in order to overcome the mere coexistence of philosophical construction and empirical concerns (SS, 41).

Here, as elsewhere, Horkheimer emphatically distances himself from the concept of totality that guides *History and Class Consciousness*. Materialism, as he declared shortly after in "Materialism and Metaphysics," admits of no knowledge of the absolute, but rather considers the totality to be unattainable; the tension between concepts and being is insurmountable (*KT*, I:48/*CT*, 28). Yet it would be mistaken, on the basis of this divergence, to jump to the conclusion that the goals Horkheimer and Lukács pursued were fundamentally incompatible. Despite his call for empirical analysis and interdisciplinary research, Horkheimer, too, adheres to the goal of historical materialism as formulated by Lukács: to trace the reified and alienated forms of contemporary society back to their human basis and show that "human beings are the producers of the entirety of their historical forms of life" (*KT*, II:192/*CT*, 244). Although Horkheimer may not share Lukács's conviction that there is a socially specified location from which "true reality" can be immediately known—the "standpoint of the proletariat"—he does indeed consider it possible that critical science, through the concerted effort of social philosophy and the individual disciplines, can produce that knowledge of the present that Lukács sees as constitutionally inherent in the proletariat. "The theory of society that provides the orientation for rational action is . . . not a simple summation of abstract, conceptual elements; rather, it is an attempt, with the help of all the individual disciplines, to trace an image of the process of social life that can lead to thoroughgoing knowledge of the critical condition of the world and to possible approaches to creating a rational order" (*KT*, I:168/*BPSS*).

This formulation shows that while Horkheimer kept his distance from Western Marxism, he ultimately pursued the same project: with the help of philosophical reflection, to get the stalled revolutionary process moving again and to promote the revolutionary subject's coming to consciousness. By no means was it Horkheimer's main purpose, as he declared in the foreword to the first issue of the *Zeitschrift für Sozialforschung*, to develop a "theory of the historical course of the current era" as such. Rather, he aimed at a theory whose methods and results are organized in such a way that humanity may "overcome its anarchic form and constitute itself as a real subject—that is, through historical deeds" (*KT*, I:78/*BPSS*). Consequently, the program of interdisciplinary materialism set out in the inaugural lecture does not simply amount to a collaboration between critical theory and the individual disciplines that would make possible reciprocal corrections on an equal footing. The point is to establish a clear hierarchy in which the individual disciplines are instrumentalized in the service of a social philosophy that obviously draws its "philosophical questions directed at the big picture" (*SS*, 41) from other sources. Despite all his assertions that the relationship must not be seen "as if it were philosophy that treated the decisive problems, thereby constructing theories that are impervious to the empirical disciplines, its own conceptions of reality, and systems encompassing the totality" (*SS*, 40), this is, in fact, just what Horkheimer proclaims. The project of researching the connection between economic, psychic, and cultural developments,

he continues just a few lines further on, is "nothing but a reformulation, better adjusted to contemporary methods and the present state
of knowledge, of the old question of the relation between particular
existence and general reason, reality and idea, life and spirit, only
now it is related to a new constellation of problems" (*SS*, 43). What
Horkheimer neglects to mention here is that not only the questions
but the answers, too, are drawn from the philosophical tradition and,
moreover, that he was profoundly committed to a particular philosophy: German idealism.

To be sure, the essays of the 1930s have a great deal to say about
materialism, social labor, material needs, the striving for pleasure, and
so on. Nor is nature completely dissolved into a social category, as in
Lukács; rather, it is acknowledged as something irreducibly material
(*KT*, I:201/*BPSS; KT*, II:159/*CT*, 210). Yet the world-historical role of
labor is justified in precisely the same way as in philosophical idealism,
particularly by Hegel. "In relating the material of apparently ultimate
facts . . . to human production," Horkheimer writes, "critical theory
agrees with German idealism" (*KT*, II:192/*CT*, 245). Analogously to
Hegel, who conceives of history as the subject's process of self-media-
tion, Horkheimer discovers in history "an active subject, however unconscious and thus inauthentic it may be" (*KT*, II:149/*CT*, 200), a
"universal subjectivity" that strives toward a determinate goal: the "rational condition," the "community of free humanity" (*KT*, II:152, 165,
166/*CT*, 203, 216, 217). This intention toward rational universality is
seen as immanent in human labor; it actualizes itself in the historical
process, in the course of which humanity acquires ever more powerful devices that make the "goal of a rational society" appear less and
less utopian. With the development of bourgeois society, claims
Horkheimer—entirely in accord with Hegel and Kant—a "superior,
rational form of the organization of humanity becomes visible" (*KT*,
II:225/*BPSS*), manifesting itself above all in the new role that accrues
to science as a productive force (*KT*, I:1ff./*CT*, 3ff.). For the first time
in history, it has become possible to "recognize the present form of
the economy and the entire culture based upon it as the product of
human labor, as the organization that humanity was capable of and
has given itself in this era." From now on, human beings can identify
with this totality and understand it "as will and reason. It is their own
world" (*KT*, II:156/*CT*, 207).

A humanism so emphatic, of course, is by no means pure Hegelianism, as Horkheimer himself made clear in his critique of the Hegelian dialectic. In terms of the philosophy of history, it is a variety of left Hegelianism. In its insistence on the open-endedness of the dialectic, it takes, in effect, a step backward from Hegel to Kant—although certainly without surrendering Hegel's historicization of the transcendental subject. Moreover, it is a left Hegelianism enriched by Feuerbach and the young Marx, for it replaces the world spirit and the cunning of reason with the historical activity of self-conscious human subjects. The materialist dialectic, as Horkheimer stresses contra Hegel, yields no finished, self-contained picture of reality. It renounces any conceptual eternalization of earthly conditions (*KT*, I:145, 241/*BPSS*).

Nevertheless, these modifications do not alter the fact that Horkheimer's critical theory is an idealist theory concerned first and foremost with "the propagation of reason," its "application to the entirety of social relations" (*KT*, I:89/*BPSS*), the "actualization of the ideal," and the "unification of particular and universal interests" (*KT*, I:97/*BPSS*)—the central features of Hegel's idea of the ethical. For Horkheimer, not idealism but imperfect idealism must be subjected to criticism—idealism that waives the realization of the ideal and prematurely comes to terms with empirical (bourgeois) reality. For him, idealism has no intrinsic relationship to bourgeois society; rather, it is intrinsically related to "*universal* subjectivity," which is to be freed—precisely with the help of "reason"—from its unconsciousness. He therefore elevates an advance along the lines prescribed by idealism to the supreme maxim of critical theory. "These days some claim that the bourgeois ideas of freedom, equality, and justice have proved to be false; yet it is not the ideas of the bourgeoisie, but conditions that do not correspond to them that have shown themselves to be indefensible. The watchwords of the Enlightenment and the French Revolution are more valid than ever" (*KT*, I:97/*BPSS*).[3]

This emphatic affirmation of the bourgeois heritage has the consequence of shutting out all those motifs in Western Marxism that aim at analyzing the intrinsic connection between this heritage and the structure of bourgeois society. Whereas in *History and Class Consciousness* Lukács had still addressed the task of discerning in the structure of the commodity relationship the "archetype of all forms of reification and all the corresponding forms of subjectivity," no trace of any such attempt will be found in Horkheimer. He is concerned not with uncovering the mediation—the presence of the social structure in the bourgeois heritage—but with precisely the opposite: with negating any mediation whatsoever through a surgically precise extraction of the universally human from the bourgeois context. In the process, he makes some critical remarks on the bourgeois heritage and the way it is treated at present. With respect to the sciences, for instance, he finds fault with the "chaotic specialization" of the academic disciplines and the "narrowing of their rationality by the increasing rigidity of social re-lationships" (*KT*, I:3/*CT*, 5); he speaks of "the fettering of science as a productive force" (*KT*, I:7/*CT*, 9) and emphatically criticizes the "*false* idealism . . . according to which it suffices to hold up the image of perfection without considering how it is to be attained." Measured against his profession of the credo of "true idealism . . . that it is pos-sible to settle reason among people and nations" (*KT*, II:310/*CT*, 270), such saving clauses alter nothing. For Horkheimer, bourgeois society is determined by the contradiction between universal-human (that is, rational) structures on the one hand and class-bound, irrational struc-tures that obscure reason on the other. The task of critical theory is to resolve this contradiction in favor of the former. It is not the type of rationality developed by bourgeois-capitalist society that comes in for criticism but rather its restriction by bourgeois institutions and property relations. "The root of these deficiencies, however, lies not in science itself, but in the social conditions that have inhibited its development and come into conflict with the rational elements im-manent in science" (*KT*, I:4/*CT*, 6).

Against this background, the later critique of "traditional theory" also proves to be far less radical than is often assumed. In Horkhei-mer's view, traditional theory—by which he understands the modern natural sciences and the theory of science from Descartes through Husserl and Carnap—has a "positive social function" that results from its fitness for its task, the mastery of nature (*KT*, II:154/*CT*, 205). Not the form of social synthesis determined by the commodity structure, as Lukács still assumed, but the formally unspecific, direct confron-tation of humanity with nature underlies the categories of traditional theory. Such categories, therefore, just like the material instruments of production, must be regarded as potential elements of a "more just, more differentiated, and more harmonious cultural totality" and are "to be developed as far as possible" (*KT*, II:154, 165/*CT*, 205, 216).

The critique that Horkheimer nevertheless directs at traditional theory does not refer to its logical structure and the way in which it is bound to the structure of capitalist society. It refers exclusively to the absolutizing of traditional theory, to its encroachment upon the field of regulative ideas concerning the "rational" organization of the whole, where critical theory has a monopoly. Horkheimer brings the critique of fetishism to bear only when scientific rationality overreaches the borders set for it and thereby endangers critical theory's claim to subsume scientific research under the transcendental "idea of the self-determination of humankind" (*KT*, II:177/*CT*, 229). Yet since he is incapable of discerning barriers or contradictions within traditional theory that offer the prospect of successfully defending the primacy of critical theory, the result is that critical theory lands in a situation as hopeless as that of phenomenology or of existential ontology, which can only apodictically proclaim the primacy of the "life-world" or of "being." There is no overlooking the fact that, already in the 1930s, critical theory's claim to recognize "historical reality" and to articulate the "interest in abolishing social injustice" (*KT*, II:194, 190/*CT*, 246, 242) exhausts itself in postulates held up to reality from outside.

The decay of such declamatory discourse proceeds rapidly from this point on. Since critical theory (by contrast with Lukács) is barred on both subjective and objective grounds from linking theoretical discourse on revolution to the practice of a party, in order to secure at least its ideological and bureaucratic perpetuation, the basis of critique becomes steadily more problematic. Similarly problematic is its attempt to overcome the irrationality and injustice of the existing relations of production and appropriation through the radicalization of reason that already exists "in itself." In view of the spread of authoritarian forms of domination, a development by no means restricted to the "totalitarian" states, at the end of the 1930s and the beginning of the 1940s Horkheimer began to revise his originally positive attitude toward traditional theory and to pursue the question of whether the structure of domination does not leave traces in this form of rationality as well. In "Notes on Science and the Crisis" (1932) he had counted science among the progressive forces of production oriented toward universality; the full unfolding of science was hindered only by something particular: the class structure. Now, however, bourgeois rationality itself appears to him more and more as something particular. Bourgeois reason, as "Reason and Self-Preservation"[4] puts it, has always been defined in relation to individual self-preservation, to which it corresponds in function and method (*KT*, III:83f.). Its purpose has always been a more rational mastery of nature, a perfecting of control over the object world—a task it could manage only through sacrifice and the renunciation of instinctual drives. Horkheimer's global affirmation of bourgeois rationality yields to an equally global abhorrence; the left Hegelian trust in historical progress gives way to a "critique of instrumental reason" inspired by Nietzsche and Freud, in which fascism is seen as the true nature of the bourgeois concept of reason finally come to light. "The new, fascist order is reason exposing itself as unreason" (*KT*, III:113).

Before we proceed from this shift in Horkheimer's thinking to consider the connection to Adorno that results from it, it is necessary to make clear the continuity that was sustained despite the changes. Although Horkheimer increasingly intensifies his critique of rationality at the beginning of the 1940s, he does not surrender his positive relationship to idealism in the process. The standard of critique is and remains "reason" in his late work as well, albeit reason that increasingly withdraws from the present and draws its strength from invocations of the religious and philosophical tradition. The concept of "objective reason," which Horkheimer juxtaposes to that of instrumental reason, is explicitly related to intellectual traditions that, like the systems of Plato and Aristotle, of scholasticism and German idealism, locate reason not merely in individual consciousness "but in the objective world as well: in the relationships between people and between social classes, in social institutions, in nature and its manifestations" (*KT*, III:123). Under the sway of this concept of reason, which Horkheimer also explicitly relates to Max Weber's conception of substantive rationality, it was still possible to do justice to things and to nature and to center the existence of human beings on such values as "humility and brotherly love, justice and humanity" (*KT*, III:158, 147). Only when instrumental, "subjective" reason, with its totalization of purposive rationality, destroyed this tradition's power to generate and confer meaning did "religious ideas and universal goals in general recede in favor of the demands of capital turnover" (*KT*, II:218/ *BPSS*).

The very fact that Horkheimer mentions religious ideas and universal goals in the same breath here is an indication that he is no longer able to ground the possibility of social critique in the fundamental contradictions of modern society. Instead, he bases it on the contradiction between two conceptions of reason, one of which—"objective reason"—is anchored in premodern, metaphysical, and religious contexts. The more radical his critique of the "spiritual imperialism of the abstract principle of self-interest" as the fundamental principle of modern society becomes, the stronger his tendency entirely to deny that it possesses reason in the full, "objective" sense and to elevate "the separation of reason from religion" to the decisive cause of the "sickness of reason" in the present (*KT*, III:129, 269).

Horkheimer does maintain a certain historical sense inasmuch as he rejects all attempts to restore the harmonious connection between science and theology. He points out that the transition from "objective" to "subjective" reason was no accident and cannot be reversed at will: "If subjective reason, in the form of the Enlightenment, dissolved the philosophical basis of convictions based on faith, which were an essential component of Western culture, it was able to do so because this basis proved to be too weak" (*KT*, III:171). Yet this important insight bears no consequences for his project of a "critique of instrumental reason," since it is precisely the idea of objective reason—which Horkheimer himself characterizes as obsolete—around which his own critique of civilization is organized. "Kant's maxim that 'The critical path alone is still open,' which referred to the conflict between rationalist dogmatism's objective reason and the subjective thought of English empiricism, is even more appropriate to the present situation. Since isolated, subjective reason is triumphant everywhere in our times, with disastrous consequences, critique must necessarily be conducted with more emphasis on objective reason than on the remnants of subjectivistic philosophy, whose genuine traditions now themselves appear objectivistic and romantic in light of the advanced state of subjectivization" (*KT,* III:268). The line that separates this conception from conservative cultural criticism is thinner than Horkheimer may have recognized.

II

Adorno's version of critical theory took shape in the 1930s under quite different auspices. Influenced by Benjamin, Adorno distanced himself from the intentions of Western Marxism even more clearly than did Horkheimer. Philosophy today, his inaugural lecture proclaims apodictically, is incapable of grasping the totality of the real by means of thought; only by way of traces and ruins can it hope to approach reality (*GS,* 1:326). Adorno replaces the conceptual reconstruction of totality, a procedure no less central for Marx than for Lukács and Horkheimer, with a nebulous conception of "philosophical interpretation" unmistakably oriented toward Benjamin.[5] Philosophical interpretation, as Adorno still claims here, does not attempt to discern the universal in the particular and to discover the "true world" behind the appearances; rather, its procedure consists precisely in an immersion in this world of appearances and in grouping its elements into configurations that provide sudden, startling flashes of truth and make possible the "awakening of the cryptic and rigidified" (*GS,* 1:357). As he later put it in "A Portrait of Walter Benjamin," which can certainly be read as a characterization of his own early work, the method of "natural history" makes it possible "not merely to awaken life that is congealed and petrified—as it is in allegory—but also to regard living things so that they present themselves as archaic, 'ur-historical,' and suddenly release their significance. Philosophy appropriates commodity fetishism for itself: all must fall under a spell and metamorphose into a thing, so that it can disenchant the monstrosity of reification" (*GS,* 10.1:243).

There is much to be said for Martin Jay's thesis that Adorno only gradually freed himself from this "extreme Benjaminism" and that Horkheimer's insistence on a simultaneously theoretical and empirical reconstruction of the social totality played a considerable role in the process.[6] Of course, Benjamin's influence on Adorno never receded entirely; it remained alive in his insistence on living, undirected experience and in a corresponding aversion to filling out the concept of "universal mediation" with a systematic analysis of society. As he asserted in his contribution to the "positivism controversy," dialectical theory must now relinquish the systematic form; and in his lecture, "Late Capitalism and Industrial Society," Adorno even doubts that contemporary society can be grasped in a coherent theory (*GS*, 8:308, 359).

Nevertheless, there is no overlooking the fact that in the course of the 1930s an idea gains steadily in significance in Adorno's writings, an idea that, as he later rightly observed, Benjamin's micrological and fragmentary method never quite managed to accommodate: the idea of "universal mediation which, in Hegel as in Marx, generates totality" (*GS*, 10.1:247). The significance Adorno accords to this conception first emerges in relatively clear form in his critique of Benjamin's "The Work of Art in the Age of Its Technical Reproducibility." Adorno accused Benjamin of a lack of dialectics and of an anarchistic faith in the self-activating forces of the proletariat—remarkably enough, by referring to Lenin, a theorist Adorno was never again to cite positively.[7] Two important further stations were the works of music criticism published in 1936 and 1938, "On Jazz" and "On the Fetish Character in Music and the Regression of Listening," in which Adorno became the first Marxist theorist since Lukács to make use of the possibilities of commodity analysis. The deciphering of the archaic element in jazz as a "second nature" mediated by the commodity structure, as well as his remarks on "pseudo-activity" and the "regression of hearing," indicate that Adorno was by no means solely concerned with aesthetic phenomena in the narrow sense but rather with nothing less than extending the theory of reification into an anthropology of industrial capitalism. The growing rift between this conceptual orientation and Benjamin's "intentionless interpretation" emerged most clearly in the often-cited letter of 1938 in which Adorno criticized Benjamin's essay on Baudelaire by describing it as "settled at the crossroads between magic and positivism."[8]

Adorno's emerging dissociation from Benjamin, however, was not only a turn to Horkheimer, as Martin Jay has argued.[9] In equal measure, it was a step beyond Horkheimer toward his own version of the critique of fetishism that Lukács had begun in *History and Class Consciousness*. Whereas Horkheimer's concept of totality is ultimately idealistic—reason "in itself" implicitly embedded in social praxis—

Adorno's interpretation of commodity analysis shows that this conception is questionable in two respects. First, it is questionable because it supposes that a unified, universal subject undergirds the bourgeois world of appearances and guarantees its essentially "human substance." What expresses itself in the figure of the transcendental subject is not at all the "idea of a rational society" (*KT*, II:258/*BPSS*) which must simply be led from being "in itself" to "for itself," but rather the universality of a functional social context that is determined by the exchange principle. "The system," in a concise formulation from *Negative Dialectics*, "is negative objectivity, not the positive subject" (*GS*, 6:31). According to Adorno, what lies concealed behind the appearances of the sphere of circulation and the bourgeois ideologies and forms of thought that correspond to it is not the world-constitutive subjectivity of idealism (and of "critical theory" as well). Instead, it is that negative universality, founded on the negation of the particular and of use value, that Marx deciphered as abstract labor, as "value." "*Das Wesen ist das Unwesen*": the essential *(das Wesen)*, so runs a paradox often used by Adorno, is therefore first and foremost a sinister trick *(Unwesen)*, an arrangement of the world that subjects all being to the rule of a real abstraction (*GS*, 6:169).

From this position, Adorno developed a critique of left-Hegelian ideology critique that can be read as a direct reply to Horkheimer's attachment to the bourgeois ideal of reason. In his 1938 lecture on Spengler, published three years later in *Studies in Philosophy and Social Science,* Adorno credited the theorists of extreme reaction with a critique of liberalism in many respects superior to the dialectical and historical version. To a large extent, the latter had criticized liberalism and liberal ideology as false promises, thereby overlooking their objective content.

The adherents of dialectical materialism . . . did not challenge the ideas of humanity, liberty, justice as such, but merely denied the claim of our society to represent the realization of these ideas. Though they treated the ideologies as illusions, they still found them illusions of truth itself. This lent a conciliatory splendor, if not to the existent, at least to its "objective tendencies." Their doctrine of the increase of societal antagonisms, or their statements about the potential relapse into barbarism, were hardly taken seriously. Ideologies were unmasked as apologetic concealments. Yet they were rarely conceived as powerful instruments functioning in order to change liberal competitive society into a system of immediate oppression. Thus the question of how the existent can possibly be changed by those who are its very victims, psychologically mutilated by its impact, has very rarely been put except by dialecticians of the Hegelian tradition, such as Georg von Lukács . . . Above all the leftist critics failed to notice that the "ideas" themselves, in their abstract form, are not merely images of the truth that will later materialize but that they are ailing themselves, afflicted with the same injustice under which they are conceived and bound up with the world against which they are set.[10]

On yet another point, Adorno goes beyond "critical theory" by placing far greater emphasis on the theme of changes in the concept of bourgeois society. Whereas in his early works Horkheimer, entirely in orthodox Marxist fashion, orients himself toward the contradiction between the forward-driving elements of intellectual and physical labor, on the one hand, and the "restricting" and "confining" relations of production on the other, Adorno turns his attention to the advancing elimination of this distinction. By comparison with use value, he argues, the negative universality of the value relationship may be something "merely thought," an appearance. "At the same time, however, that appearance is the most real of all, the formula by which the world was bewitched" (GS, 8:209). With this observation Adorno took up Marx's idea that the social mediation of the products of labor that is accomplished by value does not remain merely external to those products but enters into the very organization of production as the development of the capital relationship advances. Whereas in prebourgeois and early bourgeois society production still essentially rested on the dominance of use value as the "system-transcending concept of value,"[11] high capitalism is characterized by the "totalitarian tendencies of the social order" (GS, 8:16), which, acording to Adorno, must be understood less as a political process than as a totalizing of the sociation of value. In a society that has been thoroughly capitalized, use value is "replaced by pure exchange value, which precisely as exchange value deceptively takes over the function of use value" (GS, 14:25). Forces and relations of production enter into a new synthesis in which the moment of mediation is clearly determined by the latter. The structural differences of production, circulation, and consumption—which in the early bourgeois period designated different spheres within a social whole only apparently joined together by the money form, but in reality determined by production—are thereby done away with. "Material production, distribution, and consumption are administered jointly. Their boundaries, which once also separated mutually related spheres within the total process, thereby respecting qualitative differences, flow together. It is all one" (*GS*, 8:369).

It would certainly be one-sided to claim to see only a return to Marx in these reflections, for the idea of a mediation between the forces and relations of production certainly contradicts several motifs in Marx that amount to an uncritical hypostatization of labor. Adorno rightly criticizes Marx's all-too-optimistic trust in the historical primacy of productive forces, a trust that could be explained only as a result of his remaining attached to German idealism's affirmative construction of history. Yet this critique concerns only the "exoteric" side of Marx's theory, the theory of revolution that forms its superstructure. In *Capital*, there is already a tension between this superstructure and the "esoteric" core similar to that later found in Lukács. By abandoning this trust and showing that the theory of revolution is ultimately based on an idealistic "metaphysics of labor," Adorno does not only distance himself from Marx; at the same time, he comes closer to him than any other previous materialist theorist. "Negative dialectics" opened a space for unfolding the implications of the theory of value that, until then, had been blocked off by the dogmas of the theory of revolution. From the perspective of the theory of value, it becomes clear that the truth of capitalism lies not in the resurrection of some sort of subjectivity, as the theory of revolution had assumed, but rather in the "negativity of the universal" (*GS*, 6:57). It becomes clear that bourgeois society does not inadvertently promote the emancipation of the human species but instead tends to overcome itself by totalizing abstract sociality and thus remains subject to blind, irrational laws. "No total social subject exists. The appearance of one could be expressed in the formula that at present all social being is so completely mediated in itself that precisely the moment of mediation itself is distorted by its totality. . . . The process by which the system becomes autonomous with respect to all, even those in control, has reached an extreme" (*GS*, 8:369).

Adorno bases this thesis above all on his theory of the culture industry, the outlines of which can already be recognized in the 1930s, long before *Dialectic of Enlightenment* or Horkheimer's "Reason and Self-Preservation," in which some interpreters have claimed to find the decisive step toward a reorientation of critical theory. At a time when Horkheimer still locates "the forward-driving elements of morality" *(sic)* in the proletariat, in which not only the will to rational conditions but also the psychological ability to bring them about is being produced (*KT*, I:104/*BPSS*), Adorno is already criticizing "the empirical consciousness of present-day society, whose narrowness and dimness, to the point of neurotic stupidity, is promoted by class domination as a way of perpetuating itself."[12] In the essays on the sociology of music that appeared in the *Zeitschrift für Sozialforschung* between 1936 and 1941, Adorno pushes the theory of rationalization across the magic threshhold that still played a constitutive role in the myth of socialism in Lukács and the early Horkheimer by concentrating on the mediation between the dominant relations of production, determined by exchange value and capital, and the processes of labor and consumption. By contrast with a conception that reifies capitalist society into a plurality of layers related to one another only externally by money, law, and so on (a conception that also underlies functionalist sociology), Adorno recalls that the transition from "formal" to "real subsumption" that Marx described also fundamentally alters the spheres of production and consumption. It subjects them to what he calls a "false synthesis," the synthesis "of a destroyed subjectivity with a social power that produces, annihilates, and in annihilating objectivizes it."[13] Capitalism, in Adorno's chain of reasoning, does not only subject the individual to mechanized and standardized labor processes; through this subsumption it simultaneously destroys the preconditions of individuality by devouring the psychic energies required for the formation of ego identity. Patterns of behavior such as lack of concentration, inattentiveness, and distraction thereby become predominant in sense perception and social behavior outside the process of production, and these patterns are taken up and reinforced by the culture industry. The overwhelming force of mechanical, repetitive forms of production generates the need for relief and compensation in so-called free time, so that free time is irrevocably coupled with its opposite. The form of subjectivity that arises is no longer capable of genuine experience, which calls for exertion and an active confrontation with the object. The missing personality segments are replaced by the culture industry, which responds to the masses' need for meaningful activity, spontaneity, and immediacy with a broad palette of offers. But since these, in turn, result from standardized, leveled-down production, the needs they are supposed to satisfy are betrayed. In the context of the culture industry, activities become "pseudo-activities" in the do-it-yourself mode; the individuality that is formed is "pseudo-individuality," whose innermost secret consists in the constant renewal of the need for the ever-the-same. Under the conditions of high capitalism, consumption takes on the character of addiction, while in production the fabrication of surrogates becomes increasingly important.[14]

Nevertheless, the argument outlined here, which aims at radicalizing Marx's theory, is not consequentially pursued by Adorno. Instead, it is overlayered with a second level of discourse on the philosophy of history that can also be traced back to his early writings and that, I believe, is the precondition of his theoretical alliance with Horkheimer. In Adorno's *Kierkegaard*, the analysis of idealism, centering on the issue of fetishism, is interwoven with a second critical motif, one that aims not at a socially determined form of thought but at a pre-societal constellation: the relationship between *"Geist"* and "nature." Along with Benjamin's influence, this argument clearly shows the impact of Freud, whom Adorno had already dealt with in "The Concept of the Unconscious in the Transcendental Theory of Mind," which he had originally intended as his *Habilitationsschrift*. Adorno criticized idealism as a "historical *Trauerspiel* of mythic thought," a failed attempt by *Geist* to wrest itself free of the context of nature through sacrifice and renunciation. The "arrogance of *Geist*," which enthrones itself as a creator and elevates itself to the absolute, as Adorno already argues, is a mere appearance since it "sinks all the deeper into nature the more it believes itself to rise above it" (*GS*, 2:153, 83f.). A similar idea appears in the "Fragments on Wagner," which show the "unity of mastering nature and ensnarement in nature" to be the fundamental idea of the "Ring of the Nibelungen."[15]

These ideas, which first appear in the form of aphoristic flashes, are later constructed into a philosophy of history that overlays and sometimes represses the critique of fetishism. In the posthumously published "Reflections on the Theory of Class" (1942), which must be read as a contribution to the discussions of "The Authoritarian State" conducted in the Institute for Social Research, Adorno adopts Horkheimer's and Pollock's theses on the "liquidation of the economy" and the primacy of politics and combines them into a revision of Marx's theory. It was not the immanent lawfulness of capitalist society, founded on exchange value, that led to the authoritarian state, he believes; "rather, the old form of domination entered into the economic apparatus at times in order, once in full control over it, to shatter it and make life easy for itself. In such an abolition of classes, class domination comes into its own. History, in the image of the last economic phase, is the history of monopolies. In the image of the manifest usurpation now practiced by the harmoniously united leaders of capital and labor, it is the history of band warfare, gangs, and rackets" (GS, 8:381). These comments present a completely different view of the historical process than that found in Marx or in classical Marxism. Marx had distinguished strictly between production and domination in precapitalist societies, assuming that a penetration of exploitative relationships into the process of production came about only under bourgeois society (a process that itself first became possible through the concretization of domination in the capital relationship). Adorno flattens out this distinction: in his view, production as such is already a form of domination, and bourgeois society only intensifies this original relation of domination, whose development is assumed to have followed a straight line "from the slingshot to the megabomb" (GS, 6:314). As a consequence, the focus of his critique shifts from labor that produces exchange value to labor that produces use value; the latter, since it is based on appropriating and forming nature, in effect contains *in nuce* all the violence and oppression characteristic of social relations among human beings. The entire practice of self-preservation, along with the forms of thought related to it, falls under this verdict. According to *Negative Dialectics,* production and domination, power and knowledge are synonymous—not by virtue of their implication in a particular form of social synthesis but because their innermost principle, that of identity, commits violence "even before any social control, before any adjustment to relations of domination" (GS, 6:232)—by virtue of its mere form.

With this conception, which can grasp only the real abstraction of exchange-value production as a continuation of relations of force already inherent in the production of use values, Adorno brings critical theory so close to the naturalist, irrationalist critique of civilization and culture (which he otherwise fought so energetically) that they can hardly be distinguished.[16] To Adorno, as to Horkheimer, history appears as the persistence of its origin, as "the heritage of violence" (*GS*, 11:179), just as it did to Nietzsche or Freud, who could only conceive of history *sub specie aeternitatis* as "the eternal return of the same," the permanence of the "archaic legacy." And in the final analysis Adorno anchors this origin in nature, just as bourgeois materialism and biologism had done. His introduction to *The Positivist Dispute in German Sociology* includes the proposition that no "sacrosanct theory" (which presumably means historical materialism) permits us to rule out the possibility that "social compulsion is an animalistic, biological legacy": "the inescapable spell of the animal world reproduces itself in the brutal domination of society, which is still subject to natural history" (*GS*, 8:349). According to a parallel formulation in *Negative Dialectics*, "Human history, the advancing domination of nature, carries on the unconscious history of nature: to devour and be devoured" (*GS*, 6:348).

Adorno immediately distances himself from any Darwinistic conclusions that might be drawn from these principles, with the assurance that one cannot deduce the inalterability of compulsion from them. Yet this remains a mere assurance. The critique of fetishism, which deciphers the "natural-historical" character of society as a socially produced "appearance," is constantly at odds with the effort to locate the causes of the "dreadful ensnarement" of humanity in a natural relationship. In *Negative Dialectics*, for instance, in flagrant contradiction to views expressed elsewhere, he traces idealistic thinking to an "anthropological scheme" and ascribes to epistemology a "prehistory in the pre-intellectual, animal life of the species" (*GS*, 6:33); the rationality of identificatory reason, he later notes, is "historically dictated by the threat of nature" (*GS*, 6:174). At another point, this idea is presented in the form of a question; Adorno declares that speculation about "whether the antagonism at the origin of human society was inherited, as a prolongation of natural history—the principle *homo homini lupus*—or whether it first came about *thesei*, by convention" is "not idle." The alternative he offers, however, is no less inadequate than the "natural history" explanation: the recourse to "archaic, arbitrary seizures of power" is just as mystifying and speculative as Nietzsche's discussion of the genealogy of morals. In this discourse, according to which everything was decided by an "irrational catastrophe at the origins," there is no place for a materialist analysis of the forms of thought and of sociation (cf. *GS*, 6:315ff.). A theory of history from the perspective of Auschwitz is as untenable as one that sees it as nothing more than an accident.

III

Ever since critical theory became the object of historical analysis, the prevailing consensus has been that Horkheimer played the leading role, both institutionally and intellectually, in the Institute for Social Research,[17] a view not entirely without justification. Horkheimer did indeed exert a substantial influence far beyond the creation of an external, organizational framework; without this influence, critical theory would be unthinkable. It was Horkheimer who, taking his point of departure from Kant and Hegel, steered Marcuse away from his origins in the philosophy of existence and led him to a positive reception of the idealist tradition. It was Horkheimer who assigned a central role to psychoanalysis in the work of the institute, as represented above all by Erich Fromm's contributions. And it was Horkheimer who originated the guiding idea of ideology critique that Löwenthal applied to literary materials. Just as the various modes of production within a social formation are joined by a dominant mode of production, which constitutes the "general illumination that saturates all other colors" (Marx), so critical theory, too, is a discursive formation that receives its form from a theoretical center: Horkheimer's essays.

The influence of this center upon Adorno must not be underestimated. Such important themes as the thesis on the decline of the sphere of circulation and the end of the bourgeois individual originate from Horkheimer; central ideas in the "Fragments on Wagner" point to the influence of Horkheimer's "Egoism and the Freedom Movement";[18] and the passages in which Adorno appeals to the unfulfilled promises of bourgeois philosophy—contradicting views he holds elsewhere—can most likely be attributed to Horkheimer as well. The fact that Adorno assigns a prominent place to the concept of "domination" in his thinking from the beginning of the 1940s onward is probably also closely connected to the institute's discussions, which were shaped by Horkheimer's and Pollock's theses on the new primacy of politics. Although this motif occurs in Adorno's work earlier than in Horkheimer's, it would seem to have been Horkheimer's turn to a theory of the authoritarian state, beginning with his essay on Montaigne, that initiated systematic reflections in this direction. Adorno's "Reflections on the Theory of Class" would be similarly unthinkable without Horkheimer's "The Jews and Europe," "The Authoritarian State," and "Reason and Self-Preservation."

Yet despite the indisputable influence that Horkheimer exercised on Adorno, two things should be clear by now. First, Adorno's theoretical development proceeded more continuously than Horkheimer's, as if to confirm Benjamin's remark upon the publication of the Kierkegaard book that the author's later work would grow out of it.[19] Both strands of argumentation we have pursued in Adorno—the value-form critique of "pure sociation" and of the "second nature" produced by it, and the critique of the identity principle from the perspective of the philosophy of history—are already adumbrated there, before Horkheimer' s version of critical theory took shape. It was only at the beginning of the 1940s that Horkheimer managed a breakthrough to the critique of idealism that Adorno had formulated in his early work. Even then, he did so with serious reservations and never adopted the critique of fetishism. The critique of bourgeois rationality represents a break in the development of Horkheimer's thinking, whereas for Adorno it meant only an extension of a position already established.

Second, if we weigh the elements these authors contributed to critical theory against each other, it is Adorno's contribution that appears to provide the more promising point of departure today. Although Horkheimer provided critical theory with important impulses, his thought, down into his late work, remained so close to idealism that fundamental insights into the formal determination of thought and of sociation remained closed to him. Because Horkheimer saw idealism not as the reflexive form of an abstract society but as the preliminary appearance of truth, which he was increasingly unable to mediate with reality, he was backed into a defensive position that can scarcely be distinguished from that of late bourgeois cultural criticism. The diagnostic capabilities of critical theory increasingly yield to a posture that assigns to philosophy the task of being "the remembrance and the conscience of humanity"—in other words, a substitute religion (*KT*, 3:278). Consequently, in Horkheimer's late work one hears more about original sin, the truth of theology, and the relevance of Schopenhauer than about the architectonics of modern society.

Adorno, on the other hand, kept critical theory open to experience and diagnosis, perhaps because he had something in him of the attitude of the collector and "natural historian" that he praised in Benjamin. However inhibiting and theoretically sterile his unhistorical philosophy of history may have been, it did not prevent him from opening himself to theories, works of art, or phenomena of the culture industry in a way that is unparalleled in critical theory. No work by Horkheimer or Marcuse displays an intensity in confronting its object comparable to Adorno's studies of Husserl or Heidegger in his *Metacritique of Epistemology* and *Negative Dialectics;* none of the institute's contributions on mass culture can match the penetrating analytical acuity of *The Philosophy of Modern Music* or the studies on occultism, television, and film, whose significance for an anthropology of the industrial age has barely been recognized. Whereas in Horkheimer's work critical theory's diagnostic capacity vanished along with its revolutionary hopes, Adorno shows that the future of critical theory lies not in climbing back over "abandoned stages of reflection"[20] but in an opening to the present, even at the risk that its traditional categories and concepts will thereby be confronted with hopeless paradoxes.

Translated by John McCole

Notes

Horkheimer's texts and English translations, where available, are cited and cross-referenced according to the following key (in some cases the translations have been modified):

SS = *Sozialphilosophische Studien. Aufsätze, Reden und Vorträge 1930–1972,* edited by Werner Brede (Frankfurt, 1972).

KT, I/II = *Kritische Theorie. Eine Dokumentation,* 2 vols., ed. Alfred Schmidt (Frankfurt, 1968); CT = *Critical Theory: Selected Essays* (New York, 1972).

KT, III = *Kritische Theorie der Gesellschaft,* ed. Marxismus-Kollektiv (pirate edition, 1968), vol. 3.

BPSS = *Between Philosophy and Social Science: Selected Early Writings* (Cambridge, 1993).

GS plus volume number = Theodor W. Adorno, *Gesammelte Schriften,* ed. Gretel Adorno and Rolf Tiedemann (Frankfurt, 1970ff.).

1. On the latter, cf. Stefan Breuer, *Die Krise der Revolutionstheorie* (Frankfurt, 1977), 60ff.; Breuer, "The Illusion of Politics: Politics and Rationalization in Max Weber and Georg Lukács," in *New German Critique* 26 (1982): 67ff.; Klaus-Dieter Oetzel, *Wertab-*

straktion und Erfahrung. Versuch über das Problem einer historisch-materialistischen Erkennt-niskritik (Frankfurt/New York, 1978), 109ff.; Helmut König, *Geist und Revolution. Studien zu Kant, Hegel, Marx* (Stuttgart, 1981), 11ff. The following account is essentially based on the interpretation developed in these works.

2. Horkheimer, "Hegel und das Problem der Metaphysik," in *Anfänge der bürgerlichen Geschichtsphilosophie. Hegel und das Problem der Metaphysik. Montaigne und die Funktion der Skepsis* (Frankfurt, 1971), 90.

3. That Horkheimer's concern was a radicalization of idealism, rather than a critique of it, is clearly shown by a letter written to Pollock on September 20, 1937: "The most unpleasant discovery that materialism leads to is the circumstance that reason exists only insofar as it has a natural subject behind it. The retroactive effect of reason upon this subject is never so strong and lasting that it loses its natural character. Thus, there never arises that celebrated identity from which idealism lives. We must nevertheless attempt to produce it as far as possible." From Helmut Dubiel, *Wissenschaftsorganisation und politische Erfahrung. Studien zur frühen Kritischen Theorie* (Frankfurt, 1978), 69. English: *Theory and Politics: Studies in the Development of Critical Theory* (Cambridge, Mass., 1985) (emphasis added). This is precisely that "revolution of reason" envisioned during the *Vormärz* by Bruno Bauer and others, who broke open the Hegelian reconciliation of reason and reality and replaced it with the "terrorism of true theory" (Bauer). Adorno, in a later remark on left Hegelianism, defended theory's claim to autonomy with respect to praxis—without, however, adopting the intentions of the philosophy of identity. See Adorno, *GS*, 6:146f.

4. [Editors' note: Horkheimer originally published this essay in English under the title "The End of Reason" in *Studies in Philosophy and Social Science* 9 (1941); " Reason and Self-Preservation" is a direct translation of the German title, *"Vernunft und Selbsterhaltung."*]

5. On the Adorno-Benjamin relationship, see the definitive account by Susan Buck-Morss, *The Origins of Negative Dialectics* (Hassox/Sussex, 1977).

6. Martin Jay, *The Dialectical Imagination: A History of the Frankfurt School and the Institute of Social Research, 1923–1950* (Boston, 1973).

7. See Adorno to Benjamin, March 18, 1936, in Walter Benjamin, *Gesammelte Schriften* (Frankfurt, 1974), 1:1000ff.

8. Cf. Adorno to Benjamin, November 10, 1938, in ibid., 1096.

9. Martin Jay, *Adorno* (Cambridge, 1984), 35.

10. Adorno, "Spengler Today," *Studies in Philosophy and Social Science* 9:318–19.

11. Adorno, *Philosophische Terminologie* (Frankfurt, 1974), 2:269.

12. Adorno, "Zur gesellschaftlichen Lage der Musik," *Zeitschrift für Sozialforschung* 1 (1932):106.

13. Adorno, "Über Jazz," *Zeitschrift für Sozialforschung* 5 (1936):257.

14. See *GS*, 14:37ff.; Adorno, "On Popular Music," *Zeitschrift für Sozialforschung* 9 (1941):24ff. Adorno later also interpreted the student protest movement as a form of pseudo-activity; cf. *GS*, 10.2:786f.

15. Adorno, "Fragmente über Wagner," *Zeitschrift für Sozialforschung* 8 (1939):33.

16. On this point, see the justified critique by Habermas, *Theorie des kommunikativen Handelns* (Frankfurt am Main, 1981), 1:516f. (English: *The Theory of Communicative Action* (Boston, 1984), 1:385f.). However, Habermas overlooks the fact that the best arguments against this turn are to be found in Adorno himself; cf. my article "Die Depotenzierung der Kritischen Theorie. Über J. Habermas' 'Theorie des kommunikativen Handelns," *Leviathan* 1:132–46.

17. See Alfred Schmidt, "Die *Zeitschrift für Sozialforschung*. Geschichte und gegenwärtige Bedeutung," *Zeitschrift für Sozialforschung*, facsimile reprint (Munich, 1970), 1:5–63; Jay, *Dialectical Imagination*; and Dubiel, *Theory and Politics*.

18. See Adorno, "Fragmente über Wagner," 3. In the Foreword to the 1964 edition, Adorno himself stresses the close connection between these works; see *GS*, 13:9.

19. Walter Benjamin, *Gesammelte Schriften* (Frankfurt, 1972), 3:383.

20. Jürgen Habermas, *Erkenntnis und Interesse* (Frankfurt, 1968), 9.

11

Max Horkheimer and the Moral Philosophy of German Idealism

Herbert Schnädelbach

I

Horkheimer's work contains many passages concerning moral and morally relevant problems, but one searches in vain for a completely elaborated moral philosophy. The rudiments of one may be found primarily in "Materialism and Morality" (1933) and in various passages of the "Juliette" portion of *Dialectic of Enlightenment*. These could be quickly summarized but would not thereby be adequately elucidated. If the matter were to remain with the mere reproduction of these thoughts, one would have to reach the regrettable conclusion—given the paucity of texts—that early critical theory had an ethics deficit. Any attempt to read Horkheimer in such a way that the relevant passages open one's vision to an implicit moral philosophy—one amenable to reconstruction—must rely upon other approaches. For my own part, I choose the method of contrast: with the ethics of German idealism. In this connection, the concept of German idealism is construed broadly so as not to preclude from the very outset the possibility that it may also encompass contemporary communicative or discourse ethics, since, after all, the latter understands itself as a transformation at least of Kant's ethics. This need not be a bad thing, for *idealism* is by no means a dirty word. To be idealistic becomes an objection to an ethics only if a materialistic ethical scheme proves itself superior or more productive. This, however, is precisely Horkheimer's thesis, and if he is correct, this would have momentous significance for the current discussion of ethics. In this sense, the engagement with Horkheimer's thought is of more than mere antiquarian interest.

Already at this point, a crucial difference becomes visible between the great idealistic systems and critical theory. With Kant and Fichte, the philosophy of morality *(Moral)*—whether as a program of the critical grounding of norms or as a philosophy of virtue or ethics—is an important element of the system of philosophy as a whole, if not indeed the most important, given the primacy of practical reason. While Hegel deprecates morality in favor of the concrete ethical life, morality retains a system-constitutive position in both the *Phenomenology of Spirit* and the *Philosophy of Right.* In the older critical theory, at least, nothing plays a comparable role; ethics and morality were for it comparatively subordinate phenomena, which certainly deserved theoretical attention (it is well known that Adorno still wanted to compose an ethics) but which did not belong to the foundations of the theoretical self-understanding of critical theory. There are at least two reasons for this. The first is that materialism, the "content" of which Horkheimer had intended the critical theory of society to be [1], does not admit of a division into theoretical and practical philosophy. If "materialist theory [is] an aspect of the effort to improve human conditions," [2] then practical philosophy has become total therein, for even the most sublime theory construction is undertaken with "practical intent." [3] The omnipresence of the practical intent in the theory leaves no room for a separate theory of praxis specializing in moral problems. The other reason for the relative irrelevance of ethics in critical theory is that it sought to counter academic neo-Kantianism's tendency to reduce the whole of practical philosophy to a normative ethics and to leave the themes of "society" and "state" to the social sciences. By contrast, critical theory transfers the traditional objects of practical philosophy to a comprehensive, interdisciplinarily conceived theory of society, whose philosophical character still has to be respected. In this materialistic "unification of philosophy and science," [4] ethics and morality themselves become objects of social theory, although it becomes difficult to specify what is still supposed to be philosophical about them aside from the fact that traditionally they always have been investigated by philosophers.

Much of what Horkheimer has to say about the issue of "morality" belongs loosely to the sociology of morality. In this respect, the paramount social-historical thesis is that morality, as an independent regulator of action effective within individuals, first emerges in the course of the development of bourgeois society and will decline together with that society.[5] Moreover, Horkheimer makes a plausible case that the moral problem, as it has been formulated and discussed in bourgeois philosophy, is decipherable as a social problem: as that of the mediation between the general and the particular at the site of individual action, which remains inscrutable in the context of the bourgeois order and therefore produces in the individual's consciousness an "endless reflection and continuous upset"[6] that fundamentally cannot be overcome. Morality—understood as the stamp of bourgeois consciousness—therefore has an aporetic structure. From this perspective it becomes clear why Horkheimer's critical theory laid so little value upon being considered as applied moral philosophy. To accord a constitutive significance to morality would amount to making the problem that one wishes to solve itself into the basis for the solution to that problem. If one thematizes morality and its problems from the standpoint of its historical contingency, indeed of its practical surmountability in a future human society that no longer requires morality,[7] one would not wish to base the theory that understands itself as an element of precisely this project of transcendence on that which is to be transcended. Of course, Horkheimer here follows the motif of sublation (Aufhebung) via realization, which the young Marx applied to the whole of philosophy. In this respect, Horkheimer's theory of morality necessarily remains circumscribed within the still existing; he would not have considered the observation that his theory itself obviously contained characteristics of bourgeois morality to be a valid objection. Nonetheless, as a critical theory of morality, which pending such realization via sublation must, against its will, remain moral philosophy, this theory cannot develop such an affirmative relationship to morality that it could make the latter into its own foundation and then—as occurred in neo-Kantian ethical socialism—into the foundation of social criticism in general.

Is Horkheimer simply a moral philosopher *malgré lui?* "Morality is by no means dismissed by materialism as mere ideology in the sense of false consciousness. It is, rather, a human phenomenon which is hardly to be overcome for the duration of the bourgeois period."[8] From that perspective one could conclude that moral philosophy persists only "because the moment of its realization was missed,"[9] but even this would reveal nothing of the truth content of its object. Even if it were possible to conceive of a society that no longer needed morality—and Kant, according to Horkheimer, had anticipated precisely this [10]—it in no way follows that one could prove from this utopian standpoint that morality had been mere ideology. That aspect of morality that is to be retained in the sublation via realization cannot be untrue. Horkheimer always vigorously rejected ideological reductionism. That which Horkheimer had to say beyond social history and the critique of ideology about the truth-content or the validity of morality is the content of his moral philosophy.

It remains moral philosophy because he persistently refused to go the way of many Marxists from ethics to the metaphysics of history. The young Marx had understood communism not as a mere "ideal" but rather as "a real movement, which transcends [aufhebt] the current condition." [11] Lenin, Kautsky, and others developed this notion into an objectivistic teleology of history that made normative questions appear not just superfluous but indeed as signs of subjectivistic backsliding. Horkheimer knew that social theory and the philosophy of history alone were incapable of answering the Kantian question regarding what we ought to do. Furthermore, such theories themselves are never normatively presuppositionless, [12] and this means that even critical theory, which according to Horkheimer was best capable of orienting rational action, was determined by an interest that it itself cannot ground completely: an "interest in the elimination [Aufhebung] of social injustice." [13] Even if Horkheimer would undoubtedly have resisted characterizing this interest as merely moral—he always understood the term *morality* to refer primarily to individual or private morality—the impulses that constitute and stimulate the program of a critical theory must be examined more closely in the reconstruction of his moral philosophy.

Ethics as a philosophical discipline is distinguished from the sociology of morality not by its object but by its questions, which traditionally concern its conceptual and normative foundations. But today one can more competently investigate the conceptual structure and grounds of factual validity of a given moral teaching as a social scientist than in the role of a philosopher, for a great deal of empirical knowledge is necessary for the task. The matter is different if we switch from the perspective of the third person to that of the first person and inquire into the meaning and grounds of validity of our own action orientations not as observers but as participants. It is impossible to separate the two perspectives in Horkheimer's thought, for when he speaks of bourgeois morality, he hardly does so as if he were a traveling ethnologist discussing the Hopis; with mere critique, even critical theory cannot transcend the bounds of the bourgeois world to which it belongs.[14] The social history and critique of the ideology of morality therefore always refers to the fundamental normative conceptions to which critical theory is committed despite its genetic and diagnostic findings. The perspectives of the first and third persons can be analytically distinguished, however, and such a move commends itself methodologically if one wishes to discuss Horkheimer as a philosopher of morality.

II

The moral philosophy of German idealism is the contrasting background against which the outlines of Horkheimer's moral philosophy emerge particularly clearly; he considered it the paradigm of all idealistic moral philosophy.[15] A complete study would be necessary to elucidate in detail the way in which Horkheimer draws on Kant, Fichte, and Hegel. Kant is ubiquitous in his thought, but the presence of Hegel in his ethical reflections cannot be underestimated; above all, the viewing of morality as a phenomenon from the perspective of the philosophy of history and of social theory, and the mistrust toward the pure ought, are Hegelian legacies. In the following, I discuss the moral philosophy of German idealism by employing certain formulaic simplifications; this leaves open the possibility of taking into consideration newer approaches to ethics as well.

At least according to Kant and Fichte, morality is the very essence of generally valid and rationally justifiable precepts of action of a categorical "ought" character; their ethics are deontological, universalistic, and rationalistic.[16] It is taken as absolute that "the moral" is the "ought" (*das Gesollte*) in the sense of that to which not just anyone, but indeed the philosopher himself, is obligated.[17] The ethics of German idealism is also deontological in the more specific sense that it is prepared to understand "the moral" only as the unconditionally obligating; everything else is mere pragmatic rules. The universalistic element of this ethics consists in the fact that it considers a categorical ought possible only in commandments that appeal to all human beings, indeed to all rational beings as such; in this regard, unconditional imperatives with individual persons as addressees would be perfectly conceivable, as, for instance, if pronounced by an omnipotent God in whom the person believes. The rationalistic motif in the ethics of Kant and Fichte is inseparable from the universalistic because of their conviction that categorically compelling moral principles can only be justified as rational insofar as they are also universal, and the structure of the categorical imperative in the relationship of maxims and general law explicitly expresses this. Yet the universal and the rational are not the same; feelings and motives that are not further justifiable may also be universal, and at the latest since Schopenhauer, it is precisely the rational that stands under suspicion of being the merely particular. Furthermore, one must make distinctions within the concept of the rational itself. The ethics of German idealism is rationalistic because it holds that the moral is that which is rationally justifiable and, simultaneously, because it understands the moral itself as rational. The two are supposed to relate to each other in such a way that the rationally justifiable immediately attains the attribute of being rational itself by virtue of its mode of justification. This leap from adverb to adjective underlies all procedural justifications of ethics, including discourse ethics, but it is not plausible in the least: there may be quite rational grounds for being irrational on occasion and, alternatively, the arguments for heeding reason and not "instincts" (or at least that which we take them to be) may run out in certain cases. In general the notion that we can only rationally perceive that which we can perceive as rational is a rationalistic myth that culminated in Hegel's philosophy; as a late descendant of the principle that like can be known only by like and thus as its equal, this notion expands here into a philosophy of absolute reason that teaches (above all for the sake of its own possibility) that reason rules the world and that world history will look rationally upon anyone who looks rationally upon the world. [18] The post-Hegelian defeatism in regard to matters of reason stands completely under the spell of this principle; in Adorno, it still leads to the suspicion that philosophy as a whole, because it relies on reason, is a "gigantic tautology" that can discover nothing but itself in its object. [19] Only if one is prepared to distinguish between metaphysical and methodical rationalism will the experience of irrationality in the world alone no longer cause one to doubt the possibility of rational philosophy.[20] In ethics, boundless rationalism leads to the conception that rational moral demands are demands of reason itself, just as if commandments, which we can rationally perceive as moral, were rational in the sense that they had had their origin in reason, that in them reason gained its voice, that indeed in them reason itself became practical.[21]

Schopenhauer rebelled against this rationalism in ethics, and Horkheimer followed his lead without thereby becoming an irrationalist. As far as the deontological character of ethics is concerned, Schopenhauer is not prepared to recognize any "other origin for the introduction of the concepts of law, precept, and Ought into ethics . . . but one alien to philosophy, the Mosaic Decalogue." The concept of duty itself, "together with its relations—that is, those of law, commandment, Ought and the like—has its origin, when taken in this unconditional sense, in theological morality, and remains an outsider in philosophical morality until it adduces a definitive attestation from the essence of human nature or from that of the natural world."[22] Horkheimer adapts this thought in a materialistic fashion. His counterargument is not that an unconditional ought must always have theological roots but rather that the justification of such an ought requires recourse to an absolute (divine or human) consciousness,[23] and this course is closed off to Horkheimer the materialist *per definitionem*. For him as social theorist, "obligations . . . point back toward commandments and contracts,"[24] and he adds to this the remark, derived from Nietzsche and Freud, that the consciousness of duty, moral constraint, and unconditional ought has a quite profane origin in the internalization of social compulsion[25] and for this reason alone cannot be viewed as a divine voice or the voice of reason. For Horkheimer, categorical imperatives belong to the arsenal of idealistic moral theories every bit as much as eternal values. Hypothetical imperatives, by contrast, are not capable of making ethics into something deontic, for pragmatic rules have nothing specifically moral about them for either Schopenhauer or for Horkheimer. Schopenhauer sees in pragmatic ethics only a "clever, methodical, far-sighted egoism" at work,[26] while Horkheimer traces them back to "harmonistic illusions," for morality and prudence necessarily diverge in the world as it is.[27]

Horkheimer states tersely: "Binding moral commandments do not exist."[28] But morality exists; morality is a historical and social phenomenon, and moral consciousness is a psychic phenomenon, which the materialist has first to describe and explain. Horkheimer also relies closely on Schopenhauer in the phenomenology of morality, and this reliance leads him to reject universalistic ethical claims. The moral is not the unconditional "ought" because such a thing does not exist, and the conditional "ought" is not specifically moral. Therewith falls away the logical or systematic compulsion to seek a justification of the moral ought in the theory of morality. After the end of theology, such a justification could only be found in an agency or authority that obligates every human being as such; that is, if ethics rids itself of deontology, it can simultaneously rid itself of universalism. Morality is not a general human phenomenon but a historical one; with this observation Horkheimer shifts even Schopenhauer's nondeontic ethics of the denial of the will to live out of the universalistic perspective and into a historical one. If the history of morality is vitally linked to the emergence of bourgeois individuality, its content is vitally linked to the individual; thus, the moral itself is something individual. Horkheimer cannot be intimidated with the objection of relativism, which rears its head almost automatically at this point; he insists that the specifically moral lies precisely in that which cannot be generally expected, demanded, or compelled, and conversely he points to the extramoral origin of that which is universalistic in bourgeois morality. For him, morality is neither deontic nor ontic in general, because metaphysics—according to which the universal is also the good—ended with Schopenhauer.[29] One could almost identify critical theory as a whole with the conviction that the universal and powerful cannot be good precisely because it is universal and powerful; thus, the good in this world is to be sought in the ephemeral, the weak, the individual impulse, the exception, indeed in the improbable—in the unexpected and actually unwise goodness of individual motives and actions. The traditional theory of morality is itself traditional and not critical theory.[30] Horkheimer does not thereby deny that bourgeois morality contains the principles of freedom, equality, and justice essentially as general principles, but he recognizes at the same time that they are not primarily moral but political principles. That is, these principles could only appear as specifically moral principles, and then as the foundation of politics as well, after their transposition into a bourgeois-moral context.[31] Despite his rejection of a deontic-universalist ethics, with this argument Horkheimer can continue to subscribe to the universalistic import of the demands for freedom, equality, and justice, which admittedly he can no longer justify in terms immanent to moral philosophy. But the motives for raising these demands as general and universal today are themselves ethical, according to Horkheimer, in the sense of the not-generally-to-be-expected and enforced good;[32] they do not follow "logically" from their universalistic import alone.

With this expulsion of the universalistic aspect of bourgeois morality to the political sphere and of the ethical aspect to the individual, the Kantian linkage of morality to rationality is broken. For Horkheimer, too, reason is the universal, but the moral is not; therefore, morality can be neither grounded in reason alone nor can it be rationally justifiable in the sense of a generally valid justification. The very limits of justifiability itself result for Horkheimer the materialist from the insight that final, absolute justifications are an "idealistic delusion."[33] Not just the notion of absolute demands is incompatible with materialist thought but also the assumption of any kind of facticity from which they could derive and to which they would ultimately have to trace their justification,[34] be it God, Being, an absolute consciousness, matter, or "history." Accordingly, Horkheimer says of morality: "It does not admit of justification—neither by intuition nor by way of argument."[35] According to Horkheimer, morality cannot "be proven," and "not a single value admits of a purely theoretical justification."[36] He adds an ethical mistrust to his metaphysical mistrust toward theoretical ethical justifications; the suspicion or the fear that the moral could lose its ethical character precisely through its rationalization via rational justification. Schopenhauer had already wanted to unmask the Kantian calculus of transforming individual maxims into universal laws to see whether one then still wants them as sublime pragmatic calculation and thus as a pseudo-ethical facade on an egoistic background. Horkheimer sharpens this argument by detecting in the rationalization of the moral the workings of the rationality of mere self-preservation. For Horkheimer, pure reason in morality is instrumental reason in unadulterated form; this is detailed in the "Juliette" chapter of *Dialectic of Enlightenment*. "Self-preservation is the constitutive principle of science, the soul of the table of categories, even if it has been idealistically deduced, as in Kant. Even the ego, the synthetic unity of apperception, the agency that Kant calls the point upon which the whole of logic depends, is in truth the product as well as the condition of material existence." [37] If one attempts to justify ethics solely in this medium or upon this agency, according to Horkheimer, a formalism remains—"a flawless and vacuous procedure" [38]—which is not just an indication of the transformation of "pure" reason into unreason but also raises the question of what all this still has to do with morality. The pure ethics of reason thus appears as a late product of the dialectic of enlightenment—that is, of the triumph of a nature-dominating rationality at the price of its formalization. While Kant wanted to avoid the consequences of this process by limiting his "enlightening critique," the Marquis de Sade expressed them bluntly: [39] "Unlike its apologists, the dark writers of the bourgeoisie [40] did not attempt to deflect the consequences of the Enlightenment with harmonistic doctrines. They refused to pretend that formalistic reason stood in a closer connection to morality than to immorality." [41]

Thus, in Horkheimer's thought, the pure ethics of reason is both accomplice and victim of the domination of nature; the move from Kant to Schopenhauer is for him an advance in the self-enlightenment of reason, not a relapse into irrationality. After Schopenhauer, a materialistic moral philosophy can no longer be rationalistic in any substantive sense. It will, of course, offer justifications when it is able to do so; it will not arbitrarily shirk demands for justification, and thereby it remains rationalistic in a methodical sense. It will, however, give grounds why one cannot justify everything, and then with reasons will reject certain demands for justification. Here we are concerned with what is now referred to as an "ultimate justification" (Letztbegründung). Horkheimer considers this specifically idealistic: "While idealism occupies itself with 'constantly calling into question its own presuppositions anew' due to the independent significance that the spiritual (Geistige) holds for it, scrutiny of materialism's own presuppositions is motivated by the real difficulties into which the theory that depends upon them falls. Materialism is in these questions much less 'radical' than idealistic philosophy." [42] Plainly, Horkheimer does not reckon with the possibility that it could be inherent "real difficulties" of ethics that might compel us to attempt ultimate justifications. This becomes comprehensible against the background of his thesis that the moral element in morality is precisely the unjustifiable; an "ultimately justified" ethics would then be a contradiction in terms.

Thus, paths out of those internal difficulties of ethics must be sought in another direction.

III

With the rejection of the deontological, universalistic, and rationalistic conceptions of ethics, the fundaments of Horkheimer's materialistic moral philosophy have emerged. "We have tried to show that, according to materialism, actions do not proceed with necessity from an ultimate, absolute thesis. . . . This materialistic perspective does not have the solely negative meaning of dismissing an ethics that is to be grounded metaphysically, but rather has always been understood by materialists in the sense of recognizing the human striving toward happiness as a natural fact that needs no justification." [43] Here, according to Horkheimer, the idealistic need for justification with reasons finds a materialistic limit. This fundamental eudaemonism of materialist moral philosophy is no mere counterthesis to Kant's ethics, since Kant's privileging of the worthiness of happiness above happiness itself for its part requires recourse to the "fact of pure practical reason" in order to be plausible—a fact that, in contrast to the human striving for happiness, has the disadvantage for the materialist of not existing. [44] Materialist moral philosophy thus rests not on an absolute demand but only on a much-contested fact, from which, however, as from facts in general, nothing further follows normatively. Thus

materialism attempts to replace the justification of action with explanation via the historical understanding of the acting individual. It always sees in such justifications an illusion. If most people until now harbor a very strong need for this illusion, if they do not wish to rely merely on feelings of indignation, compassion, love, or solidarity, but rather connect their instinctual drives to an absolute world order by characterizing them as "ethical," this still in no way proves the possibility of the rational fulfillment of this need. [45]

The retreat of materialist ethics from the justification of action to interpretive explanation is no simple error, no uncontrolled discursive switch.

The lives of most people are so miserable, the privations and humiliations so numerous, efforts and rewards stand for the most part in such crass disproportion, that the hope that this earthly order may not be the only one is only too understandable. To the extent that idealism tries to rationalize this hope instead of explaining it for what it is, idealism becomes a vehicle for mystifying the instinctual renunciation compelled by nature and social relations.[46]

Ultimate justifications of action are not just illusionary but ideological; they amount to "mystification" because they seek to postpone recognition of the validity of urges toward protest and hopes for improvement until such time as their rationalization has been successfully completed—and that is never the case. For Horkheimer, morality occurs only when men profess their commitment to feelings of "indignation, compassion, love, and solidarity," and indeed precisely when there are no adequate rational grounds to feel this way.

Materialist moral philosophy is not deontological but eudaemonistic; not universalistic but individualistic and context bound; not rationalistic—thus irrationalistic? If one reduces the significance of reason for the interpretation of responsible action, the weight of emotions grows; if one limits justifications, unjustifiable decisions gain ground. Horkheimer thus falls not accidentally into the vicinity of the two most important and influential normative positions of his age: emotivism in metaethics and decisionism. Horkheimer rehabilitates the emotions; does he therefore defend a mere emotivism? In many passages, the incriminated word *decision* appears; what distinguishes him from Carl Schmitt?

Horkheimer's conception distinguishes itself from pure emotivism, first, in that it is not intended as a contrasting project to rationalism but rather is indebted to the latter for insight into its limits. Thus, materialism is not for him a straightforward counterposition to that of idealism but essentially a critique of idealism; only in this sense is the amalgamation of materialism and critical theory at all comprehensible. The materialist knows that one cannot justify everything and that reason alone—"pure" reason—is incapable of motivating real action. A "pure" ought, behind which no empirical impulses and forces stand, is for him a myth; Kant's "respect for the law" *(Achtung vor dem Gesetz)* thus appears a mere makeshift solution that nevertheless fails to appreciate the sublime figure of internalized social compulsion to which that formulation points. For Horkheimer, the fiction of purely rational motives of action, which results from idealistic system constraints, and the isolation of reason-free emotions, upon which emotivism is based, are two sides of the same coin. In the "Juliette" chapter, he describes enlightenment as a progressive process of unmingling reason and the affects, which leaves behind reason as a pure "organ of calculation" and the affects as mere natural facts: "Because reason posits no substantive goals, all affects are equally distant from its governance, and are purely natural." [47] Pure calculating reason is thus no longer capable of motivating action morally; from it flows, at worst, the coy enticement of the pure ability to command—the perverse eros of power for the sake of power. Rationality, which has been reduced to the naked logic of self-preservation, has, for Horkheimer, itself "reverted to nature," [48] because it perpetuates natural constraints instead of sundering them. The dialectic of enlightenment consists in the fact that reason, which seeks through its formalization constantly to expand its dominion, thereby regresses into the natural depravity that it hoped to avoid. Horkheimer is no pure emotivist because he knows that, before the tribunal of enlightenment passing judgment on enlightenment, neither rationalism nor emotivism has the upper hand; he therefore privileges neither pure reason nor pure feeling.

Morality cannot survive where reason and emotion are completely separated from each other. This conclusion leads Horkheimer to engage Kant's concept of "moral feeling" and reinterpret it materialistically. When Horkheimer employs the misleading formulation that ethics is a "psychic state," he means that morality is a psychic disposition that rests upon a particular, morally relevant sensibility: "Characteristic for the moral feeling is an interest that diverges from 'natural law' and that has nothing to do with private appropriation and possession." [49] The difference between proclivities toward "natural law" and moral feeling is thus also the rational kernel of Kant's distinction between actions performed out of mere inclination and those performed out of duty, but Horkheimer refuses to trace the ethical quality of the moral feeling to a psychologically inexplicable emotional effect of pure rationality, as Kant does. What makes the moral feeling ethical is something that points beyond the inclinations toward the "natural law" of the prevailing order:

The moral feeling has something to do with love . . . but this love concerns the person not as economic subject, nor as an asset belonging to the lover's property, but rather as the potential member of a happy society. This love is directed not toward the function and repute of a particular individual in bourgeois life, but toward his neediness and powers, which point to the future. Unless the aim of a future happy life for all persons, which results, of course, not from revelation but from the privations of the present, is taken up into the description of this love, it does not admit of a determination. To all, insofar as they are human beings, it wishes the free development of their creative powers. It appears to this love that living creatures have a claim to happiness, and it does not in the least request a justification or substantiation for this. . . . Not the corporal's baton but the climax of the Ninth Symphony is an expression of the moral feeling. [50]

It is important that Horkheimer does not simply link the ethical quality of the moral feeling to a utopian perspective, which increasingly slipped away from him in his later work; anyone who believes that it suffices to anticipate utopia in order to be moral reduces ethics to the philosophy of history. According to Horkheimer, it is the universalistic perspective of a claim of all to happiness—itself neither further justifiable nor in need of justification—that first makes love morally relevant as inclination, emotion, or passion.

Love in this sense is that aspect of moral feeling that makes the Other—as Kant formulated it—not a mere means but recognizes her or him as an end; she or he is an end in light of the anticipation of a liberated and happy humanity. [51] The psychic reality of this anticipation, however, is compassion, which recognizes itself in the suffering Other; therefore, the active form of such anticipation is solidarity. Like Schopenhauer, Horkheimer understands compassion not as mere emotion but as an emotional impulse mediated by insight; he is thus no pure emotivist. In *Dialectic of Enlightenment,* he delineates compassion more precisely as "the sensuous awareness of the identity of general and particular, as naturalized mediation." The time has come for an ethics of compassion because this form of mediation is the only one "that was left after the formalization of reason." [52] Precisely because compassion unites in itself the perspectives of the universal and the individual, the general and the particular, it alone—and not "pure" reason—is capable of providing the grounding for the moral. Horkheimer agrees with those critics of compassion who note that it may be used as a cover for becoming overweening or sentimental; its contrary is "bourgeois coldness," [53] not rationality per se. Reason itself is immoral insofar as it is nothing but the organon of bourgeois coldness.

If compassion and reason are not simply contraries, then the materialist need not reject justifications to the extent that he or she is forced to become a decisionist; at the same time, he or she will not believe that no decisions are necessary because everything admits of justification. Horkheimer understood the connection between absolute truth claims, relativism, and the anxiety of subjective decisions.[54] To recognize that one cannot justify everything, and that we must simply decide in those cases we cannot justify, is not to become a decisionist. Horkheimer opposes only excessive—that is, idealistic—claims to justification which necessarily lead to relativism and paralyze praxis. Moreover, he insists upon the indispensability of empirical, historical, and predictive knowledge for those decisions that can be justified to the extent that such knowledge is indeed indispensable.[55]

Just as Horkheimer's critical theory as a whole operates on the razor's edge between metaphysics and positivism,[56] his moral philosophy remains equidistant from pure rationalism, flat emotivism, and abstract decisionism. It is just as incompatible with the metaphysics of values in themselves, "pure" reason, or heroic decisions *ex nihilo* as it is with the positivism of mere feelings. Moreover, Horkheimer describes decisionism as the result of a purist disaggregation of rationally motivated decisions that divides them into their basic elements of abstract calculation, emotional motive, and purely spontaneous decision.[57] The difference between a materialistic and an emotivistic or decisionistic moral philosophy consists in the fact that the latter isolate and dramatize the emotive and voluntaristic aspects of real actions out of an idealist despondency over the insufficiency of pure reason, while the materialist reacts to this rather more calmly. This may be documented by way of the concept of interest, which Horkheimer uses in the quoted description of the moral feeling and again in crucial programmatic passages in the characterization of critical theory. The "interest in the elimination of social injustice" is for him "the materialist content of the idealist concept of reason."[58] This interest is neither a purely Kantian interest of reason *(Vernunftinteresse)*, nor a quasi-transcendental cognitive interest, nor a mere natural fact that justifies linking critical theory with naturalism.[59] Feelings and emotions such as love or compassion are as little independent of culture as are the interests of human beings. The concept of "interest" is a systematic lacuna in critical theory, and unfortunately it remains so today despite a number of studies of the concept's history.[60] The problem of the normative foundations of critical theory would look quite different today if critical theory had not for so long assumed that the concept is intuitively clear. Horkheimer, correctly, situated the concept strategically in the theory without really explicating it. Interests are not mere feelings or emotional predispositions; they are not reducible to discrete impulses of instinct or will; they must probably be conceived as rationally and cognitively elaborated dispositions of motivation and will. In such "elaboration," empirical knowledge, self-knowledge, interpretations of situations, and means-ends calculations would play a role; it is only for this reason that interests are susceptible of being changed by argument, which is not the case with instinctual impulses, for example. At the same time, the recourse to interests precludes abstract decisionism; because of the cognitive and rational aspect of interests, interest-governed decisions are never pure acts of will, which occur where the force of argument cannot reach.

In materialist moral philosophy, "interest" is a mediating concept that should integrate extremes, not the name of a principle. "Interest" is not fit to be a principle because it is itself a historically, socially, and psychically mediated phenomenon. Insofar as the materialist bases ethics on an interest, he or she is on shaky ground; but at the same time, he or she contests the notion that the ground of other conceptions of ethics is any less shaky—indeed, the materialist suspects that they are groundless. The theoretical insecurity of materialist moral principles is the price that must be paid for the insight that all moral principles have their place in concrete historical and social contexts that originate in human praxis and are therefore malleable. Horkheimer's materialist ethics is thus primarily a political ethics, which could be reduced to the formula: instead of rationalistic private morality, solidarity and politics.[61] He believes that he can look to the tradition of the moral philosophy of German idealism because Kant's ethics, at least, sets bourgeois morality in a utopian perspective that can only be redeemed by political means. According to Horkheimer, the consistency of Kant's own thinking led him beyond the limits of bourgeois morality; his thesis is that the universalistic principles implicit therein indeed turned out to be political and social principles. In this sense, Horkheimer understood critical theory not just as the critic of idealist moral philosophy but also as its heir.

IV

My sympathetic reconstruction of Max Horkheimer's implicit moral philosophy would be incomplete were it not to mention the systematic difficulties into which that philosophy brings the sympathizer. From the standpoint of Hegel, this moral philosophy appears as a critical theory of bourgeois ethical life *(Sittlichkeit)*, in the context of which morality becomes a historical phenomenon in need of explanation without thereby losing its significance for the orientation of contemporary action; the deontological, universalistic, and rationalistic self-understanding of this morality is put fundamentally in question. Horkheimer distinguishes himself from Hegel's philosophy of morality by subsuming morality under the Marxist dialectic of sublation and realization. If morality and bourgeois society belong together and if that society can no longer be understood as a moment of an overarching, concrete ethical life that is the embodiment of objective reason, then the Good cannot be exhausted by that which morally "ought to be" in the here and now but must instead point beyond it.[62] That Horkheimer not only demonstrates this utopian surplus of bourgeois morality but that he identifies with it and would like to make it into the standard of political praxis is not merely the moral or political decision of a sociologist of morality. Horkheimer gives reasons for it, and this is what makes him a moral philosopher. But Hegel's "reason in history" is no longer available to Horkheimer the materialist; the historical power of bourgeois morality tells us nothing about its reasonableness or binding force. The pure reason to which the Kantian withdraws is sufficiently suspect of formalism and thus of amorality. Whence, then, can we draw the grounds for the rescue of morality, if they are to be rational grounds?

The fact that Horkheimer himself adduces grounds shows that he does not take his own suspicion that moral justifications merely follow idealist system constraints or academic rituals of self-affirmation as the occasion for remaining at the level of moral phenomenology. Under post-Hegelian conditions, anyone who attempts to offer justifications has problems of justification, and Horkheimer has them as well. That he divides the traditional problem of morality into the two elements of "moral feeling" and "politics under universalistic principles" amounts in truth only to a displacement of the problem; this does not resolve it. Rather, two questions now arise that need to be answered without recourse to a metaphysics of history: What precisely makes moral feeling moral? And, how can the universalistic perspective of emancipatory politics be defended against skeptical objections? I would like to demonstrate briefly that at this point Horkheimer connects hermeneutic perspectives with issues of principle without thus being able to resolve the associated difficulties. Nonetheless, he points in the direction in which a resolution of the entire problem complex might be sought.

To restrict oneself to feelings when attempting to evaluate moral feeling would amount to a positivism of emotion, against which Horkheimer always stood firm. The same is true for interests—including, indeed precisely, the "interest in the rational organization of human activities" that "critical theory consciously pursues in the formation of its categories and in all phases of its development"; critical theory, according to Horkheimer, sets itself the task of "illuminating and legitimating" this interest.[63] A positivism of interests, which ultimately would amount to the political hamstringing of critical theory by that power which understood how to define this interest successfully, is thus also precluded, for interest-guided theory returns to its guiding interest and makes this interest itself into its object. This feedback loop between interest and theory, which places both moments in a reciprocally constitutive relationship and thus hinders their one-sided absolutization, could be understood as dialectical if a structural dialectics were divisible from absolute idealism. Because this is not the case, I prefer to speak here of hermeneutics, although this word has long been listed on the *index verborum prohibitorum* in Frankfurt.[64] The connection between interest and theory in Horkheimer's work is hermeneutic because they form a hermeneutic circle: the interest in rational conditions of life has the function of a preunderstanding that is constitutive of theory but itself must be "illuminated and legitimated"— that is, made comprehensible in its empirical and normative senses— by the theory so constituted. The hermeneutic circle created by interest and theory could also be described as the product of the unification of the perspectives of the first and third persons: the interest that determines the critical theorist's theory construction appears simultaneously on the side of his or her objects, and vice versa. Such a hermeneutics is materialistic because, in contrast to Heidegger and

Gadamer, it interprets its own preunderstanding not existentially but socially; critical theory understands itself not as existential destiny *(Seinsgeschick)* but rather as the intellectual dimension of real historical (or historically possible) changes that arise from the material life process. This is precisely the meaning of the thesis, which Horkheimer himself formulated, that social theory belongs a priori to its own object realm; it exemplifies a hermeneutic figure.[65]

The limits of hermeneutics as practical philosophy are drawn where reference to an existentially or socially conditioned preunderstanding is no longer adequate to the task of "illuminating and legitimating" practical intentions in more than a historical sense. What makes those conditions of life in which critical theory is interested rational? What is unjust about "social injustice," the elimination of which critical theory has made its aim? What is rational and just is not immediately obvious; nor do "moral feeling," the "critical impulse," and "practical interest" suffice as standards. The problem is that such singular and historically conditioned impulses and dispositions are not capable of constituting the universalistic dimension of the fundamental concepts of "reason" and "justice." The same is true of hermeneutic self-reflection, for it only makes clear the historical standpoint of the theoretician, conditioned by the life-world, a standpoint from which reason and justice may appear as universal principles; to consider them to *be* so would constitute an objectivistic regression by the hermeneuticist, which is all the less excusable the more uncompromisingly he understands himself as critic of ideology.

Through the critique of ideology, Horkheimer destroys the universalism of bourgeois morality and moral philosophy with reasons but attempts at the same time to rescue politically that part of it which was universalistically intended: the ideas of freedom, equality, and justice. Precisely at this point, however, he once again runs into the problem of justification, which cannot be sidestepped hermeneutically. Horkheimer is no mere hermeneuticist because he still takes seriously the problem of justification as a problem of principle. He says of critical theory that "the perspectives which it takes from historical analysis to be the aims of human activity—especially the idea of a rational organization of society, which corresponds to universal needs—are immanent in human labor, though neither individuals nor the public consciousness are aware of them in their correct form. A certain interest is required to experience and perceive these tendencies." [66] What is hermeneutic in this passage is the notion that one can extract practical aims from a properly developed historical analysis—in particular, through the feedback between the interest that is constitutive of theory and that which theory discovers; both interests ultimately refer to the same thing. No longer merely hermeneutic, on the other hand, is the thesis that the idea of a rational social organization is immanent in human labor itself; this thesis is a matter of principle, but it is nowhere rigorously justified by Horkheimer. Elsewhere he says that "the aim of a rational society, which today admittedly appears to be preserved only in the imagination, is really inherent in every human being," [67] but here too one seeks in vain for more precise details. These and similar formulations reveal that Horkheimer at least sensed a justification deficit in critical theory; he recognized that referring to the reciprocal determination of practical-political interests and critical social theory does not suffice to protect the unredeemed bourgeois ideals of freedom, equality, and justice from the suspicion of simply being culturally specific curiosities or mere ideology. As long as they simply rotate within the hermeneutic circle, the relativistic and ideology-critical skeptic remains in the right, and critical theory is then not much more than a warring faction of powerless and quickly disillusioned intellectuals.

References to human labor, to "every human being," or to a concept of humanity specific to critical theory [68] in the context of issues of justification, were mere episodes in the early Horkheimer; he later drew closer to Kantian positions once again to the extent that the political experiences of the 1930s extinguished even his weak Hegelian Marxist faith in historical "tendencies." What is the universally rational that is supposed to be "really inherent" in "every human being" if not precisely instrumental reason? In *Dialectic of Enlightenment*, Horkheimer points out the ambiguity of the Kantian concept of reason:

As the transcendental, supraindividual self, reason comprises the idea of a free, human social life in which human beings organize themselves as a universal subject and overcome the conflict between pure and empirical reason in the conscious solidarity of the whole. This represents the idea of true universality: utopia. At the same time, however, reason constitutes the court of judgment of calculation, which adjusts the world for the ends of self-preservation and recognizes no function other than the preparation of the object from mere sensory material in order to make it the material of subjugation.[69]

In *Dialectic of Enlightenment,* Horkheimer and Adorno located the rational in reason, that part of it which is not exhausted in being an organon for the domination of nature, in reason's self-reflection;[70] it should be clear that this falls far short of what Horkheimer says approvingly about Kant in the passage above. Once the critique of morality conducted by Hegel, Marx, and Nietzsche has come into the world, one can reconstruct the universalistic meaning of the main precepts of bourgeois ethics—which are also those of critical theory— only if one demonstrates, with Kant, that the ideas of a free and solidaristic human social life are inherent in reason itself as elements that cannot be thought out of existence. Merely recalling the mechanisms, consequences, and costs of nature-dominating rationalization is inadequate here. But if the rational concept of reason contains the idea of free and solidary association, then it remains to be seen what this idea represents in "every human being." At this point, the aporias of the philosophy of consciousness at least make plausible the transition to a speech- or communications-theoretical grounding of critical theory; other alternatives are not yet in sight. If one does not close one's eyes to critical theory's internal problems of justification, especially in ethics, one will no longer decry the "communications-theoretical turn" as a kind of original sin and wish to reverse it.[71]

V

On the other hand, the communicative or discourse ethics that would like to inherit and continue critical theory must consider how it wants to respond to Horkheimer's objections to an idealistic ethics. Discourse ethics is deontological, universalistic, and rationalistic in the sense that it seeks to prove that the ought is the rationally justifiable and precludes questions of motivation.[72] It must admit of being questioned by Horkheimer as to whether, if it has formulated the problem of ethics as a problem of universally binding norms, it has spoken at all of the ethical as the good. Horkheimer remains a eudaemonist because he considers a deontological ethics untenable in a postmetaphysical age; at the same time, the identification of the good with the rational must appear to him—as to Schopenhauer and Nietzsche before him—as a rationalistic prejudice. Universalistic validity claims can be raised in ethics only when one believes that the will must become purer—that is, more rational—in order to become a good will. But even if one no longer equates the good will with the pure, merely rational will, the question remains whether the rational is the good: is that which we can ground rationally therefore and exclusively for that reason good? Not only substantive but also procedural ethical rationalism leaves open the question concerning the good.

Thus, to the extent that it seeks to secure the claim to universality of binding norms in the medium of procedural rationality, discourse ethics runs the risk of losing sight of the morally good. Jürgen Habermas has taken this into account by conceding that a procedurally rational, and thus formalistic, ethics must restrict itself to normative problems of justice and must exclude evaluative questions regarding the good and proper life; at best, such an ethics can treat these questions as candidates for suggested norms with a claim to generally binding force.[73] Assuming for the moment that discourse ethics deals better with the problem of relativism than did Horkheimer's materialist moral philosophy, would it not be possible for Horkheimer to invite discourse ethicists to broaden the foundations of normative justification so that, when the rationally justified is spoken of, the good is discussed as well? In order to achieve that objective, it would be necessary to abandon pure cognitivism in the justification of norms and, without fear of falling into emotivism or decisionism, consider emotive and voluntaristic factors as well. The discourse ethicist will respond that this concerns mere motivational issues and not the validity dimension of what is at issue in the ethics debate. From Horkheimer one can learn that it is not possible simply to shunt motives into the realm of psychology if one seriously confronts the issue of interests—and not just the problematic interest of reason in itself, which Kant referred to as "moral feeling." A materialist ethics that takes interests seriously must also provide a materialistic interpretation of the Kantian interest in the generalizability of interests, without once again ending up in a position of historical relativism. What kind of interest is an interest in the just? Is it merely an interest in knowledge of what is just—in knowing the just? Does it not also include recognizing it—that is, an affective attachment to the just and the will to pursue in one's own decisions that which one knows to be just?

Horkheimer's moral philosophy can help to stimulate a critique of pure communicative reason in the ethicists' discussion of foundations. If the discourse ethicist were to take into consideration not just the communicative but also the emotive and voluntaristic conditions of real morality, he or she might perhaps once again be able to perceive the good that has fallen from view in those methodically excluded motives for recognizing that which has been discursively grounded. In "Kant's Philosophy and the Enlightenment" (1962), Horkheimer speaks of the capacity for "devotion and happiness" as forming "the precondition for concern about the welfare of the whole, for self-abnegation, indeed for comprehension of the theoretical idea." [74] Here it becomes clear that even the purely cognitive interest in the moral is no merely cognitive affair; even less so is its practically significant recognition, as ethical intellectualism would have it. Why do we even want to know what is moral? Why do we conduct discourses of justification? Horkheimer shows us that the good cannot coincide with the discursively justifiable because discursive justification itself—like critical theory as a whole, and theory in general—depends on factors that are not discursively justifiable: the capacity for "devotion and happiness" is always presupposed in the "concern for the welfare of the whole," in "self-abnegation," indeed in the "comprehension of the theoretical idea," and all this together is what constitutes the interest that critical theory itself pursues in the first place.

Thus, even the merely cognitive interest in the ethical is itself no mere cognitive affair; this is especially true when we take the "moral point of view," the perspective of universalization with "practical intent." From Horkheimer one can learn that the cognitive interest in the ethical need not necessarily be ethical, even where it is not purely cognitive. What is ethical about the universalization of maxims and interests if it can be the expression of the wholly amoral instrumental rationality of calculated self-preservation? (In a thoroughly rationalized society it is prudent to live according to generalizable precepts.) Kant did not have to confront this problem because for him the morally good coincided with the rational. But if the rational is indeed a necessary but by no means sufficient condition of the good, then universalization alone no longer suffices to make the step from rationality to morality. Horkheimer sees that the interest in morality itself must be a moral interest in order to constitute morality; opportunists and cynics can also have a practical interest in the ethical but for other than ethical reasons. The above holds a fortiori for the practical recognition of that which is known as morally good. The problem of recognition has long been discussed in the form of the question, "Why be moral?"[75] Translated into the language of discourse ethics, it reads: "Why should I even participate in ethical disputes in which it can be demonstrated to me transcendentally that through my participation in them I have always already recognized ethically relevant norms?" To seek the answer in a decision that is not further justifiable, or in a calculus of shrewdly securing one's identity,[76] would surrender the practically significant recognition of the discursively justified to motives that can by no means be characterized as morally good. In short, one can recognize the morally good for other than ethical reasons, as Kant already knew.

Horkheimer's critical theory thus reckons with emotive and voluntaristic foundations of morality and of moral philosophy because it recognizes that morality cannot be reconstructed from rationality alone. It calls these foundations "moral feeling," which it bases on the interest in the just, that is, on what discourse ethics believes it can justify in purely cognitive terms. The theory is materialistic because it claims that the good will can no longer be described as the pure will and because the ethical quality of its "moral feeling" is formed only under contingent conditions; there is no a priori guarantee for its existence. The capacity for "devotion and happiness," as an ultimately contingent cultural fact, constitutes the interest that "deviates from the natural law";[77] it is the source of motivation both for the question of the good and the just and for its recognition, but it is not only this. Because this capacity is what makes the will into the good will, it is a necessary condition of the good itself.

Translated by John Torpey

Notes

1. Cf. Max Horkheimer, *Kritische Theorie: Eine Dokumentation,* ed. Alfred Schmidt (Frankfurt am Main, 1968), I:45 (hereafter cited as *KT*).

2. Ibid., 46ff.

3. On the relationship between theory construction and practical interest, cf. ibid., II:112ff.

4. Ibid., I:55.

5. Ibid., I:71ff.; cf. also II:7ff., 62ff.

6. Ibid., I:75; cf. also 74ff.

7. Cf. ibid., I:82ff., II:76.

8. Ibid., I:79.

9. T. W. Adorno, *Negative Dialektik* (Frankfurt am Main, 1966) 13.

10. Cf. *KT*, I:82ff.

11. Karl Marx, *Deutsche Ideologie,* in S. Landshut, ed., *Die Frühschriften* (Stuttgart, 1953), 361.

12. Cf. note 3.

13. *KT*, II:190. In the original version of "Traditionelle und kritische Theorie," the passage reads: "interest in the overcoming of class domination." Cf. *Zeitschrift fur Sozialforschung* 6 (1937): 292. On the relationship between theory and interest, cf. also ibid., II:162ff., and I:91.

14. Cf. T. W. Adorno, "Kulturkritik und Gesellschaft," in *Prismen* (Frankfurt am Main, 1955), 7ff.

15. For Horkheimer's characterization of idealist moral philosophy, cf. *KT*, I:72ff.

16. These characteristics also accurately describe Hegel's conception of morality *(Moralität),* although he defines it only as an element of the concrete ethical life. On the application of these definitions to discourse ethics, see section V.

17. Once Fichte and Hegel interpreted this ought as a "mere" ought, that is, as an indicator of the finitude of the subject, an ambiguity was introduced into the matter that has tremendously burdened the ethics discussion until the present day, especially with Hegelians. Only from a teleological standpoint, which is not the Kantian, can the ought as that which obligates us be equated with the "mere" ought, that is, the still unreal, the not-yet-realized. On this, cf. Odo Marquard, "Hegel und das Sollen," in his *Schwierigkeiten mit der Geschichtsphilosophie* (Frankfurt, 1973), 37ff. Both Hegel's critique of the "mere" ought and Schopenhauer's rejection of deontological ethics as a whole play an important role in Horkheimer's ethical reflections.

18. See Hegel, *Die Vernunft in der Geschichte,* 5th ed. (Hamburg, 1955), 31.

19. See Herbert Schnädelbach, "Dialektik als Vernunftkritik: Zur Rekonstruktion des Rationalen bei Adorno," in von Friedeburg and Habermas, eds., *Adorno-Konferenz 1983* (Frankfurt, 1983), 66ff.

20. On this point, see Herbert Schnädelbach, "Über Irrationalitat und Irrationalismus," in Hans Peter Duerr, ed., *Der Wissenschaftler und das Irrational* (Frankfurt, 1981), 2:155ff.

21. Cf. Kant, *Kritik der praktischen Vernunft*, Introduction, A, 29ff.

22. Schopenhauer, *Über die Grundlage der Moral*, sec. 4, in *Werke in zehn Bänden*, Zurich edition, 6:161ff.

23. Cf. *KT*, I:39, 42.

24. Ibid., 105.

25. Cf. ibid., 92.

26. Schopenhauer, *Die Welt als Wille und Vorstellung*, vol. 1, Appendix: "Kritik der Kantischen Philosophie," in *Werke*, 2:639.

27. Cf. *KT*, I:93.

28. Ibid.; on the following, cf. 91ff.

29. Cf. Max Horkheimer, "Die Aktualität Schopenhauers," in *Zur Kritik der instrumentellen Vernunft* (Frankfurt, 1967), 256ff. (hereafter cited as *KiV*).

30. Cf. Carl-Friedrich Geyer, *Kritische Theorie: Max Horkheimer und Theodor W. Adorno* (Freiburg and Munich, 1982), 131.

31. "The concept of justice . . . is older than morality." *KT*, I:98. Cf. also Horkheimer's remarks on Kant, *KT*, I:88ff., 94ff.

32. Cf. *KiV*, 206; see also section V below.

33. *KT*, I:81. Horkheimer refers with this expression to the good will as the sole unconditional good.

34. Cf. ibid., I:42, 38ff.

35. Ibid., 93.

36. Ibid., 106.

37. Max Horkheimer and T. W. Adorno, *Dialectic of Enlightenment*, trans. John Cumming (New York, 1972), 86–87.

38. Ibid., 90.

39. Cf. ibid., 93ff.

40. Horkheimer elsewhere names Machiavelli, Hobbes, and Mandeville. Cf. ibid., 90.

41. Ibid., 117–18.

42. *KT*, I:42.

43. Ibid., 64.

44. Thus, Kant's ethics belongs to the "mere *coups de main* by reason of the conscious-ness that morality itself is underivable." *Dialectic of Enlightenment*, 85.

45. *KT*, I:44.

46. Ibid.

47. *Dialectic of Enlightenment*, 88, 89.

48. Ibid., 87.

49. *KT*, I:93. On Kant's concept of the "moral feeling," cf. *Kritik der praktischen Ver-nunft*, A, 133.

50. *KT*, I:94–95.

51. Cf. ibid. The later communicative ethics of Jürgen Habermas and Karl-Otto Apel could connect with this motif of the anticipation of the ideal and thus understand itself as the heir of critical theory.

52. *Dialectic of Enlightenment*, 101.

53. Ibid., 103.

54. Cf. *KT*, I:235–36; cf. also ibid., II:112ff.

55. Cf. ibid., I:64.

56. Cf. Alfred Schmidt, "Die *Zeitschrift fur Sozialforschung:* Geschichte und gegenwär-tige Bedeutung," in *Zeitschrift für Sozialforschung* (Munich, 1980), 1:25ff.

57. Cf. *KT*, II:128–29.

58. Cf. note 13.

59. It is my impression that the quasi-transcendental "cognitive interest" with which Jürgen Habermas argues in *Knowledge and Human Interests* and thereafter is more strongly inspired by Max Weber than by Max Horkheimer. On this, cf. Max Weber, "Die 'Ob-jektivität' sozialwissenschaftlicher Erkenntnis," pt. II, in *Gesammelte Aufsätze zur Wissen-schaftslehre* (Tübingen, 1973), 161ff.

60. Cf. *KT*, I:95ff.

61. Cf. ibid., 84–85.

62. At this point, Horkheimer implicitly offers an alternative to modern neo-Aristotel-ianism, which as the philosophical prop of our contemporary neoconservatism prefers to interpret and to ground every ethics from the standpoint of a given lived ethos; Horkheimer, too, pursues this approach, but he turns it in a critical direction. On neo-

Aristotelianism, cf. Herbert Schnädelbach, "Was ist Neoaristotelismus?" in Wolfgang Kuhlmann, ed., *Moralität und Sittlichkeit* (Frankfurt, 1986).

62. *KT*, II:193.

64. In the "Positivist Dispute," Jürgen Habermas defended as hermeneutic the dialectical position of the Frankfurt theorists.

65. Cf. *KT*, II:148ff.; in addition, see Jürgen Habermas, "Analytische Wissenschaftstheorie und Dialektik," in T.W. Adorno et al., *Der Positivismusstreit in der deutschen Soziologie* (Neuwied and Berlin, 1969), 156ff.

66. *KT*, II:162.

67. Ibid., II:199.

68. Cf. ibid., II:159.

69. *Dialectic of Enlightenment*, 83–84.

70. Cf. ibid., 38ff.

71. On this see, as interesting documentation, Lobig and Schweppenhäuser, eds., *Hamburger Adorno-Symposion* (Lüneburg, 1984).

72. Cf. Jürgen Habermas, "Diskursethik—Notizen zu einem Begründungsprogramm," in *Moralbewusstsein und kommunikatives Handeln* (Frankfurt am Main, 1983), 53ff.

73. Cf. Jürgen Habermas, "Über Moralität und Sittlichkeit: Was macht eine Lebensform 'rational'?" in Herbert Schnädelbach, ed., *Rationalität: Philosophische Beiträge* (Frankfurt, 1984), 220ff.

74. *KiV*, 206; cf. also *KT*, I:247ff.

75. Cf. F. H. Bradley, "Why Be Moral?" *Ethical Studies* (1876); Gernot Reibenschuh, "Warum moralisch sein? Zur Kritik soziologischer Moralbegründung" in Manfred Riedel, ed., *Rehabilitierung der praktischen Philosophie* (Freiburg, 1974), 2:85ff.; cf. also the citations in the Notes.

76. On this point, cf. Jürgen Habermas, "Diskursethik," 108ff. While Karl-Otto Apel never disputes the existence of a "decisionistic residual," Jürgen Habermas attempts at this point to refer the skeptic to real conditions of his survival as a person; he thus adopts a position that approaches that of Hobbes and Hobbesianism.

77. *KT*, I:93.

12

"Mystical Aura": Imagination and Reality of the "Maternal" in Horkheimer's Writings

Mechthild Rumpf

Thus it once again becomes clear that the phenomenon of the aura cannot be bound by a clear-cut definition, because it is itself the movement of desire which oversteps boundaries; its origin lies in individual and collective prehistory; its source, as the power of fantasy, is involuntary memory; its medium is the image and its longing, homesickness.

—*Marleen Stoessel,* Aura: Das vergessene Menschliche

For the feminist critique of enlightenment, discussion of the contents of Adorno and Horkheimer's "message in a bottle" has been important for some time. Upon examining some of the critical replies to the *Dialectic of Enlightenment* (1947), it becomes apparent that the fixation on this text has confined our attention to the complex and contradictory construction of the masculine constitution of the subject within critical theory. Here, however, I am interested in the "maternal," which, though it leaves no traces in the *Dialectic of Enlightenment,* was accorded a special meaning in Horkheimer's early and late texts and then made to vanish. Horkheimer's statements about maternal love contain a latent dialectic of male processes of development that was not fully thought through; to do this from a feminist point of view could open a new perspective on the dialectic of enlightenment.

The connection between phylogenesis and the ontogenesis of the male subject is thematized by Adorno and Horkheimer in an uncertain fashion:

Humanity had to inflict fearful things upon itself before the self, the identical, purposive, virile character of man was formed, and *something* of that recurs in every childhood. (*DE,* 33; emphasis added)

Man's domination over himself, which grounds his selfhood, is almost always the destruction of the subject in whose service it is undertaken; for the substance which is dominated, suppressed, and dissolved by virtue of self-preservation is none other than that very life as functions of which the achievements of self-preservation find their sole definition and determination: it is, in fact, what is to be preserved. (*DE*, 54–55)

I am concerned with this "something" because the undetermined distinction between prehistorical inheritance and socialization is the empty site at which the historico-philosophical closure of the *Dialectic of Enlightenment* potentially can be broken through. At this empty site the "maternal" receives its "mystical aura," at least up to the point where the difference is once again leveled out.

In this respect, my contribution is meant as an alternative to the reading of critical theory put forward by Jessica Benjamin.[1] One of her central theses presents too undifferentiated a view of critical theory, a view that follows from her critique of it: she argues that critical theory remains bound to a subject-object dialectic and a "monadic view of the self." In the domination of nature, Adorno and Horkheimer did not recognize the domination of women; an intersubjectively conceived dialectic of enlightenment therefore remained barred to them.

The consequences of instrumental rationality and the monadic self were worked out by the representatives of critical theory in *Dialectic of Enlightenment* for the first time, clearly and convincingly. Nevertheless, they continued to hold onto a theory of socialization that apologetically defended and redoubled these consequences. The values or norms corresponding to instrumental rationality are central to the experience of the male personality and the father's Oedipal role; Horkheimer and Adorno were apparently unable to conceive of any other form of differentiation, or even of the loss of this sort of father. Instead, critical theory insistently argued that paternal intervention, the Oedipal father, and an ego built upon the internalization of this father provide the sole possibility for differentiation. However, this argument is consistent only on the assumption that individuation and ego development can only be carried out in opposition to fundamentally dangerous archaic impulses, such as a regression to an undifferentiated state and an aggressive striving for omnipotence.[2]

Benjamin's interpretation overlooks important reflections and intentions pursued by Adorno and Horkheimer, whose critique of the masculine, bourgeois development of the self concentrates precisely on the forms and consequences of separation processes and the problematic power of the paternal principle. Her reading passes over the intersubjectively construed dimensions of the male developmental process, as Horkheimer in particular recognized them. Unless individual statements are taken out of context, he presented the father as a tragic figure rather than a savior and a guarantor of childhood autonomy and resistance. Benjamin's approach corresponds to the fundamental objections that have been raised by Jürgen Habermas; their critiques share an intersubjective focus. Beyond the critique of instrumental reason Habermas, too, can see in Adorno's and Horkheimer's texts only the totally "other," nature, or the irrational.

The critique of instrumental reason, which remains bound to the conditions of the philosophy of the subject, denounces as a defect something that it cannot explain in its defectiveness because it lacks a conceptual framework sufficiently flexible to capture the integrity of what is destroyed through instrumental reason. To be sure, Horkheimer and Adorno do have a name for it: *mimesis.* . . . Imitation designates a relation between persons in which the one accommodates to the other, identifies with the other, empathizes with the other. There is an allusion here to a relation in which the surrender of the one to the example of the other does not mean a loss of self but a gain and an enrichment. Because the mimetic capacity escapes the conceptual framework of cognitive-instrumentally determined subject-object relations, it counts as the sheer opposite of reason, as impulse.[3]

For Habermas, the "rational core" of the mimetic performance can only be revealed by carrying out the "paradigm shift" implicit in Adorno's aesthetics: Adorno described reconciliation in terms of an "intact intersubjectivity," which "is only established and maintained in the reciprocity of mutual understanding based on free recognition."[4]

Horkheimer sees the significance of the mimetic ability above all in the formative process of the subject—not, however, as the "irrational" power of "love," the opposite of reason, or the "revolt of nature."[5] I would like to pursue a motif that is suggested in his image of the "mystical aura" of the maternal ("AFG," 227f.).[6] My formulation of the problem, which I can take up here in only some of its aspects, involves an intersubjective concept of the "maternal," not the ontologizing of "female" powers. In the traces of the "maternal"—that is, in psychic representations—I am looking for those aspects of the constitution of the subject that resist the separation of reason and sensuality, of self and other, aspects in which a rupture of the subject-object structure is implicit. Horkheimer's interest in maternal love can be traced back to some of these motifs. Although he concentrates only on the male formative process, and the androcentrism of his theory is as obvious as the pathos of some passages is unbearable, he inquires into the conditions of possibility of a form of male subjectivity that is not defined by distance, egoism, abstract autonomy, and the non-recognition of the other. "The Concept of the Human" (1956), for instance, includes the following reflection:

Maternal love does not consist in feelings alone, nor even in convictions; it must find the right expression. The well-being of the infant and the trust with which it responds to the people and things around it depend, to a large extent, on the peaceful yet animated friendliness, the warmth and the smiles of the mother or of the person who represents her. Indifference and coldness, abrupt gestures, restlessness, and aversion can permanently *warp the child's relationship to objects, to people, and to the world; it can produce a frigid character devoid of spontaneity.* This was already recognized by the time of Rousseau's *Emile,* of John Locke, and even before, but it is only today that we begin to understand the connection in its many aspects. One does not need sociology to see that a mother pressed by external cares and occupations will not have the desired effect.[7] (emphasis added)

I will pursue the hypothesis that Horkheimer's interest in maternal love is not to save the "other" of reason. Rather, he seeks to establish that in the formative process of "spirit," a libidinal, noninstrumental relationship to people and objects must be preserved. On a preconceptual level, he anticipates what is today referred to as intersubjectivity. However, this idea of Horkheimer's contains an antinomy of its own, of which he was unaware, involving the difference between inner (psychic) and external reality. This theoretical problem is not fortuitous. Rather, it is an expression of his cultural and social criticism as a whole, which reproduces an ideological view of the relations between the sexes. For the woman "the division of labor imposed upon her by man was not favorable" (*DE,* 248) but for Horkheimer it becomes the only conceivable precondition of male individuation processes in early childhood. "Awareness of the task of tracing concepts back to their subjective origins" brackets out its own, male form of subjectivity (*Eclipse,* 92). As soon as Horkheimer speaks of "woman," he already sees her as the object of social and patriarchal structures—but always only as wife or mother, in relation to her child or husband. She persists in the status of "voluntary servitude"; she is the loving mother only through conscious opposition to the husband/father as

the representative of social reality. Suppressed, female subjectivity disguises itself only in the suffering of the woman.[8] All of this appears in Horkheimer as a dialectical history of a process of male emancipation that destroys its own preconditions. Thus, the thesis of the disappearance of maternal behavior results from a deductive logic rather than from social-historical analysis, which would yield a more complex, nuanced depiction of the reality of women's lives. I cannot pursue this issue here, but the results of historical and sociological research on maternal love have thoroughly shaken Horkheimer's dichotomized observation.

"Because One Cannot Learn What Love Is from What One Is Told . . ."

The blind spots in Horkheimer's thought mark specific obstructions of male subjectivity. The attempt to secure a place for the psychic representation of the "mystical aura" of the maternal within the male subject, to lend it a culturally binding language, ultimately fails in both reality and theory. This failure has to do with the fact that the imagos of the mother and the father, which are unreconciled in reality, do not relate to one another additively and integratively. In the context of asymmetrical gender relations, the social and cultural dominance of the father is institutionalized intrapsychically as well. But the failure of this theoretical effort sustains an awareness of the problematic constitution of male subjectivity. Thus, Horkheimer comprehends not only his own time in his thought but the contradictions of male self-reflection as well.

The split in Horkheimer's depiction of the mother is to be found at one such blind spot in the process of reflection. The idealized mother was supposed to be a historical occurrence, but her repressed aspects—the "bad" imagos—recur in the cultural criticism of Horkheimer, the observer of his time. There is a positive power in his thought that is formulated in his memory of his own mother:

My mother was a particularly affectionate and loving woman. And if I have encountered something of the good and the beautiful in my life, and if that may be traced in part to my manner of living, then it is probably because in my home—partly from my father, but above all from my mother—I learned about love mimetically. Because one cannot learn what love is from what one is told; it can only be learned from the gleam in the mother's eyes, from her love, from the way she speaks. And that is why precisely the family seems to me so important, and its present-day dissolution so highly problematic. I believe Freud would have agreed with me.[9]

Perhaps it is only through the level of development reached by psychoanalytic theory today that the substance of this confession can be deciphered. The interaction between mother and child is understood here as a form of practice that creates meaning prior to language; this interaction is constitutive of the ability to experience the world and to relate to it and to oneself libidinally. Here lies the utopian dimension of childhood that Horkheimer and Adorno repeatedly speak of, in various contexts, yet that eludes any positive characterization by utopian thought.[10]

The image of the maternal in Horkheimer's texts is also the metaphorical expression of a philosophical idea related to Kant's formulation that "man and, in general, every rational being exists as an end in himself and not merely as a means to be arbitrarily used by this or that will."[11] Hence, on the one hand, Horkheimer sees love as sexual desire, through which the other becomes a means; yet on the other hand, he also sees in it the possibility of realizing the Kantian idea. The recognition of the human being as an "end in him- or herself" is fundamental to Horkheimer's concept of morality, to what he calls *"moral feeling."*[12] Since for him morality does not have its source in pure reason, it relies on a motivational basis that must be anchored in the formative process of the subject. Horkheimer recognized in the mother-child interaction the experience of such a relationship not determined by means and ends. And in the complexity of early structures of meaning, he surmises, lies a wealth of prelinguistic motivations that form, in their confrontation with social reality, the basis for critique and for productive objectification of the imagination. The impoverishment of culture, according to Horkheimer, is due to the dissolution of these tensions; accommodation to reality turns into total absorption by society. In "Philosophy as Cultural Criticism" (1959) he writes:

The overcoming of the chaotic, unbound element in human beings, which includes not only uncoordinated bodily impulses but aimless spiritual ones as well, is replaced by their mere suppression and, as a reaction, by an aversion to anyone capable of allowing their impulses to play more freely. . . . In order to become a formative power of the self and the conscious, underlying motive of an autonomous life, the moral sensibility needs a protected childhood, an ability to experience things differentiatedly, to identify with happiness to which violence has been done.[13]

This is not a critique of reason that invokes its "other"; rather, Horkheimer describes a process of bifurcation that robs the self of its possibilities. The fact that he does not see the victory of spirit over the senses as cultural progress shows that he does not understand libido, sensuousness, and spirit as fixed opposites. Thus, he does not place the maternal and paternal principles in a hierarchical relationship, because for him the mother is not only an object of desire from the perspective of the child; rather, she represents successful intersubjectivity and a principle critical of society.

Marleen Stoessel's study of Walter Benjamin, *Aura: The Forgotten Human Quality*, deciphers the origin and meanings of the experience of the aura.[14] Her work also sheds light on some of Horkheimer's intentions, including his conception of the existence of the "mystical aura" of the maternal and its disappearance. The aura, the "forgotten human quality" in the movement of desire and memory, has its original model in the mother-child relationship. "It is this 'mother matrix,'" writes Stoessel, "out of which the child, through the playful movement of wish-fulfillment, continually establishes itself as both similar to her and multifarious, but not yet as an identical self separate from her."[15] The experience of the aura is linked to this phase, which precedes the "identity of the one and the same"; it arises from the trace of a memory that is concealed by the "exclusion of the other" and the "conscious possession of oneself." In the experience of the aura, consequently, the "experience of relationship with an 'other,' be it person or nature, a loosening of the boundaries of self and identity" survives. Unlike Benjamin, Horkheimer seeks the decline of the aura in the constitution of the masculine subject or, more precisely, in the loss of the mother matrix. Stoessel cites a witness to this decay who could have drawn the picture that guides Horkheimer's thought: "Thus Max Ernst shows three figures—including himself—who watch in indecent embarrassment as the mother of God spanks the infant Jesus, whose gossamer halo falls to the ground at such undignified treatment."[16]

The underlying meaning of the "mystical aura" of the "maternal" already contains the cultural transformation of nature and calls to mind a dimension of objective reason: the idea of solidary relationships among people. Therefore, Horkheimer contrasts the "maternal" with reason that has become instrumental—not, however, with reason per se. Nor does the maternal represent the realm of emotion. The cult of emotion, as a phenomenon of the culture industry, was criticized by Adorno and Horkheimer themselves in *Dialectic of Enlightenment* and by Adorno at many points in *Minima Moralia* (1951). The critique of irrationalism and the cult of emotions in Horkheimer's "Juliette" chapter in *Dialectic of Enlightenment* advances a specific concern: "Though feelings are raised in this way to the level of an ideology, they continue to be despised in reality" (*DE*, 91). When detached and separated from the concepts of reason and truth, emotion becomes an independent, "antagonistic principle" in regard to thought. But when Horkheimer counters this unresolved dualism by invoking Hegel, with whom "high philosophy discovered the claim to truth even in subjective and objective expressions which are not yet fully thought— in emotions, institutions, and works of art" (*DE*, 91)—he fails to mention how Hegel conceived of the "truth" of the institution of the family. The differential determination of the sexes is the metaphysical residue in Hegel's concept of reason. The mediation of the particular and universal is tied to the condition that the masculine subject will be recognized by the woman in his sensual and emotional needs. These "material needs" (Hegel) are a moment of subjective reason that arises from the principle of self-preservation; the "services" performed by the woman are accorded the dignity of rationality because they strengthen the concrete, bodily, and spiritual man for the "universal" tasks of objective reason:

Through their rationality, the two natural sexes receive both their intellectual and moral significance; their differences are moments of the concept. . . . The man is oriented to the family only in his material needs. The woman must provide for the man's needs, and the man's spirit must be refreshed by the woman in the family so that he can once again assert himself and represent the universal. Only idle fantasy . . . can tear the sexes away from their destiny.[17]

Inasmuch as reason appears in the immediate "morality" of the family and the institution itself becomes a moment of "objective spirit"—and thus an irreducible fact—the social and historical determination of asymmetrical gender relationships is dehistoricized. Recognition of material needs and of the concrete other are excluded from male practice and from the philosophical concept of the subject,[18] though in reality, they are—as the practice of women—subsumed by them. Horkheimer fails to see this; in many ways he is taken in by Hegel's fascinated view of the family. His critical statements about gender relations primarily address the forms of male domination and exploitation as well as "the deformation of female nature," which is seen in connection with women's historical exclusion from the status of subjects.[19]

This critique, however, does not address the question of gender difference in a fundamental way. What Horkheimer does is to give Hegel's ideology of the family a new meaning: an antagonistic, sociocritical moment has been formed in the family only by virtue of the exclusion of women from culture and society. The figures of maternal love that he outlines, therefore, follow the logic of a linear cultural pessimism; they miss the reality of woman as an empirical "subject." In the final analysis, he invokes a prehistorical myth, a myth that becomes explicable only in light of the negativity of sociocultural development—the alleged "disenchantment" of familial practice.

In any case, it seems quite clear that the collapse of the father-myth calls into question the existence of conscience as a social phenomenon. The mother who pursues a career is already something completely different than the mother whose life was essentially dedicated to the raising of children. . . . The career reifies her thoughts, just as it does in the case of the man. Add to this something else: she has equal rights. She no longer radiates love as she once did. Previously, the mother was the one who preserved *her nature in a positive sense*, through her language and her gestures. Her conscious and unconscious reactions played an important role in child rearing. They molded the child perhaps more decisively than any instructions. . . . Of course, such processes cannot be reversed. But one can try to preserve some of what has been transmitted by making the negative aspects of the change visible. That is an important task of critical theory.[20] (emphasis added)

This is the substance of one of Horkheimer's "enlightenment" gestures from the time of "Authority and the Family" (1936) onward. It inverts one of critical theory's basic philosophical maxims: that thought misses the "positive" whenever it names it. In this case, the alleged negativity depends on an idealized image of maternal love and its "mystical aura," an unscrutinized fantasy that is confused with reality.

The question is how Horkheimer can maintain that this vanishing, idealized maternal love exists when he repeatedly asserts that women are oppressed and exploited. If woman is not an end but a means, then the search for the origin of the "idea of happiness with an emancipatory intent" takes a philosophically untrue form. The self-destruction of reason through the internal and external domination of nature refers to the non-recognition of the "uniquely maternal" and to the unrealized promise of mutual recognition in the relations of the sexes.

I have spoken of the split in Horkheimer's image of the mother between the good mother of the past and the bad one of the present. Just as this figure of thought is a theoretical construction necessary for Horkheimer to grasp the problematic constitution of the male subject without plunging into the abyss of a radical analysis of gender relationships, so he never publicly cast a shadow on the memory of his own "particularly affectionate and loving" mother. Since the publication of his philosophical diary from 1925 to 1928, however, this positive force appears in a new light that confirms my thesis of a repressed "bad" mother-imago:

Insofar as the talk of "blood ties" is supposed to have a normative character and even, one-sidedly, to hold the patriarchal idea of "obedience" in its background, it belongs to the most sinister of ideological idols. . . . Ideologies are perpetuated for centuries after they have lost the breadth of their foundations! Too much could appear to be a "matter of course" to me as well, but I must not forget that my mother's sinister, malicious egotism and my father's petty and cowardly egotism would have destroyed thousands other than me. I must not forget that there is no stupidity or meanness that these people would not have mobilized against me, that they would have murdered my friend and my wife a thousand times over, without the slightest scruples, out of the most ridiculous and 'outmoded' fanaticism in the world—had fear of the laws of a society that is certainly socially advanced not tied their hands: my mother, actively and evilly; my father, in the cowardly, patient posture of the petty sinner and henpecked husband. The thought that what I am writing here is marked by affect and should be treated by psychoanalysis and individual psychology, the thought that a fourteen year old boy might talk like this should not keep me from being clear. Perhaps the fourteen year old boy is closer to the truth. Only someone completely unoriented could believe that psychoanalysis could cloud the objectivity of judgment. I must not take the matter-of-course to be too self-evident. I must not allow the traditional atmosphere to smuggle in a mood that suggests that, spiritually, anything else exists between me and my parents than a *single,* yawning, unbridgeable abyss that cannot be filled in![21]

The Puzzle of the Male Subject

The historical and theoretical contexts in which Horkheimer assessed the significance of maternal love should not be ignored, though only a brief overview of them is possible here. In the various phases of his work, the interests that motivated his analyses shifted. At the time of *Studies on Authority and the Family* (1936) and the founding of critical theory, he still held hopes of revolutionary social transformation, but from *Dialectic of Enlightenment* (1947) onward, his view of family processes changed.[22] The formulation "Authority and Family Today" (1949), therefore, seems to be a resumption of the earlier approach only at first glance. The attempt to comprehend the "incomprehensible" signals a search for the origin of fascist character structures and the psychic structure of anti-Semitism. This text briefly takes up a thesis from 1936, in which Horkheimer comes close to the truth about the constitution of the male subject. (I will return to it in the last part of this chapter.) During the early 1940s Horkheimer subjected psychoanalytic theory and orthodox psychoanalytic practice to what was in some respects a radical critique. The protocols of the discussions between Adorno and Horkheimer and the notes Horkheimer made in America include subversive fantasies.[23] The search for the "social" in the individual—that is, for repressive forces—led them, in a contradictory fashion, beyond the Oedipal complex.[24] The meaning of the maternal acquired a new dimension, one that also found expression in the development of psychoanalytic theory after Freud: the mother becomes fate, and the utopian dimensions of the subject, which were linked to emancipatory social theory, disappear. Mimesis becomes a mechanism that produces the individual's non-conflictual adjustment to a false reality.[25] But from the perspective of Horkheimer's and Adorno's metatheoretical reflections on the relationship between social theory and psychoanalysis, some of their concrete analyses can be criticized for obscuring borders. In some instances, social mediation is no longer taken into account.

The concept of instrumental reason, which is meant to characterize all human relations—not only subject-object relations or the reduction of male reason to mere self-preservation—introduces a social-theoretical analysis that, during the restoration period of the Federal Republic, tended toward the idea of a totally administered world. In comments from his late work, Horkheimer conceived the tendencies that are breaking down the family as part of a "withering away of the human" as such.[26] And he viewed the "emancipation" of women critically, on the grounds that they would become men's equals in a negative sense. This led him to envision a new barbarism, in which instrumental reason is anthropologized.[27]

Horkheimer persists in the kind of thinking that thematizes "the human" but speaks only of the male subject. Thus, he repeats old figures of thought that ascribe a progressive significance to the injustice of male domination by linking it to the "happiness of the individual" in the family.[28] The mirror image of this is the alleged negative consequence of equal rights for women, the disappearance of non-instrumental relationships. This sort of thinking makes dialectics into a masculine attitude and brings it to a stop: "For the sake of truth we must heed the fact that a number of the old cultural spheres possessed a not inconsiderable significance for the life of the individual—a significance which will one day cease to exist."[29]

The Maternal as the "Social Principle" of Prehistory

"Authority and the Family" (1936) introduced a social-psychological perspective that was supposed to capture the intrapsychic dynamics of the dominated. The internalization of what had once been the external compulsion of material conditions becomes the starting point for determining the relation of culture and society. Horkheimer grasps the historical process of internalizing external violence not simply as a form of affirmation but rather as a dialectic of accommodation and possible resistance. Taking the example of morality and romantic love, he demonstrates that social development simultaneously produced the precondition for breaking with the social order ("AF," 114). Cultural institutions—here, above all, marriage and the family—are thereby accorded a "definite, even if relative autonomy" ("AF," 59).

From the perspective of 1936, this dynamic appears to be frozen. The significance of authority can no longer be seen as historically progressive and deserving of affirmation: "The fullest possible adaptation of the subject to the reified authority of the economy is the form that reason really takes in bourgeois society" ("AF," 83). Decisive for Horkheimer is the fact that the structural transformation of authority in the family and in society works to reinforce domination and subordination, because authority is thereby robbed of its potential intersubjective dynamic, and thus of the possibility of being overcome. The physical, legal, moral, and economic strength of the father appears to the child as a naturally given status. Thus, in the family "we find anticipated in large measure the structure of authority as it existed outside the family . . . to recognize facts means to accept them" ("AF," 100–101).

Horkheimer sees rational and irrational elements inseparably joined together in the father's functions. On the one hand a "genuine social need" is satisfied, even if in "a problematic manner"—this would be the progressive moment. On the other hand, the child's respect involves "habituation to an authority which in an obscure way unites a necessary social function with power over people" ("AF," 108). The precondition of this was that the father's "powers and jurisdiction" remain clear and vivid, forming the basis for later confrontations through which the son would attempt to free himself from paternal authority. The father's status in a "family which has shrunk to a group of consumers" is communicated only by the money he earns. The social task he performs becomes invisible: "Because of this separation in space and time between professional and familial life, every bourgeois father may in social life have a very modest position and have to bend the knee to others, yet at home he will be the master and exercise the highly important function of accustoming his children to discretion and obedience" ("AF," 108).

It is crucial for the development of the authoritarian character that the child, under pressure from the father, should learn to feel that every mistake is a personal failure. "At times this has been a productive trait, namely, as long as the fate of the individual and the common good both depended, at least in part, on the efficiency of the individual" ("AF," 109). For the present era, Horkheimer formulates the negative side of this principle: people are no longer raised to "get to the root of things"; they have a masochistic tendency "to surrender their will to some sort of leader" ("AF," 110). From now on, the irrational features of paternal authority stand out against a background of opaque social relations. As a result, the father's actual behavior, whether coercive or indulgent, becomes meaningless because the "impulse of submission" is produced by the "very structure" of the family rather than by "the conscious intentions and methods of the father" ("AF," 111).

The structure of this argument is problematic. If the previous form of paternal authority united power and competence in a *"clear and vivid"* manner, this meant that the symbolic meaning of the father could not be separated from his concrete function. But if the previous form of this connection is now falling apart, this cannot mean that the behavior of actual, concrete fathers becomes unimportant, for the irrational authority of the father does not result from structural considerations alone. The resolution of the Oedipal conflict, to which Horkheimer implicitly refers, can only be grasped through the form in which it is experienced. Horkheimer reduces the significance of the father to his socially stabilizing function. He does not regard the fact that the family also includes the possibility of "acting as a human being" as a condition of the father's practice.[30] It is decisive for the further course of the argument that Horkheimer's negative image of the father provides no anticipation of a father who "loves his children's childhood." The polarity of the mother- and father-imagos is thereby fixed on the basis of a gendered division of labor.

In order to comprehend the family's "antagonistic" relation to society, Horkheimer must bring "sexual love and especially . . . maternal care" ("AF," 114) into play because all humane features have been extirpated from the father figure.

Even in the golden age of the bourgeois order, it must be remembered, there was a renewal of social life, but it was achieved at the cost of great sacrifice for most individuals. In that situation, the family was a place where suffering could be given free expression and the injured individual found a retreat within which he or she could put up some resistance. In the economy people were being reduced to mere functions of one or another economic factor: wealth or technically demanding physical or mental work. The same process of reduction to subpersonal status was going on within the family insofar as the father was becoming the money-earner, the woman a sexual object or a domestic servant . . . Within the family, however, unlike public life, relationships were not mediated through the market and the individual members were not competing with each other. Consequently the individual always had the possibility there of living not as a mere function but as a human being. ("AF," 114)

Yet since there is no "human being" as such but only human being as a contradictory unity of human and gendered being,[31] the denial of culturally codified gender differences prior to capitalist reification leads here to a false generalization of the connection between family and humanity. It remains a puzzle how the loving mother or wife can develop out of the woman's position as object. In the history of bourgeois thought, a gender metaphysics legitimated the exclusion of women from culture and society; now, for Horkheimer, this exclusion becomes the cause of a gender difference that can be formulated as a critique of society, a difference that already appears to be theoretically secured by the concept of "reification" as a category of differentiation:

In civic life, even when common concerns . . . had an essentially negative character . . . common concerns took a *positive* form in sexual love and especially in maternal care. The growth and happiness of the other are willed in such unions. A felt opposition therefore arises between them and hostile reality outside. To this extent, the family does not only educate for authority in bourgeois society; it also cultivates the dream of a better condition for mankind. In the yearning of many adults for the paradise of their childhood, in the way *a mother can speak of her son* even though he has come into conflict with the world, *in the protective love of a wife for her husband,* there are ideas and forces at work which admittedly are not dependent on the existence of the family in its present form, and, in fact, are even in danger of shrivelling up in such a milieu, but which, nevertheless, in the bourgeois system of life, rarely have any place but the family where they can survive at all. ("AF," 114–15; emphasis added)

Once more, the question arises as to the origin of the "ideas and forces" at work in maternal care and love of one's husband. Horkheimer now moves toward a new explanatory framework: "To the extent that any principle besides that of subordination prevails in the modern family, the woman's maternal and sisterly love is keeping alive a social principle dating from before historical antiquity, a principle which Hegel conceives of 'as the law of the ancient gods,' 'the gods of the underworld,' that is, of prehistory" ("AF," 118). Here Horkheimer appears to be trying to resolve the preceding antinomies. The social principle that maintains itself in maternal love is phylogenetically older than all conscious human laws. It is a mythic inheritance—embodied for Hegel in the figure of Antigone, evoked by the divine forces of Hestia and the lares—that nevertheless does not sustain itself by its own strength. The authority of the husband and the subordination of wife and children may be an objective law, but in the love of the wife and mother this law is virtually transcended. The woman is an object, but by breaking through this status, she brings her actions into an antagonistic relation to the existing order. She thinks about her son: is he to preserve the intimation of a better society, or will he later only be reminded of this intimation by his wife's protective love?

With the assertion that the mother represents a prehistoric social principle, Horkheimer touches on the question of the "sublation [Aufhebung]" of myth. Later, in 1945, he would say that "in true enlightenment, the kind that is identical to philosophy, mythology is not shouted down. Its power is placated."[32] One might vary this observation by suggesting that in the formative process of male subjectivity, this "female," prehistoric power was shouted down rather than placated. The family became the site of this captivity. The analogy to ontogenetic development is not a hasty supposition; Horkheimer himself suggests it in the theme of "Authority and the Family" and in his associations to the passage just cited: "If therapeutic psychology were what it is supposed to be, it would concentrate on the effort to uncover the moments in individual and historical life through which power (in the shape of the father or political ruler) made the person incapable of devotion to things, in order to put him all the more certainly at the mercy of things. In this role, psychology would once again become an instrument of philosophy."[33]

In his discussion of Antigone in "Authority and the Family," Horkheimer attempts to clarify two problems: the origin of the "moment of the recognizing and recognized individual self" as a social principle and its historical disappearance, both phylogenetic and ontogenetic. The tragic antithesis of family and community stands at the center of Horkheimer's critique of Hegel—not, however, the philosophical construction that makes this figure of thought possible. Antigone's fate repeats itself in Hegel's concepts in the form of the symbolic death of a female subject. The myth that Horkheimer alludes to is thereby deprived of its power. Antigone's suicide in the Sophoclean tragedy and her last words—"If this seems good to the gods, / Suffering, we may be made to know our error"[34]—are given a specific interpretation by both Hegel and Horkheimer, which can be discussed here only insofar as it relates to the following argument: "When she thus renounces all resistance, she simultaneously accepts the principle of male-dominated bourgeois society: bad luck is your own fault." ("AF," 121)

The antagonistic moment, which is supposed to be present in the woman's love as a social principle from prehistory, is conceivable only as conscious resistance. This is the point of Horkheimer's conclusion, which he attempts to link with his thesis on the modern disappearance of this resistance in the final section of "Authority and the Family" as well as in later texts.[35] Instead of asking how the "prehistoric social principle" subsists intrapsychically under the sway of paternal law, Horkheimer sees the ontogenetic root of the problematic masculine, authoritarian character in the transformation of the "female"—the alleged disappearance of the empirical basis of maternal love. He links the symbolic meaning of the maternal directly to the concrete expression of maternal behavior. Thus, for him it is logical that the utopian dimension and the moment of resistance in the male subject should disappear as soon as the "influence of a mind dedicated to the prevailing order of things" expresses itself in maternal practices. "It is not only in this *direct* way, however, that the woman exercises the function of strengthening authority. Her *whole position* in the family results in an inhibiting of important psychic energies which might have been effective in shaping the world" ("AF," 120; emphasis added).

Horkheimer now refers to the Oedipal structure, which reflects the general "devaluation of purely sensuous pleasure." Above all, "every sensuous moment" in the son's tenderness toward the mother must be "strictly banished":

Under the pressure of such a family situation the individual does not learn to understand and respect his mother in her concrete existence, that is, as this particular social and sexual being. Consequently he is not only educated to repress his socially harmful impulses (a feat of immense cultural significance), but, because this education takes the problematic form of camouflaging reality, the individual also loses for good the disposition of part of his psychic energies. ("AF," 121)

Here Horkheimer formulates an unequivocal connection between the suppression of drives and the nonrecognition of the woman in the process of the constitution of the male subject. Precisely because he does not understand the mother only as the son's libidinal object, he comes close to the truth about male identity, which must develop through separation from the mother and from previous experience because the father-imago is becoming increasingly abstract and because irrational male authority represents the socially dominant principle. Such an interpretation would not criticize the Oedipal conflict as such but only an asymmetrical and repressive form of it—the culturally specific, differential valuation of masculinity and femininity and of maternal and paternal practice. The Oedipal problematic itself does not predetermine asymmetrical gender relations; rather, such relations confer a specific, symbolic meaning on the Oedipal process and restrict the functions of the self.

The outcome of the Oedipal phase, as he outlines it in "Authority and the Family," already includes a separation of reason and sensuality: "Reason and joy in its exercise are restricted; the suppressed inclination towards the mother reappears as a fanciful and sentimental susceptibility to all symbols of the dark, maternal, and protective powers.[36] Because the woman bows to the law of the patriarchal family, she becomes an instrument for maintaining authority in this society" ("AF," 121). The context of this passage shows that Horkheimer no longer anticipates that the mother will be the "loving" woman. He defuses the explosive power of his thesis that the male resolution of the Oedipal conflict inseparably ties together the suppression of drives and the nonrecognition of the woman. This uncomfortable, almost unconscious realization must not be allowed to become a critical insight that could undermine the ideology of maternal love. What would the woman be like as a subject, seen in relation to herself? She is useful for the theory of male development only as wife and mother, in relation to husband and child. A structural ambivalence toward the mother and the socially determined contradictions of maternal practice is split apart, and the polarized images are assigned to different historic epochs. Instead, in order to solve the puzzle of the male subject, Horkheimer invokes the end of romantic love, of eroticism, and of the "mystical aura."

The antinomies in Horkheimer's thought have several causes. For one, his approach to the project of critical theory fails at the intersection where family and society are mediated. He does not relate the various analytic levels to one another in all their specific differences but rather connects them additively. He thereby loses sight of the fact that psychic reality and external reality are not mirror images of one another. Maternal practices cannot simply be deduced from structural conditions, and they do not cease to exist just because they are not represented culturally or in the male subject. The point of departure, and the key to the reproduction of the masculine character, was Horkheimer's analysis of the increasingly abstract father-imago. This was what produced the disappearance of the "mystical aura." Only the imagination of it vanishes, not the reality.

The Traces of the "Maternal" Become Invisible

In *Eclipse of Reason* (1947), Horkheimer radicalized the arguments presented above: "The triumph of subjective, formalized reason is also the triumph of a reality that confronts the subject as absolute, overpowering.... The individual, purified of all remnants of mythologies, including the mythology of objective reason, reacts automatically, according to the general patterns of adaptation" (*Eclipse*, 96–97). As a result, the "self, the abstract ego, is emptied of all substance." Nature is solely an object of control; reason and the ability to adapt become identical. Academic experiences in America now led to a shift in emphasis in Horkheimer's view of the "maternal." In *Minima Moralia* Adorno speculated about a "prehistoric intervention, which incapacitates the opposing forces before they have come to grips with each other."[37] Horkheimer sees this pre-Oedipal "a priori triumph of the collective authority," like equal rights and women's employment outside the home, as resulting from the scientization of maternal behavior and the transition to formal rationality:

The tremendous good that psychoanalytical enlightenment in all its versions has brought to certain urban groups is at the same time a further step toward a more rationalized and conscious attitude on the part of the mother, on whose *instinctual* love the child's development depends. She is transformed into a nurse, her friendliness and her insistence gradually become part of a technique. Much as society may gain by making motherhood a science, it deprives the individual of certain influences that formerly had a binding force in social life. (*Eclipse*, 110–11; emphasis added)

The scientization of "maternal love" is not a phenomenon of the "culture industry"; at that time it affected only the nonbourgeois strata.

The incursion of pedagogy into mothering was already part of the Enlightenment itself and invariably stood in opposition to uncontrolled, spontaneous maternal behavior. But these developments alone tell us nothing about maternal practices, which are determined not only by acquired knowledge but also by the child and by the mother's ability to find access to her own unconscious. As early as 1931, Alice Balint described what Horkheimer presumably meant by instinctive love: "It is therefore not so much the learning of new facts that we wish for in those who raise children, but rather a remembering of something forgotten. The precondition for a caring upbringing is at bottom nothing else but to remember what we all knew as children. We know how difficult this is to recall, but it is by no means impossible."[38] It would require a separate study to determine how this ability can be influenced, whether positively or negatively, by pedagogical and psychological "knowledge." Horkheimer justly criticizes the social intrusions upon mothering, but at the same time he treats mothers as agents of social power without reflecting on the objective conditions of their action or on their subjective motivations and affects. Yet the difference between the "ideology of the maternal role" and real maternal practices must always be kept in view.

The suspicion that the decay of the "mystical aura" might have something to do with gender relations is formulated by Horkheimer for the last time in "Authority and the Family Today" (1949).[39] His goal is the social-psychological deciphering not of instrumental reason as such but of its barbaric form, the fascist character: "More than anything else, it is the connection between subservience and coldness that characterizes the potential fascist of today" ("AFG," 280). Horkheimer sees both elements as the result of an almost complete lack of a concrete relation to the parents. Adherence to a familial paternal authority becomes abstract "once the inner substance of the family has dissolved." Submissiveness results from the repressed rebellion against the father. On the other hand, coldness manifests itself in a "disdain for empathy—empathy of the kind that more than anything else is a sign of the mother's love for her child" ("AFG," 281). Here, maternal love is an image that serves to make the contrast clear. Horkheimer is not yet making a direct connection between a lack of maternal love and disdain for empathy of the kind suggested in the following remarks:

With boys the conscious rejection of the mother's love likewise proved very significant. During his early adaptation to the demands of life the boy gets the impression that the mother, on account of her gender, represents something weak and contemptible. He senses the ambivalence in the official glorification of her, and regards her as a member of an inferior race. To a large extent, the coldness and superficiality of the authority-bound character are the emotional consequences of this rejection. Hardness, thoughtlessness, and an exaggerated air of masculinity, all of which lead to fascist political ideologies, have their roots in *a disturbed relationship to the mother, or perhaps, indeed, in the lack of any genuine relation to her.* Yet this is presumably not even the *most important consequence of the stunted relationship between mother and child* [emphasis added].

What appears to be most deeply affected is the individual's tolerance for the other sex. An anti-feminine affect, which is based on the rejection of the mother, provides the model for the later rejection of everything that is regarded as "other." The groups the fascists reject as foreign, above all the Jews, are often endowed with "feminine" traits such as weakness, emotionality, lack of self-discipline, and sensuality. Contempt for the traits of the other sex as soon as they appear among the members of one's own sex regularly appears to be bound up with a strong, generalized intolerance for all that is other. This finding leads to the supposition of a deep-rooted relationship between homosexuality,[40] attachment to authority, and the contemporary decay of the family. The strict dichotomy between masculinity and femininity, as well as the taboos on any psychological transition between the former and the latter, accords with the general tendency to think in rigid dichotomies and stereotypes. ("AFG," 282)

The coldness of the authoritarian and fascist character is depicted as the emotional consequence of the rejection of the mother, the cause of which in turn is seen in society's contempt for, or ambivalence toward, the "female." None of the social-critical dimensions that Horkheimer associated with the "maternal"—recognition of the other, "moral feeling," a binding, nonseparating power, fantasy, identification with happiness that has been done violence, and the mimetic ability—leave any trace in the development of male identity.

But the explosive effect of Horkheimer's argument is undermined by an implicit paradox: the thesis of the "rejection of the mother" is contradicted by his claim that the maternal itself has lost its substance. The relation between mother and child is said to be stunted in reality.[41] Horkheimer does away with distinctions that cannot be eliminated: the difference between psychic representations of the "maternal" and actual maternal behavior; between the mother-imago and the real mother and wife; between the "mystical aura" and social non-recognition of its meanings—indeed, contempt for them.

The place of the "mystical aura" in the development of psychic structures remains unclear in Horkheimer's work. The importance he attributes to early, prelinguistic structures of meaning shows that he sees the id as a culturally influenced, psychophysiological unity and not as nature in revolt. Horkheimer anticipated the possibility of its proximity to the ego, and its sublation in consciousness and in the practices of the masculine subject. But he was unable to conceptualize the repression of the early identification with the mother and the non-representation of the prelinguistic foundation of meaning in the male subject, because he did not consistently examine the relationship of maternal practices to paternal law against the background of asymmetrically structured gender relations. This failure is also linked to an abridged social-theoretical perspective—a frozen dialectic between the male individual and society. In *Dialectic of Enlightenment* it was the voice of de Sade that demystified the aura of the maternal by pointing to society's real interest in a structural hostility toward the tender bonds of the family (*DE*, 116–17). This idea of a latent conflict between the family and society gets lost in Horkheimer's later texts. With the psychic birth of the male individual the conflict—seen ontogenetically—has supposedly been decided: it no longer exists. In *Dialectic of Enlightenment* it was the self-empowerment of the male subject that simultaneously resulted in its self-destruction. Now it is the allegedly unmaternal mother who sends her son to ruin before he dares to think for himself.

But Horkheimer's intention was to confer upon preconceptual experiences and the mother-child interaction a language opposed to the idea of a monadic self:

The self is the product of a long process of human biological and psychological development that is repeated in highly compressed form in every individual. If this repetition takes place abruptly, in too cold and dispassionate an atmosphere, then *a separation from others* and an *unapproachability* remain characteristic of the individual until the end. Love in its true form—the kind that embraces everyone, even the enemy—still bears traces of the phase of development prior to the formation of the ego, however much the ego may have developed since. The more civilization reaches the stage at which the interplay between childlike and adult traits in the individual is disturbed on one side or the other, the more freedom is threatened—the kind of freedom that is enriched by the possibilities of identification and love.[42] (emphasis added)

Translated by Jean Keller with assistance from John McCole

Notes

Horkheimer's texts are cited and English translations, where available, are cross-referenced according to the following key (in some cases the translations have been modified):

"AF" = "Authority and the Family," in *Critical Theory: Selected Essays* (New York, 1972).

"AFG" = "Autorität und Familie in der Gegenwart" (1949), in *Zur Kritik der instrumentellen Vernunft* (Frankfurt, 1985).

BPSS = *Between Philosophy and Social Science: Selected Early Writings* (Cambridge, 1993).

CIR = *Critique of Instrumental Reason* (New York, 1974).

DE = *Dialectic of Enlightenment* (New York, 1972).

Eclipse = *Eclipse of Reason* (Oxford, 1947).

1. Jessica Benjamin, "Die Antinomien des patriarchalischen Denkens. Kritische Theorie und Psychoanalyse," in Wolfgang Bonß and Axel Honneth, eds., *Sozialforschung als Kritik* (Frankfurt, 1982); see also Jessica Benjamin, "Die Fesseln der Liebe. Zur Bedeutung der Unterwerfung in erotischen Beziehungen," in *Feministische Studien* 4 (November 1985). In English, see Jessica Benjamin, *The Bonds of Love* (New York, 1988). In my *Spuren des Mütterlichen. Die widersprüchliche Bedeutung der Mutterrolle für die männliche Identitätsbildung in Kritischer Theorie und feministischer Wissenschaft* (Frankfurt, 1989), I examine in detail the contributions of Benjamin and of Nancy Chodorow, on whom Benjamin relies.

2. Benjamin, "Die Antinomien des patriarchalischen Denkens," 446f.

3. Jürgen Habermas, *The Theory of Communicative Action* (Boston, 1987), 1:389.

4. Ibid., 340.

5. Ibid., 26.

6. For the context see note 39.

7. Horkheimer, "Zum Begriff des Menschen" (1956), in *Gesammelte Schriften* 7 (Frankfurt, 1985): 60/*CIR*, 8; cf. "Der Mensch in der Wandlung seit der Jahrhundertwende," *Gesammelte Schriften* 8: 131ff., and "Bedrohungen der Freiheit," ibid., 262ff./*CIR*, 136ff.

8. Cf. Horkheimer, "Altmodisches Problem" (1939/1940), in *Gesammelte Schriften* 12: 292f.; cf. also *DE*, 106–7.

9. Horkheimer, "Das Schlimme erwarten und doch das Gute versuchen" (conversation with Gerhard Rein, 1972), in *Gesammelte Schriften* 7:442f.

10. As Adorno once put it, "With the family there passes away, while the system lasts, not only the most effective agency of the bourgeoisie, but also the resistance which, though repressing the individual, also strengthened, perhaps even produced him. The end of the family paralyzes the forces of opposition. The rising collectivist order is a mockery of a classless one: together with the bourgeois it liquidates the utopia that once drew sustenance from motherly love." Theodor W. Adorno, *Minima Moralia. Reflexionen aus dem beschädigten Leben* (Frankfurt, 1969), 17. English translation: *Minima Moralia: Reflections from Damaged Life* (London, 1974), 23.

11. Kant, *Grundlegung zur Metaphysik der Sitten* (Stuttgart, 1963), 428, 78.

12. "Kant describes marriage as 'the union of two persons of the opposite sex for the purposes of the lifelong mutual possession of one another's sexual attributes.' . . . Modern depictions of marriage, if they have not become completely ideological, contain similar definitions. According to Freud, the sexual aim of the infantile drives (in which, according to his doctrine, the essential features of the adult's drives are already to be found) consists in 'obtaining satisfaction by means of an appropriate stimulation of the . . . erotogenic zones.' In this view, the loved one appears primarily as the means of performing this stimulation. In this respect, Freud's theory would appear to be a more detailed explication of Kant's definition of marriage.

"Moral feeling differs from this kind of love, and Kant is right to distinguish it not only from egoism, but from any such 'inclination.' His doctrine that in morality, contrary to the rule that prevails in the bourgeois world, the person is not merely a means, but always at the same time an end, describes the psychic state of affairs. Moral feeling has something to do with love, for 'love . . . [is] inherent in an end.' " Horkheimer, "Materialismus und Moral" (1933), *ZfS* 2 (1933): 181ff./"Materialism and Morality," *BPSS*.

13. Horkheimer, "Philosophie als Kulturkritik" (1959), in *Gesammelte Schriften* 7:94f.

14. Marleen Stoessel, *Aura: Das vergessene Menschliche* (Munich/Vienna, 1983).

15. Ibid., 148.

16. Max Ernst's picture dates from 1928 and is entitled 'La vierge corrigeant l'enfant Jésus devant trois témoins A.B., P.E. et le peintre.' Ibid., 190.

17. Georg Wilhelm Friedrich Hegel, *Vorlesungen über Naturrecht und Staatswissenschaft* (Hamburg, 1983), sec. 77, 96f.; cf. Hegel, *Grundlinien der Philosophie des Rechts* (Hamburg, 1983), sec. 165, 166.

18. In "Authority and the Family" (1936), Horkheimer criticizes Hegel for failing to recognize a socially relevant future in "the recognizing and recognized individual"; this would have "broken through" Hegel's system. "AF," 117.

19. Cf. "On the Concept of the Human," *Dialectic of Enlightenment*, "Altmodisches Problem," 292f., and all of Horkheimer's works on the family, especially "Authority and the Family" and "Authority and the Family Today."

20. Horkheimer, "Was wir 'Sinn' nennen, wird verschwinden" ("What we call 'meaning' will disappear"), conversation with Georg Wolff and Helmut Gumnior (1970), in *Gesammelte Schriften* 7:356.

21. Horkheimer, *Gesammelte Schriften* 11:254f.

22. "What appeared to Horkheimer and Adorno in 1944 as the end of history can be understood today as the end of an epoch without minimizing their claim. The critical theory Horkheimer formulated in the 1930s was linked to Marx's view of historical eras, according to which the end of capitalism would also mean the end of prehistory. With Auschwitz, however, prehistory exhausts the range of previous emancipatory theory. After Auschwitz, prehistory continues—nevertheless, before and after Auschwitz marks a watershed between historical epochs." Detlev Claussen, *Abschied von gestern. Kritische Theorie heute* (Bremen, 1986).

23. See Horkheimer, *Gesammelte Schriften* 12.

24. For instance, as Adorno wrote in *Minima Moralia*, "No science has yet explored the inferno in which were forged the deformations that later emerge to daylight as cheerfulness, openness, sociability, successful adaptation to the inevitable, an equable, practical frame of mind. There is reason to suppose that these characteristics are laid down at even earlier phases of childhood development than are neuroses: if the latter result from a conflict in which instinct is defeated, the former condition, as normal as the damaged society it resembles, stems from what might be called a prehistoric surgical intervention, which incapacitates the opposing forces before they have come to grips with each other, so that the subsequent absence of conflicts reflects a predetermined outcome, the a priori triumph of collective authority, not a cure effected by knowledge. . . . Underlying the prevalent health is death. All the movements of health resemble reflex-movements of beings whose hearts have stopped beating." *Minima Moralia*, 69f./ English translation, 59.

25. See notes 10, 24. Below I will show how Horkheimer sketches the image of reified and rationalized maternal behavior analogously to the motif "reason is the mimesis of death" in *Dialectic of Enlightenment*.

26. Horkheimer, "Zum Begriff des Menschen" (1956) in *Gesammelte Schriften* 7:79/*CIR*, 33.

27. "The consequences of extinguishing non-purposive thinking, of the victory of the intellect over the spirit, of the instrumental character of human relationships seem to me irreversible." Horkheimer, "Die verwaltete Welt kennt keine Liebe" (conversation with Janko Musulin, 1970), in *Gesammelte Schriften* 7:361.

28. See "Authority and the Family," in *CT*.

29. Horkheimer, "Zum Begriff des Geistes und der Verantwortung des Geistes" (conversation with Otmar Hersch, 1972) in *Gesammelte Schriften* 7:348.

30. See the passage cited in the following paragraph of this text.

31. Birgit Hohm, *Die Entzauberung des Weibes* (Pfaffenweiler, 1985), 46ff.

32. "New Yorker Notizen, 1945" in *Gesammelte Schriften* 12:301.

33. Ibid., 302.

34. G. W. F. Hegel, *Lectures on the Philosophy of History*, trans. Elizabeth S. Haldane and Frances H. Simson (London, 1892–1896), 1:441, as cited by Horkheimer in "Authority and the Family," *CT*, 121.

35. Cf. also *DE*, 114, 262ff.

36. Horkheimer is referring to Freud, "The Most Prevalent Form of Degradation in Erotic Life" (1912).

37. Adorno, *Minima Moralia,* 69/English translation, 59.

38. Alice Balint, *Psychoanalyse der frühen Lebensjahre* (1931) (Munich/Basel, 1973), 112.

39. At first Horkheimer repeats his thesis on the disappearance of maternal love: the mother's "entire attitude toward the child becomes rational; even love is treated as an aspect of pedagogical hygiene. . . . The mother's spontaneity and her natural, boundless loving care and warmth tend to dissipate. As a result, in the child's consciousness the image of the mother loses its *mystical aura* [emphasis added]. . . . Women have paid for their limited admission to the economic world of men by adopting the behavioral patterns of a totally reified society. The consequences of this extend to the most tender relations between mother and child. The mother ceases to be a soothing mediator between the child and harsh reality; instead, she becomes its mouthpiece. Once, she provided the child with a feeling of security that enabled it to develop a certain measure of independence. The child sensed that the mother reciprocated its love and somehow drew on this store of feeling its whole life long. The mother, who was cut off from the community of men and forced into a dependent position despite her idealization, represented a principle different than that of the predominant reality. Together with her child she really could dwell on utopian dreams, and she was its natural ally whether or not she wanted to be. Thus, there was a power in the life of the child that enabled it to develop its own individuality even as it adapted to the external world. Together with the circumstance that the decisive authority in the home was wielded by the father and that, at least up to a point, this authority was exercised through intellectual and moral channels, the mother's role prevented this adaptation from taking place too quickly and totally, at the cost of individuation. Today, when the child no longer experiences its mother's boundless love, its own capacity for love remains underdeveloped." "AFG," 277f.

40. Here Horkheimer seems to mean the repressed homoeroticism typical of intimate male groups. Only in this sense is Adorno's thesis comprehensible: "A great many intellectually gifted individuals are likely to be found among homosexuals; psychogenetically, this is probably because by virtue of their extreme identification with the mother they have also internalized those traits of the mother which are set up against the father, who represented a practical sense of reality." Adorno, "Sexualtabus und Recht heute" (1963), in *Eingriffe. Neun kritische Modelle* (Frankfurt, 1963), 112.

41. See note 39, as well as "Familie," in Institut für Sozialforschung, *Soziologische Exkurse: Nach Vorträgen und Diskussionen* (Frankfurt, 1956).

42. Horkheimer, "Threats to Freedom," *CIR,* 152.

13

Reason and the "Other": Horkheimer's Reflections on Anti-Semitism and Mass Annihilation

Dan Diner

Max Horkheimer has been reproached for not having devoted—before, during, and even after the National Socialist annihilation of the Jews—the kind of attention to anti-Semitism called for by its historical rank and, above all, by his own Jewish origins.[1] In light of this alleged "disinterest," the increased attention he later turned to the fate of the Jews and his reflections on anti-Semitism are denigrated as a "compensation" for his previous attitude.[2] To judge Horkheimer's position on anti-Semitism in this way is to take up a critical position outside history, outside the times, experiences and the sense of life crucial not only for Horkheimer and the original Frankfurt School but for German Jews in general: the belief that the civil emancipation of the Jews in Germany had already been accomplished and their equality as Germans actually and irreversibly established.[3] For those dedicated to emancipation, the task at hand was to overcome further barriers and socially discriminatory distinctions. The irruption of unimaginable barbarism, which went far beyond any mere retraction of the achievements of emancipation and enlightenment, profoundly contradicted their originally optimistic schemes. But in light of this optimism, it is not surprising that German National Socialism was not regarded at first as a phenomenon specifically concerning the Jews. Rather, it was considered to be one element of a general social threat, to which one reacted first and foremost as a political being, and only secondarily as a Jew.[4] Why should Horkheimer have seen things differently? Why should he have imagined the unimaginable before it occurred? And is his change of attitude in light of the destruction of the

Jews—an event, moreover, that qualitatively exceeds anti-Semitism—grounds for criticism? Gauged against the hope of emancipation and the significance of the historical rupture represented by National Socialism and the destruction of the Jews, it could hardly have been otherwise.

Horkheimer could not help but devote his attention to anti-Semitism during those terrible years. The way he went about it has led to some annoyance, particularly concerning his essay "The Jews and Europe." "Elements of Anti-Semitism," written with Adorno and Löwenthal as part of *Dialectic of Enlightenment,* has been judged quite differently. Both texts can be regarded as essential theoretical sources for analyzing a historic transformation of anti-Semitism. In addition, the theme of anti-Semitism was worked into other theoretical reflections in a dispersed, unsystematic fashion and interwoven with critical remarks on current affairs and biographical notes. These commentaries on anti-Semitism reveal a striking duality: they are both an element in the phenomenology of Horkheimer's critique of reason and the secret, biographical impetus behind the theoretical endeavor; they are at once mere material for explicating his critique of civilization and yet one of its subliminal motives as well. This duality corresponds to the significance attaching to the Jews as the primary victims of National Socialism: in being murdered *as* Jews, an event afflicting the Jewish people as a particular collective, their particularity seems to be confirmed. Yet in addition, a universal break in civilization simultaneously manifested itself. This break lies in the fact that an arbitrary and unfathomable annihilation of human beings became possible and actually took place.

The tension arising from this duality is inherent in the occurrence of mass annihilation. Its ambiguities, which already make an unequivocal judgment difficult, can be traced as a leitmotif in Horkheimer's writings and notes on anti-Semitism. This inherent tension between universal stance and particular concern is heightened by the question of what the term *Jew* means. It can signify both the concrete Jewish person and a social metaphor composed in the fantasy world of the anti-Semite. This metaphor has little to do with real Jews, although the fatality of a newly spun reality decreed that real Jews became its first victims. It is not surprising that for Horkheimer, as for other critics of anti-Semitism, the social-metaphorical significance of the Jews blends together with that of concrete Jewish persons. Of course, a mixing of social meaning with real fates is difficult to avoid. But claims for the validity of such a conflation could be made only before Auschwitz. On this point, the bureaucratically administered, industrial annihilation of the Jews necessarily brought in its wake a caesura in linguistic usage and conceptualization. Before the mass annihilation, which put a definitive end to the optimistic philosophy of historical progress, for Horkheimer—as for Marx in "On the Jewish Question"—"the Jews" did not stand for actual Jewish persons. The term bore above all an extended social meaning. After Auschwitz—after the actual destruction of the European Jews—the metaphorical and conceptual construal of term "Jew" in an extended sense receded. Since Auschwitz, common linguistic usages such as the description of phenomena from the sphere of circulation as Jewish have forfeited their dubious claim to reality.[5]

The perception and assessment of anti-Semitism necessarily take different forms from a universalistically oriented Jewish standpoint than from that of Jewish particularism. Neither of these perspectives was immune to errors and misjudgments in dealing with National Socialism. To criticize Horkheimer for having failed at the decisive moment to recognize the true significance of anti-Semitism is to insinuate that, faced with the evident significance of National Socialism, he obstinately refused to acknowledge the particularity of the problem (and of his own, very personal fate as well) by means of a distorted perception of reality and an exclusively theoretical treatment of its universal aspects. Whatever biographical truth there may be to this, when so formulated it has the ring of a retrospective valuation we would do better to refrain from, considering the monstrosity and inconceivability of the destruction of the Jews.[6] This is all the more so because the inconceivable came to be a thoroughly personal experience for Horkheimer.[7]

Moreover, critiques that base their reproaches on Horkheimer's texts on the problem of anti-Semitism and the situation of the Jews before and during the process of mass annihilation presume, without acknowledging it, the accomplished fact of genocide. The latent implication of such critiques is that the mass annihilation was foreseeable. They insinuate that anti-Semitism necessarily led to Auschwitz. If that were close to the truth, then the laxity with which Horkheimer and the predominantly Jewish members of the Frankfurt School considered (or failed to consider) anti-Semitism would be incomprehensible. But if one rejects this negative historical teleology—an alleged determinism leading from anti-Semitism to the destruction of the Jews—then it may be possible to shed light on those ambiguous mixtures of (undoubtedly eclectic) conceptual experiments and biographically conditioned perceptions in a way that does more justice to a tragic conjunction of political defeat, biographical suffering, and theoretically articulated pessimism. Once it had taken place, the mass annihilation turned the particular fate of the Jews into a universal historical event, which thereby acquired a standing all its own in the realm of theory as well. Horkheimer and Adorno rightly spoke of a "turning point in history" (*DA*, 230/*DE*, 200), but only in retrospect. No mind equipped with Western reason could have undertaken to formulate a notion of that caesura before its occurrence.

I

No statement, no passage of Horkheimer's has been worn out more than the dictum that those who do not wish to speak of capitalism should keep quiet about fascism (*JE*, 308–9/"JE," 78). Facile postfascist recipients have read out of it what Horkheimer in fact put into it—at that time, before Auschwitz. Alongside its truth claims, the statement suggestively formulates a claim to correct political action: fascism, as an authoritarian form of bourgeois political domination, cannot be fought effectively by those of its opponents who do not at the same time aim to overthrow the social relationships that spawned it. The statement contains a latent attack on liberalism; that, too, was part of its intention.

Behind this statement, which has meanwhile been reduced to an empty phrase, stands the idea that the phenomenon of anti-Semitism is not something independent but rather the particular expression of an underlying, more comprehensive context. The piece thus begins, as if with the sounding of a gong, with the statement: "Whoever wants to explain anti-Semitism must speak of National Socialism" (*JE*, 308/ "JE," 77). To dwell on the phenomenon of anti-Semitism would be as pointless as to remain fixated on fascism. Critique must detach itself from the phenomena and take aim at the origin of the prevailing order—at capitalism. This is the central claim of Horkheimer's "The

Jews and Europe." Apart from the broader implications of the piece, which ultimately has no more and no less to do with the Jews than Marx's "On the Jewish Question," Horkheimer concerns himself exclusively with the altered form of political domination represented by the figure of the "authoritarian" or fascist state. The Jews and anti-Semitism serve him as shibboleths of social reality, as a litmus test of that political transformation.[8] Yet there is more to it than that. In portraying the transition from the liberal state to the authoritarian, fascist state, Horkheimer makes statements about the Jews entirely in accord with the sentiments and convictions predominant on the left at the time.[9] These statements indicate Horkheimer's intention of denying any particularity to the fate of the Jews at the hands of National Socialism. Beyond that, puzzlingly, the piece also has a sardonic undertone. This remains true of Horkheimer's orientation at the time despite his later attempts to distance himself from this text and despite the pains taken by some interpreters to extenuate his attitude.

Against the background of the Nazis' anti-Jewish measures before the war—a policy of discrimination and expatriation but not of organized physical destruction, which began only later—Horkheimer could still sustain the speculative core of his thesis: with the liquidation of the market by the "authoritarian state," the putative agents of that market, the Jews, had lost their social significance. Horkheimer thereby insinuated that the Jews in fact constituted a leading element in the sphere of circulation. In so doing, he remained thoroughly bound up in the tradition of economistic interpretations, sociological and Marxist, of the Jewish question.[10] Yet in doing so he conflated the entirely relevant presence *of* the Jews in circulation with the significance of the Jews *for* the sphere of circulation. From the perspective of critical theory, one can see in this reasoning holdovers of traditional theory—above all, a rigorous economism. This regression may be an expression of Horkheimer's attempt to keep his distance from the Jewish problem as an existential issue by making claims to universality.[11] In the context of expectations whose basic tenor, despite all despair, was an optimistic hope for an emancipatory resolution, anti-Semitic politics in Nazi Germany was reduced to a mere ornament of the crisis. No peculiar status was to be accorded to it.

The construal of antipathy toward the Jews in Nazi Germany as the immediate expression of a decline of market relationships, above all of the sphere of circulation and the liberal world bound up with it, makes it possible to assign the events a theorizable sense when gauged by the paradigm of competitive capitalism. At any rate, when seen as an epiphenomenon of competition, anti-Semitism seems still to fit within structures of reason, if only those of instrumental reason. In this way, the events could still serve as material for a traditional critique of the intrinsic limitations of civil emancipation. Thus, Horkheimer comments that the emancipation of the Jews, a direct result of the ambiguous character of the French Revolution, of freedom and equality, was burdened from the start with the curse of its contrary. In fact, "The order which set out as the progressive one in 1789 carried the germs of National Socialism from the beginning" (*JE*, 324/"JE," 89). In the abstraction of the citizen, the anonymity of the person that results from market relationships reduced differences to insignificance. Equality ignores particularity: one hears echoes of Marx's treatment of the relationship between the individual and the universal in "On the Jewish Question" when Horkheimer points out the "humane . . . inhumanity" that manifests itself in abstract equality (*JE*, 325/"JE," 90).[12] But because emancipation proceeds as a mere function of the market economy, those who have been emancipated only by means of the attributes of circulation are overthrown with the turn from the anonymous market to naked power that lies at the core of National Socialism. Their fall results from the rivalry between the market and power—or in his later, more precise formulation, between the spheres of circulation and production. At that time, Horkheimer drew the conclusion so irritating today: "The result is bad for the Jews. They are being run over. Others are the most capable today: the leaders of the new order in the economy and the state" (*JE*, 325/"JE," 89).

The significance Horkheimer ascribes to the decline of the sphere of circulation as an explanatory framework for anti-Semitism in National Socialist Germany will not stand up to examination. Of course, it is striking that the Jews' loss of civil rights went together with their expulsion from the sphere of circulation, which until then had seemed a source of security. But to conclude that this meant the neutralization of circulation as such, amounting to a real primacy of political domination over the economy, does not accord with reality.[13] Rather, it arises from Horkheimer's identification of the Jews with the sphere of circulation as such. He infers the end of free circulation in general from the exclusion of the Jews and the revocation of their civil rights. Horkheimer was inclined to believe that National Socialism completely undermines the power of the economy because of his simplistic equation of circulation, the sphere of the market, with the capitalist economy. Only in this way can the recourse to the Jews and anti-Semitism in interpretating fascism as an undermining of the economy acquire such explanatory value for Horkheimer. The fact that the Jews did not play the role in circulation that he alleges jeopardizes his entire construction of the decline of the sphere of circulation as a significant expression of the undermining of the economy in fascism.

In explaining this connection, Horkheimer argues that the economy "no longer has an independent dynamic." It has lost "its power to the economically powerful," who now achieve their goals by noneconomic means. "Exploitation no longer reproduces itself aimlessly, via the market, but rather in the conscious exercise of domination" (*JE*, 316/"JE," 83). This finding is less than sensitive in dealing with the Jewish victims of National Socialist discrimination in the 1930s. Horkheimer assumes that both the market economy, with the liberal state that corresponds to it, and the economy of power in the fascist state share a common rationality. And since the Jews had grounded their existence as agents of circulation on this same rationality, their condemnation derived from the same justice on which their emancipation and prosperity had depended. Indeed, when the Jews "glorify the prehistory of the totalitarian state, monopoly capitalism, and the Weimar Republic, with an understandable homesickness, then the fascists are in the right against them" (*JE*, 330/"JE," 93). Everything thus stands and falls with the "type of rationality" inherent in the specific conditions of exploitation. Previously, it had accrued to the benefit of the Jews, or rather, of Jewish entrepreneurs. Now this "kind of rationality" was turning against them. For weighed by the standards of this morality, the "morality of economic power," the Jews were "found to be too light." And "this same rationality . . . has now pronounced judgment on the Jews as well" (*JE*, 324/"JE," 89).

Two moments stand out in "The Jews and Europe," moments with little significance for Horkheimer's theoretical concern with explaining fascism in the 1930s through the undermining of the economy, as a liquidation of the market, and the political expropriation of the Jews as prominent agents of circulation. One of these is the conspicuously smug tone, bordering (clearly against his own will) on satisfaction. This gesture is accompanied by a criticism of the Jews that goes beyond the purposes of analysis, in which they are set up as personifications of capitalism. These invectives would seem to have something in common. They touch something intimate in Horkheimer, arousing an antipathy he deflects into social criticism.[14] Thus he comments upon the decline of liberalism and of the democratic forms of rule and commerce as if he cared less about the actual consequences of a dismal reality than about proving himself right. Somewhat triumphantly, he holds up fascism as the "truth of modern society, which theory realized from the beginning" (*JE*, 309/"JE," 78). He deplores the obduracy of liberal citizens still not ready to concede that the cause of their political ruin lies in themselves—a truth that, after all, had long been known to them as a warning in the guise of theoretical knowledge. And the Jews? "They shed many a tear for the past." But the fact "that they fared better under liberalism does not vouch for its justice" (*JE*, 323/"JE," 88).[15] "Leniency toward the flaws of bourgeois democracy, flirting with the forces of reaction as long as they were not too openly anti-Semitic, arranging themselves with the status quo—the refugees of today already incurred guilt back then" (*JE*, 330/"JE," 93). Moreover, it would be idle to expect that misery in general, and the fate of the Jews in Germany in particular, could lead to a change of insight into their deeper causes, which lay in capitalism and its costs. In short: may the rise of fascism lead them to turn from capitalism. In this way, the victims are not entirely innocent of their own fate. "How should nouveaux riches Jews or Aryans abroad, who have always acquiesced in the impoverishment of other social and national groups, in mass poverty in home countries and colonies, in 'well-managed' prisons and insane asylums, how should they come to their senses in light of what is happening to the German Jews?" (*JE*, 326/"JE," 90–91).

This sort of moral appeal to the better insight and the goodwill of citizens, and particularly the Jews, rests above all on the universalistic assumption that although they were the first, the Jews would not be the particular victims of National Socialism, the German form of the fascist domination spreading across Europe. In retrospect, when Horkheimer voices the expectation that the oncoming universalization of barbarism will put an end to the singling out of the Jews, it seems a kind of plea that the discrimination between Jews and non-

Jews should cease. "Perhaps in the initial terror the Jews will not be noticed, but in the long run they must tremble along with everyone else at what is now coming over the earth." The longing that the Jews be spared their particular victimization is also universalistic in the way it adopts the idiom of condemning the particular: "As agents of circulation, the Jews have no future. They will not be able to live as human beings until human beings finally put an end to prehistory" (JE, 328/"JE," 92). Such desperate optimism in the face of defeat recalls the content of an incriminating aphorism in the earlier *Dämmerung*. There Horkheimer, implying that the Nazis' anti-Semitism was socially selective, reproached Jewish capitalists who were in a "blazing uproar" over anti-Jewish measures with being unable to detach themselves from the hierarchy of goods, a hierarchy that "for bourgeois Jews is neither Jewish, nor Christian, but bourgeois." Against this formal equality of Jews and non-Jews he set an emancipatory equality, which would later appear to have been horribly refuted by the events that followed: "The Jewish revolutionary in Germany puts his own life on the line, just as the 'Aryan' does, for the liberation of humanity."[16]

The universalism Horkheimer called for so emphatically was made universally untrue by the Nazis' singling out of the Jews and their total annihilation for the sake of annihilation. The conclusion to be drawn was that a break took place, a break that goes deeper than the effects of anti-Semitism alone. It meant a rupture in civilization—a practical refutation of Western rationality. Neither Horkheimer nor the other members of the Frankfurt School can be accused of not having already recognized fascism in Germany at that time, in the 1930s, as what it really was—as National Socialism on the road to Auschwitz.

II

In Horkheimer's analysis of fascism or the "authoritarian state," the critique of liberalism as a political expression of capitalism is only tentatively linked to a critique of the kind of rationality he would later call "instrumental reason." The theme of the decay of reason in Western civilization would take shape as the core of Horkheimer's social criticism during and after the war. In the process, "anti-Semitism" and "the Jews" acquired a different significance. In "The Jews and

Europe," he still traced the "authoritarian state" and the social expulsion of the Jews back to the logic of a market-transcendent, monopolistic undermining of competition. At the same time, however, he adumbrated his later leitmotiv by evoking "a kind of rationality" that had once entailed the civil emancipation of the Jews but was now turning against the Jewish entrepreneurs. Like the Jews in general, they had counted on the "utilitarian character" of political arrangements that promised calculability, predictability, and the spread of free commerce (*JE*, 325/ "JE," 78). But these were expressions of the same origin as that of fascism or the authoritarian state: the purposive-rational logic of capitalism. From this Horkheimer also concluded that anti-Semitism had utilitarian functions, as both a competitive device and a diversion from class struggle;[17] here he remained bound up in the traditional, indeed orthodox, Marxist conception of anti-Semitism. Only with the annihilation of the Jews, to which no utilitarian relation of means and ends whatsoever could be attributed, did that historical turning point arrive at which rationality, reason, and enlightenment reverse into their opposites. The Nazis' annihiliation of the Jews undoubtedly has categorical significance for this dialectic of enlightenment. Accordingly, the critique of reason and Auschwitz also stand in an epistemological context for Horkheimer,[18] even if he does not make this explicit (apart from a cautious suggestion in the introduction to *Dialectic of Enlightenment,* which makes it clear that the theses on "Elements of Anti-Semitism" address the general phenomenon of the relapse of enlightened civilization into barbarism). Anti-Semitism and the history of civilization are interwoven; anti-Semitism is the central metaphor of Western civilization. And because a practical tendency to self-destruction was inherent in that rationality from the very beginning, not only during the phase in which it emerged undisguised, a philosophical ur-history of anti-Semitism became necessary (*DA*, 22/*DE*, xvii).

In view of the triumph of fascism in Europe in 1941 and 1942, at a time when the annihilation of the Jews was still heading toward its inconceivable climax in industrialized mass murder and the connection between the persecution and executions taking place in the east and the events of the war was difficult to grasp—Horkheimer pronounced the "collapse of the root concepts of Western civilization." Central to these is the concept of reason (*VS*, 320/"EndR," 28).

Horkheimer links the destruction of reason to reason itself. His central thesis is that the origins of the decay of reason lie in the particular, dominant form of reason: a rationality that serves as a means to attain ends and thereby dissociates itself from a more encompassing reason grounded in being.

Horkheimer saw fascism as already latent in subjective or "goal-positing reason." Bourgeois society came into its own above all in its moment of absolute "self-preservation," the egoistic assertion of particular interests. Fascism was no exception but rather the intensification of the rule. As the perfection of bourgeois domination, fascism could be conceived by Horkheimer as the legitimate expression of this class-bound form of reason: "The new order represents a leap in the transformation of bourgeois domination into immediate domination, in which the bourgeois form is perpetuated. The National Socialists do not depart from this course of development" (VS, 332/"EndR," 34). The essence of the social order is still maintained, although the transactional form of exchange is replaced by the employment of brute force—the form of exchange that Neville Chamberlain called by its name when he characterized Hitler's demands at Bad Godesberg as "unreasonable." This was supposed to mean "that an equivalence of give and take should be observed. Such reason is modelled on exchange. Goals should be attained only mediately, as it were via the market, by virtue of the slight advantage which power is able to obtain by respecting the rules of the game and trading off concessions" (DA, 239–40/DE, 209–10). And because in exchange "each gets his own and yet social injustice comes of it, so too the reflexive form of the exchange economy, the dominant unreason, is just, universal, and yet particularistic, the instrument of privilege in equality. The fascist settles accounts with it. He openly represents the particular and in doing so exposes the ratio itself, which unjustly boasts of its universality, as partial" (DA, 240/DE, 210).

Both forms of appropriation—by exchange and by force—are grasped as expressions of bourgeois society. Both rest on "subjective reason" and are manifestations of self-preservation. A relationship of ends and means inheres in both—and in National Socialism as well, which Horkheimer, in the Marxist tradition of the 1930s, still conceived of as fascism. But a total rationality of economic power can no longer be discerned at the center of a fully realized National Socialism, which enacts, instead, an utterly different totality—the totality of the annihilation of the Jews.[19] From the perspective of Auschwitz, "subjective reason," which arises from the principle of asserting particular interests and realizes itself in the form of brute self-preservation, reverses into its opposite, from the fascist form of purposive utility to the comparatively manifest irrationality or, better, antirationality of National Socialism. This meant that any reaction by the total victim to the totalitarian order, any response to the Nazis governed by the cognitive forms of means and ends and of self-preservation, was thereby doomed to certain failure. National Socialism was indeed "reason, in which reason exposes itself as unreason" (*VS*, 348/ "EndR," 46).

The opposition between forms of reason set up by Horkheimer comprises various dimensions—for instance, the opposition between objective reason, which grounds being, and subjective reason oriented toward particular goals and directed at self-preservation. In addition, there is also a regressive moment, the throwback produced by disenchanted, civilizing rationality (*BV,* 28). In their atrocity toward the Jews and others, the Nazis had long since dispensed with all attributes of subjective reason, casting off the rationality of self-preservation whose utility constantly tempts even the devil, such as making deals for the sake of one's own advantage. Through the industrial mass destruction of the Jews, carried out in the shadow of the war, the Nazis succeeded in horribly refuting even the principles of subjective reason and self-preservation that determine Western civilization. The fact that their irrationality was rationally organized in the technical sense only confirms the instrumental madness of reason. The goal that had been imputed to the "economically powerful" in fascism had long since divested itself of any ostensible economic rationality. Annihilation no longer had any purpose but itself.

When the objective reason that grounds being is destroyed by subjective, purposive-rational reason; when the goal-positing reason rooted in the principle of exchange forfeits even that origin; when disenchantment results in its opposite, so that the world of calculability and predictability is swept up in destruction as the fulfillment of senselessness, then the vital question becomes how reason could have split into its contrary, component parts of mere purposive rationality and mythos. In light of such a dialectic of enlightenment, anti-Semitism, which henceforth harbors the annihilation of the European Jews at its center, acquires a more fundamental significance than the essentially functional sense previously attributed to it. Anti-Semitism and the fate of the Jews become constitutive elements of a realized totality. They become that "historical turning point" at which they once again await explanation.

The purposive moment in the explanation of purposelessness and the foundering of purposive rationality on itself remain issues in "Elements of Anti-Semitism." Utilitarian interpretations of the sort predominant in "The Jews and Europe" continue to turn up. But they are holdovers that illustrate the difficulty of making the transition to a new analysis of anti-Semitism capable both of capturing the phenomenon of hostility toward the Jews in the narrow sense and of going beyond this to a critique of civilization. Thus, one still reads of the obvious utility of anti-Semitism for purposes of domination: "It serves as a diversion, a cheap means of corruption, and an example of terror" (DA, 200/DE, 170). Its functional role in the class struggle is said to be equally evident, for the addressees of such maneuvers are "the workers" (DA, 197/DE, 168). An instrumental character is also ascribed to anti-Semitism in the statement that those "who give the orders from above" know "the real reasons" and that they neither hate the Jews nor love their "own followers" (DA, 201/DE, 171). But the pursuit of such reflections leads to the decisive turn of seeing through mere utility as a camouflage for motives that lie deeper. The allegedly rational motive for the outburst of those followers, the anti-Semitic mobs—the ostensible desire to feast on the property of the Jews—misses its target. Gain could not have been the motive. The "pitifully thin rational motive, plunder, adduced for purposes of rationalization," falls away. The purpose is meant to veil its own purposelessness, for gauged by its proposed benefits, anti-Semitism is "a luxury" for the people. The senseless deed became honest despite itself when it "became a true, autonomous end in itself" (DA, 201/DE, 172).

With the turn to the view that irrational, purposeless action makes use of rational motives to justify itself, that delusions take shape in images with a rational form, Horkheimer takes leave of "conclusive rational, economic, and political explanations and counter-arguments" in interpreting the hostility toward the Jews. The true grounds for anti-Semitism lie in the rationality involved in domination and social control. The "blind rage" produced by the unrecognized link between domination and rationality calls forth reactions that for those involved are deadly and "devoid of sense" when measured against their ostensible reason and purposive rationality (*DA*, 200/*DE*, 171). The senselessness of anti-Semitism in turn immunizes it against arguments that its rationality is deficient.[20] This is not to suggest that the traditional, functional interpretation of anti-Semitism simply vanishes from Horkheimer's work. But its exclusively instrumental character is abandoned insofar as it is classified as an irrational reflex: "Only the blindness of anti-Semitism, its lack of purpose, lends the explanation of it as a safety valve its proper measure and truth" (*DA*, 200/*DE*, 171). A blinding caused by social abstraction, anti-Semitism has no meaning. It is "an ingrained scheme, indeed a ritual murder of civilization. The pogroms are the true ritual murders" (*DA*, 200/ *DE*, 171).

III

With the departure from the paradigm of economic utility and means-ends rationality in interpreting the hostility toward the Jews, Horkheimer and Adorno begin to develop the alternative explanation of anti-Semitism as projection. The preparation of the anti-Semitic consciousness does not lie in projection in itself, since "in a certain sense all perception is projection" (*DA*, 217/*DE*, 187). "What is pathological about anti-Semitism is not projective behavior as such, but the absence of reflection in it." Anti-Semitism therefore rests on "false projection" (*DA*, 217/*DE*, 187)—to the point of paranoia.

The paranoiac perceives the outside world only in accordance with his blind purposes. He "seizes on whatever presents itself to him and fits it into his mythic web, utterly indifferent to its own characteristics." Through practical insistence, the surrounding world—the reality in which the anti-Semite's notions can find no firm hold—is modeled upon his own truth, his *idée fixe*, an inner image (*DA*, 220/*DE*, 190). Fascism elevates such behavior to the level of politics. Those who, as Jews, fall under its decrees must "first be located by means of complicated questionnaires. . . . Fascist anti-Semitism must first, in a sense, go about finding its object" (*DA*, 237/*DE*, 206–7). To "call someone a Jew amounts to an instigation to work him over until he resembles the image" (*DA*, 216/*DE*, 186). And once the anti-Semite has formed the Jew according to his image of him, he then persecutes him on account of his own fantasies, which he does not admit to himself. Instead, he attributes them to the prospective victim. In his "blind lust for murder," the anti-Semite constantly "sees the victim as a persecutor who drives him to desperate acts of self-defense." Such a rationalization is "at once both a ruse and a compulsion" (*DA*, 217/*DE*, 187). Instead of looking into himself "in order to record the protocol of his own lust for power, he attributes the 'Protocols of the Elders of Zion' to others" (*DA*, 219–20/*DE*, 189–90). "The *völkisch* fantasies of Jewish crimes, child murder, and sadistic excesses, of poisoning the nation and of international conspiracies, precisely define the anti-Semitic wish-fulfilling dream" (*DA*, 216/*DE*, 186). Once the state has been reached in which the projection can be realized politically, the psychic latency of anti-Semitism becomes a social force; fantasy is converted into reality. In the process, the "execution of evil" surpasses "even the evil content of the projection" (*DA*, 216/*DE*, 186).[21] Anti-Semites transform the world into the hell "as which they have always seen it" (*DA*, 229/*DE*, 199).

In *Dialectic of Enlightenment*, the conversion of the "psychic energy" of anti-Semitism into political reality is conceptualized as "rationalized idiosyncrasy" (*DA*, 213/*DE*, 183). What in turn underlies idiosyncrasy, as a virtually congenital loathing, is something particular, a difference, which is imparted with singular significance and concrete content by means of the Jews (*DA*, 209/*DE*, 179–80). This difference is rendered public via the sphere of circulation and the "artificially increased visibility of the Jews," through which the reactions of populist, anti-Semitic rebels are diverted from the domination that is the true object of the "rebellion of oppressed nature." The rebels produce a semblance of emancipation by organizing themselves as equals against the particular. In this way "anti-Semitism as a popular movement" is always also "leveling" (*DA*, 199/*DE*, 170)—although, of course, it is the kind of leveling that finds perverted fulfillment in a racially defined national community. By means of anti-Semitism, therefore, the rebellion originally directed against domination ultimately accrues to its benefit (*DA*, 215/*DE*, 185).

Demonstrating the relationship between equality and anti-Semitism is an essential concern of the critique of progress and rationality that

Horkheimer carried out with Adorno. Elements of the critique of liberalism and the internal limitations of civil emancipation already formulated in "The Jews and Europe" are carried over into it, only now the earlier polemical, political cutting edge is replaced by a pessimistic general statement on the philosophy of history. Equality and emancipation, with their assimilatory tendencies—"in effect, a second circumcision" (*DA*, 198/*DE*, 169)—made the Jews politically visible in the first place. From then on, they were released into a homogeneous world shaped by others, leaving them unprotected in a way previously unknown to them. Their particular attributes were not absorbed without remainder into the sphere of the new generality. They could belong to that generality only as Germans, Frenchmen, and so on, denying their Jewish particularity. Moreover, liberalism put the Jews in an even more exposed position inasmuch as it granted them possessions by guaranteeing property and allowed them equality before the law as human beings but as Jews denied them political rights and thereby "sovereign authority" (*DA*, 201/*DE*, 172). Thus, from the very beginning it was the unhappy "meaning of human rights to promise happiness where there is no power" (*DA*, 201/*DE*, 172).

Paradoxically, the emancipation of the Jews, which accorded them equal status as human beings, was accompanied by the emergence of political anti-Semitism in the bourgeois national state. This simultaneity was no mere accident or caprice but an expression of political equality despite persisting, unacknowledged difference. Formal equality, which made comparison possible, first forced existing differences out into the open. With the formal fulfillment of emancipation, therefore, the appearance of political anti-Semitism heralded the end of the Jews' civil equality. Inasmuch as the Jews stood out from the anonymity of the general public and from that "which fits into the purposive nexus of society" (*DA*, 209/*DE*, 180), their existence compromised "the existing generality by their lack of adjustment" (*DA*, 198/*DE*, 169). This dubious triumph of the particular—not to yield to social rationalization in the form of the predominant attributes of universality—attracts the hostility of those who, as bearers of universality, no longer possess any particularity. They believe they can secure a particularity of their own only by constituting themselves as a mythic counterimage to the Jews. And to constitute themselves as a hypostatized particular through racial fictions, they model the Jews into a "counter-race" by means of a projective reversal. What results is by no means "natural" but rather "that reduction to the nature-like, to naked violence, to the obdurate particularity which, under the prevailing order, is precisely the general." It is general insofar as the fictive racial affiliation becomes an attribute of the "self-assertion of the bourgeois individual integrated into the barbaric collective," proceeding irresistibly forward on the way "to naked oppression and to reorganization as the hundred-percent pure race" (*DA*, 198/*DE*, 169).

Horkheimer and Adorno attempted to interpret the fact that precisely the Jews had become the preferred object of persecution, and the counterimage for purposes of self-definition, by means of the element of idiosyncrasy: "violence was ignited endlessly by the mark which violence had left on them" (*DA*, 213/*DE*, 183). The Jews are persecuted because they bear the stigma of persecution. There is no more substantial motive than the compulsion to persecute. Thus, for instance, the "desecration of cemeteries is not an excess of anti-Semitism; it is anti-Semitism itself" (*DA*, 213/*DE*, 183). So, too, the projection onto the Jews of "all the horrors of primeval times, which civilization has overlaid" (*DA*, 215–6/*DE*, 186) represents only a rationalization of the repetitive compulsion to confirm the idiosyncrasy through continued persecution.

The particular, the non-identical, which eludes assimilation to the universal, highlights historically accumulated idiosyncratic features by means of equality and comparability. In the eyes of the compulsive persecutor, it comes to be associated with attributes seemingly free of the grim mastery of nature—"happiness without power, earnings without work, a homeland without boundaries, religion without myth" (*DA*, 229/*DE*, 199). The paradox of representing the helplessly persecuted and powerless as both keepers of the grail of happiness and virtuosos of concealed domination finds expression in the phantasmic certainty that a "conspiracy of lecherous Jewish bankers finances Bolshevism" and that the good life is a sign of happiness. "The image of the intellectual joins up with this; the intellectual seems to think, which others begrudge themselves, and his brow does not pour with the sweat of toil and physical strength. The banker and the intellectual, money and mind, the exponents of circulation, are the denied wish-images of those mutilated by domination, whom domination uses to perpetuate itself" (*DA*, 202/*DE*, 172). And through this projective burdening of the Jews as the embodiment of the nonidentical, the biblical myth of the chosen people found dreadful fulfillment in their destruction to the extent that "fascism made it come true" (*DA*, 197/ *DE*, 168).

In their assessment of what constitutes the nonidentical in Western civilization and attaches to the Jews in the perception of the anti-Semite, Horkheimer and Adorno oscillate between features projectively attributed to the Jews alone, which direct hatred toward them, and the Jews as the incarnation of particularity as such. Anti-Semitism is thereby generalized, however, into a prejudice against any bearers of difference whatsoever. In line with this extended interpretation of anti-Semitism, at the end of their essay they define it as a mere technique that domination makes use of to secure its hold. It is the "ticket mentality" that, as the enemy of all difference, directs itself against the nonidentical particular in order to shore up the generality. Thus, not only the anti-Semitic ticket as such would be anti-Semitic but the ticket mentality per se. "The rage against difference, a *ressentiment* on the part of the mastered subjects of the mastery of nature which is teleologically inherent in the ticket mentality, is always ready to strike out at the natural minority, even when for the moment this threatens the social minority" (*DA*, 238/*DE*, 207).

The idiosyncrasy that adheres to the particular, performing manipulative services that help to secure domination, looms out of the depths of the past into those social formations for which Horkheimer and Adorno describe the significance of anti-Semitism. It stems from a source that only seemed to have been overcome by secularization and disenchantment—the source of the Christian religion. To assert its ongoing efficacy as a source of hostility toward the Jews is to undercut the classical distinction, stemming from the Enlightenment, between religious anti-Semitism and its political or racial varieties. Insisting on such continuity, however, does not mean endorsing the thesis of the transhistorical character of anti-Semitism. Rather, what Horkheimer and Adorno point out is the stubborn persistence of myths that merely dye their vestments in worldly colors but otherwise retain their magical significance. Such myths recur as a secularized, rationalized idiosyncrasy whose origins lie in the relationship of the Christian religion to the Jews. Horkheimer and Adorno believe that "the religious animosity which propelled the persecution of the Jews for two thousand years" could hardly have been extinguished completely. "The zeal with which anti-Semitism denies its religious tradition testifies, instead, that the religious tradition secretly lives on within it—no less deeply than profane idiosyncrasy was once inherent in religious zeal" (*DA*, 206/ *DE*, 176).

The secularizing of occidental civilization in fact amounts to Christianity made worldly. For all the efforts at enlightenment, the culture that results remains Christian in its form and its conceptions of value. Enlightenment brought about the transformation of a religious, universally oriented nexus of civilization into national cultures supported by national states in which Christianity, secularized and rationalized, remains the underlay—altered, warped, and concealed.

The modern state in which the Jews were emancipated was an avowedly Christian state. Thus, it is not surprising that religion "was not liquidated, but incorporated as a cultural asset" (*DA*, 206/*DE*, 176). In the process, the anti-Judaic effect of Christianity, the *ressentiment* against the Jews that generates the religion, was also preserved.[22] While it found expression in political form, its psychic energies continued to be nurtured by an older source.

The origin of the opposition between the Jews and Christianity[23] is seen as rooted in Christianity's unfulfilled claim that Jesus, the human being, was God (*DA*, 207/*DE*, 177). According to this, the redemption of the world, which depends on the arrival of the Messiah, has already been accomplished. But since the world has not changed despite his arrival, it becomes obvious that Christianity rests on "a non-binding promise of spiritual salvation" (*DA*, 208/*DE*, 178). That which was represented as spiritual being proves, in the face of spirit, to have been natural being. Christ, the spirit become flesh, would thus be no more than an idolized shaman, and Christianity itself exposed as a "spiritualization of magic" (*DA*, 207/*DE*, 177). Christianity thus splits off into a special cultural realm, and by contrast with Judaism, a belief hardly distinct from general and rational self-assertion, it becomes a religion—"in a certain sense, the only one." "Christianity's claim to represent progress beyond Judaism" thereby proves to be "a relapse behind Judaism" (*DA*, 206/*DE*, 166).

The religious origin of anti-Semitism is located in the Christians' feeling that their eschatalogical expectations have been disappointed, so that they must begin, with a bad conscience, to talk themselves into

Christian belief. They are constantly reminded that the redemption they claim has not arrived by those who have denied it from the start. "The adherents of the religion of the father are hated, as those who know better, by the adherents of the religion of the son. It is the antipathy toward spirit of a spirit that is rigidifying as salvation. The thorn in the side of the Christian enemies of the Jews is the truth that withstands calamity without rationalizing it, holding fast to the idea of unearned blessedness against the course of the world and the order of salvation, which are actually supposed to bring it about." Thus, the Christian promise of redemption can be made true only in its inversion—through the calamity of the Jewish adversaries. "Anti-Semitism is supposed to confirm the truth of the ritual of belief and history by inflicting it upon those who reject its truth" (*DA, 209/DE,* 179). Secularized traces of Christian anti-Judaism are mixed in with Western civilization in the form of idiosyncrasy. The ill will toward the non-identical persists.

The "Elements of Anti-Semitism" indeed remained no more than elements—approaches, theses, and ideas that were not synthesized into a theory but served rather as material, as additional evidence for the overarching theme of this phase of Horkheimer's thought, the thesis on the "limits of enlightenment." The individual arguments, scarcely organized, are shaped by diverse approaches.[24] They remain marked by the economistic interpretation of anti-Semitism, thought to have been overcome, which is balanced out by psychoanalytic interpretations.[25] Yet they sometimes come together in ways that go far beyond mere preliminary reflections.

One such high point is the thesis that the specifically economic motive for bourgeois anti-Semitism is "to disguise domination in production" (*DA,* 202/*DE,* 173). Underlying this definition of anti-Semitism is the Nazi defamation, seemingly confirmed by appearances, built on a distinction between "exploiting" and "producing" capital. "Exploiting" capital, identified with the sphere of circulation, is ascribed to the Jews, whereas "producing" capital stands for the incarnation of supposedly pure production and is racially equated with Aryanism. Horkheimer and Adorno demonstrate the extent to which such a perception is socially conditioned. Industrialists, who pass off their economic operations in the sphere of production as productive labor, thus posing as "producers," turn out to be the concealed exploiters.

The swindle succeeds because the employer does not rake in his profit on the open market, where appropriation takes place visible to all, but at the very "source" of the creation of wealth—in production. "As a functionary of the class," the employer, whether industrialist or bureaucrat, sees to it that "he does not get the short end of the stick when his labor force works." The labor contract conceals the "exploitative nature of the economic system," the appropriation of surplus value (*DA*, 203/*DE*, 174). "The industrialist has his debtors, the workers, in the factory where he watches over them and checks their services before advancing them their money. They notice what has really happened only when they find out what they can buy for it. . . . The merchant presents the workers with the promissory note they signed for the industrialist. He plays the bailiff for the whole system, taking upon himself the odium for the others. The accountability of the sphere of circulation for exploitation is a socially necessary appearance" (*DA*, 204/*DE*, 174). Once the market has revealed how few goods are allotted to the value of labor, the plundering gets thrown into an even harsher light when the merchant—with all supposedly being equal—publicly promotes goods that those who are in fact unequal cannot afford. "The guilty party for the entire system is easy to find. One cries 'Stop! Thief!' and points to the Jew. He is indeed the scapegoat, not merely for individual maneuvers and machinations, but in the comprehensive sense that the economic injustice of the entire class gets blamed on him" (*DA*, 203/*DE*, 174).

A theory of bourgeois anti-Semitism based on the identification of the Jews with the sphere of circulation differs considerably from the sort of economistic explanation characteristic of "The Jews and Europe." In the latter, the hostility to the Jews was traced back to the fascist undermining of the economy that takes place in National Socialism as a form of fascism—that is, to a literal decline in the significance of the sphere of circulation. The Nazis' anti-Semitic policies are thereby interpreted as the result of the Jews' loss of their economic position, employing an immediate, sociological, and empirical conception of competition. In "Elements of Anti-Semitism," the motif of the sphere of circulation recurs but in a completely different role. No longer are the Jews simply equated with it. The fact that they do not have a monopoly on circulation is acknowledged; nonetheless, the public image of social exploitation, which arises from the sphere of circulation, becomes attached to the Jews "because they remained confined in it for too long" (*DA, 204/DE, 174*). As a consequence, the Jews became a metaphorical concretization of the sphere of circulation.

Only when apparent social realities are translated in terms of the meaning of social metaphors does the comprehensively economic interpretation avoid the narrowly economistic turn that leads it astray. To be sure, traces of the earlier interpretation are still to be found. So, for instance, "Elements of Anti-Semitism" continues to suggest that the Jews occupied positions of economic power that they lost only with the undermining of the economy and the decline of "liberalistic forms of enterprise" (*DA, 229/DE, 199*). A historical survey of the significance of the Jews as "colonizers of progress" (*DA, 204/DE, 175*)—however accurate it may appear to be—strays from the analytical intention when employed as evidence for a history of the supposedly rational origins of anti-Semitism. At the end of the essay, the authors relapse not only behind the element of the inconceivable in the annihilation of the Jews but behind their own—above all, Horkheimer's—critique of reason as well. The historical logic dictated by economic rationality they once again invoke is entirely in line with "The Jews and Europe." They once again speak of the "administration of totalitarian states" as mere "executors of economic verdicts long since decreed," which "consign untimely segments of the population to extermination" (*DA, 237/DE, 206*).

IV

In the postwar years and until his death in 1973, Max Horkheimer addressed the question of anti-Semitism in basically aphoristic form. A strong personal identification with the Jewish victims of the National Socialists' mass annihilation is evident in these writings; notably, he makes no direct attempt to seek relief by theoretically generalizing the experience. Insofar as theoretical concerns are raised, the universalizing approach to anti-Semitism already accorded primacy in *Dialectic of Enlightenment* predominates—the moment of the socially "nonidentical" that is embodied by the Jews. The nonidentical expresses itself, for instance, in the will to justice, thus becoming the "enemy of all things totalitarian."[26] Horkheimer associates "justice" with two things: a fundamental, moral justice and the justice constituted by fair exchange. Both forms of justice contradict "state capitalism in the East" no less than "Western monopolistic society."[27] This is seen as "one of the roots of world-wide anti-Semitism."[28] The entire existence of the Jews points toward a "society of the free and equal, but not a national community."[29] And because they are bound to trade and liberalism, to relationships between individuals, and to the bourgeoisie, the Jews also incarnate the justice of fair exchange. Anti-Semitism would thus arise because the Jews, with every one of their gestures, serve as reminders of the henceforth general mode of existence to all those who seek to deny their own participation in the forms of a society founded on exchange. They "compromise the lie which pervades society" and are therefore endangered everywhere.[30]

Along with the stigmata of exchange, which attach to the Jews as the "hated mirror image" of society as such and in which an antitotalitarian moment also finds expression, it is the particularity of the Jews—and even more, an "essentiality" that others imagine them to possess—that contributes to the hatred of them. Their mere existence as "God's chosen people" gives offense, because in bearing witness to a spiritual God they relativize everything "that parades as absolute." Perceiving the Jews essentially as Jews "arouses a lust for revenge which not even death can appease."[31]

Whereas the religious metaphor stands for one side of the origins of anti-Semitism—for the nonidentical, for sublimated nature—the psychoanalytic interpretation of anti-Semitism points to the other side, the psychic representation of domination embodied by the Jews as an expression of the abstract, of civilization. "Unconsciously," this representation serves "as the quintessence of unmastered, hated prohibitions"; it is part of the "suppressed, negative side of ambivalent sexuality, of unsublimated, barbaric promiscuity." In these respects, anti-Semitism belongs "essentially to the primitive instincts negated by civilization."[32]

Horkheimer's political remarks on the ongoing effect of the past on the present in Germany must be read in the context of this systematics of projective reversal as a moment in the origins of anti-Semitism. Horror about the occurrence of mass annihilation might not lead, as one would wish, to a moral integration and working through of guilt; instead, paradoxically, it can lead to an anti-Semitic form of release from guilt. This would result from the fact that although (or because) the Jews were victims, they are closely associated with the thought of the catastrophe. Through the thoughts of violence committed by Germans and against Germans, the roles get exchanged in the unconscious. "Not the murderer, but the victim is guilty"[33]—guilty because he represents the atrocities and testifies to the reality of what happened. To rid oneself of him would be to free oneself of the inner representation of guilt as well. "Overcoming a narcissistic insult is infinitely more difficult, and even the generation that was not involved still suffers from a wound it does not know of."[34]

Anti-Semitism is not a thing of the past; the climax of mass annihilation was not the end of it. "It has not spent its force, but only shown its horrifying effects. The belief that it has passed is naively optimistic."[35] By contrast with such pessimism, the practical and pedagogical gestures of assistance against anti-Semitism expected of Horkheimer have the ring of enlightened helplessness.[36] More candid is his despairing biographical confession, "After Auschwitz": "We Jewish intellectuals who escaped death by torture under Hitler have only one task: to help see to it that such horrors never recur and are never forgotten, in solidarity with those who died under unspeakable torments. Our thought, our work belongs to them; that we escaped by accident should make our solidarity with them not doubtful, but more certain. Whatever we experience must stand under the sign of the horrors intended for us as for them. Their death is the truth of our life; to express their despair and their longing, we are there."[37] Until the end, Horkheimer remained committed to the compelling longing that runs like a guiding thread through his life: to see to it "that the murderer not triumph over the innocent victim."[38]

Translated by John McCole

Notes

In order to portray Horkheimer's changing position on anti-Semitism, I have focused my account on a few texts drawn from the years 1939–1944/45. This meant forgoing treatment of his position on Judaism in general as well as related themes, such as the analysis of authority or of the significance of religion.

This essay was written in 1984 when I was teaching at Odense University in Denmark. The text remains basically unchanged, despite some shifts in perspective since then. It does not take into account subsequent literature on the topic such as Detlev

Claussen, *Grenzen der Aufklärung* (Frankfurt, 1987) or Rolf Wiggershaus, *Die Frankfurter Schule* (Munich, 1987).

Horkheimer's texts and English translations, where available, are cited and cross-referenced according to the following key (in some cases the translations have been modified):

DA = "Dialektik der Aufklärung" (completed 1944), in Horkheimer, *Gesammelte Schriften*, 5:16–290; *DE* = *Dialectic of Enlightenment* (New York, 1972).

VS = "Vernunft und Selbsterhaltung" (written Winter 1941–1942), in Horkheimer, *Gesammelte Schriften*, 5:320–50; "EndR" = "The End of Reason," in Arato and Gebhardt, eds., *The Essential Frankfurt School Reader* (New York, 1982), 26–48.

JE = "Die Juden und Europa" (written in early September 1939) in Horkheimer, *Gesammelte Schriften*, 4:308–331/"*JE*" = "The Jews and Europe," in Stephen Bronner and Douglas Kellner, eds., *Critical Theory and Society: A Reader* (New York, 1989), 77–94.

BV = "Zum Begriff der Vernunft" (written 1951, published 1952) in Horkheimer, *Gesammelte Schriften*, 7:22–35.

KiV = *Zur Kritik der instrumentellen Vernunft* (first part written 1944 and originally published in 1947 as *Eclipse of Reason*) (Frankfurt, 1967); *Eclipse* = *Eclipse of Reason* (Oxford, 1947) and *CIR* = *Critique of Instrumental Reason* (New York, 1974).

N = *Notizen 1950–1969 und Dämmerung* (Frankfurt, 1974); *DD* = *Dawn and Decline: Notes 1926–1931 and 1950–1969* (New York, 1974).

1. Martin Jay, "The Jews and the Frankfurt School: Critical Theory's Analysis of Anti-Semitism," in Jay, *Permanent Exiles: Essays on the Intellectual Migration from Germany to America* (New York, 1985), unsympathetically stresses the young Horkheimer's "*facile dismissal of specifically Jewish problems*" (90; emphasis added).

2. Ibid., 91. Elsewhere, Jay falls prey to a misunderstanding with substantive foundations by interpreting Horkheimer's resignation after the annihilation of the Jews as a turn toward a profession of Zionism: "Not until after the war did Horkheimer come to the melancholy conclusion that Zionism had been the only way out for the Jews of Europe," Jay, *The Dialectical Imagination: A History of the Frankfurt School and the Institute of Social Research, 1923–1950* (Boston: 1973), 308, n. 92. Horkheimer's passage actually reads: "The Zionist movement, which no longer trusts in the prospects of pluralism and the culture of the autonomous individual in Europe, constitutes the radical, yet resigned reaction of the Jews to the possibilities opened up during the past century. It is a sad aspect of the history which has since transpired—sad both for the Jews and for Europe—that Zionism was proven right," "The German Jews," *CIR*, 110. The approach taken by Erich Cramer, *Hitlers Antisemitismus und die "Frankfurter Schule." Kritische Faschismustheorie und geschichtliche Realität* (Düsseldorf, 1979), is problematic. An ex post facto perspective does not enable one to trace the dramatic entwinement of theory and existential experience.

3. Jay, *The Dialectical Imagination*, 32, points out that at the time the Jewish members of the Institute denied that their Jewish origins had any significance whatsoever.

4. Thus, before the war Horkheimer attributed no significance to anti-Semitism in its own right (Jay, *The Dialectical Imagination*, 133); only in 1939 did the institute draw up a project for a study of anti-Semitism, printed in *Studies in Philosophy and Social Science* 9 (1941):124ff.

In a discussion with me, Cilly Kugelmann pointed out the paradox that it was precisely Jews such as Horkheimer, whose orginal reasons for fleeing from National Socialism were above all political, who left Germany early enough to escape the collective death sentence the Nazis passed upon the Jews. Those Jews, however, who perceived themselves above all as Jews did not yet see sufficient grounds to leave Germany in the first phase of the Nazis' rule. It was thus precisely their self-image as Jews that, in the context of National Socialism, became part of a biographical trap. This inversion of Jewish sensibility, on the one hand, and behavior that turned out to be correct in light of National Socialism, on the other, should do something to qualify critical judgments of the members of the Frankfurt School on the issues of anti-Semitism and the persecution of the Jews.

5. Eva G. Reichmann reports that Horkheimer found the republication of the text, which appeared in a bootleg edition in 1967, to be "particularly embarrassing." He had avoided having the article reprinted because it contained "formulations" that might be misunderstood. See Reichmann, "Max Horkheimer the Jew: Critical Theory and Beyond," in *Yearbook of the Leo Baeck Institute* (1974), 19:181ff., 187.

6. In a late remark, Horkheimer implicitly made clear the difference in the approach to the phenomenon of National Socialism in its various phases: "The fact that National Socialism came to power in Germany is explicable, although what it did is inconceivable," *N*, 161, in the aphorism "Deception," 1961–1962.

7. "People like me, not just generally like me, but specifically, that is, Jews, who looked and thought like Jews, like my father and my mother and like me, for the very reason that they were like that, at the end of years of awful fear, after unspeakable humiliations, inconceivable forced labor, beatings, and torment, were slowly tortured to death by the thousands in the concentration camps, because they looked and thought like Jews, kept in awful fear and finally tortured to death. . . . I should find satisfaction and peace in myself because my life testifies to senseless, unearned chance, the injustice, the blindness of all of life, because I should be ashamed still to be here," *N*, 202, "One Who Escaped," 1966–1969.

8. Julius Carlebach, *Karl Marx and the Radical Critique of Judaism* (London, 1978), explores the intellectual and social background of the actively assimilatory attitude toward the Jews predominant on the traditional left. In an extended discussion, he takes a positive position on Horkheimer (234ff.).

9. Helmut Dubiel and Alfons Söllner characterize the text as "a political essay rather than a theoretical text"; moreover, Horkheimer treats German fascism in "an astonishingly economistic manner." See "Die Nationalsozialismusforschung des Instituts für Sozialforschung" in *Wirtschaft, Recht und Staat im Nationalsozialismus* (Frankfurt am Main, 1981), 13, 12. Dubiel had earlier assessed the text differently, stating that Horkheimer adopted the "continuity thesis" formulated by Pollock and Marcuse in 1933–1934— fascism as the political form adequate to fully developed monopoly capitalism—and "specified it with the greatest possible precision and compactness in 'The Jews and Europe.' " Further, "the phenomenon of anti-Semitism as well, particularly the National Socialist form, is explained politically and economically." See Helmut Dubiel, *Wissenschaftsorganisation und politische Erfahrung. Studien zur frühen kritischen Theorie* (Frankfurt am Main, 1978), 62. English: *Theory and Politics: Studies in the Development of Critical Theory* (Cambridge, Mass., 1985).

10. Among these, above all Werner Sombart, *Die Juden und das Wirtschaftsleben* (Munich/Leipzig, 1928; Otto Heller, *Der Untergang des Judentums* (Vienna/Berlin, 1931); Abraham Léon, *Kapitalismus und Judenfrage* (Munich, 1971). For a critical examination of Sombart and Max Weber, see Toni Oelsner, "The Place of the Jews in Economic

History as Viewed by German Scholars," in *Yearbook of the Leo Baeck Institute* (1962), 7:183ff.

11. Jay, "The Jews and the Frankfurt School," 91.

12. Julius Carlebach finds that Marx, in "On the Jewish Question," helped bring about an intellectual breakthrough for the anti-Semitic stereotype of the trader as Jew. See *Karl Marx and the Radical Critique of Judasism*, 148ff. He provides an annotated bibliography to Marx's "On the Jewish Question," 438–49.

13. Ernst Fraenkel has shown how, in the Nazi state, the sphere of circulation and the corresponding forms of commerce and law could continue to function unimpaired despite political dictatorship and the exclusion of the Jews. See Fraenkel, *Der Doppelstaat* (Frankfurt am Main, 1974).

Barbara Brick and Moishe Postone, in their critique of the equation of capitalism with the market, have demonstrated how critical theory's reliance on a form of "traditional Marxism" is a theoretical weak point. See chapter 9 in this book.

14. The significance of the socialization conflict for Horkheimer and other representatives of the Frankfurt Institute in the development of their socially critical attitude has been pointed out by Hans Dieter Hellige, "Gesellschaftskonflikt, Selbsthass und die Entstehung antikapitalistischer Positionen im Judentum. Der Einfluss des Antisemitismus auf das Sozialverhalten jüdischer Kaufmanns- und Unternehmerssöhne im Deutschen Kaiserreich und in der K. u. K.-Monarchie" in *Geschichte und Gesellschaft* 5 (1979): 476ff., 517. Helmut Gumnior and Rudolf Ringguth, *Max Horkheimer* (Reinbek, 1973), 7–9, cite an early biographical document in which his strong, emotional rejection of his own social origins finds expression: "Who is complaining about suffering? You and I? We are cannibals complaining that the flesh of the slaughtered gives us stomachaches. . . . You sleep in beds, wear clothes produced by people who are starving, people we drive with the tyrannical whip of our money, and you don't know how many women have fallen at the machine which produces the material for your 'cutaway.' Others are burned alive by poisonous gasses, so that your father continues to get the money you use to pay for your therapy—and you find it awful that you can't read more than two pages of Dostoyevsky. We are monsters, in fact we're not tormented enough. It's downright ridiculous, as if a butcher in the slaughterhouse were to brood about his white apron getting bloody." Letter to his cousin Hans, unpublished, Horkheimer Archive, Stadt- und Universitätsbibliothek Frankfurt.

15. In *Dämmerung* (1934), whose aphorisms date to the period from 1926–1931, Horkheimer's formulations on the Jews were far more pointed and intransigent. Under the Title "Belief and Profit," he wrote: "The Jewish capitalists get all worked up about anti-Semitism. They say that what they hold most sacred is under attack. But I think that they get so unspeakably annoyed only because something about them is being threatened that yields no profit, yet cannnot possibly be changed. If contemporary anti-Semitism were aimed at religion rather than 'blood,' many of those who are most outraged at it would renounce this unprofitable thing they hold most sacred 'with a heavy heart.' " *N*, 260/*DD*, 43.

16. Ibid.

17. On the presumedly instrumental significance of anti-Semitism, he writes: "The hatred of the Jews belongs to the ascendant phase of fascism. . . . It is used as a means of intimidating the populace by showing that the system will stop at nothing. Politically, the pogroms are aimed more at the spectators than at the Jews." *JE*, 328/"JE," 92.

18. "If it did not itself sound cynical with respect to what happened at Auschwitz, then one might speak of Auschwitz as the *thema probandum* of critical theory; Auschwitz is the immediate evidence for the validity of the basic thesis of the historical construction in *Dialectic of Enlightenment,* according to which civilization itself calls forth the anti-civilizational, the destructive, and intensifies it in the further course of history." Carl-Friedrich Geier, *Kritische Theorie. Max Horkheimer und Theodor W. Adorno* (Freiburg/Munich, 1982), 13.

19. "No analysis of National Socialism which cannot explain the extermination of the European Jews does justice to it." Moishe Postone, "Nationalsozialismus und Antisemitismus," in *Merkur,* no. 1/1982, 13.

20. "The attempt to convert an anti-Semite is to some extent a contradiction in terms." Horkheimer, "The German Jews," *CIR,* 117.

21. In a discussion following Horkheimer's lecture "Über das Vorurteil" ("On Prejudice") (Cologne/Opladen, 1963), Alphons Silbermann formulated the thesis that "prejudice is part of the structure of society" (35–36). It cannot be made to disappear, but it must be kept from reaching an "explosive state." Horkheimer responded by asking Silbermann a question directed at the distinction between psychic latency and the social circumstances that actualize that latency: "Do you believe that prejudice itself exploded, that prejudice itself is the grounds for explosion?" Silbermann responded affirmatively and elaborated: "I believe that the program of education—'enlightenment' is not a particularly good term—that the educational program, call it a 'fight' against something or whatever you will, can only aim at keeping social prejudice from becoming explosive. It will never disappear, because it's a social given, inherent in human beings on both psychological and sociological grounds. . . . It's not a matter of anti-Semitism, it's a question of social prejudice."

22. Hatred of the Jews "is the secret resentment of one's own religion." Ibid., 34.

23. Horkheimer later corrected his original thesis that religious anti-Semitism was connected with Christianity. "With Christianity? Kierkegaard would say: with the Christians. For the hate practiced by Christians in the world is not immanent to Christianity." Ibid., 33.

24. Leo Löwenthal also collaborated on the first three of the seven sections of "Elements of Anti-Semitism." See Jay, "The Jews and the Frankfurt School," 281, n. 34.

25. Ibid., 96.

26. Max Horkheimer, *Die Sehnsucht nach dem ganz Anderen. Ein Interview mit Kommentar von Helmut Gumnior* (Hamburg, 1970), 11.

27. The aphorism "Hated Mirror Image." *N,* 101/*DD,* 165.

28. Horkheimer, *Die Sehnsucht nach dem ganz Anderen,* 11.

29. *N,* 101/*DD,* 165.

30. Ibid.

31. The aphorism "On Anti-Semitism." *N,* 28/*DD,* 131.

32. The aphorism "On the Metaphysics of Hatred of the Jews." *N* 164.

33. Horkheimer, "The German Jews." *CIR*, 116.

34. Ibid. See also the aphorism "Eine besondere Art des Antisemitismus" ("A Particular Kind of Anti-Semitism"), which alludes to an identification with his parents.

35. Horkheimer, "Über das Vorurteil," 10.

36. "I believe that when a young person has been instilled with an abhorrence of these horrors, it is not necessary to speak above all of the atrocities commmitted upon the Jews." Ibid., 33.

37. The aphorism "After Auschwitz." *N*, 213.

38. Horkheimer, *Die Sehnsucht nach dem ganz Anderen*, 62.

14

Mass Culture and Aesthetic Redemption: The Debate between Max Horkheimer and Siegfried Kracauer

Martin Jay

One of the most persistent images in the extensive literature on the intellectual migration is that of a group of elitist cultural mandarins, who were shocked and appalled by the banality, vulgarity, and emptiness of the mass culture they first encountered in exile. Even leftist émigrés, so the conventional wisdom has it, were often extremely hostile to what one historian of the migration calls "the new opiates of the people."[1] There can be little doubt that many German intellectuals, whatever their political inclinations, did find American mass culture abhorrent, especially when they found themselves in such egregious centers of it as southern California.[2] And it is no less true, as the famous analysis of "one-dimensional man" by Herbert Marcuse demonstrates,[3] that Marxists often considered what they saw as pseudo-popular culture to be an obstacle to class struggle in their adopted country.

What can be questioned, however, is the assumption that such critiques derived from a prior ignorance of or distaste for mass culture and a corresponding reverential attitude toward its presumed opposite, the high *Kultur* identified with German *Bildung*, for, as several historians of the Weimar Republic have demonstrated,[4] a vigorous debate over mass culture was already well underway in the immediate post–World War I period, if not before. Even more important, many Weimar leftists, future émigrés among them, welcomed the crisis of high culture that accompanied the end of the Second Reich and cheered the new democratic, technological, modernist mass art they hoped would replace it. Although generally hostile to the popular *völkisch* art of nostalgia that competed with this modernist alternative, they by no means rejected the possibility of a progressive version of mass culture. Inspired in part by the experiments of the Soviet avant-garde, and in part by the American cultural innovations in movies, sports, and jazz that flooded Germany after 1918, many Weimar leftists sought to combine the best of both egalitarian cultures to create what one historian of their efforts calls "simultaneous futures" for Germany.[5]

The social underpinnings of the traditional concept of culture were called into question as many Weimar intellectuals reflected on the change in their own conditions hastened by the inflation of the early postwar years. No longer able to envisage themselves as members of an elite *Bildungsbürgertum* above the social fray, they sought ways to reconceptualize their role as active participants in the creation of a modern mass culture commensurate with or even in advance of the new political regime. Unlike the cultural spokesmen of the Wilhelmine Social Democratic party, who tended to support traditional high culture and merely advocated its extension to the proletariat,[6] they recognized that a radically new culture had to be created to replace its exhausted predecessor.

What form that creation was to take became a bone of vigorous contention on the Weimar left, and it remained one even under the changed conditions produced by the emigration. By that time official Communist cultural policy, in the Soviet Union and among its followers, had taken a drastically conservative turn with the coming of socialist realism as the party line in aesthetic matters.[7] As a result, the most innovative contributors to the ongoing debate came from the ranks of the unaffiliated "homeless" left of Weimar, who were even more isolated from working-class politics after migrating to America.

Two of the most representative figures in that discussion were Max Horkheimer and Siegfried Kracauer, whose work has never been systematically compared.[8] Because what each represented is so different, contrasting them now will help us grasp the full range of attitudes in the migration toward the issue of mass culture. Although many in their circle of friends and acquaintances, such as Theodor W. Adorno, Leo Löwenthal, Ernst Bloch, Walter Benjamin, and Bertolt Brecht, also wrote extensively on the same questions, Horkheimer and Kracauer are particularly interesting to contrast in light of a dichotomy introduced by the German literary critic Peter Bürger in his *Theory of* the Avant Garde.[9] They are almost perfect embodiments of the opposition Bürger posits between the normally synonymous terms *modernism* and the *avant-garde.*

Modernism, for Bürger, emerged out of the aestheticism of the late nineteenth century, which radically separated art from life. *L'art pour l'art* meant that the institution of art was to be contrasted with other social and cultural practices by its utter indifference to ethical, instrumental, utilitarian, or political concerns. Although modernism called into question the traditional image of the coherent, closed organic work of art by problematizing its formal and linguistic assumptions, it nonetheless remained wedded to the model of aesthetic autonomy underlying that tradition. The avant-garde, in contrast, attacked the very institution of art itself, challenging its alleged differentiation from the larger lifeworld out of which it arose. Rather than resting content with a work-immanent approach that radicalized only artistic technique, such avant-garde movements as dadaism, surrealism, and constructivism sought to subvert the assumption that art was an independent subsystem of the social and cultural whole. In so doing, especially in its more explicitly political moments, the avant-garde hoped to harness the utopian energies of art to revolutionize life, thus overcoming the pernicious division of labor characteristic of bourgeois modernization.

Without turning Bürger's suggestive dichotomy into too rigid an opposition, it is nonetheless very helpful in making sense of the differences between Horkheimer and Kracauer, in particular of their respective attitudes toward mass culture. By following out the contrasting implications of their positions, we can also better understand their potential pitfalls after their importation to America, for it was in the émigré context that the optimistic expectations of the Weimar left, both modernist and avant-garde, were ultimately dashed.

Unlike the more celebrated aesthetic debates of their contemporaries,[10] the implicit quarrel between Horkheimer and Kracauer has never been treated because it left behind so few obvious residues. Despite their common friendships with Löwenthal and Adorno, the two men were on cool personal terms from the late 1920s. Kracauer, in his capacity as the *feuilleton* editor of the prestigious *Frankfurter Zeitung,* declined Horkheimer's request to write an article defending the Institute for Social Research from the charge that it was controlled by

Communists.[11] Later, after their respective power statuses were reversed during the migration, Horkheimer was reluctant to forget this slight and others like it.[12] Although Kracauer's desperate financial situation during his exile, first in Paris and then in New York, meant he was compelled to swallow his pride and appeal to the Institute for support, he never received enough to make him overcome the bitterness he felt toward Horkheimer. Tensions were increased by the way in which the work he submitted to the Institute was treated, in particular by Adorno.[13] Although the Institute was instrumental in helping him acquire the precious affidavit that allowed him to leave France for America, Horkheimer, contrary to one historian's account, did not play a central role in the process.[14]

Beyond these personal and at times petty reasons, the tensions between the two men had more substantive sources. As Wolfgang Schivelbusch has noted,[15] even in Weimar their contrasting intellectual situations had an impact. Kracauer, trained as an architect rather than an academic and, after 1920, employed as a journalist, was much more personally involved with the phenomenon of mass culture than Horkheimer, who remained within the mandarin university world, even if in a heterodox enclave. Moreover, as a journalist in the volatile economic atmosphere of the Weimar Republic, Kracauer did not have the financial security assured Horkheimer by his parents' wealth and the institute's private endowment. In his "On the Writer," published in the *Frankfurter Zeitung* in 1931,[16] Kracauer contended that all unaffiliated writers felt economic pressures to become like journalists and thus abandon transcendent, absolute questions in favor of more timely and mundane ones. Horkheimer, to be sure, was also drawn to problems in everyday life, as the aphorisms he pseudonymously published under the title *Dämmerung* in 1934 illustrate.[17] But if a number of these do discuss issues too trivial for traditional philosophers, with few exceptions mass culture is ignored. And elsewhere in his writings, Horkheimer was able to focus at length on the larger problems Kracauer's *feuilletons* could only glancingly address.

Kracauer, to be sure, was himself schooled in philosophy and social theory—well enough, in fact, to instruct the young Adorno in Kant shortly after the end of the war. But the theorists who most influenced him, Georg Simmel and Max Scheler, only reinforced his fascination with the surface manifestations of reality, which might be read phenomenologically to reveal their meaning. His hostility toward the more totalizing or dialectical thinkers to whom Horkheimer was attracted was sufficiently strong to allow Benjamin to call him "an enemy of philosophy" in 1923.[18] Whereas Horkheimer's fascination with Schopenhauer and Hegel meant that he was drawn away from the phenomenal world to the allegedly more essential realities beneath, which he then interpreted in increasingly Marxist terms, Kracauer, even when he too was influenced by Marxism, preferred to search for meaning on the level of appearances.

Perhaps the most fundamental source of their disagreement over mass culture was their different susceptibility to its lures. Many years later, Adorno would remember that "Kracauer's interest in the mass psychology of film was never merely critical. He had in himself some of the naive visual delight *(Sehlust)* of the movie-goer; even as he makes fun of the 'little shop girl,' he sees in her a form of his own reaction."[19] In contrast, Horkheimer, like Adorno himself, rarely showed anything but visceral distaste for all variants of mass culture, at least in his published writings both before and after his migration to America.

The perspective from which that animus came was not, however, that of a mandarin defender of elite culture, who spurns its antithesis because it provides mere entertainment to the uneducated. Like Kracauer, Horkheimer had little use for the idealist defense of *Bildung* per se, with its tendentious opposition between culture and civilization and its ascetic disdain for sensual gratification. In his seminal essay of 1936, "Egoism and the Freedom Movement: On the Anthropology of the Bourgeois Era," he coined the phrase "the affirmative character of culture"[20] to describe its essentially conservative function as a consolation for actual suffering. Warning against the Social Democratic contention that its benefits should be spread to the masses, he wrote: "This undialectical view, which adopts the whole cultural concept of the bourgeoisie, its ascetic scale of priorities, and its concept of morality, but remains ignorant of its great artistic achievements, has dominated the reform strivings even of progressive nineteenth-century political parties down to this day, made thinking shallow and finally also contributed to defeat."[21] Marcuse's influential essay "The Affirmative Character of Culture," which appeared in the *Zeitschrift für Sozialforschung* the following year, spelled out the implications of this argument in greater detail.[22] Although even affirmative high culture preserved a moment of protest by maintaining the utopian impulse in art, it turned it in the direction of compensation for the very nonutopian conditions of everyday life by restricting culture to a sphere above material reality. Like religion in Marx's celebrated analysis, high culture was a distorted expression of protest, which nonetheless functioned as a kind of opiate to dull the pain of class society.

Or rather, high culture in its traditional forms functioned in this way, according to Horkheimer, Marcuse, and their Frankfurt School colleagues. Hence they preferred its modernist successor, which was less "affirmative" than traditional culture, even if it too failed to find an immediate link between art and life. The modernist dissolution of the organic, holistic work of art, its self-conscious baring of the devices that such works had drawn on to create their illusions, meant such art could no longer function as a positive model of harmony into which the aesthetic consumer could escape as a refuge from unhappiness in the real world. By its still dogged insistence on the possibility of art, even in this antiorganic form, modernism did maintain some hope for a different social reality in the future, but it did so only by denying the comforting belief that harmony, if only on the level of art, was possible today.

The modernist movement to which Horkheimer himself was initially drawn was the expressionism of the 1910s, in particular the ethical-libertarian version of it represented by such journals as Franz Pfemfert's *Die Aktion*.[23] Like Adorno, whose debt to the same source has recently been emphasized by Eugene Lunn,[24] Horkheimer was especially sensitive to the crisis of individual subjectivity registered by the expressionists. About later movements like Neue Sachlichkeit, surrealism, or constructivism—the movements Bürger identifies with the avant-garde rather than modernism—Horkheimer had certain reservations because he saw them cheerfully accepting the demise of the subject in the name of an allegedly collective successor. In *Dämmerung*, one of his harshest aphorisms was directed against the Neue Sachlichkeit of the mid-1920s, whose championing of the concrete he linked to the philosophical flight from relational thinking of the same years in the work of Scheler and others.[25] Both movements neglected the social and historical context of the isolated objects they sought to valorize.

Horkheimer was no less suspicious in *Dämmerung* of attempts to create a politically charged popular art, such as the revolutionary theater of Piscator and Brecht. "The reason the theater cannot have a lasting revolutionary effect," he argued, "is that it turns the problems of the class struggle into objects of shared contemplation and discussion. It thus creates harmony in the aesthetic sphere. But proletarian consciousness must break through that harmony; that is one of the principal tasks of political activity."[26] When such plays really pose a political threat, he concluded, they will no longer be allowed to be performed. Until then, they merely provide a way for well-intentioned bourgeois audiences to salve their consciences.

As for the cinema, which held so much promise for Kracauer, the only aphorism in *Dämmerung* dealing with it stressed its compensatory function as a way to avoid confronting real suffering. "Of course, there are people that shed tears over 'Sonny Boy' at the movies," Horkheimer wrote. "And they do that at the very moment that, in the service of their own interests, real persons are slowly being tortured to death, simply because they were suspected of fighting for the liberation of mankind. Photography, telegraphy, and the radio have shrunk the world. The populations of the cities witness the misery of the entire earth. One would think that this might prompt them to demand its abolition. But simultaneously, what is close has become the faraway. Now, the horror of one's own city is submerged in the general suffering, and people turn their attention to the marital problems of movie stars."[27] Thus, even the documentary potential of the film, its ability to record the actual misery of the world, could have a counterproductive impact. Like Lukács with his distaste for mere reportage in the proletarian novels of the 1920s,[28] Horkheimer was suspicious of any attempt to combine political tendentiousness with a fetishistic emphasis on the unmediated "facts" of the world as it was.

Horkheimer's own aesthetic alternative did not become fully apparent until after his migration to America, when his collaboration with Adorno began to bear real fruit.[29] The essay "Art and Mass Culture," published in the last volume of the institute's journal in 1941,[30] shows his solidarity with Adorno's thinking on these subjects and his distance from Kracauer's. Written as a critique of the American philosopher Mortimer Adler's lame attempt to elevate cinema into the pantheon of transhistorical art forms, the essay begins by noting the historical differentiation of "pure" art from the life world. The social basis of this split, according to Horkheimer, was "the private atomic subject"[31] who had not yet been reduced to a cog in the economic or technological machine. The aesthetic judgment made by such a subject, as Kant had noted, contained a moment of genuinely disinterested humanism, which pointed toward a possible future of human solidarity. Thus, "an element of resistance is inherent in the most aloof art. . . . Art, since it became autonomous, has preserved the utopia that evaporated from religion."[32]

But the private realm that sustained such aesthetic judgments and the very existence of autonomous art, Horkheimer then warned, has been increasingly undermined, especially because of the crisis of the family. As he frequently lamented throughout this period, the family no longer functioned as "a kind of second womb, in whose warmth the individual gathered the strength necessary to stand alone outside it."[33] Instead of being socialized by the family, the child is directly manipulated by mass culture, whose effect is to bring about the "disappearance of the inner life."[34] As a result of these changes, Horkheimer concluded, "man has lost his power to conceive of a world different from that in which he lives. This other world was that of art. Today it survives only in those works which uncompromisingly express the gulf between the monadic individual and his barbarous surroundings—prose like Joyce's and paintings like Picasso's *Guernica*."[35]

Here the examples Horkheimer chose demonstrate his bias for modernist rather than avant-garde works, in Bürger's sense. Such works as Joyce's and Picasso's, he contended, have given up the communicative function of art and express instead the isolation of the bourgeois subject in crisis. Rather than trying in vain to build a new social order like certain avant-garde experiments, they "abandon the idea that real community exists; they are the monuments of a solitary and despairing life that finds no bridge to any other or even to its own consciousness. . . . The work of art is the only adequate objectification of the individual's deserted state and despair."[36] In other words, only culture in its negative rather than affirmative state can sustain the utopian impulse in art.

As for the pseudo-populist attempts of Adler to celebrate film as the mass art of the present, comparable to the great art of the past,

Horkheimer had only contempt. Introducing the phrase that was to become so central in his collaborative project with Adorno, *Dialectic of Enlightenment*, he scornfully wrote, "What today is called popular entertainment is actually demands evoked, manipulated and by implication deteriorated by the cultural industries. It has little to do with art, least of all where it pretends to be such."[37] No less questionable, Horkheimer continued, was Adler's neo-Aristotelian praise for the imitative function of film, for all it reproduces is the bad reality of the present. The same attitude was expressed in *Dialectic of Enlightenment* a few years later, where he and Adorno contended, "Real life is becoming indistinguishable from the movies. The sound film, far surpassing the theater of illusion, leaves no room for imagination or reflection on the part of the spectator, who is unable to remain within the structure of the film, and yet ruminate uncontrolled by the exact details without losing the thread of the story: hence the film forces its victims to equate it directly with reality."[38]

Although Adorno seems to have moderated his hostility to films somewhat in his last years,[39] there is no evidence to suggest that Horkheimer ever did. In the posthumously published aphorisms, *Notizen,* he continued to argue that "all art has the quality of affording pleasure without first referring men to reality, as does the modern cinema. This draws interest only from real life and thus becomes its instrument."[40]

In so arguing, Horkheimer demonstrated how distant he always remained from Kracauer's view of mass culture in general and the cinema in particular. Unlike Horkheimer, Kracauer was optimistic about the disruptive, oppositional potential in film, whose realistic capacities he particularly praised. As an avant-gardist in Bürger's sense, he was highly sympathetic to the threat this new mass medium posed to the aesthetic hierarchies of traditional culture. Interestingly, his appreciation of this challenge was shared by the authorities in Wilhelmine Germany when cinema first appeared as a mass entertainment in 1895. As Gary Stark has recently demonstrated,[41] the German government quickly acted to regulate and censor what it saw as an inflammatory stimulus to lower-class unrest. No less anxious were the guardians of German *Bildung,* who assailed the cinema as a particular threat to that paragon of high culture, the theater. In fact, it was not until World War I that the German authorities began to recognize another potential in films: the manipulative one that the Nazis were to bring to perfection a generation later.

Kracauer, to be sure, was himself aware of the cinema's ambiguous implications. In the celebrated and controversial discussion of the Weimar cinema written in his American exile, *From Caligari to Hitler*,[42] Kracauer showed himself keenly sensitive to the sinister potential of film even before it was taken over by the Leni Riefenstahls of the Nazi era. Here, in fact, he explicitly drew on much of the same social and psychological analysis that had motivated the Frankfurt school's work on authority and the family in the 1930s. Both Horkheimer and Erich Fromm, formerly an institute figure, were cited by Kracauer as sources for his interpretative content analysis of the Weimer cinema.[43]

But Kracauer's other major exile reflection on cinema, *Theory of Film: The Redemption of Physical Reality* (1960), demonstrated his allegiance to an alternative vision of film that directly contradicted Horkheimer's. It was precisely the reflective, mirroring quality of cinema that he found most compelling. Stressing its kinship with photography, he insisted that "films cling to the surface of things. They seem to be the more cinematic the less they focus directly on inward life, ideology, and spiritual concerns. This explains why many people with strong cultural leanings scorn the cinema. . . . Plausible as this verdict sounds, it strikes me as unhistorical and superficial because it fails to do justice to the human condition in our time. Perhaps our condition is such that we cannot gain access to the elusive essentials of life unless we assimilate the seemingly non-essential?"[44] It was for this reason that the film's "redemption of physical reality" was more progressive than its attempts to ape the high art of the past, in particular the theater. Indeed, as he had argued in *From Caligari to Hitler*,[45] it was only when the cinema began to abandon its true vocation and tried to "elevate" itself to the level of art that its potential for abuse was first opened.

In 1960, when *Theory of Film* appeared, Kracauer had long since abandoned his radical inclinations. But even during his most leftist period, during the waning years of the Weimar Republic, he staunchly defended the emancipatory effect of the cinema's revelation of surface realities. Unlike Horkheimer and other more Hegelian Marxists such as Lukács, he never employed a concept of reification to condemn appearances as distorted, fragmentary, and static misrepresentations of the deeper, more dialectical realities beneath. Hostile to the category of totality so crucial to Hegelian Marxism, he went so far as to claim in his study of Jacques Offenbach, written in the 1930s, that surfaces are the "place where petrifaction least occurs."[46] Even Adorno, who came to have his own suspicions about Hegelian Marxist notions of totality and reification, chastised Kracauer for his utter indifference to their importance.[47] Although he may have emphasized that film in a capitalist world had to be understood as a commodity and therefore drew the conclusion that film criticism must also be social criticism,[48] Kracauer never lost his faith in the truth-telling potential of film per se.

In fact, his optimism about the nature of the cinema spilled over as well to his social analyses, however much they may have been influenced by his leftist sympathies. In the Weimar period, he was most concerned with the new audience for the film, which he noted was especially attractive to the growing group known as the *Angestellten*, the white-collar workers whose susceptibility to right-wing irrationalism he probed in one of his most telling works.[49] But elsewhere, he jettisoned the class-specific nature of his analysis and spoke more generally of the "homogeneous metropolitan public"[50] who went to the movies. In the eyes of later, more orthodox Marxist commentators like Helmut Lethen,[51] this loss of specificity meant an unfortunate neglect of the still potent difference between the proletariat and other groups in society, whose goals and social functions were by no means identical. *Die Angestellten* were not, after all, the real producers in society and therefore could not be counted on to revolutionize it in the way the working class might.

Whether Kracauer ever really thought the new homogeneous public for films would be radicalized by them or merely believed, in ways that Marxists like Lethen did not, that mass culture was effacing class differences is uncertain. But it is clear that he found much to praise in the way that the audience reacted to the films they saw. In a 1926 essay, "Cult of Distraction: On Berlin Movie Theaters,"[52] he defended *Zerstreuung*, "diversion" or "distraction," as a healthy mode of perception in the modern world. As Simmel had argued, the typical experience of the urban dweller was that of discontinuous sense impressions, which flickered across the consciousness of the passive subject. Films, Kracauer contended, were the appropriate medium to register that experience. As such, they gave the lie to the traditional notions of artworks as organically closed totalities.

In so arguing, as Miriam Hansen has pointed out,[53] Kracauer was anticipating the argument of Walter Benjamin in his widely discussed essay, "The Work of Art in the Age of Mechanical Reproduction," whose similar defense of distraction aroused the ire of Adorno.[54] Both Benjamin and Kracauer were hopeful about the political implications of the decline of the traditional aura around the work of art and welcomed its reintegration with the life world. Kracauer, in fact, seems to have had even less nostalgia for the lost aura than Benjamin in certain of his moods. The two friends were also closer to each other than to either Adorno or Horkheimer in their praise for the revolutionary Soviet film-makers of the 1920s, especially Pudovkin and Eisenstein, whose collective rather than individualist view of the new medium they applauded.[55] And finally, like Benjamin, Kracauer was immensely impressed by the arguments of the Soviet playwright Sergej Tretjakov, who visited Berlin in 1931. As Hugh Ridley has argued, Kracauer's "On the Writer" and Benjamin's "Author as Producer," written three years later, both show the impact of Tretjakov's emphasis on the new role of the intellectual as a participant in the class struggle rather than an aloof observer of it.[56]

Tretjakov, a former futurist turned Marxist, was a perfect embodiment of what Bürger has called the avant-garde rather than modernism. Kracauer's enthusiasm for him demonstrates how much he too can be situated in the same camp. Although he did not write extensively on the avant-garde movements of his day, the influence of surrealism has been detected in certain of his writings by Benjamin and other commentators.[57] And despite his explicit distaste for the disillusioned and cynical qualities of the Neue Sachlichkeit,[58] there were echoes of its objectivist sobriety in such works as his novel *Ginster*.[59] Kracauer spoke truer than he knew when he referred to himself jokingly to Adorno as the "derrière-garde of the avant-garde"[60] in the 1920s.

No better testimony of the affinity can be offered than his celebrated essay on the Tiller Girls, a group of precision dancers from America who toured Germany in 1927. "The Mass Ornament" begins with a characteristic plea for the value of investigating the "simple

surface manifestations of an epoch."[61] As trivial as the Tiller Girls may seem, Kracauer argued, they reveal two fundamental aspects of contemporary reality. First, in their capacity as deindividualized, ornamental cogs in a cultural machine, they bear witness to the transformation of a people or a community into a mass. According to Kracauer, "only as parts of a mass, not as individuals who believe themselves to be formed from within, are human beings components of a pattern."[62] As such, the Tiller Girls express a sinister potential in modern life, whose implications Kracauer himself would later spell out in an unpublished essay on fascist propaganda he submitted to the *Zeitschrift* and in his supplement to *From Caligari to Hitler* on "Propaganda and the Nazi War Film."[63] What Benjamin later made famous as the "aestheticization of politics" was adumbrated in the aesthetic transformation of individuals into parts of a technological mechanism.[64]

But second, the Tiller Girls also expressed for Kracauer a potentially progressive tendency in modern life, which paradoxically derived from their relation to the process of capitalist modernization. With specific reference to the Taylorist methods of organizing labor that were so controversial in the 1920s, Kracauer contended that "the mass ornament is the aesthetic reflex of the rationality aspired to by the prevailing economic system."[65] Although at first glance such an observation might appear congruent with his initial argument about the negative implications of the Tiller Girls, which would put him in the same camp as Horkheimer and the Frankfurt School, Kracauer took it in the opposite direction. "Certain intellectuals," he wrote, "have taken offense at the emergence of the Tiller Girls and the image created by the stadium pageants. Whatever amuses the masses, they judge as a diversion of the masses. Contrary to such opinion, I would argue that the *aesthetic* pleasure gained from the ornamental mass movements is *legitimate*."[66] The source of that legitimacy, he continued, is its mimetic content, even if the reality it imitates may in some sense be impoverished. Thus, "no matter how low one rates the value of the mass ornament, its level of reality is still above that of artistic productions which cultivate obsolete noble sentiments in withered forms—even when they have no further significance."[67]

What made this mimesis potentially progressive for Kracauer was his surprisingly positive attitude toward the larger process of rationalization itself, a process whose demythologizing and disenchanting effects he welcomed. "The kind of thinking which is associated with the present economic system," he argued, "has made possible a domination and use of self-contained nature which was not granted to any earlier epoch. The fact that this thinking makes the exploitation of nature possible is not decisive here—if human beings were merely exploiters of nature then nature would have triumphed over nature—but what is decisive here is that this process allows for greater independence from natural conditions and in this way makes room for the interjection of reason. We owe the bourgeois revolutions of the last hundred and fifty years precisely to this kind of *rationality*."[68] Capitalism, to be sure, is only a stage in the process that will have to be surpassed. For, "the rationale of the capitalist system is not reason itself but obscured reason."[69] But there is no going back to mythical thinking or a lost oneness with nature; indeed, the problem is that "capitalism does not rationalize too much, but *too little*."[70]

The mass ornament, Kracauer then contended, is itself problematic not because it is a rationalization of life but because it still retains certain mythological features. Most important, its human components are unable to express themselves, remaining instead mute and passive. But it would be wrong to try to remedy this deficiency by holding on to an outmoded notion of private expression, the traditional idea of high culture with its myth of the artistic genius, for it is no longer possible to reconstitute the social conditions that would allow such individualized art to be viable. "The privileged individuals, who do not accept the fact that they are an appendage to the prevailing economic system, have not even understood the mass ornament as a sign of this system. They dismiss the phenomenon while continuing to edify themselves at fine arts events, untouched by the reality present in the stadium pattern. The masses, who so spontaneously took to the pattern in openly acknowledging facts in their rough form, are superior to those intellectuals who despise it."[71] Yet what remains mythological about even this superior understanding, Kracauer had to admit, is the ultimately meaningless quality of the abstract rationality of both capitalism and the mass ornament, which opens the way to an irrational manipulation of the masses. "Reason," he wrote, "is impeded when the masses into which it should penetrate yield to emotions provided by the godless mythological cult. Its social meaning is much like that of the Roman *circus games* sponsored by tyrants."[72]

But if an "unobscured" reason is to be achieved in the future, Kracauer concluded, the only hope is to carry through the process of rationalization of which capitalism and mass art are a necessary stage. The esoteric work of art cannot provide a refuge for utopian hopes; only the exoteric work—in Bürger's sense, the avant-garde work—is the artwork of the future. Turning back to discredited elite versions of art is merely "a flight from reality. The process leads directly through the mass ornament, not away from it. It can move forward when thinking sets limits to nature and produces human beings in a way reason would produce them. Then society will change. Then, too, the mass ornament will vanish and human life itself will assume the traits of that ornament which expresses itself in the folk tales, face to face with truth."[73]

From the perspective of Horkheimer's later work, with its defense of esoteric modernism rather than exoteric avant-gardism, it is easy to see certain problems in Kracauer's argument. Not only did he fail to appreciate sufficiently the costs in the rationalist domination of nature, which were spelled out in *Dialectic of Enlightenment*, so too was his linear notion of capitalist rationality as a necessary stage in the transition to a genuinely rational future highly questionable. Indeed, it smacked of the orthodox Marxist philosophy of history that Kracauer in so many other respects found troubling.

When Kracauer lost the vestiges of his earlier radicalism during his exile in America, the defiantly optimistic note in such essays as "The Mass Ornament" was also jettisoned. What remained, however, was Kracauer's insistence on the importance of surface realities and the mass cultural redemption of them. In *Theory of Film* in particular, this emphasis was powerfully present, although now expressed in an elegiac, even melancholic mood noted by many commentators.[74] As I have argued elsewhere,[75] Kracauer began to adopt the disillusioned, even cynical attitude of the Neue Sachlichkeit at its most apolitical, the very attitude he had condemned in the 1920s. Now the collapse of art into life produced nothing utopian at all, or, more precisely, the redemption of physical reality led nowhere in social terms.

In the larger perspective provided by Peter Bürger, we can understand Kracauer's development as a striking example of the miscarriage of the avant-garde project to realize the critical potential in art by destroying its autonomy and reuniting it with the lifeworld. The most compelling current version of that failure is the postmodernist art that is fully at peace with late capitalist society.[76] Despite the hopes of Kracauer and others like him, the deinstitutionalization of art has meant a false sublation or *Aufhebung* of its negative and critical potential. Distraction has shown itself to be far more conformist in implication than either Kracauer or Benjamin had hoped.

Can Horkheimer's modernist alternative, which was shared by most other members of the Frankfurt School,[77] be said to have fared any better? As the work of art progressively deconstructs itself as a coherent, integral whole, is there anything left that can function as even the negative placeholder of utopian impulses? Adorno himself, who is often criticized for clinging to a modernist aesthetic in the face of its decay, was forced to acknowledge the aging of the "new music" of the Schoenberg school, which had served as his model of critical art.[78] Near the end of his life, Horkheimer also seems to have understood the problem. In an aphorism published in his *Notizen,* he concluded, "Today abstract art is to surrealism as positivism is to the Enlightenment. It no longer has any enemies."[79] Even the most intransigently noncommunicative modernist art, he came to realize, was not immune to being integrated into affirmative culture by the marketplace. It was thus perhaps why he turned in his last years, after his return to Germany, to another possible locus of negation, religion.[80] If in 1941 he could write, "Art, since it became autonomous, has preserved the utopia that evaporated from religion," his controversial ruminations on theology suggest that he may ultimately have reversed the formula.

It is clear that Horkheimer's modernist reliance on autonomous art as a reliable counterweight to mass culture has shown itself to be as historically limited as Kracauer's avant-garde belief that the collapse of art into the lifeworld would be a way-station to a rational future. The possible alternatives to these positions are not themselves very promising. One might still call for a deliberately engaged political art of the kind that Brecht or Hanns Eisler advocated, but the meager impact of attempts to apply their ideas in the 1960s suggests the limits of this approach. Or one might insist on covert utopian impulses latent in even the most seemingly conformist mass culture, as have more recent leftist critics like Fredric Jameson, Stanley Aronowitz, and Douglas Kellner.[81] The culture industry may well be not as totalitarian as Horkheimer and Adorno assumed in their bleaker moments. But whether it allows more than pockets of what one commentator has called "artificial negativity"[82] remains very much to be seen. Or one might follow Habermas and combine a Horkheimer-like insistence on the viability of esoteric, modernist art with a Kracauer-like contention that aesthetic rationalization is part of a more global process of social rationalization, which will preserve some differentiation rather than try to end it prematurely. But here too, problems remain with the relationship between the still disparate spheres of the modern totality, as well as with the nature of rationalization in each sphere.[83]

However one assesses the promise of these attempts, it is difficult to quell the doubt that we may have recently come to the end of an epoch in Western cultural history, an epoch in which art was assigned a privileged function as a radical, even utopian force capable of playing a leading role in changing society. Its inaugural document may have been Schiller's *Letters on the Aesthetic Education of Man* in 1795, whereas Adorno's *Aesthetic Theory* of 1970 possibly served as its unintended epitaph. Whatever the final verdict on this enormously ambitious project may be, it is clear that the implicit debate between Horkheimer and Kracauer, whose outlines this essay has tried to trace, must be read as an important chapter in the story as a whole. The sobering lessons provided by their very different attempts to harness art for radical purposes make it difficult not to wonder if its end may be near.

Notes

1. Anthony Heilbut, *Exiled in Paradise: German Refugee Artists and Intellectuals in America from the 1930's to the Present* (New York, 1983), chap. 6.

2. See, for example, the account of Arnold Schoenberg's distaste for Los Angeles in Jarrell C. Jackman, "German Emigres in Southern California," *The Muses Flee Hitler: Cultural Transfer and Adaptation, 1930–1945* (Washington, D.C., 1983), 97.

3. Herbert Marcuse, *One-Dimensional Man: Studies in the Ideology of Advanced Industrial Society* (Boston, 1964).

4. John Willett, *Art and Politics in the Weimar Period: The New Sobriety, 1917–1933* (New York, 1978); Anton Kaes, Introduction to *Manifeste und Dokumente zur deutschen Literatur 1918–1933*, ed. Anton Kaes (Stuttgart, 1983).

5. John Zammito, "Simultaneous Futures and the Berlin Avant Garde," in *Literature and History*, ed. Leonard Schulze and Walter Wetzels (Lanham, Md., 1963), 145–56.

6. For accounts of SPD cultural policies in the Wilhelmine era, see Vernon L. Lidtke, "Naturalism and Socialism in Germany," *American Historical Review* 79, 1 (February 1974):

14–37; Frank Trommler, "Working-Class Culture and Modern Mass Culture before World War I," *New German Critique* 29 (Spring–Summer 1983): 57–70.

7. Helga Gallas, *Marxistische Literaturtheorie: Kontroversen im Bund proletarisch-revolutionärer Schriftsteller* (Neuwied, 1971).

8. For individual discussions of Horkheimer, see Helmut Gumnior and Rudolf Ringguth, *Max Horkheimer in Selbstzeugnissen und Bilddokumenten* (Reinbek bei Hamburg, 1974); Franz Lienert, *Theorie und Tradition: Zum Menschenbild in Werke Horkheimers* (Bern, 1977); and Anselm Skuhra, *Max Horkheimer: Eine Einführung in sein Denken* (Stuttgart, 1974). See also the general accounts of the Frankfurt School in Martin Jay, *The Dialectical Imagination: A History of the Frankfurt School and the Institute of Social Research, 1923–1950* (Boston, 1973), and David Held, *Introduction to Critical Theory: Horkheimer to Habermas* (Berkeley, 1980). Kracauer has been less well served by historians. For a general overview of his career, see Martin Jay, "The Extraterritorial Life of Siegfried Kracauer," *Salmagundi* 31–32 (Fall 1975–Winter 1976): 49–106. A list of other articles on him can be found in the special issue of *Text + Kritik* 68 (October 1980) devoted to him.

9. Peter Bürger, *Theory of the Avant Garde*, trans. Michael Shaw (Minneapolis, 1984).

10. *Aesthetics and Politics: Debates between Bloch, Lukács, Brecht, Benjamin, Adorno*, ed. New Left Review (London, 1977); see also Eugene Lunn, *Marxism and Modernism: An Historical Study of Lukács, Brecht, Benjamin, and Adorno* (Berkeley, 1982).

11. Conversation with Leo Lowenthal, Berkeley, September 18, 1973.

12. See the discussion in Martin Jay, "Adorno and Kracauer: Notes on a Troubled Friendship," *Salmagundi* 40 (Winter 1978): 50.

13. Kracauer was particularly upset by Adorno's editing of his manuscript "Masses and Propaganda" in 1938; see the letters of Kracauer to Adorno, August 20, 1938, and Kracauer to Horkheimer, August 20, 1938, in the Kracauer *Nachlass*, Schiller Nationalmuseum, Marbach am Neckar.

14. Horkheimer is given the credit by Jörg Bundschuh, "Als dauere die Gegenwart eine Ewigkeit; Notizen zu Leben und Werk von Siegfried Kracauer," *Text + Kritik* 68 (October 1980): 8. From the evidence in the Kracauer archive and conversations with his old friends, it would seem that Adorno, Lowenthal, and Pollock at the institute and Meyer Schapiro, the art historian, and Iris Barry of the Museum of Modern Art's Film Library were all more helpful than Horkheimer.

15. Wolfgang Schivelbusch, *Intellektuellendämmerung: Zur Lage der Frankfurter Intelligenz in den zwanziger Jahren* (Frankfurt, 1982), 50.

16. Reprinted in *Text + Kritik* 68 (October 1980): 1–3.

17. Heinrich Regius (pseud. for Horkheimer), *Dämmerung* (Zürich, 1934); reprinted in *Notizen 1950 bis 1969 und Dämmerung. Notizen in Deutschland*, ed. Werner Brede (Frankfurt, 1974); partial English translation as *Dawn and Decline. Notes 1926–1931 and 1950–1969*, trans. Michael Shaw (New York, 1978).

18. Cited by Theodor W. Adorno, "Der wunderliche Realist," *Noten zur Literatur III* (Frankfurt, 1965), 86. Kracauer willingly accepted this title and in fact approvingly extended it to Benjamin in return. See his 1928 essay "Zu den Schriften Walter Benjamins," reprinted in *Das Ornament der Masse: Essays* (Frankfurt, 1963), 249–55.

19. Adorno, "Der wunderliche Realist," 94. A similar reproach is made by Heide Schlüpmann, "Kinosucht," *Frauen und Film* 33 (October 1982): 47.

20. Horkheimer, "Egoism and the Freedom Movement: On the Anthropology of the Bourgeois Era," *Telos* 54 (Winter 1982–1983): 51. For an account of the importance of this essay, see my introduction to it in the same issue.

21. Ibid.

22. Herbert Marcuse, "The Affirmative Character of Culture," in *Negations: Essays in Critical Theory*, trans. Jeremy J. Shapiro (Boston, 1968). Marcuse acknowledges the origin of the essays title on p. 277.

23. See his early works in *Aus der Pubertät. Novellen und Tagebuchblätter*, ed. Alfred Schmidt (Munich, 1974). Schmidt stresses the importance of Pfemfert on p. 363. Significantly, Pfemfert was hostile to the cinema during this time. See his "Kino als Erzieher," *Die Aktion* (June 19, 1911, reprinted in Anton Kaes, ed., *Kino-Debatte: Literatur und Film 1909–1929* (Tübingen, 1978), 59–62.

24. Lunn, *Marxism and Modernism*, 195–98, 261–67.

25. Horkheimer, "The New Objectivity," in *Dawn and Decline*, 97. Horkheimer did not explicitly attack the other avant-garde movements, as Adorno often did in the case of Surrealism. In fact, Leo Lowenthal recalls more ambivalence on his part than on Adorno's. Conversation, Berkeley, June 1984.

26. Horkheimer, "Revolutionary Theater or 'Art Reconciles,' " in *Dawn and Decline*, 55.

27. Horkheimer, "Unlimited Possibilities," in *Dawn and Decline*, 19.

28. For an account of Lukács's hostility toward the proletarian novels of the Weimar left, see Russell Berman, "Lukács' Critique of Bredel and Ottwalt: A Political Account of an Aesthetic Debate of 1931–1932," *New German Critique* 10 (Winter 1977): 155–78.

29. Adorno arrived in New York in February 1938 and moved with Horkheimer to Los Angeles in 1941, where he and Horkheimer worked together on *Dialectic of Enlightenment*.

30. Horkheimer, "Art and Mass Culture," *Studies in Philosophy and Social Science* 9, 2 (1941), reprinted in Horkheimer, *Critical Theory: Selected Essays* (New York, 1972), from which the following citations are quoted.

31. Ibid., 273.

32. Ibid., 274–75.

33. Ibid., 276.

34. Ibid., 277.

35. Ibid., 278.

36. Ibid., 279.

37. Ibid., 288.

38. Horkheimer and Adorno, *Dialectic of Enlightenment*, trans. John Cumming (New York, 1972), 126 (translation corrected from original edition, p. 151).

39. See his "Transparencies on Film," *New German Critique* 24–25 (Fall–Winter 1981–1982), with an excellent introduction by Miriam Hansen. Adorno did not relax his hostility to Kracauer's emphasis on the realistic nature of the film in this essay, which he claimed had its roots in the German *Jugendstil*'s hostility to subjectivity (202), but he did acknowledge that the montage capacity of film and its ability to interact with other media give it a progressive potential.

40. Horkheimer, "Kunst und Kino," *Notizen 1950 bis 1969 und Dämmerung. Notizen in Deutschland,* 11; not included in the English translation.

41. Gary D. Stark, "Cinema, Society and the State: Policing the Film Industry in Imperial Germany," in Gary D. Stark and Bede Karl Lackner, eds., *Essays on Culture and Society in Modern Germany* (College Station, Texas, 1982).

42. Kracauer, *From Caligari to Hitler: A Psychological History of the German Film* (Princeton, 1947).

43. Ibid., 10–11.

44. Kracauer, *Theory of Film: The Redemption of Physical Reality* (London, 1960), x–xi.

45. Kracauer, *From Caligari to Hitler,* 18.

46. Kracauer, *Jacques Offenbach und das Paris seiner Zeit* (Amsterdam, 1937), 219. The remark is cited by Karsten Witte, "Introduction to Siegfried Kracauer's 'The Mass Ornament,'" *New German Critique* 5 (Spring 1975): 63, where he notes that it is missing from the English translation.

47. Adorno, "Der wunderliche Realist," 107. For an account of Adorno's critique of Hegelian Marxism, see Martin Jay, *Marxism and Totality: The Adventures of a Concept from Lukács to Habermas* (Berkeley, 1984), chap. 8.

48. Kracauer, "Über die Aufgabe des Filmkritikers," in *Kino: Essays, Studien, Glossen zum Film,* ed. Karsten Witte (Frankfurt, 1974), 9.

49. Kracauer, *Die Angestellten,* in Kracauer, *Schriften* (Frankfurt, 1971), vol. 1.

50. Kracauer, "Kult der Zerstreuung. Über die Berliner Lichtspielhäuser," *Das Ornament der Masse,* 313.

51. Helmut Lethen, *Neue Sachlichkeit 1924–1932: Studien zur Litratur des "Weissen Sozialismus"* (Stuttgart, 1970), 103.

52. See note 50.

53. Miriam Hansen, "Early Silent Cinema: Whose Public Sphere?" *New German Critique* 29 (Spring–Summer 1983): 180.

54. Walter Benjamin, "The Work of Art in the Age of Mechanical Reproduction," in *Illuminations: Essays and Reflections,* ed. Hannah Arendt, trans. Harry Zohn (New York,

1968). Adorno's response appeared in "On the Fetish-Character in Music and the Regression of Listening," in *The Essential Frankfurt School Reader,* ed. Andrew Arato and Eike Gebhardt (New York, 1978).

55. Kracauer, *Kino,* sec. II on Soviet film; Benjamin, *Moskauer Tagebuch* (Frankfurt, 1980), 107, 123.

56. Hugh Ridley, "Tretjakov in Berlin," in *Culture and Society in the Weimar Republic,* ed. Keith Bullivant (Manchester, 1977), 154, 157.

57. Benjamin, *Gesammelte Schriften* (Frankfurt, 1977), 3: 226–27; Gerwin Zohlen, "Text-Strassen," *Text + Kritik* 68 (October 1980): 71.

58. See, for example, his critique in *Die Angestellten,* 287.

59. Kracauer, *Ginster* (Frankfurt, 1963); original published in 1928.

60. Quoted in Adorno, "Der wunderliche Realist," 89.

61. Kracauer, "The Mass Ornament," *New German Critique* 5 (Spring 1975): 67.

62. Ibid., 68.

63. Kracauer, "Masse und Propaganda. Eine Untersuchung über die faschistische Propaganda" (Paris, 1936), Kracauer Archive, Schiller National Museum, Marbach am Neckar. For a short summary, see Karsten Witte's introduction to "The Mass Ornament," 62. "Propaganda and the Nazi War Film," in *From Caligari to Hitler,* first written in 1942.

64. Benjamin, "The Work of Art in the Age of Mechanical Reproduction," 244. For an interesting account of the fascist aestheticization of technology, see Jeffrey Herf, "Reactionary Modernism: Some Ideological Origins of the Primacy of Politics in the Third Reich," *Theory and Society* 10, 6 (November 1981).

65. Kracauer, "The Mass Ornament," 70.

66. Ibid.

67. Ibid.

68. Ibid., 71.

69. Ibid., 72.

70. Ibid.

71. Ibid., 75.

72. Ibid.

73. Ibid., 76.

74. See, for example, Rudolf Arnheim, "Melancholy Unshaped," in *Toward a Psychology of Art* (Berkeley, 1972).

75. Jay, "The Extraterritorial Life of Siegfried Kracauer," 79f.

76. See the critique of postmodernism by Fredric Jameson, "Postmodernism and Consumer Society," in *The Anti-Aesthetic: Essays on Postmodern Culture,* ed. Hal Foster (Port Townsend, Wash., 1983).

77. See, for example, Herbert Marcuse, *The Aesthetic Dimension: Toward a Critique of Marxist Aesthetics* (Boston, 1978).

78. Adorno, "Modern Music Is Growing Old," *Score* 18 (December 1956).

79. Horkheimer, "Mind, Art and the Bourgeoisie," in *Dawn and Decline,* 180.

80. For an account of this turn, see Rudolf Siebert, "Horkheimer's Sociology of Religion," *Telos* 30 (Winter 1976–1977).

81. Fredric Jameson, "Reification and Utopia in Mass Culture," *Social Text* 1 (Winter 1979); Stanley Aronowitz, *The Crisis in Historical Materialism: Class, Politics and Culture in Marxist Theory* (South Hadley, Mass., 1981); Douglas Kellner, "Critical Theory, Commodities and the Consumer Society," in *Theory, Culture and Society* 1, 3 (1983).

82. Paul Piccone, "The Crisis of One-Dimensionality," *Telos* 35 (Spring 1978).

83. For a discussion of Habermas's attempt, see Martin Jay, "Habermas and Modernism," *Praxis International* 4, 1 (April 1984).

15

The Failure of Self-Realization: An Interpretation of Horkheimer's *Eclipse of Reason*

Georg Lohmann

Overshadowed by the brilliance of *Dialectic of Enlightenment,* Horkheimer's *Eclipse of Reason,* which originated at the same time and was delivered as a series of lectures at Columbia University during the last months of the war, has fallen into the background of the history of critical theory.[1] Yet the title of the German translation by Alfred Schmidt has become a familiar symbol of its program: *The Critique of Instrumental Reason (Kritik der instrumentellen Vernunft)* became the emblem of critical theory after World War II, although familiarity with the title has often stood in inverse proportion to acquaintance with the text. Of course, it was possible for this study to slip into the shadows of attention not least because, according to Horkheimer's own statements, the ideas presented or developed in it had already been formulated in "The End of Reason" (1941), his last essay for the *Zeitschrift für Sozialforschung.*[2] This chapter seeks to retrieve the text from this marginal position without, however, putting it into competition with *Dialectic of Enlightenment.*

The early critical theory of the 1930s had embodied a belief in the possibility of a better, socialist society through the potential historical agency of the working class, and this will for revolutionary change was embodied in the Institute's program of interdisciplinary social research. This optimism was shaken at the end of the 1930s by three historical experiences. The barbarity of fascism, the establishment of Soviet state capitalism with the tyranny of Stalinism, and the stability of capitalism through the integrative power of mass culture together led to a radical reexamination of the underlying assumptions that informed the concept of critique employed in the 1930s.[3] *Eclipse of Reason* can be viewed as Horkheimer's principal work of disillusioned self-criticism from the second phase of critical theory.[4] Surprisingly, while distancing or even detaching itself from the program of social research, this self-criticism led to a social philosophy that heightened and generalized its theoretical claims. Horkheimer and Adorno now saw the present catastrophes rooted in a single process of the self-destruction of reason that had dominated the whole development of Western civilization. Therefore, the goal of *Eclipse of Reason* was "to inquire into the concept of rationality that underlies our contemporary industrial culture" (13/v).[5] But since it could not develop another, positive concept of reason, the critique of instrumental reason could not be certain of its own activity and, in the end, became entangled in ambiguities and aporetic justifications. The self-understanding of critique was so overshadowed by the "dark . . . future perspective of reality" that it no longer had the confidence to make the transition to a transformative praxis (cf. 14/vi, 171f./183f.) but rather saw its main effect in bringing about a reflective pause.

Both this return to *theoria* freed from action and its aporetic result, which will be demonstrated, raise the question of whether the difficulties of criticism may not have been caused by a certain overextension of the program. It might also be asked whether part of the program is not more than the whole and whether central intentions in the work's approach might be maintained and defended against the justified criticism of its aporetic outcome. Therefore, in an interpretation that closely follows the text, I will attempt to secure those critical intentions that, I believe, were not invalidated by the failure of the general program.

I

Horkheimer begins by presenting what he considers to be the currently prevailing conception of reason. According to this conception, the rational is defined as whatever is useful. In particular, what is rational is the appropriate means to given ends. Ends themselves are considered rational only insofar as "they serve the subject's interest in relation to self-preservation" (15/4). This conception of reason makes reason itself, as an instrument of self-preservation, subordinate. Thus,

Horkheimer also calls the subjective conception of reason instrumental. Subjective reason is negatively characterized by the fact that "the idea that an aim can be reasonable for its own sake . . . is utterly alien to [it]" (15/4). By this is meant not an "abstinence from reflection upon ends" generally but rather that a specific kind of justification or determination of ends has become alien.[6]

The alternative is represented by a competing conception of reason now invoked only within the history of philosophy. Horkheimer calls it, schematically, objective reason. Examples are the "great philosophical systems" of metaphysics and ontology, from Plato and Aristotle through scholasticism and German idealism. They derive the definition of humanity from the rationality of a comprehensive totality—the cosmos, being, or the idea of a highest good (cf. 16/4, 22/11, and throughout). The objectively rational is not only that which exhibits a "structure inherent in reality" (22/11) but also the resulting claim upon humanity. Objective reason is ultimately "the ability to reflect upon such an objective order" (ibid.). Its assertions make a trans-subjective, universal, and absolute claim to rationality. Viewed historically, this latter aspect brings about the replacement of "mythology as false objectivity" (18/7) by the ontological systems of objective reason. But this process of enlightenment also entails a process in which objective reason "dissolves its own objective content" (23/13). Reason's enlightened attempt to secure the objectivity of its assertions leads it to become aware of subjectivity, which it had always already contained as the guarantee of certainty (cf. 18/7). This subjectivization of the conditions of knowledge also makes the contents of knowledge subjective. Just as his locating of objective reason within the history of philosophy blurs essential differences, Horkheimer "narrates" the emergence of subjective from objective reason rather than offering a systematic account of it.[7]

If subjective reason is characterized by the purposive-rational determination of ends, where any given rational end becomes a possible means to subjective self-preservation, then objective reason is characterized by the concept of the end in itself and by substantive rationality. As Horkheimer himself indicates, this difference resembles Weber's distinction between "functional and substantive rationality" (17/6).[8] Whereas Weber works out the increase in rationality that this distinction makes possible, Horkheimer wants to describe the loss that results when the concept of the end in itself and substantive rationality disappear from the discourse of rationality. But Horkheimer himself holds that objective reason belongs irrevocably to the past. It is not only that, historically, reason has become ineffective in reality but that its claims do not stand up to the theoretical critique of subjective reason. Although objective reason cannot claim to encompass all of reason or the complete truth, Horkheimer interprets the European process of enlightenment as the growing domination of the subjective concept of reason at the expense of an irrevocably obsolete objective conception. His criticism is thus burdened from the outset with an uncertainty regarding the validity of its own standard. Horkheimer engages in critique in order to demonstrate the negative consequences of this loss. In a first, preliminary approximation, one can say that for Horkheimer the loss of ends in themselves can be seen in the experience of a lack of satisfaction and joy (cf. 42/35–36), ultimately leading to a loss of autonomy and freedom; the desubstantialization of reason, on the other hand, goes together with the experience of a loss of meaning, leading to a weakening of the binding force of rational assertion and to relativism. Together with the weakening of capacities for criticism and contradiction, both moments result in a reduction of reason to the ability to adapt skillfully to the given order of things.

Like Weber, Horkheimer interprets this historic process of change as the disintegration of knowledge of the totality. The metaphysically grounded unity of objective reason—the rational interdependence of God, world, and soul—breaks down into separate "cultural domains" that possess no encompassing rationality and in which the formal rationality of the sciences goes together with the irrationality of morality, art, and religion (28/18).[9] Horkheimer therefore traces the historical process of the separation of religion from reason, which while relieving religion from philosophical assaults, also lent it an ambiguous sort of neutrality. Thus, too, he alludes to the dissolution of political ideas such as tolerance (28f./18f.), majority rule (35/29), justice, and equality, which lose their spiritual roots in a single unified reason and, as isolated and formalized concepts, threaten to switch into their opposites. Moreover, the "inability to establish an objective order" (45/38) also affects the self-esteem of modern forms of life (43f./36f.), the possibilities of aesthetic experience, and the content of works of art.

For Horkheimer, pragmatism exemplifies the transformation of the sciences under the ascendancy of subjective reason, and he criticizes its subordination of truth-claims to the "criterion of satisfying the subject" (cf. 58/52). In all of this he tacitly follows Georg Lukács's generalization of Marx's reification thesis to all social and cultural spheres.[10] Horkheimer interprets this splitting up of objective reason as both causing and reinforcing an omnipresent cultural crisis and questions whether it can be analyzed by its own rational methods. Can this cultural crisis be conceptually understood and overcome with the help of the modern sciences? In the second chapter, "Conflicting Panaceas," Horkheimer investigates this question by examining the controversy between two contemporary schools of philosophy. He takes logical positivism as an extreme school of subjective reason and neo-Thomism as a model attempt to rehabilitate objective reason. Both are questioned as to their claims of being able to heal the cultural crisis.[11] Against "the rapidly disintegrating hierarchy of generally accepted values" (66/61), neo-Thomists seek artificially to revive the absolute values of objective reason. But thereby, Horkheimer finds, the "absolute becomes itself a means" of compensation for what is lacking in prevailing subjective reason. Positivists, as Horkheimer refers to the early Rudolf Carnap, Ernest Nagel, and Sidney Hook, view the cultural crisis as resulting "from a loss of confidence in scientific method" (64/60). Against this "loss of nerve" they pose the "identity of truth and science" (75/72) as their principle but without being able—so Horkheimer argues—to justify this principle itself. A lack of critical self-reflection and a tendency toward conformism follow from this "worship of the institutionalized sciences" (79/76).

The cures proposed by both schools thus confirm the parceling out of genuine reason; in their respective one-sidedness, they cannot halt the decay of values. Rather, they aggravate the causes of the cultural crisis by weakening the potential for comprehensive criticism. Although at the conclusion of this chapter Horkheimer speaks of "autonomous reason" as if it could serve him as an explicable standard in his own role as judge in this controversy, in fact his refutation of the cures operates with no such comprehensive concept of reason. Rather, his strategy is to point out the internal contradictions of each school. As "conflicting panaceas" they are discredited as proposals for alleviating the cultural crisis (cf. 92/91).

II

Consequently, Horkheimer does not think he can call upon the contemporary schools of philosophy. It is therefore understandable that he attempts to find another reference point at which the process of the destruction of reason is evident and from which it can be criticized, if not revised. And it is in the bearer of instrumental reason, the "autonomous subject," that Horkheimer sees the effects of the self-destruction of reason manifested. He investigates the constitutive process of this subject in the third chapter, "The Revolt of Nature." Here, the individual's relationship to his or her inner nature stands in the foreground. The chapter begins with a reformulation of the thesis already developed in *Dialectic of Enlightenment:* humanity strives to dominate nature for the sake of its mere self-preservation and passes over into the domination of other humans; and the human subject, the more it subjugates external nature in this fashion, is compelled to subjugate the nature within it and thus to deny itself (94/93). In both works, the thesis is specifically that modern civilization turns even this revolt of subjugated inner nature to its advantage.

Horkheimer's description of the disempowerement of nature can be elucidated in terms of the same features he used in characterizing the destruction of objective reason—an indication that here, for him, nature stands in for objective reason (cf. 162/173). That subjugated nature is "stripped of all intrinsic value or meaning" can be read as a kind of *desubstantialization* (101/101). What gets lost in the process is that "substance," which is nothing other than "that very life as functions of which the achievements of self-preservation find their sole definition and determination—that is, precisely what is supposed to be preserved" (*DdA,* 71/*DE,* 54–55).[12] But it is lost in the sense that humanity "cuts itself off from the awareness of itself as nature" (*DdA,* 70/*DE,* 54). As a result, "the telos of its own life becomes distorted and opaque." As with the dissolution of objective reason, here the "definition of humanity" is lost. The self constituted through the subjugation of its own nature is in no position to understand nature as a text to be brought to language (which would call for *Geist,* reason, and philosophy)—a text that, "if rightly read, will unfold a tale of infinite suffering" (122/126). The consequence of this loss of the definition of humanity is an inability to perceive the meaning of suffering and even, in a certain sense, to perceive suffering itself.[13] In the same way, a self thus constituted is prevented from projecting itself positively toward the telos of human natural history.[14] Rather, according to Horkheimer, it regresses to the original stage of its natural history, to that type of animalistic-organic life that maintains itself through unconscious mimetic adaptation to its environment (cf. 112/115; *DdA*, 212/*DE*, 180).[15]

This is in turn linked to the second element, the *loss of ends in themselves,* since nature is viewed completely as a means of subjective self-preservation. It is "an empty nature degraded to mere material, mere stuff to be dominated, without any other purpose than that of this very domination" (97/97). With regard to outer nature, the respect and responsibility that would otherwise be due to life regarded as an end in itself is lost. Horkheimer elucidates the resulting indifference toward nature with reference to the "fate of the animals in our world" (cf. 130f./135f.). With respect to inner nature, the loss of ends in themselves is, beyond that, a fundamental disqualification of the freedom of the self-preserving individual, which finally changes into heteronomy. Horkheimer captures this in the paradoxical formula of "self-preservation without the self." By this he means that the subject that maintains itself through the control and manipulation of external nature can only accomplish this insofar as it also brings its own inner nature under control. Only by doing so is it in a position to develop the self-discipline and capacity for adaptation necessary for dominating external nature. Horkheimer equates the structure of domination of external nature with that of inner nature (which has been justly criticized). Both are cases of domination as heteronomous determination. But whereas the heteronomy of outer nature has only a metaphorical meaning, the heteronomous determination of inner nature has a specific sense. This nature is expressed in one's sensual impulses, drives, and immediate inclinations, which strive for fulfillment and satisfaction. Heteronomy, in this case, means preventing or sublimating their satisfaction for the sake of other goals. But these other goals are merely possible means through which the subject maintains itself; they are means for its competence in the domination of nature and not goals that satisfy the inner nature of the subject through the realization and development of its natural abilities. This does not mean that there are two ontologically distinct worlds of ends and means; rather, what is decisive is that this repression of inner nature can be made clear by the manner in which the subject sets its goals. What is excluded is a type of self-determination in which the subject satisfies its natural impulses, develops and creatively augments its abilities, and thereby acquires the strength for autonomy and self-assertion through inner, affective gratification. The result of the self-preservation criticized by Horkheimer is a kind of self-determination in which the subject selects goals supplied to it by the rationality of the domination of nature, goals it pursues without experiencing inner satisfaction.

On the one hand, the quantitative range of possibilities for subjective choice is thereby increased; but on the other hand, this "accretion of freedom has produced a change in the character of freedom" (98/98). Just as the interchangeability of what can be selected shows that no goal is any longer aspired to for its own sake (see 101/101), so the adapted self's inability to be satisfied shows that it does not succeed but fails along this path toward its self-preservation.

One can thus speak of a "liquidation of the subject" (94/93) only in a limited sense: what is done away with is the "supposedly autonomous individual" (96/96) who can resist and criticize reality (see 110f./111f.). What remains is the individual who must submit to reality, who must accommodate himself in order to maintain himself. Horkheimer generalizes this diagnosis to the whole process of civilization: "This deliberate (as opposed to reflexive) making of oneself like the environment is a universal principle of civilization" (113/115).

However, the repressed and degraded nature within humanity, Horkheimer surmises, "seems to be taking its revenge" (103/104). In order to make this thesis plausible, Horkheimer draws a parallel between the psychoanalytic conception of the father-child relationship and the relationship between civilization and the individual.[16] Just as the unpleasurable repression of the child's natural impulses leads to an enmity against the father, so the adapted individual harbors a latent resentment against civilization, since he neither has the capacity for autonomous resistance nor are "the renunciations of instinctual urges expected from him . . . adequately compensated" (109/111). The revolt of repressed instinctual desires leads to "officious conformity or to crime" (111/114). Modern civilization can make use of this rebellion and the resulting compulsion to conform by unleashing it in the service of its system. Horkheimer makes this clear in the case of National Socialism (117f./121f.) and the popular Darwinism of American culture (120f./123f.). Both absolutize nature at the expense of reason and individual autonomy. The former does so in order to unleash a "satanic synthesis of reason and nature" (119/122) in the manipulable masses, the latter in order to establish a false equation between nature and reason through the slogan of "survival of the fittest."

For Horkheimer, however, the telos of reason is not an identity with nature, which only degrades reason, but rather reconciliation with it. Reconciliation means "assisting and supporting nature" in such a way that at the same time "independent thought" (123/127) is set free. Here the critique of instrumental reason postulates as genuine reason a contemplative theory over which critique, according to its own insights, can no longer exercise control. Moreover, the goal of this reason, reconciliation, is marked by a "spirit of humility" (120/124) toward nature. With the call for an "understanding of nature in and for itself" (102/103) in the "remembrance of nature in the subject" (*DdA*, 55/*DE*, 40), Horkheimer and Adorno must forgo a theoretical explication of their goal, which secretly "proclaims a Being of nature independent of the subject."[17] The grounds of this twofold rehabilitation of "an objectivistic ontology of nature" and classical *theoria*[18] lie in an undifferentiated approach to the analysis of individual self-preservation. Horkheimer restricts the process of human work upon nature to that of an individual subject who represses his or her inner nature in the categories of the domination of outer nature. As a result, the qualities particular to the socially organized domination of nature go unnoticed, as does the difference between work upon external nature and the intrapsychic process of instinctual repression.[19] Horkheimer also neglects the fact that the individual self develops not only through the renunciation of instincts but also by engaging in social interaction and that civilizational imperatives do not affect the child directly through the commands of the father.[20] It is especially limiting to project the whole history of civilization out of the categories of individual self-preservation qua repression of inner nature. At this point, as Michael Theunissen has pointed out, society and history are demoted in favor of nature, which gains theoretical priority.[21] In the end, all these limitations and failures to differentiate overburden the critique with aporetic justificatory claims that can no longer be redeemed.[22]

III

One can reject the burden of proof imposed by these generalizations and still attempt to place the negative aspects of the predominance of instrumental reason into another framework. Horkheimer himself undertakes such an argument in the fourth chapter, "Rise and Decline of the Individual." Against the contours of a view of the "true individual," which he derives from the history of ideas, he traces the decline of the individual in modern civilization. This reliance on the history of ideas leads one to expect that the standard by which Horkheimer measures the negativity of this decline makes only a historically relative truth claim. Of course, the argumentation does not only pursue this line within intellectual history. It becomes interwoven with further themes: the modifications of modern self-realization and an interpretation of individual suffering, solidaristic compassion, and resistance informed by Schopenhauer. Horkheimer takes up these themes because he cannot ground his critique in reality on the basis of reflections drawn from the history of ideas alone.

In his historical sketch of the "category of the individual" Horkheimer employs a general interpretive framework: the quality of the individual's self-relation is correlated with her or his critical relationship to society, and both dimensions are used to assess the rise and decline of the individual. In a few vaguely sketched stages, Horkheimer follows the history of the rising individual: from the "prelude" in the ancient hero (125/131), through the Greek citizen as the "individual par excellence" (126f./131f.) and the Christian individual with the "doctrine of the immortal soul" (132/137), to the prototypical individuality of the "independent entrepreneur" of the liberal era (133f./139f.). I want to draw attention to only two decisive transformations that, according to Horkheimer, have determined the category of the individual.

The individual has been considered autonomous ever since Socrates attributed the individual's conscious choice of his or her life conduct to conscience. The degree of one's deliberate, ethical life conduct also determined one's self-sufficiency and one's power to assert oneself against social demands. With its doctrine of the indivisible and "immortal soul [as] an image of God" (132/137), Christianity elevated the individual worth of every person, but at the same time it relativized "concrete, mortal individuality." In Christianity, the conflict between the "denial of the will to self-preservation on earth" and the "preservation of the eternal soul" is eased through "the repression of vital instincts" (132/137f.). The "new ideal," to which the individual orients herself through internalization, is the "Christian doctrine of love, of *caritas*" (ibid.). Through it, the autonomous life conduct of the individual is oriented to the communicative relationship of neighborly love.

The modern individual looks to programs of self-realization to compensate for the loss of a determination of humanity that results from the dissolution of objective reason.[23] The degree of autonomous self-realization is shown by the individual's power to resist social demands. This delineation, however, is not supposed to result in complete isolation, separation, or atomization. For this reason, Horkheimer must specify a moment in the individual's movement of self-relation—which he treats as the sole source of independence—that still directs the realization of the individual to the social generality, as in Kant's "humanity within us" and Christianity's ideal of *caritas*.

The individuality of the "independent entrepreneur," with which Horkheimer concludes his historical précis of the rising individual, is characterized by a moment that at least potentially goes beyond subjective reason. In order to exercise foresight in protecting her or his property, each person is forced "to encourage independent thinking" (134/140). This corresponds to the "idle thinking" that requires leisure and peaceful contemplation[24]—characterizations that indicate that such thinking has the character of an end in itself. On the other hand, this moment of the bourgeois individual, however ideological, is supposed to put him in a position "to serve the interests of society" (134/140).

But it is not compelling to locate the basis for the modern individual's ability to transcend the predominance of subjective reason through self-realization solely in the "use of the intellectual functions" (135/140). In a brief excursus I would like to indicate another mode of modern self-realization that Horkheimer goes into only negatively, insofar as it is destroyed in the culture industry. It is best exemplified in the development of autonomous art and involves individualization "as an experiment with oneself, as a truly purposeless way in which the individual comes to experience what he is."[25] Here too—so one could interpret this experimental self-realization—it is in the experience of activities undertaken as ends in themselves that the individual goes beyond her or his given self-knowledge. That can happen through independent thinking but also through other modes of activity and expression. Activities that are performed only as means for the realization of pregiven ends would, of course, be aspects of self-realization but not ones in which the individual experiments and is open to new experiences. The disclosure of new structures of reality and new moments of self-understanding, an openness to experience and an opening up of the subject through the experience of activities that are (also) performed as ends in themselves—these things indicate an aesthetic conception of modern self-realization. They are seen as the expression of individual spontaneity, the self-realization of an authentic self,[26] and suggest that the unity of self-realization be described in terms of aesthetic categories, as a successful combining of elements.

Yet the happiness of successful self-realization provides no objective criteria for whether the happiness of one is also to be linked to the happiness of others and, if possible, to the happiness of all. With respect to the intersubjective conditions of modern self-realization, then, from this aesthetic position Horkheimer can only postulate a mutual effort not to make one another into means but rather to respect one another mutually as ends; he cannot, however, convincingly ground such respect in the modes of experimental self-realization. "The creation of a social condition in which one is not made the means of another is at the same time the fulfillment of the concept of reason, which now threatens to disappear in the split between objective truth and functional thinking."[27] We will see that he attempts to develop the moment of modern self-realization oriented to social universality from another, indeed contrary position—namely, individual suffering. The decline and "contemporary crisis of the individual" come about, according to Horkheimer, because in fully developed capitalist societies, the economic basis for individuality no longer depends on the autonomous action of the individual but on one's integration into social and economic organizations and one's ability to adapt to them. However, behavior adapted to the organized and bureaucratized social environment also affects the individual's self-referential relation.

It requires a sacrifice of the "hope of ultimate self-realization" (135/141).

The modes of self-realization are transformed into culturally pre-determined forms of life that, despite their diversity, are essentially similar and stripped of the character of being ends in themselves. Imitation and adjustment, which ensure survival in the social relations of production, are repeated in mass culture. There is no longer a "cleavage between culture and production" (138/145); the "gigantic loudspeaker of the culture industry" only duplicates the conformist pressures of a wretched economic reality.[28] Despite apparent plurality, this leveling encompasses all social classes, "the lower as well as the higher social groups, the worker no less than the businessman" (137/143). Thus, Horkheimer sees the assimilation of labor unions to the model of profit-oriented businesses (cf. 141/148) as the height of the working class's integration as a "new force in social life" (143/150).

He illustrates the decline of the autonomous individual with the figure of the engineer[29]—perhaps the symbol of this age—who is said to understand things not for their own sake but rather "in accordance with their being fitted into a scheme, no matter how alien to their own inner structure," and to adopt this same principle for his own self-understanding (144/151). The individual thereby loses his or her historically developed capacities for resisting and criticizing social demands. But he or she also loses certain self-referential capacities, especially the ability to experience something as something new and through such experiences to overcome oneself and expand one's horizons. He or she is "closed to dreams of a basically different world" (143/150). Where culturally reinforced societal pressures to repeat and imitate force individuals into the schemas offered by society (cf. 151/158), the decay of experience brings with it a loss of awareness that self-realization has been impoverished, and thus a loss of awareness of the suffering that means. The "discouragement of our time," Horkheimer put it later (1954), is found in the fact "that today people no longer permit themselves to experience the suffering caused by social conditions, but rather accommodate themselves to what is inflicted on them, if not actually approve of it."[30] Servile adaptation, poverty of experience, imperviousness to the qualitatively new, and an inability to suffer are the marks of a reification become total. The self-realization of individuals loses the character of being an end in itself. Instead, as Horkheimer concludes, individuals become "an agglomeration of instruments without a purpose of their own" (144/ 151).

IV

The decline of the individual through the domination of an all-encompassing instrumental rationality is diagnosed from the perspective of the history of ideas, but it would be disastrous if this pessimistic diagnosis of the times came true. If reification were so hermetically sealed, there would no longer be anyone who could indict and resist the decline.[31] According to its own premises, this critique, developed out of the history of ideas, is only one opinion among others, and if all were happy, its relative truth would not even be contested by anyone—even if this happiness were, as the critic believes, illusory. But Horkheimer does not reckon on a completely closed world of instrumental reason. He believes "that the individual, despite everything, does not entirely disappear in the new impersonal institutions." This hope,[32] which also finds expression in his claim "that man is still better than the world he lives in" (151/159), is admittedly linked to a precarious thesis and a historical experience of horror.

Contrary to all social pessimism, "there are still some forces of resistance left within man" and "the spirit of humanity is still alive, if not in the individual as a member of social groups, at least in the individual as far as he is let alone" (135/141). This thesis, surprising at first, becomes more comprehensible when interpreted in connection with motifs from Schopenhauer, who, as is well known, influenced Horkheimer throughout his life.[33] The individual who is "let alone" is first of all the individual who, without any comfort and without any metaphysically derived meaning, lives with his or her finitude and mortality. He or she is the suffering individual, whose sufferings are not appeased by society's false offers of happiness. Wherever there is still an experience and awareness of individual suffering, there is also, according to Schopenhauer's admittedly metaphysical doctrine, compassion "in the sense of being directly motivated by the suffering of another."[34] The spirit of humanity that Horkheimer sees persisting in the individual, the non-Christian echo of the Christian soul, is this "solidarity with those who are suffering, the community of humanity abandoned in the universe."[35]

For this reason Horkheimer can also say that the misery of "workers of earlier days," when they still suffered from their oppression, was the "misery of individual human beings, and therefore linked them with any miserable people in any country and any sector of society" (142/149). The solidarity of compassion, one might say, kindled by the observation of individual suffering, links—in a negative way— the self-realization of one individual with that of another and, finally, with that of all individuals. Human beings would thus experience their solidarity not in happiness but in misfortune, suffering, and pain. Pain "leads the resistant and the wayward, the phantast and utopian back to themselves. It reduces them to the body, to part of the body. Pain levels and equalizes everything, man and man, man and animal."[36] Horkheimer notes this solidarity-producing effect of compassion when, with Schopenhauer, he sees individual suffering as the spur to the struggle for "the abolition of misery."[37] "But the capacity to suffer from what is wrong is one of the preconditions for things getting better."[38]

Horkheimer vehemently resists the view that the negation of suffering—which defines happiness for him, as for Schopenhauer and Freud[39]—can be used retroactively for the constitution of meaning.[40] That is precisely his general critical reservation against all systems of objective reason, against metaphysics, religion, or the philosophy of history, which seek to compensate for the senselessness of suffering by elevating it into some larger framework. In such ideological justifications of injustice and suffering, Horkheimer sees, rather, a weakening of the power of resistance and of the commitment to abolishing suffering (cf. 162/174). There is thus no positive, absolute concept of the good or of happiness against which Horkheimer measures the negativity of suffering. This is, of course, correct, since happiness is not a directly intended result of our will but rather shows that in the realization of what we will, we ourselves are truly at stake.

What is it, then, that defines the negativity of suffering? According to Schopenhauer, "suffering" occurs when the human will is "restrained by an obstacle standing between it and its present goal."[41] Although for Schopenhauer "all striving [arises] . . . from deficiency," and even if there is "no ultimate goal of striving, thus no measure or purpose of suffering," the will's respective goals must be viewed as satisfactory and good for the subject in order for its hindrance to be experienced as an evil. Schopenhauer thinks—and Horkheimer seems to agree—that the degree of suffering (that is, the measure of its negativity) depends on the will's respective degree of consciousness. "Thus, to the same degree as knowledge becomes clear, and consciousness is heightened, so too the agony increases, an agony which therefore achieves its highest degree in man and, further, is greater there as knowledge becomes more clear, as man is more intelligent; thus it is the genius who suffers the most."[42] However, this view is convincing only if the degree of knowledge means the degree of valuation, the validity of the reasons for the respective goals, and not simply an increase in consciousness. Such value judgments, which may be more or less deliberate, are always subjective valuations that express what the subject considers good or valuable. Thus, where suffering is "consciously" experienced in this sense, it refers to the failure or hindrance of a true, deliberate willing of, first, goals that the subject considers good, and then of that which is good for the subject as a whole—self-realization.

Subjective valuations have an affective component that makes it clear that what is willed is value-relevant and reveals the negativity of the failure of self-realization.[43] The failure to attain particular goals shows itself in feelings such as disappointment, displeasure, and indifference, which afflict us when we do not achieve something we want. In the negative feelings and negative dispositions we experience as suffering, we can see that by being hindered in the realization of our goals, we are hindered in our self-realization. Dispositions—unhappiness and suffering, negatively, and happiness and satisfaction, positively—reveal the success or failure of self-realization.

Horkheimer treats this, though inadequately, under the heading of "the repression of inner nature." In the discontentment of inner nature, we may recognize a sign that the individual's manner of self-preservation does not involve his or her true self. But Horkheimer does not adequately take into consideration these affective components of suffering. According to the negative findings of his cultural criticism, the capacity to suffer is lost under the domination of instrumental reason, since individuals are prevented from becoming sufficiently aware of the goals of their self-realization. But the possibility of individual suffering could not be precluded simply by a manipulation of consciousness; there would have to be a similarly total heteronomy of affects and dispositions. That is difficult to imagine, for many reasons. Of course, the culture industry manipulates the socially valid forms of expressing suffering,[44] and thereby also the experience of suffering itself. It manipulates the individual and social interpretation of suffering, but that presupposes that there is individual suffering to begin with.

Even Horkheimer, who does not believe that the "state of delusion" will become total, ties his hopes to actual historical suffering. In the often-quoted closing paragraph of the fourth chapter, Horkheimer summons his historical witnesses, whose sufferings point to the "core of true individuality" (152/161):

The real individuals of our time are the martyrs who have gone through infernos of suffering and degradation in their resistance to conquest and oppression, not the inflated personalities of popular culture, the conventional dignitaries. These unsung heroes consciously exposed their existence as individuals to the terroristic annihilation that others undergo unconsciously through the social process. The anonymous martyrs of the concentration camps are the symbols of the humanity that is striving to be born. The task of philosophy is to translate what they have done into language that will be heard, even though their finite voices have been silenced by tyranny. (152/161)

But the horrendous suffering in the concentration camps was not always necessarily connected with solidarity and resistance. Barrington Moore has proposed a nuanced, differentiated analysis of the relationship of suffering, solidarity, and resistance that shows the conditions (for example, strong religious or political convictions, cultural definitions of suffering, mechanisms for the suppression of revolt, and so on) under which victims will take up resistance and how far they will solidarize with others in their situation.[45] In any case, this historical analysis suggests an empirical refutation of Schopenhauer's thesis of an immediate connection between individual suffering and compassion. Thus, too, the claim with which Horkheimer builds this thesis into his overall conception is also dubious. The "true individual," because he or she experiences suffering consciously, is supposed to pass directly over to compassion and universal solidarity (the "community of humanity abandoned in the universe") with the sufferings of others. But such a generalization of compassion does not automatically result from beholding the sufferings of others. Often we feel compassion, but sometimes only indifference, toward their suffering. Even spontaneous and "natural compassion" requires deliberation in order to be applied correctly. It must "be an active, reflective attitude, which involves a concept of others' welfare and suffering."[46] But the latter implies a specific interpretation of both the existentially inevitable suffering of mortal human beings and the avoidable suffering inflicted by people on one another. Against the background of this interpretation of the human condition, human beings, as creatures capable of suffering, are objects of compassion. As such, they are respected in view of their capacity to experience suffering, a respect expressed in the obligation not to harm and to help in need. The universalization of natural compassion then means the universalization of respect for human beings as being capable of suffering.[47]

Animals, however, are also capable of suffering; they, and possibly even further domains of living nature, can be the object of such universal respect.[48] From this perspective Horkheimer's call for a reconciling association with nature can be given a completely plausible interpretation: what is meant is respect for all beings of living nature that are capable of suffering (and, in part, of self-determination), a respect revealed in compassion for the suffering of animals, and beyond that results in the moral obligation not to harm and to help in need.

Philosophical reflection on compassion for the suffering of another thus does not lead to a "core" of individuality that directly implies universalization but rather makes it clear that the universalization of compassion depends on a deliberate disposition to respect beings capable of suffering—an attitude that, for its own part, depends on specific interpretations of the human condition. The task of philosophy would then be to inquire into the possible grounds—that is, into the truth-claim—of the universalization of this disposition. To that extent it is still unclear whether and how the intended solidarity of compassion can be derived, together with the goal of true self-realization, from conscious individual suffering.

V

In the two preceding chapters on "The Revolt of Nature" and "Rise and Decline of the Individual," the sufferings of damaged nature and

failed self-realization were invoked to demonstrate the negative character of the domination of instrumental reason; their proper interpretation was defined as the task of philosophy. But in the final chapter
of his study, "On the Concept of Philosophy," Horkheimer does not
really take up the task he has set himself. To be sure, he reiterates
that "philosophy is at one with art in reflecting passion through language and thus transferring it to the sphere of experience and memory" (167/179), but the precise meaning of this is not clarified by simply
invoking the "genuine mimetic function" of language.[49] What was
needed was to provide a theoretical explication of mimesis in order to
demonstrate the truth-claims of critique.[50] Thus, the definition of
philosophy as interpreter of the suffering inflicted on nature and humanity by the domination of instrumental reason remains merely
programmatic.

Instead, Horkheimer relies on the possibility of a self-criticism of
reason, which is supposed to undertake the true goal of philosophical
thinking: "to essay a reconciliation" (153/162). Two approaches to this
definition of philosophy can be distinguished. The first sees the task
of philosophy in a denunciatory self-criticism of the competing conceptions of reason and remains within a strict (historical) relativism.
The second approach aims at recovering a comprehensive concept of
reason through which the critique of instrumental reason could be
justified. The first approach sets the tone for the entire chapter. I
would like to show how it passes over into the second approach without being able to meet the requirements appropriate to it.

In the controversy between competing conceptions of reason, philosophy can neither deliver prescriptions nor decide by definition (cf.
155f./165f.). Horkheimer sees its task as being "to foster a mutual
critique" (163/174). Since, according to his diagnosis, subjective reason prevails in the present, "critique must necessarily be carried on
with an emphasis on objective reason" (ibid.). Horkheimer himself
has thus far criticized instrumental reason from this perspective. He
sees the relative right of objective reason, which his one-sided critique
brings to bear, in "the insight that self-preservation can be achieved
only in a supra-individual order, that is to say, through social solidarity" (164/176). But in light of the way Horkheimer has conceived subjective self-preservation throughout the text to this point—under the
categories of the domination of nature by a singular individual—he
can introduce the idea of an orientation toward social univer-

sality only by defining humanity in a way that must appear to violate individual autonomy. This is precisely what characterizes the obsolescence of objective reason, the dissolution of its "substantive" truth-claim. Faced with this difficulty in his one-sided criticism, Horkheimer then seeks out various possible solutions but leaves their contradictory presuppositions undiscussed.

An immanent critique that negates prevailing rationality's truth-claim and the "brash claims of reality" (170/182) remains strictly relativistic, itself unable to call on an absolute reason. It pursues "the salvation of relative truths from the ruins of false absolutes." But insofar as it points out the self-contradictory character of the respective conceptions of reason, it is also destructive. Its critique is "the denunciation of what is currently called reason" (174/187); in the final sentence of the work, Horkheimer calls this the "greatest service reason can render" (ibid.). An example of such criticism would be the rebuke to the claims of one-sided scientific doctrines to heal the cultural crisis (cf. 63f./58f., 170/182). The demonstration that the instrumental reason of subjective self-preservation ultimately destroys the individual whose self-realization it originally aimed to promote is also denunciatory. Yet this finding yields no objectively justifiable alternative. It shows only that these approaches do not work.[51]

A second attempted solution rehabilitates the concept of the critique of ideology. "On the one hand it [philosophy] appraises society by the light of the very ideas that it recognizes as its highest values; on the other, it is aware that these ideas reflect the taints of reality" (167/178). These ideas raise a "universal claim" (166/178) over against the particular interests of individuals. Claim and reality are compared with one another, but it remains an open question whether the ideas justly make a claim to reason or do so only historically, de facto. The self-understanding of this relativistic critique of ideology is admittedly paradoxical; it was precisely the argument of Adorno[52] and Horkheimer that an immanently conducted critique of ideology will come up empty if cultural ideas merely duplicate social reality and there is no longer any difference between ideological claim and false reality. Therefore, Horkheimer sees himself compelled to presuppose "that at this stage of complete alienation the idea of truth is still accessible" (165/177).

What is decisive is the underlying concept of truth. In the tradition of Platonism, Horkheimer defines it as "the correspondence of name and thing," "language and reality" (168/180). Of course, "genuine philosophy," within which this concept of truth "dwells," would also have to have at its disposal criteria for correspondence, and hence a nonideological concept of reason. But then the denunciatory version of the self-criticism of reason has already passed over into the attempt to recover a comprehensive concept of reason.

Horkheimer sees this concept preserved, in however distorted a form, in the "great ideals of civilization—justice, equality, freedom"; "they are . . . the only formulated testimonies we possess" (169/182). Philosophy is to secure for itself the rational potential of these ideas; though it denies their claim to "ultimate and eternal truth," it grants "that the basic cultural ideas have truth values" (170/182). This view is contradictory. If in critically examining the relation between ideal and reality philosophy can "transcend them" (ibid.), then it may do so only when, on the side of the ideals, its criterion of truth is justified. The "basic difference between the ideal and the real" (171/183) characteristic of this "true philosophy" is at the same time a relapse into metaphysics.[53]

Adorno, consequentially, transferred the theoretical intention of truth to the mimetic capacity.[54] And in *Negative Dialectics*, he showed why, in his view, truth defined as the correspondence between concept and reality reinstates the domination of identity thinking.[55] By contrast, Horkheimer persists with aporetic "on the one hand, on the other hand" constructions. He can only evoke a concept of reason able to wield a concept of truth that would heal the "disease of reason." It would have to be a form of reason that is not infected with the disease of "reason in civilization as we have known it thus far" (164/176), hence a form of reason that is genetically prior to all reason that, from the outset, has borne the subjugation of nature as its mark of Cain.[56] He believes of such a form of reason, oriented to reconciliation with nature, that "by being the instrument of reconciliation, it will be more than an instrument" (165/177)—a paradoxical formulation, which once more only points out the failure of the attempt to recover a comprehensive concept of reason.

In his careful reconstruction of the critique of instrumental reason, Jürgen Habermas has given a severe account of its aporetic outcome and convincingly demonstrated why Horkheimer and Adorno had to run aground in these aporias insofar as they wanted to reinstate a universal concept of reason. They set out the critique of instrumental

reason in the categories of a philosophy of consciousness that itself
has no other conceptual apparatus at its disposal than that which can
be derived from the cognitive and instrumental relationship between
subject and object.[57] From this perspective, validity claims are assimilated to claims to power.[58] The failure of attempts to use this conceptual apparatus for a theoretical explication of undistorted subject-subject
relationships indicates to Habermas the need to carry out a "paradigm shift" from the philosophy of consciousness to a pragmatic theory of communication. By doing so, he can secure a comprehensive
and differentiated concept of rationality able to serve as a standard
for the critique of instrumental reason. In the differentiated program
of critical social theory, in which Habermas joins with the early critical
theory of the 1930s, the content of the critique of instrumental reason
is reconstructed in terms of the loss of meaning and freedom.[59]

Yet the negative phenomena that sparked Horkheimer's critique
seem peculiarly pale against the background of a universal concept of
communicative rationality, for a communicative, procedural reason
loses its grasp when dealing with the evaluation of autonomously chosen forms of life as a whole.[60] In Habermas's view, the success of an
autonomously determined project of self-realization cannot be decided by moral standards of justice but only by the criteria of the good
life, if only these were at our disposal.[61] But it was precisely in the
phenomena of failed self-realization that Horkheimer demonstrated
the negativity of instrumental reason. The reading of the text attempted here seeks to insist on this intention of Horkheimer's.

Translated by Kenneth Baynes and John McCole

Notes

1. Max Horkheimer, *Eclipse of Reason* (New York, 1947); German translation by Alfred
Schmidt, "Zur Kritik der instrumentellen Vernunft," in Horkheimer, *Zur Kritik der
instrumentellen Vernunft. Aus den Vorträgen und Aufzeichnungen seit Kriegsende* (Frankfurt
am Main, 1967), 11–174.

2. [Translator's note: "The End of Reason" was originally published in English in *Studies in Philosophy and Social Science* 9 (1941); it has been reprinted in Andrew Arato and
Eike Gebhardt, eds., *The Frankfurt School Reader* (New York, 1982).]

3. See Helmut Dubiel, *Wissenschaftsorganisation und politische Erfahrung. Studien zur frühen Kritischen Theorie* (Frankfurt, 1978), 87ff. English translation: *Theory and Politics:
Studies in the Development of Critical Theory* (Cambridge, 1985), 69ff.

4. On the phases of Horkheimer's theoretical development, see Gerd-Walter Küsters, *Der Kritikbegriff der Kritischen Theorie Max Horkheimers* (Frankfurt/New York, 1980), 196, and Alfred Schmidt, *Drei Studien über Materialismus. Schopenhauer, Horkheimer, Glücksproblem* (Frankfurt/Berlin/Vienna: 1979), 81ff; on the periodization of critical theory, Dubiel, *Theory and Politics;* and on the history of critical theory, Martin Jay, *The Dialectical Imagination: A History of the Frankfurt School and the Institute of Social Research, 1923–1950* (Boston, 1973).

5. Page references in parentheses within the text refer to the German translation, "Zur Kritik der instrumentellen Vernunft," followed by the English, *Eclipse of Reason* (see note 1, above).

6. Thus Hermann Lübbe sees the great danger not in an inability to set goals but in the uncontrolled consequences of progress, which then fall under the competence of the technocratic intelligentsia. "Instrumentelle Vernunft. Zur Kritik eines kritischen Begriffes," in Lübbe, *Fortschritt als Orientierungsproblem* (Freiburg, 1975), 87. On this "conservative critique" of Horkheimer, see Georg Lohmann, "Den Schuh muß man ja nicht anziehen. Zur Zivilisationsphilosophie Hermann Lübbes," *Katabole* 2 (1981).

7. See, for example, transitions in the text that employ temporal phrases: "For a long time . . . was prevalent (16/4); "This process was gradually extended . . ." (18/7); "Later the concept of reason . . ." (30/21), and others.

8. Cf. Jürgen Habermas, *Theorie des kommunkativen Handelns* (Frankfurt, 1981), 1:225f., 461ff. English translation: *The Theory of Communicative Action* [= *TCA*] (Boston, 1987), 1:157f., 345ff.

9. Ibid., 102f., 463f./*TCA*, 1:66f., 346f.

10. See Georg Lukács, *Geschichte und Klassenbewußtsein* (Darmstadt/Neuwied, 1981), 170ff. English translation: *History and Class Consciousness* (Cambridge, 1971). On the interpretation of the theory of reification within critical theory, see Habermas, *Theorie des kommunikativen Handelns,* 1:474ff./*TCA,* 1:355ff. On Lukács's theory of reification, see Lohmann, Authentisches und verdinglichtes Leben. Neuere Literatur zu Georg Lukács' *Geschichte und Klassenbewußtsein*," *Philosophische Rundschau* 30, no. 3/4 (1983): 253–71, and Lohmann, *Indifferenz und Gesellschaft. Eine kritische Auseinandersetzung mit Marx* (Frankfurt, 1991).

11. Horkheimer relies here upon a contemporary collection of essays, Y. H. Krikorian, ed., *Naturalism and the Human Spirit* (New York, 1944).

12. *DdA* = Max Horkheimer and Theodor W. Adorno, *Dialektik der Aufklärung* (Amsterdam, 1947); *DE* = *Dialectic of Enlightenment* (New York, 1972).

13. Cf. Küsters, *Der Kritikbegriff der Kritischen Theorie Max Horkheimers,* 108f.

14. On the concept of natural history in Adorno, see Friedemann Grenz, *Adornos Philosophie in Grundbegriffen* (Frankfurt, 1974), 57ff., 160ff.

15. For a critique of this conception, see Axel Honneth, *Kritik der Macht. Reflexionsstufen einer kritischen Gesellschaftstheorie* (Frankfurt, 1985). English translation: *The Critique of Power: Reflective Stages in a Critical Social Theory* (Cambridge, 1991), 39ff.

16. For the influence of psychoanalysis on critical theory, see Wolfgang Bonß, "Psychoanalyse als Wissenschaft und Kritik. Zur Freudrezeption der Frankfurter Schule,"

in Wolfgang Bonß and Axel Honneth, eds., *Sozialforschung als Kritik* (Frankfurt, 1982), and especially Jessica Benjamin, "Die Antinomien des patriarchalischen Denkens. Kritische Theorie und Psychoanalyse," in Bonß and Honneth, eds., *Sozialforschung als Kritik.*

17. Michael Theunissen, *Gesellschaft und Geschichte. Zur Kritik der Kritischen Theorie* (Berlin, 1969), 18; cf. also W. Leiss, "The Problem of Man and Nature in the Work of the Frankfurt School," *Philosophy and Social Sciences* 5 (1975): 163ff., and Habermas, *Theorie des kommunkativen Handelns,* 1:508f./*TCA,* 1:379f.

18. Cf. Theunissen, *Gesellschaft und Geschichte,* 19.

19. Cf. Honneth, *Critique of Power,* and Küsters, *Der Kritikbegriff der Kritschen Theorie Max Horkheimers,* 179f.

20. Cf. Honneth, *Critique of Power.*

21. Theunissen, *Gesellschaft und Geschichte,* 18f.

22. Cf. also Thomas Baumeister and Jens Kulenkampff, "Geschichtsphilosophie und philosophische Ästhetik," *Neue Hefte für Philosophie* 5 (1973).

23. Cf. Michael Theunissen, *Selbstverwirklichung und Allgemeinheit* (Berlin/New York, 1982).

24. Cf. Horkheimer, "Vernunft und Selbsterhaltung," in H. Ebeling, ed., *Subjektivität und Selbsterhaltung* (Frankfurt, 1976), 61.

25. Theunissen, *Selbstverwirklichung und Allgemeinheit,* 2.

26. Cf. Bernhard Lypp, "Selbsterhaltung und ästhetische Erfahrung," in Burkhardt Lindner and W. Martin Lüdke, eds., *Materialien zur ästhetischen Theorie Theodor W. Adornos* (Frankfurt, 1979).

27. Max Horkheimer, *Sozialphilosphische Studien,* ed. Werner Brede (Frankfurt, 1972), 57.

28. On changes in Horkheimer's concept of culture, see Jay, *The Dialectical Imagination,* 212ff.; Dubiel, *Theory and Politics;* and J. F. Schmucker, *Adorno—Logik des Zerfalls* (Stuttgart, 1977), 81f. For the various interpretations and changes in the concept of culture, see chapter 8 in this book. On the theory of mass culture, see Douglas Kellner, "Kulturindustrie und Massenkommunikation. Die Kritische Theorie und ihre Folgen," in Bonß and Honneth, eds., *Sozialforschung als Kritik;* for a critical analysis, see Habermas, *Theorie des kommunikativen Handelns,* 2:571ff./*TCA,* 2:389ff.

29. Hermann Lübbe saw this as a "defamation" against which the technocratic intelligentsia should be defended. "Instrumentelle Vernunft," 121ff.

30. Horkheimer, *Sozialphilosphische Studien,* 202f.; cf. Küsters, *Der Kritikbegriff der Kritischen Theorie Max Horkheimers,* 141ff.

31. On the thesis of a hermetically sealed society, see Schmucker, *Adorno—Logik des Zerfalls.*

32. It is at the same time the "redemption of the hopeless." On the theological motives for this hope, see Wiebrecht Riess, "Die Rettung des Hoffnunglosen," *Zeitschrift für philosophische Forschung* 30 (1976): 69–81.

33. Alfred Schmidt, in particular, has always pointed this out. For example, see Schmidt, *Drei Studien über Materialismus,* 81ff., and chapter 2 in this book.

34. Arthur Schopenhauer, "Preisschrift über die Grundlage der Moral," in Schopenhauer, *Sämtliche Werke,* ed. W. Freiherr von Löhneysen (Darmstadt, 1980), 3:743.

35. Horkheimer, "Die Aktualität Schopenhauers," in *Zur Kritik der instrumentellen Vernunft,* 258–59. English translation: "Schopenhauer Today," in Horkheimer, *Critique of Instrumental Reason* (New York, 1974), 75. Cf. also Horkheimer, *Kritische Theorie: Eine Dokumentation* (Frankfurt, 1968), 1:46, 95.

36. Horkheimer, "The End of Reason," in Arato and Gebhardt, eds., *The Frankfurt School Reader,* 46.

37. Cf. also "Die Aktualität Schopenhauers," 259/"Schopenhauer Today," 75.

38. Horkheimer, *Sozialphilosophische Studien,* 203; cf. Horkheimer, *Kritische Theorie,* I:259ff.

39. Cf. Alfred Schmidt, *Drei Studien über Materialismus,* 172f.

40. Cf. Horkheimer, *Kritische Theorie,* 1:259 and Schopenhauer, *Die Welt als Wille und Vorstellung,* in *Sämtliche Werke,* 1:438. On the relation between happiness and suffering, cf. also Werner Post, *Kritische Theorie und metaphysischer Pessimismus. Zum Spätwerk Max Horkheimers* (Munich, 1971), 101f. Horkheimer disagreed with Walter Benjamin over the question of the significance of past suffering, an exchange that Helmut Peukert has vividly reconstructed in *Wissenschaftstheorie—Handlungstheorie—Fundamentale Theologie* (Frankfurt, 1978), 305ff.

41. Schopenhauer, *Die Welt als Wille und Vorstellung,* 425.

42. Ibid., 425f., 406.

43. On moods and affects as disclosing the will's valuations, see Ursula Wolf, "Über den Sinn moralischer Verpflichtung" (Habilitationsschrift, Freie Universität Berlin, 1983), 192ff., published as *Das Problem des moralischen Sollens* (Berlin/New York, 1984).

44. Cf. Horkheimer and Adorno, *Dialectic of Enlightenment,* 120ff.; see also Schmucker, *Adorno—Logik des Zerfalls,* 94f.

45. Barrington Moore, *Ungerechtigkeit. Die sozialen Ursachen von Unterordnung und Widerstand* (Frankfurt, 1982), esp. 99f. English original: *Injustice: The Social Bases of Obedience and Revolt* (White Plains, 1978).

46. Wolf, "Über den Sinn moralischer Verpflichtung," 89.

47. Ibid., 156f.

48. Ibid., 166f.

Georg Lohmann

49. On the concept of mimesis, see Lypp, "Selbsterhaltung und ästhetische Erfahrung" and Baumeister and Kuhlenkampff, "Geschichtsphilosophie und philosophische Ästhetik." What is interesting here is that since language mimetically "reflects the longings of the oppressed and the plight of nature," Horkheimer sees the reconciling achievement of philosophy in its transference of this reflection into the "sphere of experience and memory" (167/179). But in this lies a return to the "*vita contemplativa*" (cf. Theunissen, *Gesellschaft und Geschichte*, 19f.) as well as a reference to that "anamnestic solidarity" at stake in Horkheimer's 1937 exchange with Benjamin (cf. Peukert, *Wissenschaftstheorie*, 305f.).

50. Cf. Habermas, *Theorie des kommunikativen Handelns*, 1:512/*TCA*, 1:382–83.

51. This refusal to sketch a positive alternative draws on motifs from the Jewish prohibition against images; on this theological motif, see Reiss, "Die Rettung des Hoffnungslosen," and Schmidt, *Drei Studien über Materialismus*, 115f.

52. Cf. the later formulations in Adorno, *Prismen. Kulturkritik und Gesellschaft* (Frankfurt, 1955), 30. English translation: *Prisms* (Cambridge, 1967).

53. Cf. Theunissen, *Gesellschaft und Geschichte*, 19.

54. However, Horkheimer also refers to this attempt at a solution; cf. above and 167/179.

55. For a critique of Adorno, see Theunissen, "Negativität bei Adorno," in Ludwig von Friedeburg and Jürgen Habermas, eds., *Adorno-Konferenz* (Frankfurt, 1983).

56. See Habermas, "The Entwinement of Myth and Enlightenment: Rereading the *Dialectic of Enlightenment*," *New German Critique*. (1982).

57. Cf. Habermas, *Theorie des kommunikativen Handelns*, 1:519f./*TCA*, 1:387f.

58. Cf. also Habermas, "The Entwinement of Myth and Enlightenment."

59. Cf. Habermas, *Theorie des kommunikativen Handelns*, 2:445ff./*TCA*, 2:301ff.

60. See Lohmann, "Authentisches und verdinglichtes Leben," 267f.

61. Cf. Habermas, *Theorie des kommunikativen Handelns*, 2:163, and elsewhere/*TCA*, 2:106.

Bibliography of Horkheimer's Works

A comprehensive, chronological bibliography of the first publications of Horkheimer's works from 1922 to 1985 has been compiled by Gunzelin Schmid Noerr, "Bibliographie der Erstveröffentlichungen Max Horkheimers," in Alfred Schmidt and Norbert Altwicker, eds., *Max Horkheimer heute: Werk und Wirkung* (Frankfurt, 1986), 372–83. An extensive bibliography of works by and about Horkheimer, including translations, is projected to appear in volume 18 of Horkheimer, *Gesammelte Schriften* (Frankfurt: S. Fischer, forthcoming).

In German (and Publications Originally in English)

Arranged chronologically by date of publication

"Zur Antinomie der teleologischen Urteilskraft." Dissertation, Frankfurt am Main, 1922.

Über Kants Kritik der Urteilskraft als Bindeglied zwischen theoretischer und praktischer Philosophie. Habilitationsschrift, Frankfurt am Main, 1925. Leipzig and Frankfurt am Main: J. B. Hirschfeld, Arno Pries, 1925.

Anfänge der bürgerlichen Geschichtsphilosophie. Stuttgart: Kohlhammer, 1930.

"Ein neuer Ideologiebegriff?" *Archiv für die Geschichte des Sozialismus und der Arbeiterbewegung* 15, 1 (1930): 1–34.

"Hegel und das Problem der Metaphysik." In *Festschrift für Carl Grünberg zum 70. Geburtstag,* 185–97. Leipzig, 1932.

Dämmerung. Notizen in Deutschland. (Published under the pseudonym Heinrich Regius.) Zürich: Oprecht & Helbling, 1934.

Studien über Autorität und Familie. Edited by Max Horkheimer. Paris: Alcan, 1936.

    "Vorwort."
    "Allgemeiner Teil" (later republished in *Kritische Theorie* under the title "Autorität und Familie").

Zeitschrift für Sozialforschung (= *ZfS*). Volumes 1–9. Edited by Max Horkheimer. Leipzig, Paris, New York, 1932–1941. Volumes 8 and 9 (1939–1941) under the title *Studies in Philosophy and Social Science (SPSS)*. (Facsimile reprint: Munich: Kösel, 1970; Munich: Deutscher Taschenbuch Verlag, 1980.)

"Bemerkungen über Wissenschaft und Krise," *ZfS* 1 (1932).

"Geschichte und Psychologie," *ZfS* 1 (1932).

"Materialismus und Metaphysik," *ZfS* 2 (1933).

"Materialismus und Moral," *ZfS* 2 (1933).

"Zum Problem der Voraussage in den Sozialwissenschaften," *ZfS* 2 (1933).

"Zum Rationalismusstreit in der gegenwärtigen Philosophie," *ZfS* 3 (1934).

"Zu Bergsons Metaphysik der Zeit," *ZfS* 3 (1934).

"Bemerkungen zur philosophischen Anthropologie," *ZfS* 4 (1935).

"Zum Problem der Wahrheit," *ZfS* 4 (1935).

"Egoismus und Freiheitsbewegung (Zur Anthropologie des bürgerlichen Zeitalters)," *ZfS* 5 (1936).

"Zu Theodor Haecker: Der Christ und die Geschichte," *ZfS* 5 (1936).

"Der neueste Angriff auf die Metaphysik," *ZfS* 6 (1937).

"Traditionelle und kritische Theorie," *ZfS* 6 (1937).

"Philosophie und kritische Theorie" (with Herbert Marcuse), *ZfS* 6 (1937).

"Montaigne und die Funktion der Skepsis," *ZfS* 7 (1938).

"Die Philosophie der absoluten Konzentration," *ZfS* 7 (1938).

"Die Juden und Europa," *ZfS* 8 (1939/40).

"The Social Function of Philosophy," *SPSS* 8 (1939/40).

"The Relation between Psychology and Sociology in the Work of Wilhelm Dilthey," *SPSS* 8 (1939/40).

"Notes on Institute Activities," *SPSS* 9 (1941).

"Research Project on Anti-Semitism," *SPSS* 9 (1941).

"Art and Mass Culture," *SPSS* 9 (1941).

"The End of Reason," *SPSS* 9 (1941).

"Autoritärer Staat." In *Walter Benjamin zum Gedächtnis* (hectographed typescript), 123–161. New York/Los Angeles: Institut für Sozialforschung, 1942.

"Vernunft und Selbsterhaltung." In *Walter Benjamin zum Gedächtnis* (hectographed typescript), 17–60. New York/Los Angeles: Institut für Sozialforschung, 1942.

"Sociological Background of the Psychoanalytic Approach." In *Anti-Semitism: A Social Disease*, 1–10. Edited by Ernst Simmel. New York: International Universities Press, 1946.

Dialektik der Aufklärung. Philosophische Fragmente. With Theodor W. Adorno. Amsterdam: Querido, 1947; Frankfurt am Main: S. Fischer, 1969. (Originally under the title "Philosophische Fragmente" (hectographed typescript). New York/Los Angeles: Institute of Social Research, 1944.)

Eclipse of Reason. Oxford: 1947.

Bibliography

"Ernst Simmel and Freudian Philosophy." *International Journal of Psychoanalysis* 29 (1948):110–13.

Studies in Prejudice. Volumes 1–5. Edited by Max Horkheimer and Samuel Flowerman. New York: Harper and Brothers, 1949–1950.

"The Lessons of Fascism." In *Tensions that Cause Wars,* 209–42. Edited by Hadley Cantril. Urbana: University of Illinois Press, 1950.

Survey of the Social Sciences in Western Germany: A Report on Recent Developments. Washington, D.C.: Library of Congress, 1952.

Sociologica II. Reden und Vorträge. With Theodor W. Adorno. Frankfurt am Main: Europäische Verlagsanstalt, 1962.

"Soziologie und Philosophie" (1959).

"Philosophie als Kulturkritik" (1959).

"Ideologie und Handeln" (1951).

"Verantwortung und Studium" (1954).

"Über das Vorurteil" (1961).

"Schopenhauer und die Gesellschaft" (1955).

"Die Aktualität Schopenhauers" (1961).

"Zum Begriff der Vernunft" (1952).

Zur Kritik der instrumentellen Vernunft. Aus den Vorträgen und Aufzeichnungen seit Kriegsende. Edited by Alfred Schmidt. Frankfurt: Fischer Athenäum, 1967.

"Zur Kritik der instrumentellen Vernunft" (German translation of *Eclipse of Reason*; see above).

"Zum Begriff des Menschen" (1957).

"Kants Philosophie und die Aufklärung" (1962).

"Theismus—Atheismus" (1963).

"Religion und Philosophie" (1967).

"De anima" (1967).

"Die Aktualität Schopenhauers" (1961).

"Autorität und Familie in der Gegenwart" (1949).

"Die Zukunft der Ehe" (1966).

"Über die deutschen Juden" (1961).

"Zur Ergreifung Eichmanns" (1960).

"Ansprache an das Hohe Haus" (1954).

"Feudalherr, Kunde, Fachmann" (1964).

"Bedrohungen der Freiheit" (1965).

Kritische Theorie. Eine Dokumentation. 2 vols. Edited by Alfred Schmidt. Frankfurt am Main: S. Fischer, 1968. Contains all of Horkheimer's essays from the *Zeitschrift für Sozialforschung* (see listing above), except "Die Juden und Europa." Also includes "Autorität und Familie," "Vorwort zur Neupublikation," and "Brief an den S. Fischer Verlag."

Die Sehnsucht nach dem ganz Anderen. Interview, with commentary, by Helmut Gumnior. Hamburg: Furche, 1970.

Vernunft und Selbsterhaltung. Frankfurt am Main: S. Fischer, 1970.

Verwaltete Welt. Conversation between Horkheimer and Otmar Hersche. Zürich: Die Arche, 1970.

Sozialphilosophische Studien. Aufsätze, Reden und Vorträge 1930–1972. Edited by Werner Brede. Frankfurt am Main: Fischer Athenäum, 1972.

"Ein neuer Ideologiebegriff?" (1930).

"Die gegenwärtige Lage der Sozialphilosophie und die Aufgaben eines Instituts für Sozialforschung" (1931).

"Zum Begriff der Vernunft" (1952).

"Schopenhauer und die Gesellschaft" (1955).

"Soziologie und Philosophie" (1959).

"Philosophie als Kulturkritik" (1959).

"Zum Begriff der Freiheit" (1962).

"Macht und Gewissen" (1962).

"Über den Zweifel" (1969).

"Bemerkungen zur Liberalisierung der Religion" (1971).

"Pessimismus heute" (1971).

"Schopenhauers Denken im Verhältnis zu Wissenschaft und Religion" (1972).

"Universität und Studium. Akademisches Studium" (1952).

"Begriff der Bildung" (1952).

"Fragen des Hochschulunterrichts" (1952).

"Verantwortung und Studium" (1954).

Gesellschaft im Übergang. Aufsätze, Reden und Vorträge 1942–1970. Edited by Werner Brede. Frankfurt am Main: Fischer Athenäum, 1972.

"Autoritärer Staat" (1942).

"Lehren aus dem Faschismus" (1950).

"Politik und Soziales" (1950).

"Invarianz und Dynamik in der Lehre von der Gesellschaft" (1951).

"Vorurteil und Charakter" (with Theodor W. Adorno) (1952).

"Der Mensch in der Wandlung seit der Jahrhundertwende" (1960).

"Über das Vorurteil" (1961).

"Der Bildungsauftrag der Gewerkschaften" (1962).

"Gedanken zur politischen Erziehung" (1963).

"Die Psychoanalyse aus der Sicht der Soziologie" (1968).

"Marx heute" (1968).

"Kritische Theorie gestern und heute" (1970).

Aus der Pubertät. Novellen und Tagebuchblätter. Munich: Kösel, 1974.

417

Bibliography

Notizen 1950 bis 1969 und Dämmerung. Notizen in Deutschland. Edited by Werner Brede and introduced by Alfred Schmidt. Frankfurt am Main: S. Fischer, 1974.

Humanität und Religion. Correspondence and conversation with Hugo Staudinger. Würzburg: Naumann, 1974.

Gesammelte Schriften. 18 vols. Edited by Alfred Schmidt and Gunzelin Schmid Noerr. Frankfurt am Main: S. Fischer, 1985ff.

1: *"Aus der Pubertät. Novellen und Tagebuchblätter," 1914–1918* (1988).

2: *Philosophische Frühschriften 1922–1932* (1987).

3: *Schriften 1931–1936* (1988).

4: *Schriften 1936–1941* (1988).

5: *"Dialektik der Aufklärung" und Schriften 1940–1950* (1987).

6: *"Zur Kritik der instrumentellen Vernunft" und "Notizen 1949–1969"* (1991).

7: *Vorträge und Aufzeichnungen 1949–1973* (1985).

8: *Vorträge und Aufzeichnungen 1949–1973* (1985).

9: *Nachgelassene Schriften 1914–1931* (1987).

10: *Nachgelassene Schriften 1914–1931* (1987).

11: *Nachgelassene Schriften 1914–1931* (1987).

12: *Nachgelassene Schriften 1931–1949* (1985).

13: *Nachgelassene Schriften 1949–1972* (1989).

14: *Nachgelassene Schriften 1949–1972* (1988).

15: *Briefe 1913–1939* (in preparation).

16: *Briefe 1940–1949* (in preparation).

17: *Briefe 1950–1973* (in preparation).

18: *Bibliographie und Register* (in preparation).

English Translations

Arranged alphabetically by title

Books and Collected Essays

Between Philosophy and Social Science: Selected Early Writings. Translated by G. Frederick Hunter, Matthew S. Kramer, and John Torpey. Cambridge, Mass.: MIT Press, 1993.

"The Present Situation of Social Philosophy and the Tasks of an Institute for Social Research."

"Materialism and Morality."

"Egoism and the Freedom Movement: On the Anthropology of the Bourgeois Era."

"History and Psychology."

"A New Concept of Ideology?"

Bibliography

"Remarks on Philosophical Anthropology."

"The Problem of Truth."

"The Rationalism Dispute in Current Philosophy."

"Montaigne and the Function of Skepticism."

"Beginnings of the Bourgeois Philosophy of History."

Critical Theory: Selected Essays. Translated by Matthew J. O'Connell and others. New York: Seabury Press, 1972.

"Notes on Science and the Crisis."

"Materialism and Metaphysics."

"Authority and the Family."

"Thoughts on Religion."

"The Latest Attack on Metaphysics."

"Traditional and Critical Theory."

Postscript (to "Traditional and Critical Theory"; originally Horkheimer's contribution to Horkheimer and Marcuse, "Philosophie und kritische Theorie," *ZfS* 6 [1937]).

"The Social Function of Philosophy."

"Art and Mass Culture."

Critique of Instrumental Reason: Lectures and Essays since the End of World War II. Translated by Matthew J. O'Connell and others. New York: Seabury Press, 1974.

Foreword (to *Zur Kritik der instrumentellen Vernunft*).

"The Concept of Man."

"Theism and Atheism."

"The Soul."

"Schopenhauer Today."

"The Future of Marriage."

"The German Jews."

"The Arrest of Eichmann."

"Feudal Lord, Customer, and Specialist."

"Threats to Freedom."

Dawn and Decline: Notes 1926–1931 and 1950–1969. Translated by Michael Shaw. New York: Seabury Press, 1974. Contains selections from *Notizen 1950 bis 1969 und Dämmerung: Notizen in Deutschland.*

Dialectic of Enlightenment. With Theodor W. Adorno. Translated by John Cumming. New York: Seabury Press, 1972.

Individual Essays

"The Authoritarian State." Translated by the People's Translation Service, Berkeley, mediated by Elliot Eisenberg. In Andrew Arato and Eike Gebhardt, eds., *The Essential Frankfurt School Reader*, 95–117. New York: Continuum, 1982.

Bibliography

"Authoritarianism and the Family Today." In *The Family: Its Function and Destiny*, 359–74. Edited by R. N. Anshen. New York: Harper, 1949.

"Egoism and the Freedom Movement: On the Anthropology of the Bourgeois Era." Translated by David J. Parent. *Telos* 54 (Winter 1982–1983): 10–60.

"The End of Reason." In Arato and Gebhardt, eds., *The Essential Frankfurt School Reader*, 26–48.

"The Jews and Europe." Translated by Mark Ritter. In Stephen Bronner and Douglas Kellner, eds., *Critical Theory and Society*, 77–94. New York: Routledge, 1989.

"Materialism and Morality." Translated by G. Frederick Hunter and John Torpey. *Telos* 69 (Fall 1986): 85–118.

"On the Concept of Freedom." *Diogenes* 53 (Spring 1964): 73–81.

"On the Problem of Truth." Translated by Maurice Goldbloom. In Arato and Gebhardt, eds., *The Essential Frankfurt School Reader*, 407–43.

"Schopenhauer Today." Translated by Robert Kolben. In *The Critical Spirit: Essays in Honor of Herbert Marcuse*, 55–71. Edited by Kurt H. Wolff and Barrington Moore, Jr. Boston: Beacon Press, 1967.

"The State of Contemporary Social Philosophy and the Tasks of an Institute for Social Research." Translated by Peter Wagner. In Bronner and Kellner, eds., *Critical Theory and Society*, 25–36.

Acknowledgments

Alfred Schmidt, "Max Horkheimer's Intellectual Physiognomy."

Abridged translation of "Einleitung" to Max Horkheimer, *Notizen 1950 bis 1969 und Dämmerung: Notizen in Deutschland,* ed. Werner Brede (Frankfurt: S. Fischer, 1974), xix–lxx.

Jürgen Habermas, "Remarks on the Development of Horkheimer's Work."

German original: "Bemerkungen zur Entwicklungsgeschichte des Horkheimerschen Werkes," in Alfred Schmidt and Norbert Altwicker, eds., *Max Horkheimer heute: Werk und Wirkung* (Frankfurt: Fischer Verlag, 1986), 163–79.

Hauke Brunkhorst, "Dialectical Positivism of Happiness: Horkheimer's Materialist Deconstruction of Philosophy."

German original: "Dialektischer Positivismus des Glücks. Max Horkheimers materialistische Dekonstruktion der Philosophie," *Zeitschrift für Philosophische Forschung* 43, 2 (April–June 1989): 318–30.

Wolfgang Bonß, "The Program of Interdisciplinary Research and the Beginnings of Critical Theory."

Revised version of Wolfgang Bonß and Norbert Schindler, "Kritische Theorie als interdisziplinärer Materialismus," in Bonß and Axel Honneth, eds., *Sozialforschung als Kritik: Zum sozialwissenschaftlichen Potential der Kritischen Theorie* (Frankfurt: Suhrkamp Verlag, 1982), 31–66.

Thomas McCarthy, "The Idea of a Critical Theory and Its Relation to Philosophy."

Original contribution.

Wolf Schäfer, "Stranded at the Crossroads of Dehumanization: John Desmond Bernal and Max Horkheimer."

Original contribution.

Axel Honneth, "Max Horkheimer and the Sociological Deficit of Critical Theory."

Abridged and revised version of chapter 1 in Honneth, *Kritik der Macht. Reflexionsstufen einer kritischen Gesellschaftstheorie* (Frankfurt am Main: Suhrkamp Verlag, 1985); En-

422

Acknowledgments

glish: *The Critique of Power. Reflective Stages in a Critical Social Theory*, trans. Kenneth Baynes (Cambridge, Mass.: MIT Press, 1991).

Moishe Postone and Barbara Brick, "Critical Theory and Political Economy."
Revised version of "Critical Pessimism and the Limits of Traditional Marxism," *Theory and Society* 11, 5 (1982): 617–58.

Stefan Breuer, "The Long Friendship: On Theoretical Differences between Adorno and Horkheimer."
Original contribution.

Herbert Schnädelbach, "Max Horkheimer and the Moral Philosophy of German Idealism."
German original: "Max Horkheimer und die Moralphilosophie des deutschen Idealismus," in Alfred Schmidt and Norbert Altwicker, eds., *Max Horkheimer heute: Werk und Wirkung* (Frankfurt: Fischer Verlag, 1986), 52–78; this translation originally appeared in *Telos* 66 (Winter 1985–1986): 81–101.

Mechthild Rumpf, "'Mystical Aura': Imagination and the Reality of the 'Maternal' in Horkheimer's Writings."
Expanded and revised version appeared in Rumpf, *Spuren des Mütterlichen* (Frankfurt: Materialis Verlag, 1989), 15–51.

Dan Diner, "Reason and the 'Other': Horkheimer's Reflections on Anti-Semitism and Mass Annihilation."
German original: "Aporie der Vernunft. Horkheimers Überlegungen zum Antisemitismus und Massenvernichtung," in *Zivilisationsbruch. Denken nach Auschwitz*, ed. Dan Diner (Frankfurt: Fischer Verlag, 1988), 30–54.

Martin Jay, "Mass Culture and Aesthetic Redemption: The Debate between Max Horkheimer and Siegfried Kracauer."
Previously in Jay, *Fin-de-Siècle Socialism and Other Essays* (New York/London: Routledge, 1988), 82–96. German original in Ilja Srubar, ed., *Exil, Wissenschaft, Identität: Die Emigration deutscher Sozialwissenschaftler 1933–1945* (Frankfurt: Suhrkamp, 1988).

Georg Lohmann, "The Failure of Self-Realization: An Interpretation of Horkheimer's *Eclipse of Reason*."
Original contribution.

Contributors

Seyla Benhabib is Professor of Government at Harvard University. She is the author of *Critique, Norm, and Utopia: A Study in the Foundations of Critical Theory* (New York, 1986) and *Situating the Self: Gender, Community, and Postmodernism in Contemporary Ethics* (New York, 1992). She is coeditor, with Drucilla Cornell, of *Feminism as Critique* (Minneapolis, 1987).

Wolfgang Bonß is Senior Research Associate at the Institut für Sozialforschung in Hamburg. He is the author of *Die Einübung des Tatsachenblicks. Zur Struktur und Veränderung empirischer Sozialforschung* (Frankfurt, 1982) and coeditor, with Axel Honneth, of *Sozialforschung als Kritik. Zum sozialwissenschaftlichen Potential der Kritischen Theorie* (Frankfurt, 1982).

John McCole is Associate Professor of History and of Social Studies at Harvard University. He is the author of *Walter Benjamin and the Antinomies of Tradition* (Ithaca: Cornell University Press, 1993).

Alfred Schmidt is Professor of Philosophy at the Johann Wolfgang Goethe University of Frankfurt. His works include *Drei Studien über Materialismus. Schopenhauer. Horkheimer. Glücksproblem* (Munich, 1977); *Zur Idee der Kritischen Theorie. Elemente der Philosophie Max Horkheimers.* (Munich, 1974); *Emanzipatorische Sinnlichkeit. Ludwig Feuerbachs anthropologischer Materialismus* (Munich, 1976); *Geschichte und Struktur. Fra-*

gen einer marxistischen Historik (Munich, 1971), published in English as *History and Structure: An Essay on Hegelian-Marxist and Structuralist Theories of History*, translated by Jeffrey Herf (Cambridge, Mass., 1981); and *Goethes herrlich leuchtende Natur* (Munich, 1984). He is coeditor, with Norbert Altwicker, of *Max Horkheimer heute: Werk und Wirkung* (Frankfurt, 1986) and coeditor, with Gunzelin Schmid Noerr, of Max Horkheimer, *Gesammelte Schriften* (Frankfurt, 1985ff.).

Jürgen Habermas is Professor of Philosophy at the Johann Wolfgang Goethe University of Frankfurt. Among his most important publications in English are *Knowledge and Human Interests* (Boston, 1971); *Legitimation Crisis* (Boston, 1975), and *The Theory of Communicative Action* (Boston, 1984 and 1987). More recently the following works have appeared in English: *The Philosophical Discourse of Modernity* (Cambridge, Mass., 1987); *On the Logic of the Social Sciences* (Cambridge, Mass., 1988); *The Structural Transformation of the Public Sphere* (Cambridge, Mass., 1989); and *Moral Consciousness and Communicative Action* (Cambridge, Mass., 1990). His most recent book is *Faktizität und Geltung. Beiträge zur Diskurstheorie des Rechts und des demokratischen Rechtsstaats* (Frankfurt, 1992).

Hauke Brunkhorst is Visiting Professor of Political Science at the University of Duisburg and Privatdozent in Sociology at the University of Frankfurt. He is the author of numerous articles on the sociology of culture and critical theory. His most recent publications include *Der Intellektuelle im Land der Mandarine* (Frankfurt, 1987); *Theodor W. Adorno. Dialektik der Moderne* (Zürich, 1990); *Der Entzauberte Intellektuelle. Über die neue Beliebigkeit des Denkens* (Hamburg, 1990); he is coauthor, with Gertrud Koch, of *Marcuse zur Einführung* (Hamburg, 1987).

Thomas McCarthy is Professor of Philosophy at Northwestern University. He is the author of *The Critical Theory of Jürgen Habermas* (Cambridge, Mass., 1978) and most recently of *Ideals and Illusions: On Reconstruction and Deconstruction in Contemporary Critical Theory* (Cambridge, Mass., 1991). He is the general editor of the series "Studies in Contemporary German Social Thought," MIT Press. Together with David Hoy, he is completing a book on *Critical Theory* for the Blackwell series on Debates in Philosophy.

Wolf Schäfer is Professor of History at the State University of New York at Stony Brook. He has published in the areas of social history, history and philosophy of science and technology, and in global history. He is the author of *Die unvertraute Moderne* (Frankfurt, 1985), and editor and coauthor of *Finalization in Science: The Social Orientation of Scientific Progress* (Boston, 1983). His *Ungleichzeitigkeit als Ideologie. Beiträge zur historischen Aufklärung* is forthcoming in 1994.

Axel Honneth is Professor of Political Philosophy at the Freie Universität Berlin. He is the author of *Kritik der Macht. Reflexionsstufen einer kritischen Gesellschaftstheorie* (Frankfurt, 1985), published in English as *The Critique of Power: Reflective Stages in a Critical Social Theory*, translated by Kenneth Baynes (Cambridge, Mass., 1991); *Die zerissene Welt des Sozialen. Sozialphilosophische Aufsätze* (Frankfurt, 1990); *Kampf um Anerkennung. Zur moralischen Grammatik sozialer Konflikte* (Frankfurt, 1992); and coauthor, with Hans Joas, of *Social Action and Human Nature* (Cambridge, 1988). He is coeditor, with Urs Jaeggi, of *Theorien des historischen Materialismus* (Frankfurt, 1977) and, with Wolfgang Bonß, of *Sozialforschung als Kritik. Zum sozialwissenschaftlichen Potential der Kritischen Theorie* (Frankfurt, 1982).

Moishe Postone is Dean of Undergraduate Studies at the School of Social Sciences, Collegiate Division, of the University of Chicago and Associate Professor of Sociology there. He is the author of numerous articles on political economy, critical theory, and Marxism. His book on Marxian social theory, *Time, Labor, and Social Domination: A Reinterpretation of Marx's critical theory*, is forthcoming from Cambridge University Press (1993).

Stefan Breuer teaches sociology at the Hochschule für Wirtschaft und Politik in Hamburg. He is author of *Sozialgeschichte des Naturrechts* (Opladen, 1983); *Der archaische Staat. Zur Soziologie charismatischer Herrschaft* (Berlin, 1990); *Max Webers Herrschaftssoziologie* (Frankfurt, 1991); and *Die Gesellschaft des Verschwindens. Von der Selbstzerstörung der technischen Zivilisation* (Hamburg, 1992).

Herbert Schnädelbach is Professor of Philosophy and Social Theory at the University of Hamburg. Among his publications are *Erfahrung,*

Begründung und Reflexion (Frankfurt, 1971); *Geschichtsphilosophie nach Hegel* (1974); *Reflexion und Diskurs* (Frankfurt, 1977); and *Vernunft und Geschichte* (Frankfurt, 1987). His *Philosophy in Germany, 1831–1933* has been translated and published in English (Cambridge, 1984).

Mechthild Rumpf is Assistant Professor of Sociology at the University of Hannover. She is the author of *Spuren des Mütterlichen. Die widersprüchliche Bedeutung der Mutterrolle in Kritischer Theorie und feministischer Wissenschaft* (Frankfurt, 1989) and coeditor of the journal *Feministische Studien*.

Dan Diner is Professor of History at the Gesamthochschule Essen and at the School of History, University of Tel-Aviv. He is the author of *Israel in Palästina* (Königstein/Ts., 1980); editor of *Ist der Nationalsozialismus Geschichte? Zu Historisierung und Historikerstreit* (Frankfurt, 1987) and *Zivilisationsbruch. Denken nach Auschwitz* (Frankfurt, 1988); and coeditor, with Dirk Blasius, of *Zerbrochene Geschichte: Leben und Selbstverständnis der Juden in Deutschland* (Frankfurt, 1991).

Martin Jay is Professor of History at the University of California at Berkeley. He is the author of *The Dialectical Imagination. A History of the Frankfurt School and the Institute of Social Research, 1923–1950* (Boston, 1973); *Marxism and Totality* (Berkeley, 1984); *Adorno* (Cambridge, Mass., 1984); *Permanent Exiles* (New York, 1985); *Fin-de-Siècle Socialism* (New York, 1988); and *Force Fields: Between Intellectual History and Cultural Critique* (New York, 1993).

Georg Lohmann is Assistant for Philosophy at the Freie Universität Berlin. He is the author of *Indifferenz und Gesellschaft. Eine kritische Auseinandersetzung mit Marx* (Frankfurt, 1991) and coeditor, with E. Angehrn, of *Ethik und Marx* (Königstein/Ts., 1986).

Index

Index

Studies in Contemporary German Social Thought

Thomas McCarthy, General Editor

Jürgen Habermas, *The Structural Transformation of the Public Sphere: An Inquiry into a Category of Bourgeois Society*

Jürgen Habermas, editor, *Observations on "The Spiritual Situation of the Age"*

Axel Honneth, *The Critique of Power: Reflective Stages in a Critical Social Theory*

Axel Honneth and Hans Joas, editors, *Communicative Action: Essays on Jürgen Habermas's* The Theory of Communicative Action

Axel Honneth, Thomas McCarthy, Claus Offe, and Albrecht Wellmer, editors, *Cultural-Political Interventions in the Unfinished Project of Enlightenment*

Axel Honneth, Thomas McCarthy, Claus Offe, and Albrecht Wellmer, editors, *Philosophical Interventions in the Unfinished Project of Enlightenment*

Max Horkheimer, *Between Philosophy and Social Science: Selected Early Writings*

Hans Joas, *G. H. Mead: A Contemporary Re-examination of His Thought*

Reinhart Koselleck, *Critique and Crisis: Enlightenment and the Pathogenesis of Modern Society*

Reinhart Koselleck, *Futures Past: On the Semantics of Historical Time*

Harry Liebersohn, *Fate and Utopia in German Sociology, 1887–1923*

Herbert Marcuse, *Hegel's Ontology and the Theory of Historicity*

Gil G. Noam and Thomas Wren, editors, *The Moral Self*

Guy Oakes, *Weber and Rickert: Concept Formation in the Cultural Sciences*

Claus Offe, *Contradictions of the Welfare State*

Claus Offe, *Disorganized Capitalism: Contemporary Transformations of Work and Politics*

Helmut Peukert, *Science, Action, and Fundamental Theology: Toward a Theology of Communicative Action*

Joachim Ritter, *Hegel and the French Revolution: Essays on the* Philosophy of Right

Alfred Schmidt, *History and Structure: An Essay on Hegelian-Marxist and Structuralist Theories of History*

Dennis Schmidt, *The Ubiquity of the Finite: Hegel, Heidegger, and the Entitlements of Philosophy*

Carl Schmitt, *The Crisis of Parliamentary Democracy*

Carl Schmitt, *Political Romanticism*

Carl Schmitt, *Political Theology: Four Chapters on the Concept of Sovereignty*

Gary Smith, editor, *On Walter Benjamin: Critical Essays and Recollections*

Michael Theunissen, *The Other: Studies in the Social Ontology of Husserl, Heidegger, Sartre, and Buber*

Ernst Tugendhat, *Self-Consciousness and Self-Determination*